EYEWITNESS TRAVEL

DORDOGNE, BORDEAUX
& THE SOUTHWEST COAST

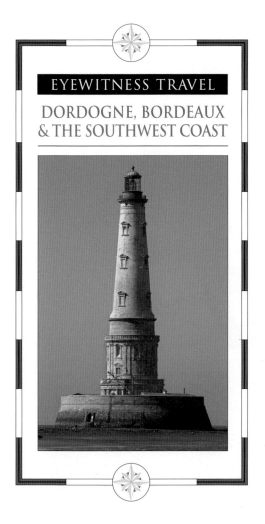

EYEWITNESS TRAVEL

DORDOGNE, BORDEAUX & THE SOUTHWEST COAST

LONDON, NEW YORK,
MELBOURNE, MUNICH AND DELHI
www.dk.com

PRODUCED BY Hachette Tourisme, Paris, France

EDITORIAL DIRECTOR Cécile Boyer-Runge
SERIES EDITOR Catherine Laussucq
PROJECT EDITOR Amélie Baghdiguian
EDITOR Aurélie Pregliasco
ART DIRECTOR Éric Laubeuf
DESIGNERS Maogani
CARTOGRAPHY Cyrille Suss

MAIN CONTRIBUTORS
Suzanne Boireau-Tartarat, Pierre Chavot, Renée Grimaud,
Wilfried Lecarpentier, Santiago Mendieta, Marie-Pascale Rauzier

PHOTOGRAPHY
Philippe Giraud, Pierre Javelle, Éric Guillemot

Dorling Kindersley Limited
PUBLISHING MANAGERS Jane Ewart, Fay Franklin
PROJECT EDITOR Cécile Landau
ENGLISH TRANSLATION Lucilla Watson
DTP Jason Little, Conrad van Dyk
CARTOGRAPHY Casper Morris
PRODUCTION Louise Daly

Reproduced in Singapore by Colourscan
Printed and bound at Toppan Printing Company, China.

First published in Great Britain in 2006
by Dorling Kindersley Limited
80 Strand, London WC2R 0RL

Reprinted with revisions 2008

Copyright © 2006, 2008 Dorling Kindersley Limited, London
A Penguin Company

A CIP CATALOGUE RECORD IS AVAILABLE FROM THE BRITISH LIBRARY.

ISBN: 978 1 40532 743 5

FLOORS ARE REFERRED TO THROUGHOUT IN
ACCORDANCE WITH EUROPEAN USAGE; IE THE "FIRST FLOOR"
IS THE FLOOR ABOVE GROUND LEVEL.

NOTE: THE FRENCH NAME OF AQUITAINE IS USED TO DESCRIBE
THE AREA COVERED BY THIS GUIDE.

Front cover main image: View of Rocamadour from the Alzou Valley

**The information in every
DK Eyewitness Travel Guide is checked regularly.**
Every effort has been made to ensure that this book is as up-to-date
as possible at the time of going to press. Some details, however,
such as telephone numbers, opening hours, prices, gallery hanging
arrangements and travel information are liable to change. The
publishers cannot accept responsibility for any consequences arising
from the use of this book, nor for any material on third party
websites, and cannot guarantee that any website address in this
book will be a suitable source of travel information. We value the
views and suggestions of our readers very highly. Please write to:
Publisher, DK Eyewitness Travel Guides,
Dorling Kindersley, 80 Strand, London WC2R 0RL, Great Britain.

CONTENTS

Decorative panel, the Pink Chamber,
Château de Roquetaillade, Gironde

INTRODUCING
AQUITAINE

Bunches of ripe grapes in a
vineyard in Bordeaux

◁ The village of Saint-Cirq Lapopie

The port of Hendaye, Pays Basque

AQUITAINE REGION BY REGION

Traditional dovecote of the Lot-et-Garonne

Decorative detail of the interior of the Grand-Théâtre de Bordeaux

Château de Puyguilhem, in the Dordogne

Église Saint-Jean-Baptiste in Saint-Jean-de-Luz

INTRODUCING
AQUITAINE

DISCOVERING AQUITAINE

Aquitaine lies along the Atlantic coast. Its silver beaches stretch 270km (170 miles) from the Gironde estuary to Biarritz and the Spanish border. Behind them, the pine forests and waterways of the Landes spread out towards the bucolic river valleys of the Lot and Dordogne. Some

Grapes ripening

of France's most famous vineyards are located here, interspersed with grand châteaux and Romanesque churches. In the south lie the wild Pyrenees of the Pays Basque and Béarn, where traditions remain strong. These two pages give a flavour of the regions, plus a quick guide to their highlights.

Château de la Rivière and its sunbaked vineyards, near Bordeaux

Grand architecture includes the imposing **Château de Hautefort** *(see pp104–105)* and the fortified town of **Rocamadour** *(see pp120–23)*. **Périgueaux** *(see pp98–101)* is the principal town in the region. It has a well conserved medieval heart, as does the engaging market town of **Sarlat** *(see pp114–117)*, which draws visitors with its truffle and *foie gras* fairs.

GIRONDE

- **Stately Bordeaux**
- **Rolling vineyards and fairytale châteaux**
- **Birdlife and beaches of the Arcachon Basin**

This is the heart of Aquitaine. Its capital, **Bordeaux** *(pp66–73)*, is an historic wine port beside the River Gironde. Essentially a Neo-Classical town of wide avenues and stone monuments, its Grand Théâtre is a prime example, built on the site of a Gallo-Roman temple. Great wines have been exported from its riverside warehouses all over the world, including **Médoc**, **Margaux** and **Saint-Émilion** *(see pp74–5* and *pp80–81)*. A tour of the grand wine estates in the area is a must. The ancient *bastide* towns and the grand châteaux of **Roquetaillade** *(see pp86–7)* and **Cazeneuve** *(see pp92–3)* also merit a tour.

For nature lovers there's the impressive **Arcachon Basin** *(see pp62–3)*, with its

oyster beds, vibrant birdlife, expansive dunes and golden beaches that stretch the length of the coast.

PÉRIGORD AND QUERCY

- **Fertile Dordogne Valley**
- **Romantic gardens of the Manoir d'Eyrignac**
- **World-famous caves**
- **Dramatic Rocamadour**

This inland region is a rich area of woodlands, caves and deep gorges cut by the Lot and Dordogne rivers, making it a popular country holiday spot. A canoe is a great way to explore the delightful **Dordogne Valley** *(see pp116–17)*. For a romantic stroll, head for the **gardens of the Manoir d'Eyrignac** *(see pp110–11)*.

Get back to more primitive nature by exploring the myriad underground caves. Some of the world's most famous cave paintings are here in **Lascaux** *(see p108)*, and there are a large number of prehistoric sites in the area.

LOT-ET-GARONNE

- **Delicious Agen prunes and Duras wines**
- **Ancient *bastide* towns**
- **Château de Bonaguil**

The rolling countryside here has been described as the "orchard of Europe", and is famous for its **Agen prunes** *(see p153)* and the Duras wines of the amiable **Pays du Dropt** *(see pp144–5)*. The Lot, Garonne and Baïse rivers are augmented by canals to ensure there's

The Dordogne river flowing past the Château de Castelnaud

plenty of river activity to enjoy. There are no cities in the region, but the *bastide* towns and Romanesque churches are waiting to be explored, as are the medieval **Château de Bonaguil** *(see pp148–9)*, the Renaissance **Château de Duras** *(see p144)* and some of France's prettiest villages. Catch a game of rugby in **Agen** *(see pp158–61)*, the French capital of the sport and a busy university town.

The *bastide* town of Villeneuve-sur-Lot, straddling the Lot river

LANDES

- **Wide, white beaches and crashing Atlantic waves**
- **Forests, parks and waterways**
- **Spa towns and bullrunning**

This is big beach country: the brilliant white sands of the Côte d'Argent stretch down the Atlantic coast for more than 100km (63 miles), attracting windsurfers and sun-bathers to resorts such as **Biscarrosse** and **Mimizan** *(see p174)*. Waterways wind inland where you can punt your way up the quiet backwaters teeming with otters and birds.

A visit to the **Parc Régional des Landes de Gascogne** *(see pp170–73)* is essential. In this extensive conservation area re-creations of traditional farming methods show how life used to be lived here.

Make a reviving stop at one of the area's famous spa towns, such as **Dax** *(see p178)*, where people have been

taking the waters since Roman times. Dax is also a major bullrunning centre along with Saint-Sever and **Pomarez** *(see p179)*, with its bull-running museum. For more culture, visit the **Église Sainte-Quitterie-du-Mas** in Aire-sur-l'Adour *(see p181)* and don't forget to sample some potent **Armagnac** *(see p183)*.

PAYS BASQUE

- **Glamorous Biarritz**
- **Culture in Bayonne**
- **Ancient pilgrim routes**
- **Dramatic gorges**

With its own dialect and unique traditions, the Pays Basque is one of France's most intriguing regions. On the sandy coast sits glitzy **Biarritz** *(see pp194–5)*, which has lost none of its Edwardian grandeur. The main town of **Bayonne** *(see pp188–93)*, just inland on the Nive river, is a cultural gem, with a handsome cathedral, an excellent art museum as well as a raucous August festival.

The Pyrenees show many signs of the **pilgrim route** *(see pp206–207)* to Santiago de Compostela in Spain, which passes this way, trailing medieval churches, hospitals and monuments. You might be tempted to take a ride in the hills on one of the local *pottock* ponies *(see p198)*. Vertiginous limestone **gorges** *(pp210–11)* in the higher mountains provide dramatic walking country.

Biscarrosse, exemplary of the wide beaches on the Landes coast

BÉARN

- **Soaring Pyrenean peaks**
- **Scenic mountain train ride**
- **Elegant and regal Pau**

The most mountainous area in the region reaches a high point at the 2,884m- (9,465ft-) high **Pic du Midi d'Ossau** *(see pp234–5)*, with its snow-tipped ridges, tarns and high summer pastures. Experienced climbers flock here, but families can also enjoy the slopes on a high-altitude scenic train trip to the **Lac d'Artouste** *(see p231)*. Beneath the peak extends the **Ossau Valley** *(see pp230–33)*, which has its own distinct customs and wildlife, including bears and vultures. The capital of Béarn is the elegant town of **Pau** *(pp220–23)*, trimmed with parks and gardens and topped by a castle that once held the royal court of Navarre.

The soaring Pic du Midi d'Ossau in the Pyrenees, Béarn

Putting Southwest France on the Map

From the Gironde Estuary in the north to the border with Spain in the south, the southwest corner of France, known to the French as Aquitaine, covers an area of 41,300sq km, (15,900sq miles) and stretches out along the Atlantic seaboard for 270km (170miles). The region has around 2,908,000 inhabitants, about 5 per cent of the population of France, with an average of 70 people per sq km (190 per sq mile). Of its five *départements* – the Dordogne, Gironde, Landes, Lot-et-Garonne and Pyrénées-Atlantiques – the Gironde is by far the most densely populated.

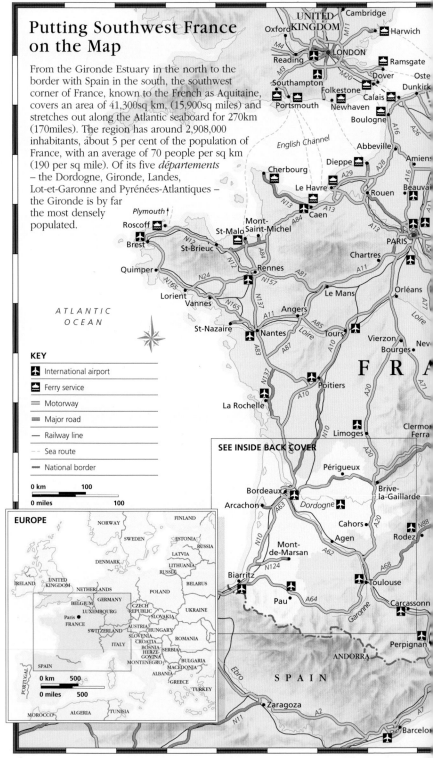

KEY

✈ International airport

⛴ Ferry service

═ Motorway

▬ Major road

— Railway line

--- Sea route

▬ National border

0 km   100

0 miles   100

SEE INSIDE BACK COVER

EUROPE

◁ *Le Fandango*, by Perico Ribera, in the Musée Basque, Bayonne

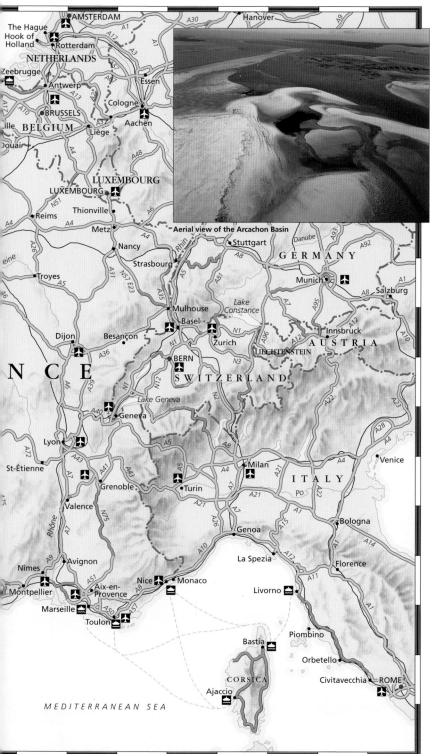

Aerial view of the Arcachon Basin

A PORTRAIT OF AQUITAINE

This culturally diverse region, known to the French as Aquitaine, is a mosaic of varied landscapes, bordered by the Atlantic to the west and the Iberian Peninsula to the south. Sited at the crossroads of a number of major routes, it has absorbed many influences over the centuries. Each of its separate areas has its own distinctive heritage; some even have their own language. Bordeaux, renowned for its wines, is the region's chief city and economic hub.

Aquitaine can be divided into six main areas: Périgord-Quercy (covered by the Dordogne and Lot *départements*) and the Gironde to the north; the Landes and Lot-et-Garonne in the centre; and the Pays Basque and Béarn (together forming the *département* of Pyrénées-Atlantiques) in the far south.

In addition to their shared history (particularly in the case of the Dordogne and Quercy), these areas have a great deal in common. They are all wine-producers and are particularly noted for their cultural heritage, sporting achievements and vernacular architecture.

Traditional Béarn dress

The Romans aptly named the region *Aquitania*, a "land of water". Its abundant rainfall not only accounts for the lush vegetation but has also helped create some of France's most productive farming land.

Extending from the Spanish border as far north as the river Loire, the region covers a total of 41,309 sq km (15,945 sq miles). Its 270-km (170-mile) Atlantic coastline, which stretches from Pointe de Grave in the north to Hendaye at the foot of the Pyrenees, also makes it one of France's main tourist attractions, the focal point of which is the Arcachon Basin.

Surfers enjoying the majestic breakers of the Atlantic coastline

◁ The village of Carennac, in the Dordogne valley

A *borie*, a small stone hut with conical roof, characteristic of the landscape of the Vézère valley

Inland, beyond the wall of dunes that runs parallel to the coast, lie many unspoilt areas, where land-use is tightly controlled. Dotted with lakes and marshes, another striking feature are the great green valleys carved out by the regions three main rivers, whose rich alluvail deposits continually enrich the soil. In the north, the Garonne meanders across the Agenais to join the Dordogne, flowing out from the Périgord, and spills out into the Gironde estuary. In the south, the Adour winds through the Pyrenees towards the sea.

The abundance of water has drawn people to Aquitaine since prehistoric times. Sites such as the Lascaux caves in the Dordogne, and finds like the Venus of Brassempouy in the Landes provide ample evidence of this.

NATURAL RESOURCES

Despite the many features that are common to the region as a whole, its most striking characteristic remains its great diversity. This is most evident in the uneven distribution of the population, nearly 44 per cent of which is concentrated in the largely urban Gironde. Outside the major cities, such as Bordeaux and its suburbs, Libourne, Mont-de-Marsan, Pau, Agen and Bayonne, the population is clustered in small towns and isolated villages, particularly in the Landes.

The extensive areas of highly fertile land support a thriving agricultural economy. This accounts for 5.3 per cent of the region's revenue – slightly ahead of construction, at 4.9 per cent – and 83 per cent of the land is given over to farming. In addition to cereals – including maize (the Landes being France's largest producer) – many other crops are now grown. These include kiwi fruit on the banks of the Adour, tobacco around Bergerac and Marmande, walnuts in the Périgord, and plums (the famous *prunes d'Agen*) in the Agenais. Livestock is also important: lamb from the Pays Basque, (also renowned for its cheeses), foie gras and other *confits* from the

Pottoks, the wild mountain ponies of the Pay Basque

Biarritz, a coastal resort since the 19th century

Dordogne, poultry from Saint-Sever and the Landes, and beef from Chalosse and Bazas are some of the best-known produce. In addition, there is the wine industry, around three-quarters of which is concentrated in Gironde. The region is one of the foremost producers of quality *(appellation d'origine contrôlée)* wines in France.

The entrance to
Cos d'Estournel

Timber is also an important resource. The region contains Europe's largest forested area of around 1.8 million ha (4.4 million acres), which provides pine – for construction and making paper – as well as oak, chestnut and beech. And finally, with four major ports, the Gulf of Gascony and the many estuaries and water courses, fishing, along with fish- and oyster-farming is a key earner too.

THE ROLE OF INDUSTRY

Industry accounts for 17 per cent of the region's wealth. The Latécoère aircraft factory was set up at Biscarrosse,

in the Landes, in 1930, and the region remains at the forefront of the aeronautics and spacecraft industry. Civil and miltary aircraft, helicopters and onboard systems – notably for the Ariane space rocket – are built either by large industrial consortiums or one of their 600 specialist subcontractors. This sector generally works closely with research scientists and developers, particularly those based at universities. The region boasts several important centres of learning, some of European importance. Chemicals, electronics, manufacturing (of shoes, for example), metallurgy and local crafts such as traditional Basque textiles, are other aspects of this wide-ranging industrial heritage.

However, Aquitiane's main source of wealth is its service sector, which accounts for 72.9 per cent of the economy. It depends largely on tourism and is expanding rapidly. Each year around 6 million visitors, 1 million of them from abroad, come to sample the region's natural attractions and architectural wonders, as well as its many festivals. Yet despite this huge influx, the dynamism and independent spirit of Aquitaine's diverse and distinct cultural heritage has been neither weakened nor compromised.

Pilgrims on the road to Santiago de Compostela

Basque supporters of Biarritz's rugby team

A CULTURAL MOSAIC

According to the theory advanced in the early 18th century by the philosopher Baron de Montesquieu – one of Aquitaine's most illustrious sons – a region's political system and character are dictated by local, natural and human factors, such as altitude, topography, latitude, distance from the sea, language, and so on. The land of Aquitaine, can be seen as a perfect illustration of this theory. Few parts of France boast so many different, deeply rooted cultures and languages.

Even the constant flow of foreign pilgrims, from the 11th century onwards, on route to the shrine of St James at Compostela, did little to dilute this focus on local tradition. As the region lay at the crossroads of the four main pilgrimage routes (from Paris via Tours; from Vézelay; from Le

Statue in the Parc
Théodore-Denis, in Dax

Puy-en-Velay; and from Arles via Toulouse), churches and hostels were built for those that passed through. Many fine examples remain, such as the Cathédrale Saint-André in Bordeaux and the Cathédrale Saint-Étienne in Périgueux, and have been declared World Heritage Sites. But despite their general Romanesque or Gothic styling, such grand buildings still have a distinctly local look.

The Pays Basque, in the south, has a particularly strong sense of indentity. This is expressed by the use of its own language, Euskara (which is taught in all schools), by its unique wooden-framed houses or *etxe (see p22)* and by its nationalist movement. In Béarn, at the foot of the Pyrénées to the east, Béarnese is spoken, especially in Oloron-Sainte-Marie, the home of the Basque beret. In central area of the Landes – a mixed landscape of river valleys, expanses of forest and long beaches backed by lakes and streams – local traditions live on most spectacularly in the bull-running festivals that have taken place since 1850. The Agenais, despite its relatively small size, has also preserved its local identity. It is noted for its gastronomic specialities,

The Stèle de Roland, at the Col d'Ibañeta, erected for Charlemagne's nephew, defeated by the Gascons

The classical and the modern in Bordeaux

such as its famous *prunes d'Agen*. The Périgord boasts a number of stately châteaux and prehistoric caves that reflect the area's unique character. It is also bisected by the river Dordogne, along which the traditional craft known *gabares* still sail.

Until well into the 15th century, Gascon was the main language of the the Gironde, and the use of local languages persists throughout Aquitaine. You will come across people who speak Occitan and Bordeaux has its own distinct patois, Bordeluche, although it is beginning to die out.

A "EUROPEAN" REGION

But such strong ties to their ancient roots do not mean that the people of Aquitaine have turned their backs on the rest of the world or the future. In 2003, the government of France unveiled plans for a new road and rail link, running from west to east across the southern part of the country. This will open up the entire region to eastern and southeastern Europe. It

already sits at the crossroads of the major trade routes between northern France and the Iberian Peninsula, and the Mediterranean and North Africa to the south. For centuries, people as well as goods have passed through, mostly via Bordeaux or Bayonne, and this traffic continues to enrich the region both economically and culturally. All this places Aquitaine firmly at the heart of modern Europe. However, a measure of the strength of the region's highly distinctive character is that it has always been able to absorb new influences and successfully blend them with the unique traditions of its past.

Château de la Brède, birthplace of Charles, Baron de Montesquieu

Plants and Animals of Aquitaine

Golden eagle

The southwest of France lies on the flight path of many thousands of migratory birds. These include barnacle and greylag geese, wigeon, avocets, ringed and grey plovers, knots and curlews. Venture up into the high mountainous areas and you are likely to spot golden (or booted) eagles, and bearded, griffon and Egyptian vultures along with animals such as chamois and marmots (introduced around 1950). Here too you will find some of the region's most beautiful flowers: gentians, yellow poppies, Pyrenean fritillary, lilies and irises. Down along the coast, sea holly and sea lilies, along with gillyflowers and convolvulus, lie scattered among the dunes, while toadflax, yellow bedstraw, hawkweed and Bayonne vetch appear almost everywhere.

Wood pigeons *pass through on their annual migration south over the Pyrenees to spend the winter in Spain. Since the Middle Ages, they have been hunted for food, as they fly by.*

SANDY COASTLINE
From Pointe de Grave, south of the the River Adour, sandy dunes stretch for 230km (140 miles), reaching a height of 100m (330ft) at Le Pyla. These dunes support vegetation typical of sandy conditions, including sea holly, sea lilies, golden rod, lucerne, spurge and sometimes shrubby horsetail.

ESTUARIES AND COASTAL MARSHLAND
From November to March, thousands of migratory birds come to the estuaries of the Gironde and the Bidassoa, the marshland of the Blayais and the northern Médoc, the Arcachon Basin, the Arguin sandbank and the Baie de Fontarrabie. While most fly on southwards, some spend the winter there.

Bayonne vetch *grows on the coastal dunes. This rare leguminous plant is now protected.*

Greylag geese *rest in the region every autumn, on their annual migration south.*

The pied oystercatcher *patrols the beaches in search of the cockles, mussels, winkles and crabs that make up the bulk of its diet.*

The avocet *uses its curved beak to search for small crustaceans in the shallow waters of the coastal marshes.*

AQUITAINE'S FISH

Gilt-head bream, black and red sea bream, sea bass, conger eels, blue sharks, bonito, coley, sole, turbot and dabs are found in abundance in the waters along the region's 300-km (190-mile) long coast. Shad, lamprey and eel are taken from the estuaries of the Gironde and the Adour. Tuna and anchovy are a major part of the catch off the shores of the Gulf of Gascony, where today around 2,000 fishermen in more than 400 fishing vessels ply their trade.

Shad *have increased greatly in number since the protection of their breeding grounds on the river at Bergerac and installations at the the Tuillères dam have created new spawning areas. The annual catch is around 200–400 tonnes.*

Sturgeon *swim up river estuaries between March and June, to breed in the spawning grounds of the Dordogne and the Garonne. Some of the eggs will be harvested, then sifted, washed and tossed in salt to produce caviar.*

FORÊT LANDAISE

Consisting mostly of maritime pines and covering more than 1 million ha (2.5 million acres), this is the largest forest in Europe. The trees were planted in the dunes in the 19th century to help stop sand from them being washed inland. Pine resin, which was tapped until 1990, was once a major source of income in the Landes.

PYRENEAN MOUNTAINS

The rocky outcrops about halfway up the Massif des Arbailles and the Forêts d'Iraty are home to capercaillie, woodpeckers, golden eagles and bearded, griffon and Egyptian vultures. Grouse and marmots can be found in the stony areas. Brown bears, which are becoming increasingly rare, live in the high valleys of the Aspe and the Ossau.

The common crane *is a regular visitor to the area around the Bidassoa estuary. Several hundred overwinter from November to March in Landes, particularly in the firing ranges at Le Poteau.*

The bearded vulture *inhabits the Haute Soule and the high Aspe valley.*

Maritime pines *have male cones, which are evident in early summer.*

The griffon vulture *usually nests in the Massif de la Pierre-St-Martin, in the Nive valley (see pp198–9), in the Aldudes valley (see pp202–203) and in the Forêt des Arbailles (see p208).*

Religious Architecture

The four ancient pilgrimage routes to Santiago de Compostela in Spain pass through the southwest corner of France (see pp206–207). This alone has helped to promote a remarkable tradition of religious architecture. No fewer than 19 historic buildings across the region have been declared World Heritage Sites by UNESCO. Hostelries for the many pilgrims journeying to Compostela, as well as fortified churches and impressive abbeys, were constructed as early as the 7th century. Several were later endowed with majestic cathedrals or great domed churches, fashioned in the Gothic and Renaissance styles.

Façade of the church at Dax, in the Landes

ROMANESQUE (7TH–11TH CENTURIES)

The region's Romanesque buildings are of several types. The fortified churches of the Périgord obviously played a defensive role. Others, like l'Hôpital-Saint-Blaise, in the Pays Basque, served as hostels for pilgrims travelling on the route to Compostela. Also typical of the Romanesque architecture of the southwest are great abbeys like those at Cadouin, Moirax, La Sauve-Majeure and Saint-Sever.

Doorway of the 11th-century Église Sainte-Foy, Morlaàs

Enclosed belfry, built in brick

Cathédrale Sainte-Quitterie, *in Aire-sur-l'Adour, was built in the 12th century and up until the 18th century was remodelled several times. It combines Romanesque and Gothic elements.*

Buttress

Doorway framed by a broken arch surmounted by a tympanum

Octagonal belfry

Arm of the central transept

Star-shaped window

The church of l'Hôpital-Saint-Blaise, *a hostel for pilgrims on the route to Compostela, was built from schist and yellow sandstone. Romanesque and Byzantine styles mix at this World Heritage Site.*

Restored Romanesque façade

Columned portal

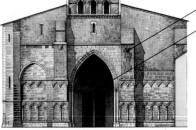

The church at Moirax, *in Lot-et-Garonne, formed part of a Cluniac priory. It is a fine example of Romanesque architecture of the 11th and 12th centuries. The central, projecting part of the façade is surmounted by an open belfry, which is in turn crowned by a pointed roof.*

DOMED CHURCHES (11TH–12TH CENTURIES)

From the 11th century, many churches in southwest France, particularly in the Ribérac region, were built with Byzantine-style domes, although they were still laid out to a Romanesque plan. With five domes arranged in the shape of a Greek cross, the Cathédrale Saint-Front, in Périgueux, serves as a good example, despite later alterations. Others are the Église Sainte-Marie in Aubiac and the Église Sainte-Croix in Oloron-Sainte-Marie, which has a Moorish-style ribbed dome.

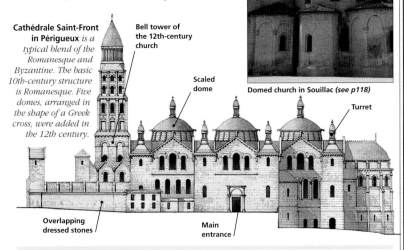

Cathédrale Saint-Front in Périgueux *is a typical blend of the Romanesque and Byzantine. The basic 10th-century structure is Romanesque. Five domes, arranged in the shape of a Greek cross, were added in the 12th century.*

Bell tower of the 12th-century church

Scaled dome

Domed church in Souillac *(see p118)*

Turret

Overlapping dressed stones

Main entrance

GOTHIC TO RENAISSANCE (13TH–16TH CENTURIES)

In the Aquitaine, the transition from the Romanesque to the Gothic was gradual. This can be seen in the remodelling of the region's cathedrals, such as the Cathédrale Saint-André in Bordeaux. The Cathédrale de Bazas, built from 1233, was one of the first to use Gothic styling.

15th-century Gothic doorway at Cathédral de Bazas

Cathédrale Saint-André in Bordeaux, *consecrated in 1096, has a Romanesque nave with Gothic spires and towers. Renaissance styling can be seen in elements such as the buttresses and former rood screen.*

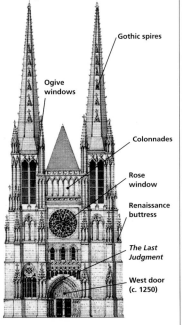

Gothic spires

Ogive windows

Colonnades

Rose window

Renaissance buttress

The Last Judgment

West door (c. 1250)

Vernacular Architecture

Mask motif, Bordeaux

Because Aquitaine is made up of several, often contrasting, regions, local architecture has evolved to suit a wide range of lifestyles and geographical conditions. The buildings that are typical of Aquitaine range from half-timbered Landes houses and Basque *etxes* to Perigordian farmhouses and dovecotes. While a variety of traditional styles can be seen dotted across the countryside, urban houses such as the *échoppe bordelaise* and Arcachon villa reflect the social and economic development of particular towns and cities.

The bow window, a feature of some Arcachon houses

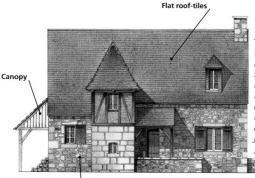

Flat roof-tiles

Canopy

Limestone walls

The Perigordian farmhouse *is a highly practical country dwelling. The design varies slightly according to the precise locality, but these sturdily built houses are usually divided up to allow separate areas for human habitation, for keeping animals and for storing crops, allowing family life and farm work to take place all under one roof.*

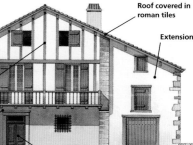

The *etche* (or etxe) *is the most common type of house in the Pays Basque. There are several variations, including those typical of Soule and Basse-Navarre. The most typical is the Labourd type (right) which is usually white with coloured half-timbering.*

Roof covered in roman tiles

Extension

Blueish-green or deep red half-timbering

Emban (canopy)

East-facing entrance

Emban (canopy)

Façade with windows

Half-timbering with cob or brick in-fill

Landes houses *have a distinctive outline, with low-pitched roofs and half-timbering. They are often set in an* airial *(a clearing surrounded by pines) and are east-facing for protection against storms coming in off the Atlantic.*

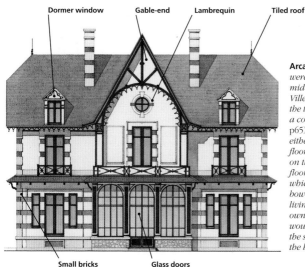

Dormer window   Gable-end   Lambrequin   Tiled roof

Small bricks   Glass doors

Arcachon houses
were first built in the mid-19th century in the Ville d'Hiver district of the town, which is now a conservation area (see p65). *These houses have either one or two upper floors. The servants lived on the "damp" lower floor. On the first floor, which sometimes has a bow window, were the living rooms. The owners of the house would always sleep on the second floor, under the high-pitched roof.*

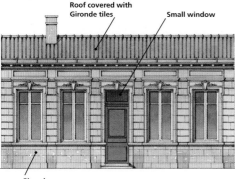

Roof covered with
Gironde tiles   Small window

Gironde
limestone

The *échoppe bordelaise* *is a single-storey building, sometimes with a small garden at the rear. It is highly typical of Bordeaux and its environs, where there are over 10,000 examples. Échoppes were originally relatively humble houses in working-class areas of the city, but later became comfortable middle-class homes.*

DOVECOTES

Particularly common in the Lot-et-Garonne, dovecotes form a distinctive element in the rural architecture of southwest France. A vestige of life in former times, they housed birds, whose droppings, known as *colombine* (from *colombe*, meaning "dove"), would be collected and used as fertilizer. Because keeping doves depended on owning a fairly large amount of land, dovecotes also signalled that the owner must be wealthy. They were built in various shapes and sizes, in brick or stone, sometimes with half-timbering and usually with a roof. Constructed either on the ground or set on columns, most were located in open countryside, where the smell and sound of the birds would not offend. Dovecotes were also integrated into other buildings, in the form of large cavities or turrets, and some were built in towns, within *bastides* like Monflanquin, where the birds were probably also used as a source of food.

A dovecote on stilts, for protection against predators

Bastide Towns

Picture from *Statuts et Coutumes d'Agen*

Between 1220 and 1370, the counts of Toulouse and King Edward I of England, ordered nearly 300 fortified towns *(bastides)* to be built in south-western France. Laid out to a set plan, they were established for political and economic as well as military reasons. Through them it was possible to bring together local populations and to maximize yields from agricultural land. A reciprocal agreement between the founder of a *bastide* and the owner of the surrounding land safeguarded the rights of each. The bastide was governed by a bailiff, who represented the king.

Entrance to the *bastide* of Penne-d'Agenais

Charretières, wide thoroughfares built especially for carts, served as the main routes into the central main square.

The church, *an integral element of a* bastide, *served as a refuge during times of danger and place of safekeeping for the relics of saints. With a belfry, small arches, machicolation and corner turrets, some churches were formidable fortresses.*

Houses *were originally just two stories high, the upper floor providing the living quarters. On the ground floor was a craftsman's workshop or a shopkeeper's store.*

Traversières were the smaller streets, set at right angles to the *charretières*.

The market hall, *a square wooden structure, was always sited in the main square. The upper floor was sometimes used to house the town council.*

The main square was the focal point of life in the *bastide*. This convenient and practical space was the location of the town's administrative centre. Fairs and markets were also held here.

The street lay-out *included not just the wide* charretières *and smaller* traversières, *but* carreyrous, *alleyways that ran along the backs of houses, and* andrones, *the narrow spaces between houses, designed to prevent fires from spreading.*

Couverts, *or arcaded galleries with living quarters above, formed a shaded walkway running around the main square.*

Timber-framed walls *of houses were filled in with cob, baked earth or bricks.*

A TYPICAL BASTIDE

In contrast to most small medieval towns with their narrow, winding streets, *bastides* were built to a highly rigid formula, and are all remarkably similar. Laid out on a rectangular or square plan, depending on the lie of the land, they have straight streets that intersect at right angles to form a checkerboard pattern. The houses, built on plots of a roughly even size, were generally long and narrow, with a courtyard or a small garden either at the back or front.

Bullfighting and Bullrunning

For centuries bullfighting and bullrunning have been popular sports in southwest France, especially in the Landes. Such secular activities were often part of religious festivals, particularly the feast of Saint-Jean in Saint-Sever, and that of Sainte-Madeleine held in Mont-de-Marsan. Although a document dating from 1289 mentions bullrunning in the streets of Bayonne, its rules had not yet been standardized, and both bullrunners and spectators would take part. It was not until the 19th century that the practice of bullrunning, as it can be seen today, was formalized. The sport of bullfighting arrived in the region from Spain around the same time, with the first French fight taking place in the Saint-Esprit district of Bayonne on 21 August 1853.

Poster for a bullfight in Bayonne in 1897

*The **paseo** is the opening ceremony before a bullfight. The matadors parade in the bullring, followed by their assistants and by the picadors.*

The *montera* is worn during the first two tercios.

The suit of lights, the richly embroidered bullfighter's attire, can weigh up to 10kg (22lb).

Inserting the banderillos *may be done by the* maestro *(the matador) himself, or by a* banderillero, *a member of the* cuadrilla, *the matador's team.*

BULLFIGHTING

Pitting a bull against a matador, a bullfight *(lidia)* consists of three phases *(tercios)*. In the first, the *tercio des piques*, the bull is teased with a cape *(above)*, after which the picadors prick the animal with their lances to provoke it to fight. Then come the *tercio des banderilles* and finally the *faena*, when the matador makes elegant passes at the bull with the *muleta*, a small piece of red fabric that acts as a lure. Finally, the matador kills the bull with a sword.

Working with the red cape *is the most exciting phase of the bullfight. The bullfighter's skill in using a variety of passes thrills the audience.*

The bull is killed *by a technique known as* al volapié, *in which the matador leaps onto the bull.*

The **leap** *is one of the bullrunner's two main gymnastic moves. Here he is executing a daring backward spiral, the most recently introduced move.*

The **écart** *is bullrunning's other main move. It involves avoiding the charging bull by swerving to one side.*

BULLRUNNING

This colourful spectacle demands both courage and agility. The *écarteur* (bullrunner) avoids the charging bull, the *coursière*, by executing balletic moves of varying complexity; elegance and the degree of risk being highly admired. Today, a rope is attached to the bull to control it more as it charges. The animal's horns are trimmed and the performance no longer ends with its slaughter.

The **écarteur** wears white trousers and a bolero decorated with gold or silver leaf.

One *coursière* may be used in around 20 bullruns a year, over a period of at least 10 years.

The **saut périlleux** *(daring leap), admired for its technical and artistic qualities, arouses the bull's aggression.*

The **rope** is held by the *courdayre*, who controls the charging bull.

The **saut de l'ange** *(angel's leap) over the bull, is one of the most widely used moves.*

WHERE TO WATCH A BULLFIGHT OR BULLRUN

Most bullfights and bullruns take place from March to October. While bullrunning can easily be seen in many towns and villages in the Landes, there are relatively few bullrings. Some of the most prestigious ones are in the following towns:

Bayonne
Avenue des Fleurs.
Map A4. **Tel** *(05) 59 46 61 00.*

Dax
Bd Paul-Lasaosa.
Map B4. **Tel** *(05) 58 90 99 09.*

Mont-de-Marsan
Bd de la République.
Map C4. **Tel** *(05) 58 75 39 08.*

Saint-Sever
Butte de Morlanne.
Map C4. **Tel** *(05) 58 76 34 64.*

Basque Traditions

Basque cross on traditional dress

The Basque people are fiercely proud of their cultural heritage and ancient language, Euskara, whose origins remain vague. The strength of this sense of national identity can be clearly seen at the many local festivals, such as those held in Bayonne, that involve dancing, singing, music and parades in which traditional red and white Basque costumes are worn and the Basque flag is carried. Jousting and other sports also feature, including trials of strength, boat races – in vessels very similar to ancient whaleboats – and tests of the speed and skill demonstrated in *pelota*, the well-known Basque ball game.

IKURRIÑA

The Basque flag – the *ikurriña* – was designed in the late 19th century in Euskadi, the Basque name for Biscay. Its red background symbolizes the Basque people. On this sits a white cross, (symbolizing Christianity), superimposed over a green cross of St Andrew (symbolizing the law). Along with the Euskara language, the flag is one of the most potent symbols of Basque national pride.

Weights lifted by Basque strongmen can exceed 200kg (440lb).

Basque strongman contests *consist of seven separate tests of strength. One of these is stone-lifting. Such contests take place both in the Pays Basque, in France, and in Euskadi, in Spain.*

Thigh protectors, pads made of fabric, prevent bruising when the weightlifter rests heavy stones on his thighs.

Bands of Basque musicians *help create the atmosphere at Bayonne's festivals and during bullrunning contests.*

The txistu, *a flute-like instrument with three holes, is played with one hand.* Txistu *music is played at many religious ceremonies.*

Soka-tira *is a game of tug-of-war involving two teams of eight to ten people.*

BASQUE LITERATURE

With 790,000 Basque-speakers, 40,000 of whom live in France, Basque literature is enjoying a revival. Some 100 publishers and almost 300 authors have published about 1,500 titles a year since 1975. Authors such as Bernardo Atxaga are keen to keep Basque literature alive and to spread awareness of it around the world. Remarkably, his novel *Obabakoak* has been translated into 25 languages.

Basque edition of novel *Obabakoak*

The alarde *is a parade in which hundreds of young people in traditional Basque dress march to the sound of flutes.*

The Zamalzain, *or horse-man, is a character in the annual masquerade that takes place in the Basque region of Soule. Hosted by a different village each year, this itinerant carnival in Basque costume begins and ends with brilliantly performed dances.*

Basque songs *are an aspect of every kind of festivity, from pastoral festivals and masquerades to* bertxulari *contests, when singers improvise on a given theme.*

BURIAL RITES

The circular crosses that were erected to mark graves in Basque cemeteries date back to the Middle Ages. However, they are thought to predate Christianity. These funerary stones, with their disc-shaped heads, are decorated with a square and a circle, which together symbolize the transition from life on earth to the world beyond. They are decorated with religious motifs, inscriptions in Latin or Basque, and tools or implements relating to the trade of the deceased.

Circular crosses over graves in a Basque graveyard

Vineyards in Aquitaine

Bordeaux is widely regarded as the wine capital of the world. The area's fertile soil, gentle climate, and age-old methods of production, as well as sea and river trade, have each contributed to this distinguished status. Pauillac, Pessac-Léognan, Pomerol, Saint-Émilion and Sauternes, are all wines of international renown. But Aquitaine's vineyards produce other fine wines. These include Bergerac, Buzet, Côtes-de-Duras, Monbazillac, Jurançon and Irouléguy. There is also Armagnac, the famous dry brandy, and the spirit, Floc de Gascogne.

Wine barrel, 18th century

Château Lafite Rothschild at Pauillac, producer of the finest Médoc wines

Grape harvest at Château Latour, in the Médoc

VINEYARDS

The vineyards of Aquitaine fill the region's wide river valleys. While the Garonne flows through the vineyards of Bordeaux and Agen, the Dordogne bisects those of Bergerac. Near the Pyrénées, the vineyards of Tursan, Pacherenc and Madiran are irrigated by the Adour, and those of Jurançon by the Gave de Pau.

The Irouléguy vineyards *lie south of Bayonne, around Saint-Étienne-de-Baïgorry and Saint-Jean-Pied de-Port. They produce fruity white, red and rosé wines.*

Arcachon

Dax

Bayonne

Peyrehorade

Salie de-Béa

St-Étienne-de-Baïgorry • Irouléguy

0   40 km

0   40 miles

WINE FACTS

Location and Climate
The vineyards of Bordeaux have two major advantages: well-drained soil and a temperate climate, with heavy rainfall in winter and plenty of sunshine in summer and autumn. The subsoil, which consists of clay and limestone, is highly suitable for vine-growing.

Grapes
Around Bordeaux, the main grapes are Cabernet-Sauvignon, Merlot and Cabernet Franc for red wine, and Sémillon and Sauvignon for white wine.

Great Vintages
In the 20th century, the years 1945, 1947, 1949, 1953, 1959, 1970, 1988, 1989 and 1990 produced some exceptional vintages throughout the region. More recently, Saint-Émilion and Pomerol vintages of 1995, 1998, 2000 and 2001 were outstanding, as were the Médoc and Graves vintages of 1995, 1996, 1999, 2000, 2003 and 2005. Sweet white wines like Loupiac, Sauternes and Cérons were excellent in 1996, 1998, 2001, 2002 and 2003. Whites like Graves and Pessac-Léognan of 1997, 2000, 2001, 2002 and 2005 were also memorable.

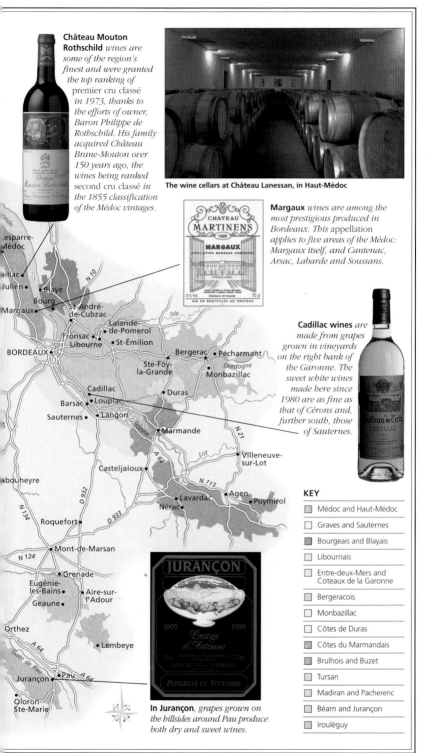

Château Mouton Rothschild *wines are some of the region's finest and were granted the top ranking of* premier cru classé *in 1973, thanks to the efforts of owner, Baron Philippe de Rothschild. His family acquired Château Brane-Mouton over 150 years ago, the wines being ranked* second cru classé *in the 1855 classification of the Médoc vintages.*

The wine cellars at Château Lanessan, in Haut-Médoc

Margaux *wines are among the most prestigious produced in Bordeaux. This* appellation *applies to five areas of the Médoc: Margaux itself, and Cantenac, Arsac, Labarde and Soussans.*

Cadillac *wines are made from grapes grown in vineyards on the right bank of the Garonne. The sweet white wines made here since 1980 are as fine as that of Cérons and, further south, those of Sauternes.*

In **Jurançon**, *grapes grown on the hillsides around Pau produce both dry and sweet wines.*

KEY

- Médoc and Haut-Médoc
- Graves and Sauternes
- Bourgeais and Blayais
- Libournais
- Entre-deux-Mers and Coteaux de la Garonne
- Bergeracois
- Monbazillac
- Côtes de Duras
- Côtes du Marmandais
- Brulhois and Buzet
- Tursan
- Madiran and Pacherenc
- Béarn and Jurançon
- Irouléguy

AQUITAINE THROUGH THE YEAR

In Aquitaine, every season has its attractions. In spring the landscape becomes lush and verdant, and many open-air festivals take place. With traditional as well as modern singing and dancing, these festivals celebrate the region's culture and history. Summer marks the start of the bullfighting and bullrunning

Basque pelota player

season in the Landes, as well as a number of important sporting events. Autumn and winter are punctuated by festivals showcasing local specialties and marking the grape harvest. This is also when carnivals and masquerades take place in the Pays Basque.

SPRING

In spring, and particularly during school holidays, the region's coastal resorts come to life. Many of the traditional festivals also take place at this time of the year.

MARCH

Bi Harriz Lau Xori *(late March)*, Biarritz. Concerts, dancing and film, celebrating the language Euskara.
Le Chaînon Manquant *(late March–early April)*, Figeac. Dance, plays, music and other art forms. This popular event, with professional artistes, also showcases new talent.

APRIL

Fête des Soufflaculs *(early April)*, Nontron. A medieval festival in which the town's inhabitants chase each other through the streets, dressed in nightgowns, in order to ward off evil spirits.

Festival Art et Courage *(mid-April)*, Pomarez. A major event at the Landes' great bullrunning mecca *(see p27)*.
Bayonne Ham Fair *(week before Easter)*, Bayonne. Hundreds of local hams are put on display. Music is provided by Basque bands.
Festival des Vallées et des Bergers *(late April–early May)*, Oloron-Sainte-Marie. A two-day festival with groups singing in Béarnais.

MAY

Terre d'Images *(early May)*, Biarritz. An international event, with exhibitions and workshops devoted to travel and photography.
Wine and Cheese Fair *(8 May)*, Monflanquin. A showcase for growers and producers of southwestern specialities *(see pp256–7)*.
Herri Urrats *(mid-May)*. Dancing, singing and other activities, set around the 4-km (3-mile) perimeter of the lake at Saint-Pée-sur-Nivelle.

Poster advertising Bayonne's programme of festivals

SUMMER

During the summer, large numbers of visitors flock to the coast. Inland, many towns and villages host festivals. Some of these, such as the grand events that are held in Bayonne, Dax and Mont-de-Marsan, draw huge crowds.

Festival d'Art Flamenco, Mont-de-Marsan

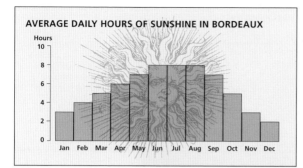

Sunshine Chart

The Gironde enjoys just over 2,000 hours of sunshine a year. The sunniest days are concentrated in the summer months, although winds blowing in from the northwest off the Atlantic help to cool the air. From October to February, parts of the region are often cloaked in fog.

JUNE

Jurade *(3rd Sunday in June),* Saint-Émilion. A medieval ceremony, revived in 1948, when the season's wine is tasted and given the official Saint-Émilion seal.

Festival d'Art Flamenco *(late June–early July),* Mont-de-Marsan. Six-day flamenco festival with dancing, music and storytelling.

Internationaux de Cesta Punta Professionel *(June–August),* Saint-Jean-de-Luz. Professional players compete on open courts.

JULY

Fête du Vin *(late June)* and **Fête du Fleuve** *(early July),* Bordeaux. Two festivals, held in alternate years, with sports, wine tastings and exhibitions.

Fête de la Transhumance *(early July),* Ossau valley. Traditional singing and dancing, with tastings of cheeses and *garbure* (a soup).

La Félibrée *(early July),* Dordogne. A celebration of the Occitan language and culture; location varies.

Fêtes de la Madeleine *(mid-July),* Mont-de-Marsan. A festival with a Spanish

Transhumance, marked by a festival, in the Ossau valley

flavour, in honour of the town's patron saint.

Festival des Jeux du Théâtre *(mid-July–early August),* Sarlat. An open-air drama festival.

Bataille de Castillon *(mid-July–mid-August).* Elaborate reconstruction of this battle of 1453 *(see p41).*

Fête aux Fromages Fermiers *(late July),* Aspe valley. The town of Etsaut shows its ewes'-milk cheeses *(see p209).*

Nuits Atypiques de Langon *(late July).* A festival of world music, with instruments ranging from *peuhl* flutes to balalaïkas.

Fête de l'Huître *(July–August),* Arcachon basin. An opportunity to sample the area's famous oysters and see oyster farmers in traditional dress.

AUGUST

Mimos *(1st week),* Périgueux. World-famous international

contemporary mime festival.

Fêtes de Bayonne *(early August).* A five-day non-stop fiesta with bullrunning, Basque orchestras and banqueting in the bodegas, a children's day on Thursday, and a major bullfight on Sunday.

Féria de Dax *(mid-August).* With traditional celebrations and bullfighting, this is one of the region's most famous festivals.

Journées Médiévales *(mid-August),* Monflanquin. Medieval music and dancing.

Festival de Force Basque *(mid-August),* Saint-Palais. Strongmen of the Pays Basque compete in trials of strength *(see p28).*

Rip Curl Pro *(mid-August),* Hossegor. An international surfing championship *(see p279).*

Lacanau Pro Surf *(mid-August).* World surfing championship.

Festival du Périgord Noir *(throughout August).* Baroque and classical music performed in historic buildings and some more unusual places.

An enthusiastic crowd at the Féria de Dax

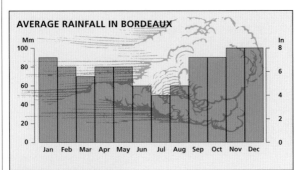

AVERAGE RAINFALL IN BORDEAUX

| | Jan | Feb | Mar | Apr | May | Jun | Jul | Aug | Sep | Oct | Nov | Dec |

Rainfall

Aquitaine is a fairly wet region, where it generally rains all year round, although it is usually wetter in winter than in summer. Rainfall tends to be gentle rather than heavy. The average annual rainfall in the Gironde area is between 70cm (27in) and 100cm (39in).

Saint-Émilion's *jurats* **(winetasters) at the top of the Tour du Roy**

AUTUMN

In the early autumn, the weather is usually still warm enough for outdoor activities. All over southwest France, the grape harvest is about to begin, and many colourful gatherings take place, celebrating the local wines. Art, dancing and regional specialities also have their own festivals.

SEPTEMBER

Le Temps d'Aimer *(September)*, Biarritz. Celebrating the art of dance, from classical ballet to hip-hop.
Académie Internationale de Musique Maurice Ravel *(mid-September)*, Saint-Jean-de-Luz and Ciboure. Young musicians perform pieces by great French composers both classical and modern.
Fête du Sel *(mid-September)*, Salies-de-Béarn. A world barrel-lifting championship organized by the Jurade du Sel *(see p217)*.
Jurade *(late September)*, Saint-Émilion. Linked with the tasting ceremony held in June *(see p33)*, this part of the *Jurade* involves measuring the annual grape harvest.

OCTOBER

Foire aux Fromages and Marché à l'Ancienne *(first weekend in October)*, Laruns. With street performances, singing, dancing and period dress, the village re-creates the age of Henri IV *(see p43)*.
Championnat de France de Course Landaise *(early October)*. This event, which takes place at a different bullring each year, marks the close of the bullrunning season.
Fête du Piment *(late October)*, Espelette *(see p199)*. Garlands of the area's famous sweet

Pepper motif, Fête du Piment, Espelette

red peppers are blessed and hung on the façades of houses. Basque strongman contests and enthronings into the local brotherhood also form part of the celebrations.

NOVEMBER

Festival du Film *(early November)*, Sarlat. Screenings, awards ceremonies and seminars and training sessions for budding producers and directors given by professional filmmakers.
Festival Novart Bordeaux *(November)*. A major showcase for all types of contemporary art.
Festivolailles *(late November)*, Saint-Sever. A poultry and foie gras fair aimed at gourmets and connoisseurs. Prizes are awarded for the finest fowl and for the best pâtés on show.

Performance at the Temps d'Aimer, a dance festival in Biarritz

AVERAGE TEMPERATURES IN BORDEAUX

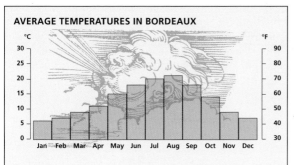

Temperatures
Because of its oceanic climate, the Gironde has relatively mild winters and pleasantly warm summers. The average temperature in January is 5–7 °C (41–45 °F), and in July and August, 19–21 °C (66–70 °F). For about three weeks a year, temperatures can rise as high as 30°C (96°F).

WINTER

With Christmas on its way, celebrations begin in earnest. Locally made handicrafts and delicacies fill the many Christmas markets that are held.
This is also the season for making foie gras, which is honoured with a whole range of festivities.

DECEMBER

Fête des Vignerons en Jurançon *(mid-December)* Jazz and rock evenings, a local delicacies market, a meal prepared by the Toqués du Terroir (local gourmet society) and wine tastings.

Masquerade dancer, La Soule

Olentzero *(mid-December).* This festival grew out of the pagan practice of marking the winter solstice. Olentzero, a Basque folk character, assumed the status of Father Christmas in the 1960s. According to legend, Olentzero comes down from the mountains, and delivers firewood to towns and villages so that no-one should be cold.

JANUARY

Masquerades *(first Sun in January to first Thu in Lent),* La Soule. This ritualized dance carnival takes place on successive Sundays, in a different village each time.

The main dance, the *Godalet Dantza* (Glass Dance), is performed around a glass of wine. The festival ends in Tardets, where all masqueraders gather.
Foire aux Pottoks *(last Tue and Wed in January),* Espelette. A horse fair, where *pottoks* (small Basque horses) are traded *(see p198).* It takes place twice a year.
Carnivals *(Candlemas to the start of Lent or Easter),* throughout the Pays Basque. Towns and villages come to life with music, dance and colourful parades. A common scene is the ritual awakening of a bear, which heralds the beginning of springtime.

FEBRUARY

Jumping International *(early February),* Bordeaux. Covering everything there is

The Pyrénées-Atlantiques have several winter sports resorts

to know about the world of horses, this takes place at the Parc des Expositions, at the same time as the exhibition Chevalexpo. It is a major event in the international showjumping circuit, attracting many famous names, and includes a competition for disabled riders.
Fête des Bœufs Gras *(mid-February),* Bazas. Dating from the 13th century, when Edward I, king of England, ruled Aquitaine, this festival takes place on the Thursday before Shrove Tuesday to mark the end of the carnival season and the approach of Lent. Immaculately groomed oxen, their horns decorated with ribbons and flowers, are weighed, then paraded, before being judged in front of the cathedral. Once the prizes have been awarded, there is an exhibition of winners, followed by a great banquet at which beef is served. All the animals on display are of a local breed that is thought to have originated in Spain.

PUBLIC HOLIDAYS

New Year's Day
(1 January)
Easter Sunday and Easter Monday
Ascension (sixth Thursday after Easter)
Labour Day (1 May)
Victory Day (8 May)
Bastille Day (14 July)
Assumption (15 August)
All Saints' Day (1 Nov)
Armistice Day (11 Nov)
Christmas Day (25 Dec)

THE HISTORY OF AQUITAINE

The Romans gave the name Aquitania to the southwest corner of France, meaning "near the sea" or "water-rich". In the 13th century, the English called it Guyenne. Now known to the French as Aquitaine, its borders have shifted constantly over the centuries. It has served as a melting pot where different peoples have met and intermingled, creating a region marked by sharp contrasts and diversity. Yet the whole region shares a unifying characteristic: a rich cultural heritage stretching back to the beginning of history.

THE DAWN OF HUMANITY

Of all regions of France, Aquitaine is by far the most important in terms of prehistory. This is most true of the Périgord, an area with an almost unique cluster of major prehistoric sites.

Around 400,000 BC, the first hunters arrived in the Vézère valley, in the Dordogne, where they lived in rock-shelters in the limestone cliffs and where they made flint tools. Today, traces of their activities have been discovered at over 150 sites and in some 50 decorated caves. Thanks to

Venus of Laussel

the discovery of the rock-shelter at Le Moustier, we have an insight into the life and religious rituals of prehistoric hunters from around 80,000–30,000 BC. At the Cro-Magnon site in Les Eyzies, artefacts from 35,000–10,000 BC have revealed the amazingly high level of skill attained by early man. A similar sense of wonder comes from looking at the cave paintings, depicting mammoths, horses and reindeer, at Lascaux, and the female figurines, such as the so-called Venus figures, found at Laussel in the Dordogne and at Brassempouy in the Landes.

During the Neolithic period, the population grew. People began to settle in villages and grow crops and domesticate animals. Their craft skills developed. They wove woollen cloth, worked with wood and leather, and made metal tools and weapons, first from copper, then later from bronze. In the Médoc, around 1,500 BC, large bronze axes were being produced.

Cave painting of a bison at Lascaux

TIMELINE

400,000 BC The first humans settle in the Vézère valley	120,000 BC Tools become markedly more complex and regular in shape	35,000–10 000 BC Cro-Magnon Man makes more sophisticated tools and weapons

400,000 BC	200,000 BC	100,000 BC	50,000 BC	10,000 BC
	About 200,000 BC Tools designed for a specific purpose, such as scrapers and awls, begin to be made		*Venus of Brassempouy*	**18,000–15,000 BC** Cave paintings at Lascaux

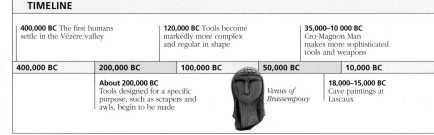

◁ The marriage of Louis XIV and Maria Theresa of Austria on 9 June 1660 at Saint-Jean-de-Luz, by Laumosnier

ROMAN GAUL

In the early 3rd century BC, the Gauls (a Celtic people), began to settle in southwest France, which at the time was sparsely populated. They integrated rapidly with the indigenous population, settling mainly around urban centres such as Burdigala (now Bordeaux) and Aginum (now Agen). Their leaders established trade links with Narbonensis, a Roman province in southern Gaul, and began to import goods from Italy, including wine. But in 52 BC, the Romans defeated the Gauls at the Battle of Alesia. This marked the beginning of Roman dominance in southwest France. Villas with large agricultural estates were established on the banks of the region's great rivers, and a building programme began in the towns, where amphitheatres, aqueducts and temples (a vestige of which is the Tour de Vésone in Périgueux) were constructed. Gallo-Roman civilization was born. However, the end of the 3rd century saw the first of many

Marble statue of Diana, Gallo-Roman period

invasions by Germanic tribes from the east. The population took refuge behind hastily constructed ramparts, and another turbulent period in the history of Aquitaine began.

A DARK AGE

At the beginning of the 5th century, a series of invasions led to the Visigoths making Aquitaine part of their kingdom in 481. They, in turn, were expelled by the Franks. It was around this time that Christianity was beginning to take hold in the towns and cities, although it did not really become widespread in the region until as late as the 11th century. But this period did see the start of the construction of some of Aquitaine's first great abbeys and churches. After the death of their king, Clovis, in 511, Frankish (Merovingian) control was weakened by the division of the region into separate administrative areas. Taking advantage of this, the Vascons, a people from the Pyrenees who are sometimes equated with the

---

ROMAN VILLA AT PLASSAC

From around the 1st century BC, the Romans established agricultural estates all over what is now southwest France. Each centred around a villa complex, which included the owner's house, accommodation for estate workers and various farm buildings. All around was agricultural land, where cereals were cultivated and, from the 1st century AD, vines were also grown. Excavations carried out between 1963 and 1978 at the site of a Gallo-Roman villa near Plassac, at the head of the Gironde estuary, revealed the foundations of a house built by a wealthy landowner from Italy in AD 14–20. The house, which was later modified several times, was richly decorated with materials, such as marble, that had been imported from North Africa.

Roman mosaic in the Musée d'Aquitaine, Bordeaux

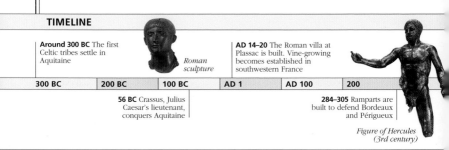

Basques, invaded in 580, settling in an area between the Garonne river and the Pyrenees, which became known as Gascony in the 7th century. A hundred years later, the Arabs arrived, but they were repulsed at Poitiers by Charles Martel in 732. Then the Carolingians annexed the territory, but their rule was relatively short-lived. In the mid-9th century, the Normans sailed up the Adour, Dordogne and Garonne rivers, pillaging and ravaging towns, churches and monasteries as they went. Bordeaux was torched in 848. Gallo-Roman civilization was broken and gradually it withered away.

Merovingian buckle

Some religious buildings, like the Cathédrale Saint-Front in Périgueux, were now being built in the Byzantine-Romanesque style. Most churches were also lavishly decorated with ornate mosaics sculptures and frescoes. But from the 13th century onward, there was a general downturn in religious architecture, although the great Gothic cathedrals of Bordeaux, Bazas and Bayonne were rebuilt in the 14th century, following the devastation of the Hundred Years' War.

Thanks to Philip the Fair, a firm ruler and accomplished diplomat, Bertrand de Got, Archbishop of Bordeaux, was elected Pope in 1305, as Clement V. His position allowed him to bestow favours on the Gascon clergy. He also initiated the construction of the great châteaux at Roquetaillade, Fargues, Budos and at Villandraut, in the Gironde, where he was a regular visitor.

SPREAD OF CHRISTIANITY

During the 11th and 12th centuries, political stability returned and the population began to increase. Churches and monasteries were now springing up all over the southwest of France. The Abbaye de la Sauve-Majeure was founded by Gérard de Corbie in 1079 and at the time of his death, around 1095, it had more than 300 monks and exercised control over about 20 priories. As religious communities in the region began to multiply, more and more land was being cleared in order to build abbeys and monasteries, especially along the main pilgrim routes going southward through France and the Col de Roncevaux pass over the Pyrenees to Santiago de Compostela.

Bertrand de Got, who became Pope Clement v in 1305

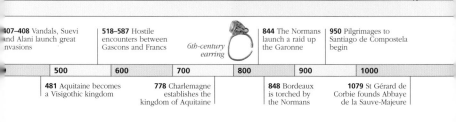

| 407–408 Vandals, Suevi and Alani launch great invasions | 518–587 Hostile encounters between Gascons and Francs | *6th-century earring* | 844 The Normans launch a raid up the Garonne | 950 Pilgrimages to Santiago de Compostela begin |

| 500 | 600 | 700 | 800 | 900 | 1000 |

| | 481 Aquitaine becomes a Visigothic kingdom | 778 Charlemagne establishes the kingdom of Aquitaine | 848 Bordeaux is torched by the Normans | 1079 St Gérard de Corbie founds Abbaye de la Sauve-Majeure |

English Rule in France

In 1137, Eleanor of Aquitaine, daughter and heiress of William X, Duc d'Aquitaine, married Louis VII, later king of France. However, as Eleanor had not only failed to produce a royal heir but also led a life that displeased her husband, the marriage was dissolved in 1152. A few months later Eleanor married Henry Plantagenet who, in 1154, became Henry II of England. Apart from the French enclaves of Armagnac and Béarn, the duchy of Aquitaine was now under English rule. Hostilities between the French and the English in the region began in 1328 and continued until 1453, when the English were soundly defeated at the Battle of Castillon.

Eleanor and Louis VII

ENGLISH AQUITAINE (1362)

▨ *Armagnac and Béarn (p212)*

EDWARD I OF ENGLAND PAYS HOMAGE TO PHILIP THE FAIR
Philip the Fair became king of France in 1285 and, as custom dictated, Edward I, king of England, paid homage to him for the territory that he held within the French kingdom.

King of France

King of England

Arms of Bordeaux
The Grosse Cloche, the bell tower of the town hall in Bordeaux that was built in the 13th century, is surmounted by the three leopards of England. At the foot of the Grosse Cloche the waters of the Garonne flow by. The crescent motif in the water is an allusion to the port of Bordeaux.

Eleanor of Aquitaine
Eleanor had two daughters by Louis VII of France, and seven children, including Richard the Lionheart and King John, by her second husband, Henry II of England. She eventually left Henry and returned to her native Aquitaine, where she was a patron of the arts, especially of troubadours writing songs and poetry in the courtly love tradition. She was buried in the Abbaye de Fontevraud, near Angers, in 1204.

The Black Prince

In 1337, the King of France claimed Aquitaine, because Edward III of England had refused to pay homage to him. Edward's son, Edward of Woodstock, also known as the Black Prince, took up arms to defend the English position. He even had local support, in Bordeaux, where he had been well received two years earlier, for upholding the city's special privileges. Under him, the English triumphed at the Battle of Crécy in 1346 and the Battle of Poitiers in 1356, where the French king, John the Good, was taken prisoner. Aquitaine was made into a principality and granted autonomous powers.

Siege of Duras

The French siege of Duras came to symbolize the numerous attacks that Bertrand du Guesclin launched on the English in Aquitaine. At Du Guesclin's death in 1380, the English controlled only Bordeaux and Bayonne.

Fleur-de-lis, symbol of French royalty

Battle of Castillon

At the beginning of the 15th century, the English regained part of Aquitaine and, from 1438, major battles resumed. They were brought to an end in June 1451, when the French took Bordeaux, and in 1453, at the Battle of Castillon, when Charles VII finally expelled the English from Guyenne. This marked the end of the Hundred Years' War.

Courtiers

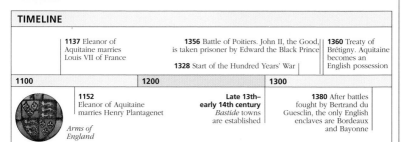

TIMELINE

1100		1200		1300	
	1137 Eleanor of Aquitaine marries Louis VII of France		**1356** Battle of Poitiers. John II, the Good, is taken prisoner by Edward the Black Prince		**1360** Treaty of Brétigny. Aquitaine becomes an English possession
			1328 Start of the Hundred Years' War		
	1152 Eleanor of Aquitaine marries Henry Plantagenet		**Late 13th–early 14th century** *Bastide* towns are established		**1380** After battles fought by Bertrand du Guesclin, the only English enclaves are Bordeaux and Bayonne

Arms of England

LORDS, PEASANTS AND THE BOURGEOISIE

For much of the Middle Ages, Aquitaine was under English rule. Defending this position against French claims to the territory led to almost continuous conflict and the construction of many castles, particularly in the Périgord, including Beynac and Castelnaud. Each of these great fortresses belonged to a lord, who was either under the protection of the king of France or the king of England. Bertran de Born (born in 1140), the famous troubadour and lord of Hautefort, described this warring, 12th-century society in his writings: men lived for hunting and battle, for finery and for the love of a noble woman. As a castle-owner, Bertran deplored the expansion of farmland: not only did it encroach on woodland, it also allowed new villages to be established and merchants and the bourgeoisie to grow rich, so reducing lordly power. Waging war was thus the foremost occupation of noblemen, who were permanently seeking new ways of maintaining their knightly lifestyle.

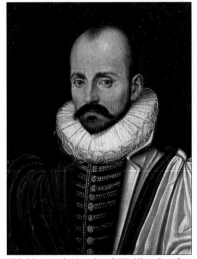

Troubadour of Aquitaine

At the same time, the rapid population expansion that occured in the 13th and 14th centuries caused towns and cities to double in size. Large towns like Bayonne, Périgueux and Sarlat, as well as smaller ones like Mussidan and Ribérac, were granted charters that gave their inhabitants certain privileges. Freed from obligations to an overlord, the bourgeoisie could now take part in public life. In the 11th and 12th centuries, with the encouragement of the Church and of enterprising lords, land clearance increased. Peasants were called on to make the land suitable for agriculture, creating what were known as *sauvetés* (as at Sauveterre-de-Guyenne, in the Gironde). In return for this work, they would be granted special favours.

REBIRTH OF INTELLECTUAL LIFE IN THE 16TH CENTURY

In the 16th century, writers such as Michel Eyquem de Montaigne (1533–92), Étienne de La Boétie (1530–63), Pierre de Bourdeilles, a priest and the lord of Brantôme (1538–1614), Blaise de Lasseran de Massencome, lord of Monluc (1500–77) and Joseph Juste Scaliger (1540–1609), contributed to a rebirth of intellectual

Michel Eyquem de Montaigne (1533–92), author of the *Essays* and member of the Parlement de Bordeaux

TIMELINE

1441 The University of Bordeaux is established

1462 The Parlement de Bordeaux is founded

1523 The Generality of Guyenne is created

Arms of Guyenne

GUYENNE

1450

1500

1453 Battle of Castillon

1498 Printing begins in Périgueux

life in southwest France. Many of them were well travelled and knew Latin. The introduction of printing to Périgueux in 1498, and the founding of the Collège de Guyenne in 1533, contributed to the diffusion of new ideas. Agen, Nérac and Bordeaux became intellectual centres, where humanism was now the central tenet of philosophical thought. While Marguerite of Navarre worked on her *Heptameron*, Montaigne would have spent many long days in the "library" of his château composing his *Essays*.

Jeanne d'Albret, mother of Henri IV

CATHOLICS VERSUS PROTESTANTS

Calvinist doctrine began to spread in Aquitaine from 1532. Marguerite of Navarre and her daughter Jeanne d'Albret, as well as many members of the nobility, such as the Duras, the La Force and the Gramont families, contributed greatly to its diffusion. The towns of Nérac, Oloron, Sainte-Foy, Agen and Bergerac gradually became bastions of Protestantism. The king of France condemned this so-called reformed faith and, from 1562, Catholics and Protestants all over France, and particularly in the southwest, began to attack each other. With the death of Jeanne d'Albret, the crisis deepened. Her son Henri of Navarre (1559–1610), later Henri IV of France, then became leader of the Protestant cause.

AQUITAINE AND THE KINGS OF FRANCE

After the Hundred Years' War, the king of France gradually gained control of the southwest by establishing a range of governing institutions, including the Parlement de Bordeaux in 1462, and the Generality of Guyenne in 1523. Military governors and intendants, acting on behalf of the king, inforced royal power. However, at the end of Louis XIII's reign, strife broke out in the countryside. In the Périgord in 1637, *croquants* – peasants who revolted against rising taxes – challenged the

HENRY OF NAVARRE

To help bring about reconciliation between Protestants and Catholics, the marriage of Henry of Navarre and Marguerite de Valois took place in Paris on 18 August 1572. But the union was not well received and on 24 August 1572, St Bartholomew's Day, Protestants in Paris for the occasion were massacred by extremist Catholics. Henry of Navarre saved his own life by renouncing his religion. Three years later he returned to his birthplace in southwest France, where he led the Protestant army in countless battles, including the Battle of Coutras in the Gironde. Henry became king of France on the death of Henri III. To bring stability to the country, he renounced his Protestant faith again in 1593, issuing the Edict of Toleration in Nantes in 1598.

Henry of Navarre

1560 Jeanne d'Albret establishes Calvinism in Pau

1598 Edict of Nantes

1610 Henri IV is murdered and Louis XIII becomes king with Marie de Médici as regent

Joseph Juste Scaliger

1600

1559 Birth of Henry of Navarre in Pau

1580 Montaigne's *Essays* are published

1620 Béarn becomes part of France

Pierre de Bourdeilles

Château Trompette, built to subdue Bordeaux

ruler of France during Louis XIV's minority) flourished. This opposition, known as *l'Ormée* in Bordeaux, was firmly suppressed and Bordeaux's citizens were obliged to submit to greater royal control. To help enforce this rule, Château Trompette was built at the entrance to the city, on the foundations of the old fortress built by Charles VII. Revolts against rising taxes were also put down.

excessive authority and rights of the aristocracy and of the local salt-tax collectors. The *croquants* fought against troops of the Duc d'Épernon, governor of Guyenne, but their efforts were largely overshadowed by the activities of the Fronde (1649–53), a rebellious movement led by aristocrats and parliamentarians seeking to gain more independence from the grip of royal power. *Mazarinades* (pamphlets against Cardinal Mazarin, the effective

THE SUGAR ISLANDS, THE SOUTHWEST'S ELDORADO

Between the beginning of the 18th century and the French Revolution, trade with the West Indies boomed. Indigo, annatto, cocoa, coffee, cotton and, most of all, sugar arrived at Bordeaux by boat, to be distributed all over France and throughout Europe. This activity either took the form of two-way trade or, from 1750, as triangular trade: ships would stop on the African coast to pick up slaves, who were were then exchanged in the West Indies for exotic goods that

The Port of Bordeaux and Foreign Relations by Frédéric de Buzon (1925)

TIMELINE

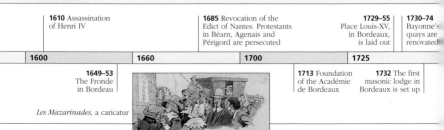

1610 Assassination of Henri IV	**1685** Revocation of the Edict of Nantes. Protestants in Béarn, Agenais and Périgord are persecuted	**1729–55** Place Louis-XV, in Bordeaux, is laid out **1730–74** Bayonne's quays are renovated

1600   **1660**   **1700**   **1725**

1649–53 The Fronde in Bordeau	**1713** Foundation of the Académie de Bordeaux	**1732** The first masonic lodge in Bordeaux is set up

Les Mazarinades, a caricatur

were brought back to Bordeaux. Many merchants who grew rich from the slave trade built elegant town houses or purchased estates on which they built fine residences in fashionable styles. One such example is the Château de Nairac in Barsac. Bordeaux, as well as the areas further inland, which traded their produce in the West

Bordeaux in the 18th century, France's premier port

Indies, prospered both from the wealth of goods arriving from the islands and also from expanding trading links with northern Europe. Some merchants opted to buy plantations in Santo Domingo, which would be run by a manager or a younger son. All this trade in the 18th century made Bordeaux into France's foremost port.

THE AGE OF ENLIGHTENMENT

Intellectual life in southwest France in the 18th century was mainly restricted to academies, learned societies (whose members were scholars and scientists), artists and men of letters. There were academies in Bordeaux, Pau and Agen, and a looser association in Périgueux. It was in such circles, made up of the intellectual elite from the nobility and the bourgeoisie, that new ideas developed, particularly the philosophy of Montesquieu. Certain members of the nobility, such as Sarraut de

Boynet et Journu in Bordeaux, Charles de Borda in Dax and the Chevalier de Vivens in Clairac, were as interested in science and medicine as they were in the arts and music. New ideas also took root in masonic lodges, where social divisions tended to be blurred.

At the same time, under the impetus of the aristocracy and public officials, towns and cities in southwestern France underwent a programme of regeneration. Street lighting was installed in Bayonne in the second half of the 18th century. Bordeaux's old city walls were knocked down to make way for ornamental gates and squares, such as Place Louis-XV (better known as Place de la Bourse). Footpaths were created and gardens were laid out.

Bordeaux, the capital of Guyenne, became a beacon for civic improvement in the southwest. In 1780, the Grand-Théâtre, commissioned by the Maréchal Duc de Richelieu, governor of Guyenne, and designed by Victor Louis, was

Montesquieu, writer, politician and native of Bordeaux

Decorative mask, Bordeaux (18th century)

1743–57 Marquis de Tourny, intendant of Bordeaux, lays out the city's elegant squares and boulevards

1748 The first edition of Montesquieu's *Spirit of Laws* appears

1771 Peak of Bordeaux's maritime trade

1780 Inauguration of the Grand-Théâtre, Bordeaux

1745   1775   1785

Trading vessel in Bordeaux

The Grand-Théâtre in Bordeaux, built by Victor Louis and inaugurated in 1780

unveiled, opposite the Allées de Tourny. All over the region, but particulary in Bordeaux, many aristocrats and merchants now owned two houses; they would spend the winter in town and the summer in a château or country residence. Many of them regularly travelled to Paris, bringing back new ideas on land management, on how to entertain and on how to dress, as well new attitudes towards hygiene and new knowledge about medicine. For example, in the second half of the 18th century, the Comte de Lur Saluces brought wallpaper back to Uza and decided to better his estate by installating an ironworks there.

FROM THE GIRONDINS TO NAPOLEON

The southwest's entire economy, which was based on trade with the West Indies, collapsed during the French Revolution. Although highly unpopular with the aristocracy, the fall of the Ancien Régime was, however,

THE GOLDEN AGE OF WINE-PRODUCTION IN AQUITAINE

Between the late 17th and early 18th centuries, the nobility began purchasing wine estates not only in the Médoc, the Sauternes and the Graves, but also outside the Bordeaux area, including Clairac, in the Lot-et-Garonne, and at Monbazillac, in the Dordogne. They turned wine-production into a major industry, building great cellars and, with the help of knowledgeable estate managers, laying down high-quality wines for export to the West Indies, England and northern Europe. The leaders in this enterprise were Monsieur de Pontac in the 17th century, and the Marquis de Ségur, the Comte de Lur Saluces and his wife the Comtesse de Sauvage d'Yquem in the 18th.

Comte de Lur Saluces

Comtesse de Sauvage d'Yquem

TIMELINE

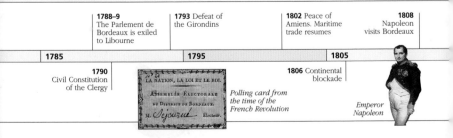

1788–9 The Parlement de Bordeaux is exiled to Libourne

1793 Defeat of the Girondins

1802 Peace of Amiens. Maritime trade resumes

1808 Napoleon visits Bordeaux

1785   1795   1805

1790 Civil Constitution of the Clergy

LA NATION, LA LOI ET LE ROI.
ASSEMBLÉE ELECTORALE
DU DISTRICT DE BORDEAUX.
M. *Sejouzui* Electeur.

Polling card from the time of the French Revolution

1806 Continental blockade

Emperor Napoleon

welcomed by a newly created nobility and bourgeoisie that was open to fresh ideas. Members of Bordeaux's parliament had been the first to question royal power by opposing the edict allowing provincial assemblies to be set up. In August 1787, Louis XVI ordered them to be exiled to Libourne. In Bordeaux, this decision marked the beginnings of the French Revolution, as it brought about a short-lived solidarity between the aristocracy and the common people.

Pierre-Victurnien Vergniaud, a Girondin who was guillotined during the Terror

This soon degenerated as a result of the Civil Constitution of the Clergy (July 1790) and the meagre harvests that blighted the southwest in 1791. The deputies for the Gironde, among whom were several lawyers who were renowned for their eloquence, had the ear of the National Assembly. While the Convention was being drawn up, such Girondins as Vergniaud, Guadet and Ducos rose to prominence, standing up for economic liberalism and decentralization.

However, on 2 June 1792, the Girondins found themselves in the minority, and power passed to their opponents. Several were then arrested, while others escaped and even managed to organize a federalist rebellion. In October 1793, Vergniaud was guillotined, along with other deputies for the Gironde. Guadet fled to Normandy, then hid in Saint-Émilion, his native town, before being arrested and guillotined in June 1794. The Reign of Terror was a painful episode for Bordeaux, where many were killed.

In other towns and cities in the southwest, the leaders of town councils were often more successful in blurring their differences with the central authorities. After the fall of Robespierre, former federalists who had escaped the Terror were reinstated, and the political situation stabilized under the Directoire, the Consulate and the Empire.

However, the upper classes remained hostile to Napoleon, as the Continental blockade made trading from Bordeaux even more difficult. Restricting maritime traffic (most particularly the export of wine), it hampered relations with England and other northern European countries, which

Bordeaux in the 19th century (the Pont de Pierre was completed in 1821)

1815 The Duchesse d'Angoulême makes a triumphal entry into Bordeaux

The painter Goya y Lucentes, who died in Bordeaux

1820

1830

12 March 1814 The English enter Bordeaux

1828 Death of Goya in Bordeaux

Entry of the Duc and Duchesse d'Angoulême into Bordeaux in 1815

(except in the Pyrenees), the region was also suffering from a shortage of manpower. Many people were also leaving to try their luck elsewhere: large numbers of Basques and people from Béarn left to seek their fortune in the United States, while the inhabitants of the Dordogne and Garonne valleys migrated north, to the Paris region.

were Bordeaux's main trading partners. In March 1814, English troops arriving from Spain were favourably received by Bordeaux's inhabitants, who were now free of the imperial yoke and who welcomed the end of the Napoleonic Wars.

DOWNTURN IN THE EARLY 19TH CENTURY

After the French Revolution and the Empire, Aquitaine slowly emerged from its torpor. The population gladly returned to monarchic rule, symbolized by the triumphal entry into Bordeaux of the Duc and Duchesse d'Agoulême in March 1815. But the economic outlook remained uncertain. Poor energy sources and a lack of raw materials held back the region's industrial development. Communication channels were still inadequate and underdeveloped, particularly in the Landes, which appeared to have been bypassed by the Industrial Revolution and remained largely rural. With a low birthrate

The economist and parliamentarian Isaac Pereire, by Léon Bonnat

EXPANSION DURING THE SECOND EMPIRE

Thanks to the Pereire brothers, two enterprising financiers, Aquitaine did, however, blossom economically. Their efforts and lobbying had widereaching consequences: the pine forests of the Landes were greatly enlarged, fruit- and vegetable-growing and tobacco-farming were introduced in the Garonne valley and, in 1855, Bordeaux wines received their first official classification according to quality. In line with the huge increase in the region's wine exports, the ports of Bordeaux and Bayonne expanded and, with the development of the coastal resorts of Arcachon and Biarritz, tourism grew. Parallel to this economic growth was the rapid expansion of the various networks of communication, most particularly the railways. Whereas in the early 19th century it would take someone travelling from Bordeaux in a sluggish horse-drawn wagon 14 hours to reach the Arcachon Basin, after the construction of the

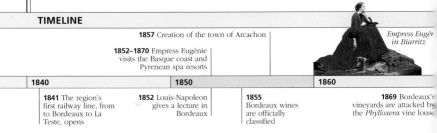

TIMELINE

1857 Creation of the town of Arcachon

1852–1870 Empress Eugénie visits the Basque coast and Pyrenean spa resorts

Empress Eugénie in Biarritz

1840	1850	1860

1841 The region's first railway line, from to Bordeaux to La Teste, opens

1852 Louis-Napoleon gives a lecture in Bordeaux

1855 Bordeaux wines are officially classified

1869 Bordeaux's vineyards are attacked by the *Phylloxera* vine louse railway, it took only two. Meanwhile, town planning was going on everywhere. Boulevards were laid out in Bordeaux, Périgueux, Agen and Pau, and railway stations became a standard feature of 19th-century cities. Aquitaine had also become a magnet for an élite who sought to emulate the Emperor and Empress: Eugénie stayed at Biarritz on a number of occasions, and visited the Pyrenean spa resorts several times. The imperial couple also spent time at Arcachon. Finally, in 1857, Napoleon III passed a law making it compulsory to clean up huge tracts of land and plant them with maritime pines. He even set up an experimental plantation at Solférino. In 50 years, the forested areas of Aquitaine increased threefold, exceeding 1 million ha (2,471,000 acres). The vast open expanses of the Landes, which until then had been given over to sheep-farming, disappeared along with the emblematic shepherd on stilts.

Poster for the Exposition Maritime Internationale de Bordeaux, held in 1907

THE THIRD REPUBLIC

Bordeaux became the capital of France on three occasions: in 1871, 1914 and 1940, when governments moved there to escape German invasions. At such times, the Grand-Théâtre was requisitioned as a makeshift parliament. In the interwar years, radical ideas spread throughout the Gironde, particularly in the Dordogne and the Lot-et-Garonne. In Bordeaux, Adrien Marquet, the city's neo-Socialist mayor, was very popular but tarnished his image by becoming involved with the Vichy regime in 1940. Bordeux also hosted great exhibitions, such as the renowned Exposition Maritime Internationale of 1907. The

Shepherds on traditional stilts in the Landes, before the area was turned over to forestry

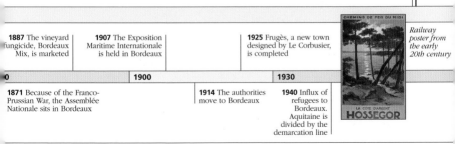

1887 The vineyard fungicide, Bordeaux Mix, is marketed

1907 The Exposition Maritime Internationale is held in Bordeaux

1925 Frugès, a new town designed by Le Corbusier, is completed

Railway poster from the early 20th century

0   **1900**   **1930**

1871 Because of the Franco-Prussian War, the Assemblée Nationale sits in Bordeaux

1914 The authorities move to Bordeaux

1940 Influx of refugees to Bordeaux. Aquitaine is divided by the demarcation line

German troops outside Bordeaux's Grand-Théâtre, July 1940

and other towns and cities of the southwest. This influx caused serious hardship. After the Armistice of June 1940, the region was bisected by a demarcation line and, until 1942, Bordeaux and the whole Atlantic coast were occupied by the enemy. The French Résistance gradually came together, but the Gestapo and the French militia harshly cracked down on it. Fearing an Allied landing, the Germans installed a string of military bunkers, known as the Atlantic Wall, all along the coast. When Général de Gaulle returned to France in 1944, he visited Bordeaux in the September, where he praised all those whose efforts had helped to liberate the country.

city also benefited from an economic boost created by its thriving food-processing and shipbuilding industries. Industrial centres began to multiply elsewhere in the south-west, with ironworks established at Le Boucau, on the Adour river, and metalworks in Fumel. One firm, the Compagnie du Midi, started the process of bringing more modern facilities to the region by building hydroelectric dams in the Pyrenees. However, this was brought to a halt by the economic crisis of the 1930s and the looming conflict of World War II.

Général de Gaulle in Bordeaux in 1944

THE DARK YEARS

After the Spanish Civil War, many Republican refugees, fleeing Franco's dictatorship, crossed the border into southwest France. When the country fell to Germany in May 1940, and the Germans occupied northern France, the French government, along with large numbers of French and Belgian refugees, hastily settled in Bordeaux

LATE 20TH CENTURY

After 1945, and until the mid-1970s, severe unrest plagued southwest France. Political life was dominated by Jacques Chaban-Delmas, a Gaullist "baron" who was nicknamed the Duc d'Aquitaine. During the 1950s, the country was severely hit by a rural exodus. The rearing of ducks and culti-vation of maize, however, developed in the Périgord and the Landes. Italian immigrants, whose knowledge and expe-rience helped to boost the region's agricultural potential, were especially

Jacques Chaban-Delmas

TIMELINE

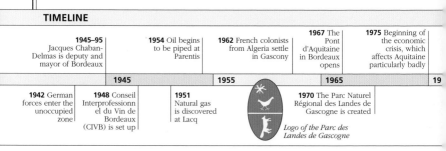

1945–95 Jacques Chaban-Delmas is deputy and mayor of Bordeaux

1954 Oil begins to be piped at Parentis

1962 French colonists from Algeria settle in Gascony

1967 The Pont d'Aquitaine in Bordeaux opens

1975 Beginning of the economic crisis, which affects Aquitaine particularly badly

1945   **1955**   **1965**   19

1942 German forces enter the unoccupied zone

1948 Conseil Interprofessionn el du Vin de Bordeaux (CIVB) is set up

1951 Natural gas is discovered at Lacq

1970 The Parc Naturel Régional des Landes de Gascogne is created

Logo of the Parc des Landes de Gascogne

instrumental in this development. A similar process occurred after 1962 when colonists, returning from the newly independent Algeria, set up fruit- and vegetable-growing farms along the region's main rivers. In the Bordeaux area, the Conseil Interprofessional du Vin de Bordeaux (CIVB), established in 1948, secured foreign markets for the region's wines. By contrast, at the end of the 1960s there was a downturn in some traditional industries and many firms were forced to close. Shoe factories, metalworks and some food-processing plants were particulaly badly affected.

However, the discovery of natural gas at Lacq and of oil deposits at Parentis in the early 1950s helped to boost the economy in the south of the region, turning Pau into a major industrial centre. The aeronautics companies Dassault and SOGERMA, and the car-maker Ford, also set up factories in greater Bordeaux.

In the early 1970s, the global oil crisis drove many factories out of business. Yet the process of modernization continued in towns and cities: certain sites, like Mériadeck in Bordeaux,

Alain Juppé, re-elected mayor of Bordeaux in 2006

became important business centres, while Agen became a focus for agricultural production. Communications networks (such as TGV Atlantique) opened up the region, placing it firmly on the European economic stage.

The 1970s also saw tourism take off around the Arcachon Basin and in the Pays Basque, where it is now the main money-spinner. The opening of the Parc Naturel Régional des Landes de Gascogne and the Parc National des Pyrénées has helped draw in thousands of visitors. And there has been an influx of people buying holiday homes, particularly in the Périgord, drawn by the variety and beauty of the landscape, as well as the mild climate.

A tram, symbol of Bordeaux's modernity, on the city's Pont de Pierre

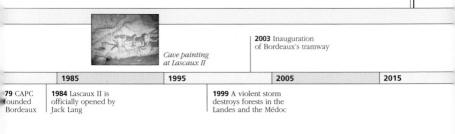

Cave painting at Lascaux II

2003 Inauguration of Bordeaux's tramway

| 1985 | 1995 | 2005 | 2015 |

79 CAPC founded Bordeaux

1984 Lascaux II is officially opened by Jack Lang

1999 A violent storm destroys forests in the Landes and the Médoc

AQUITAINE REGION BY REGION

Aquitaine at a Glance

The sandy beaches of Aquitaine, which stretch all along its Atlantic coastline and around the Arcachon Basin, attract large numbers of visitors every summer. In the south, the Pyrenees offer spectacular scenery and mountaineering. And, in addition, the whole region is alive with history, being full of picturesque *bastide* towns, historic fortresses, stately châteaux and majestic abbeys. Bordeaux, the capital, owes its wealth to its local wines. Thanks to their superb quality, the city has become the focus of the most prestigious wine trade in France.

Château Margaux *produces one of the world's finest wines. Besides its great vineyards, the estate includes an elegant Neo-Classical château and wine cellars with unusual vaulting.*

ATLANTIC
OCEAN

Blaye

Bordeaux•

Arcachon

GIRONDE

The Landes coast *is a long, more or less straight stretch, lined with sandy beaches that attract many summer visitors. Landes pines are adapted to this soil, covering around 1 million ha (2.5 million acres), Europe's largest forested area.*

GULF OF GASCONY

Mont-de-Marsan•

LANDES

• Dax

Bayonne•

Saint-Jean-de-Luz

PYRÉNÉES-ATLANTIQUES

Pau•

Oloron-
Sainte-Marie

BÉA

PAYS BASQUE

Basque folk traditions *are an important aspect of Aquitaine's cultural identity. The white shirt and trousers, red sash and scarf, and beret, are mostly worn at traditional festivals.*

◁ Fort de Socoa at Saint-Jean-de-Luz

Château de Beynac *is set on a high hill, and commands breathtaking views of the Dordogne river. The castle is in an interesting example of medieval fortified architecture.*

0 km   30
0 miles   30

Périgueux

DORDOGNE

Sarlat

ourne   • Bergerac

PÉRIGORD · QUERCY

Marmande

Cahors •

LOT-ET-GARONNE

• Agen

The *bastide* town of Monflanquin, *set on a hill overlooking the Lède river, dates from the 13th century. Laid out to an oval plan, it consists of a grid of streets, with a central square lined with arcaded galleries. It is one of the most picturesque bastide towns in the Lot-et-Garonne.*

Pic du Midi d'Ossau, *which rises to 2,884m (9465ft), is inhabited by wild goats. For experienced mountaineers, it is one of the best places to climb in the Pyrenees.*

GIRONDE

Ｆ*rom the banks of the Garonne and the Dordogne to the port of Bordeaux, the capital city, and from Libourne in the north to Bazas in the south, the Gironde's prestigious vineyards cover a substantial part of the region. The Gironde also has a rich and varied cultural heritage, along with a long stretch of sandy coastline that is perfect both for relaxing and for enjoying watersports.*

The great waves crashing on to the sandy beaches of Gironde's Atlantic seaboard offer surfers and other watersports enthusiasts near perfect conditions. Similarly, the banks of the Gironde estuary are a paradise for anglers, and are also lined with a succession of prestigious wine-producing châteaux and some of the world's best Romanesque and Gothic architecture. Thanks to its many fine buildings, Bordeaux, the region's largest port in the 18th century, still retains an atmosphere that is both majestic and elegant.

The Romans were among the first to exploit the Gironde's potential. They laid out vineyards on the hillsides, where they built sumptuous villas. Today Bordeaux wines include many world-class *appellations*, from Médoc to Saint-Émilion, and from Graves to Sauternes. Pioneering medieval monks erected prestigious abbeys, such as the Abbaye de Saint-Ferme and Abbaye de Sauve-Majeure. Status was conferred on the region when Pope Clement V laid claim to territory in Uzeste and Villandraut. And in their turn, the English rulers established the *bastide* towns such as Monségur and Sauveterre-de-Guyenne.

The late 19th century witnessed the discovery of the health-giving benefits of the sea air at Arcachon and Soulac, and the coming of the railways, making the region accessible. Yet, although the Arcachon Basin is now a prime holiday destination, traditional trades like oyster-farming remain important to the economy.

Finally, the Gironde boast links to many illustrious Frenchmen, including the philosopher Montesquieu, the writer Montaigne, the painter Albert Marquet and the novelist François Mauriac.

A flat-bottomed fishing smack, typical of the Arcachon basin

◁ *The Triumph of Concord*, an allegorical statue on the Monument aux Girondins in Bordeaux

Exploring the Gironde

Covering an area of around 10,700 sq km (4130 sq miles), the Gironde is named after the estuary at the confluence of the Dordogne and Garonne rivers. It is known mainly for its capital city, Bordeaux, and for the Arcachon Basin, but the region also has many vine-growing areas that produce some of the world's most famous wines. Dotted across the landscape are numerous châteaux in a variety of architectural styles, as well as many elegant cathedrals, churches and *bastide* towns. The Gironde's Atlantic coast and its lakesides are ideal for cycling, swimming and other watersports.

THE REGION AT A GLANCE

Abbaye de Saint-Ferme **㉗**
Arcachon **❼**
Arcachon Basin
  pp62–3 **❻**
Barsac **㉟**
Bazas **㊶**
Blasimon **㉔**
Blaye **⓯**
Bordeaux pp66–73 **❾**
Bourg-sur-Gironde **⑯**
Cadillac **㉜**
Castillon-la-Bataille **㉒**
Cazeneuve pp92–3 **㊴**
Dune du Pyla **❽**
Entre-deux-Mers **⑳**
Fort-Médoc **⓭**
Graves **㉞**
Lacanau **❺**
La Brède **㉝**
Lac d'Hourtin Carcans **❹**
La Réole **㉙**
La Sauve-Majeure **㉑**
Libourne **⑰**

Malle **㊱**
Margaux **⑪**
Monségur **㉘**
Moulis-en-Médoc **⑫**
Pauillac **⑭**
Phare de Cordouan **❶**
Pointe de Grave **❷**
Rauzan **㉓**
Roquetaillade pp86–7 **㉚**
Sainte-Foy-la-Grande **㉕**
Saint-Émilion p78 **⓲**
Saint-Macaire **㉛**
Sauternais **㊲**
Sauveterre-de-Guyenne **㉖**
Soulac-sur-Mer **❸**
Uzeste **㊵**
Villandraut **㊳**

Tours
Tour of the Médoc **❿**
Vineyards of
  Saint-Émilion **⓳**

PHARE DE CORDOUAN ❶

POINTE DE GRAVE ❷

SOULAC-SUR-MER ❸

St-Vivien-de-Médoc

Phare de Richard

Montalivet-les-Bains

Vendays-Montalivet

Lesparre-Médoc

N21

D101   D3

Hourtin-Plage

Hourtin

LAC D'HOURTIN CARCANS ❹

Carcans

Étang de Cousseau

D3

Lacanau-Océan

Lac de Lacanau

LACANAU ❺

Ste-Hélène

Le Porge

D3   D5

Arès

D106

Andernos-les-Bains

ARCACHON BASIN ❻

Marcheprime

N250

ARCACHON ❼

Gujan-Mestras

Cap Ferret

A660

DUNE DU PYLA ❽

Salles

D3

Bayonne

ATLANTIC OCEAN

Gironde

0 km   15

0 miles   15

SEE ALSO

Picturesque fishermen's huts on stilts in the Arcachon basin

For additional map symbols *see back flap*

Château Rayne-Vigneau, surrounded by vineyards, one of many elegant country residences in the Sauternais

GETTING AROUND

Bordeaux, capital of the Gironde, has an international airport at Mérignac. The TGV (high-speed train) links Paris and Bordeaux in three hours, stopping at Libourne, and continuing to Arcachon (four hours) in the high season. The A10 motorway from Paris to Bordeaux runs through the Gironde. The A63, and its continuation, the A660, connects Bordeaux and the Arcachon basin to the west. From Bordeaux, the A89 runs to Libourne and continues eastward into the Gironde.

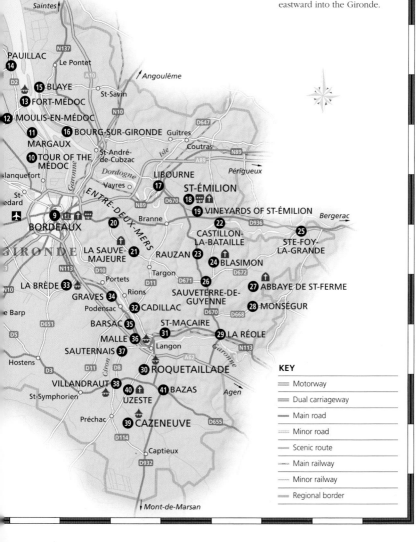

KEY

═══	Motorway
═══	Dual carriageway
───	Main road
┅┅┅	Minor road
───	Scenic route
╼╾╼	Main railway
───	Minor railway
═══	Regional border

Phare de Cordouan ❶

The lighthouse's elegant silhouette rises up against the skyline 7km (4 miles) to the west of Pointe de Grave. Designed by Louis de Foix, work on it began in 1584, although ten years later Henri IV had the original plans

Detail of the chapel

altered. In 1611, a Renaissance-style tower was added and, in 1789, the engineer Teulère increased the height to 67.5m (220ft). The lighthouse was declared a historic monument in 1862 and, because of its restrained classical style, soon became known as the "Versailles of the Sea".

VISITORS' CHECKLIST

Road map B1. 🚢 *Pointe de Grave.* **Tel** *(05) 56 09 62 93.* ⬤ *Apr–Oct: daily.* ⬤ *Fri & when keepers change over. Timetable depends on the tide.* 🎫 📷

Lantern
The beam from the 2,000-watt light can be seen from a distance 40km (25 miles).

Stair well

Chapelle Notre-Dame-de-Cordouan
The stained-glass windows date from the 19th century.

Entrance

Visiting the lighthouse
At low tide, the 260-m (850-ft) long causeway, leading up to the lighthouse, is accessible by boat.

AN ENGINEERING FEAT

The lighthouse is encircled by an outer wall 41m (135ft) long and 8.3m (27ft) high. This entire structure is supported by 2,000 piles that were sunk into the ocean bed.

King's Apartments
In the Renaissance style, these are on the first floor.

Doric columns frame the monumental portico.

Parapet

Outer stairway

An elegant coastal-resort villa at Soulac-sur-Mer

Pointe de Grave ❷

Road map B1. 🚌 ⛴ *Le Verdon-sur-Mer.* 🛈 *Pointe de Grave (05) 56 09 61 78.* **www**.littoral33.com

The lighthouse here, the **Phare de Grave**, houses the Musée du Phare de Cordouan et des Phares et Balises, with exhibits illustrating the daily life of a lighthouse-keeper. The 107 steps to the top of the 28-m (92-ft) tall lighthouse, lead to a platform with panoramic views of the Phare de Cordouan out at sea, the beaches along the coast and the port at **Le Verdon**.

Gaulish cult figure of a wild boar

🔦 **Phare de Grave**
Tel *(05) 56 09 61 78.* ⬜ *Jul–Aug: daily.*

Environs
About 15 km (9 miles) south-east of Pointe de Grave is the **Phare de Richard**, with its lighthouse and oyster museum.

🔦 **Phare de Richard**
Tel *(05) 56 09 52 39.* ⬜ *Apr–Oct: daily.* 📷

Soulac-sur-Mer ❸

Road map B1. 🏛 *2,819.* 🚉 🚌 🛈 *68 rue de la Plage (05) 56 09 86 61.* 🏪 *daily.* **www**.soulac.com

Backed by a forest and fronted by the ocean, Soulac developed during the Second Empire (1852-70), when a resort served by the railway line was built here. Attractive villas sprang up in the late 19th and early 20th centuries. Soulac has fine sandy beaches, the Plage Amélie and Plage la Négade. The latter is a nudist beach (like the one at Vendays-Montalivet 18km/12 miles) away).

A UNESCO World Heritage Site, the **Basilique Notre-Dame-de-la-Fin-des-Terres** lies on the route taken by pilgrims travelling from Britain to Santiago de Compostela. This great 12th-century Romanesque church has superb modern stained-glass windows and carved capitals.

The **Musée d'Art et d'Archéologie** contains exhibits of prehistoric, Gaulish and Gallo-Roman artefacts, as well as contemporary paintings and sculptures.

🏛 **Basilique Notre-Dame-de-la-Fin-des-Terres**
⬜ *daily.*

🏛 **Musée d'Art et d'Archéologie**
1 avenue El-Burgo-de-Osma. ***Tel*** *(05) 56 09 83 99.* ⬜ *Apr–Sep.* ⬜ *Wed in Apr–Jun & Sep.* 📷

Lac d'Hourtin-Carcans ❹

Road map B1. 🛈 *Place du Port, Hourtin-Port (05) 56 09 19 00.* **www**.hourtin-medoc.com

Some 17km (11 miles) long and with a surface area in excess of 7,500 ha (18,000 acres), this lake is one of the largest in France. Its shores are a good place to spot wildlife, such as herons, foxes, rabbits and hares. Plants include Dortmann lobelia and several insect-devouring species, such as sundew and pitcher plants.

Environs
The nearby resort of **Carcans-Maubuisson** offers tennis, cycling, horse riding and water-sports. It also has a museum of local culture, the Maison des Arts et Traditions Populaires.

Lacanau ❺

Road map B2. 🏛 *3,182.* 🚌 🛈 *Place de l'Europe, Lacanau-Océan; (05) 56 03 21 01).* 🏪 *Wed am.* **www**.lacanau.com

With a surface area of 2,000ha (5,000 acres), the Lac de Lacanau is ideal for sailing and sailboarding. For over 20 years, Lacanau-Océan has hosted a stage of the world surfing championship. It also has a large number of early 20th-century seaside villas, particulary in rue Faugère.

Environs
The **Étang de Cousseau**, 5km (3 miles) northeast of Lacanau, is a lake with a nature reserve.

Summer visitors on the long sandy beach at Lacanau-Océan

Arcachon Basin ❻

Lying between the Dune du Pilat and the tip of Cap-Ferret, the Arcachon Basin forms a huge triangle more than 100km (60 miles) long. Being almost completely enclosed it is like the Gironde's inner sea. At high tide, it holds 370 million cu m (1,300 million cu ft) of water, with a surface area of 156 sq km (60 sq miles). At low tide, only about a quarter of this remains, as the water recedes to reveal sandbanks, mudflats and salt meadows. The Basin is an important sanctuary for many birds, including the pied oyster-catcher, the common curlew and the great cormorant, as well as for migratory birds, such as sandpipers, avocets and graylag geese, that pass through the nature reserves at the Banc d'Arguin and the Parc Ornithologique du Teich. All around the basin are small oyster-farming communities.

Ticket-seller's hut

Sailing in the Arcachon Basin

Huts on stilts
These wooden houses on stilts are known as maisons tchanquées in Gascon, "tchanque" meaning "stilts". They can be seen all around the Arcachon Basin.

At low tide, the water level in the basin recedes to reveal sandbanks

```
0 km            1
0 miles         1
```

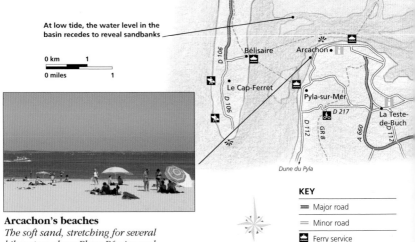

Lège-Cap-Ferret

D 106E3

Arès

D 106

GR 8

RF

D 106

Le Canon

L'Herbe

Île aux Oiseaux

D 106

Bélisaire

Arcachon

Le Cap-Ferret

Pyla-sur-Mer

D 106

D 217

La Teste-de-Buch

D 112

GR 8

A 660

Dune du Pyla

Arcachon's beaches
The soft sand, stretching for several kilometres along Plage Péreire and Plage du Moulleau, two of the Arcachon beaches, makes them a paradise for summer visitors. These safe, family-friendly shores are perfect for swimming.

KEY

▬	Major road
═	Minor road
⛴	Ferry service
🛈	Tourist information
✗	Nature reserve
✲	Viewpoint

A *pinasse*
*Swift and stable, pinasses are designed to safely
navigate the shallow waters that conceal the Basin's
sandbanks.*

BORDEAUX
06

D 215

dernos-
-Bains

Taussat •

Lanton

Certes

D 3E10

D 3E5

Audenge •

Gujan-
Mestras •

Parc
Ornithologique
du Teich •

Le Teich •

Biganos •

Facture •

Eyre

D 3

N 250

BORDEAUX

650

D 650E2

A 660

BAYONNE

Shipping in the basin
Fishing boats, yachts, pinasses and the motor cruisers that provide a regular service between Arcachon and Cap-Ferret are part of the ceaseless traffic that criss-crosses the Basin.

Parc Ornithologique du Teich
This bird sanctuary was created in 1971 to preserve a natural habitat and protect a number of bird species.

OYSTER-FARMING IN THE BASIN

Oyster-farming in the waters here developed in the 1860s, when the first experimental oyster beds were installed by the naturalist J-M Coste. It takes several years for oysters to reach maturity. Spat (larval oysters) are grown on lime-washed tiles. In spring, the spat are detached from the tiles and transferred to oyster-beds, about 4–5km (2.5–3 miles) out to sea, and left to grow. It takes 18 months to three years for the larval oysters to reach maturity. They are then washed and packed into creels, ready to sell. The Arcachon Basin produces around 8–10,000 tonnes of oysters a year.

An oyster-farm worker in the early 20th century

Exploring the Arcachon Basin

This shallow, tidal gulf is surrounded by a variety of different landscapes.

Gujan-Mestras

ℹ *19 avenue de Lattre-de-Tassigny (05) 56 66 12 65.* **⊠** *Wed.* **✳** *Foire aux Huîtres (first two weeks in Aug).*
This small town has seven harbours. Producing 55 per cent of all the oysters farmed in the Basin, it is the local capital of oyster farming. The **Maison de l'huître**, an information centre, is located in Larros harbour. *Pinasses*, long slender boats made of Landes pine, are anchored in the channels here.

🏛 Maison de l'Huître
Tel (05) 56 66 23 71. ⧖ *Jun–Aug: daily; Sep–May: Mon–Sat.* 🖼 🎫

🐦 Lège-Cap-Ferret Peninsula

ℹ *1 avenue du Général-de-Gaulle (05) 56 03 94 49.*
Sandy beaches stretch for 22km (14 miles) along the western side of this thickly wooded peninsula. On its eastern side, which faces onto the Basin, there are sheltered beaches at Claouey, Grand-Piquey, Petit-Piquey and Piraillan. The unspoilt oyster-farming villages of **Canon** and **L'Herbe**, can be explored on foot. Most of their tiny cottages are now second homes. The Moorish-style chapel at L'Herbe is all that remains of the Villa Algérienne, a grand residence located between La Vigne and L'Herbe, that was demolished in 1965.

A fisherman's hut, with a square dipping-net

The peninsula's smartest resort is at **Phare du Cap-Ferret**. The lighthouse here, with a curious red lantern, looks out over the basin from a height of 53m (174ft).

📷 Phare du Cap-Ferret
Tel (05) 57 70 33 30. ⧖ *Apr–Sep: daily; Oct–Mar: Wed–Sun.* 🖼 🎫

🦅 Île aux Oiseaux

Lying 3km (2 miles) north of Arcachon, this island is named for the many sea birds that flock here. The island is also an oyster-farming centre, and is popular with hunters, who lie in wait for their prey in hides. Raised on stilts, these wooden huts are known as *cabanes tchanquées*, from the Gascon word *"tchanque"*, meaning "stilt".

🦅 Parc Ornithologique du Teich

ℹ *Place Pierre-Dubernet, Le Teich (05) 56 22 80 46.* **✳** *Fête du Delta (week-end nearest to 14 Jul).* 🎫 *through Maison de la Nature (05) 56 22 80 93.*

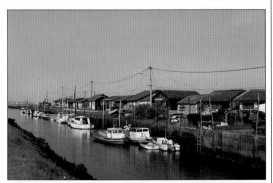
Audenge, an oyster-farming coastal village, with colourfully painted huts

This 120-ha (300-acre) nature reserve, on the Basin's wildest shores along the Eyrre Delta, was created around the brackish waters of abandoned salt meadows. Up to 260 species of migratory birds can be seen here throughout the year. Heron, wild ducks, egrets, storks, swans, and bluethroats may be observed in a natural setting, with salt-loving plants such as false willow and tamarisk growing nearby.

🐦 Domaine de Certes

ℹ *Audenge; (05) 56 26 95 97.* 🎫 *naturalist guides (free of charge).*
The fish-farming shallows at Certes consist of large expanses of fresh and salt water, covering around 400ha (990 acres) and interconnected by the odd patch of dry land. Sea bass, grey mullet and sea bream are farmed here. The estate was purchased by the Conservatoire du Littoral in 1984. A footpath runs along the coast, and birdwatchers will be able to see a wide variety of species, including herons, cormorants and ducks, in their natural habitat.

Andernos-les-Bains

ℹ *Esplanade du Broustic (05) 56 82 02 95.* 🚌
This family-oriented resort nestles on the northeastern shore of the Basin. Although there is no water here at low tide, Andernos is still very popular, and is crowded with visitors in summer. When the tide is in, its many small beaches are ideal for relaxing and swimming.

The resort also has an oyster-farm and a marina at Le Bétey, with a 232-m (761-ft) jetty, the longest in France. On the shore stand the ruins of an Early Christian basilica and the Église Saint-Éloi, a charming church with a 12th-century apse.

Seagull

Arcachon ❼

Road map B2. 🏃 *11,854.* 🚉 🚌
🚢 *(for Cap-Ferret).* 🛈 *Esplanade
Georges-Pompidou (05) 57 52 97 97.*
🏪 *daily.* 🎭 *Le Printemps d'Arcachon
(Mar); 18 Heures à la Voile et
Tchanquetas (end Jun–beg Jul); Fêtes
de la Mer (14–15 Aug).*

It was thanks to Napoleon III,
who fell in love with the
place, that Arcachon began to
develop as a coastal resort.
This process was completed
by the arrival of the railway in
1857. Arcachon is one of the
most spread-out towns in
France, covering 20,000ha
(49,420 acres) and almost
merging with neighbouring
La Teste-de-Buch. A marina
was built in the 1960s, and
the long pier on the busy
seafront serves as the town's
central meeting place.

In Parc Pereire, modern
villas, set in exquisitely kept
gardens, look down onto the
coast road. At the **Musée-
Aquarium**, beside the beach

The ever-changing Dune du Pyla, currently 117m (384ft) high

and near the casino, visitors
can view exhibits on the local
marine life that is found in
local waters.

🏛 **Musée-Aquarium**
2 rue du Professeur-Jolyet. **Tel** (05) 56
83 33 32. ◻ *daily.* ⬤ *Nov–mid-Feb.*

Château Deganne, now Arcachon's casino

Dune du Pyla ❽

Road map B2. 🛈 *Rond-Point du
Figuier, Pyla-sur-Mer (05) 56 54 02 22.*

This is literally France's
most moving monument.
About 3km (2 miles) long,
500m (550ft) wide and
117m (384ft) high, the Dune
du Pyla is the highest sand
dune in Europe. It overlooks
the Banc d'Arguin and is
covered with beachgrass,
sea holly, gilly flowers and
convolvulus. It was formed
partly by the action of
westerly winds, which lift and
blow the sand from the banks
along the valleys. In 1855, its
was only 35m (114ft) high,
but grows by 1–4m (3–13ft)
a year. From the top of the
dune, there is a splendid
view of the Forêt de la Test
and the Atlantic Ocean.

PRICELESS ARCHITECTURAL HERITAGE

The Ville d'Hiver (Winter Town) at Arcachon was created by the
Pereire brothers, bankers who had settled in the region. In 1862, they
purchased some 400ha (988 acres) of wooded dunes above Arcachon,
which they divided into plots. They commissioned the architect
Régnaud and the landscape designer Alphand to build handsome
villas suitable for the visitors who came to Arcachon for health
cures – the resinous air was renowned for its therapeutic qualities.
Surrounded by pines and sheltered from the wind, the Ville d'Hiver
comprised 300 villas. Every one is different: Moorish villas, colonial
residences and neo-Gothic manor houses cluster round place des
Palmiers. Cornices, corbelling, fretted gables, balconies with pierced
wooden balustrades, and semicircular and dormer windows grace
these elegant structures. In the 19th century, visitors here included
the Italian writer Gabriele D'Annunzio, at Villa Saint-Dominique, and
the composer Charles Gounod, who frequently stayed at Villa Faust.

A villa at Arcachon

Street-by-Street: Bordeaux ❾

Built on a curve of the river Garonne, Bordeaux has been a major port since pre-Roman times, but today there is little evidence of this long history. Always a forward-looking place, the city underwent a radical transformation in the 18th century. Today its industrial and maritime sprawl is scattered around a mix of grand boulevards and noble, Neo-Classical squares. Facing directly on to the waterfront lies the place de la Bourse, flanked by a row of elegant wine-merchants' houses, originally built to mask the medieval slums that once lay behind. The magnificence of the Esplanade des Quinconces sweeps down to the river, offering a fine view of the lavishly decorated Monument aux Girodins from the quayside. Also striking is the place des Grands-Hommes, near the Église Notre-Dame, a rare example of town planning in Bordeaux at the time the Revolution.

Église Notre-Dame was begun in 1684 and completed in 1707.

Bar à Vins and Ecole du Vin du CIVB hold professional wine tastings.

★ **Grand-Théâtre**
The façade of this building (1773–80) is decorated with statues of the nine Muses, and the goddesses Juno, Minerva and Venus.

★ **Place de la Bourse**
A masterpiece of architectural harmony, this square is flanked by two majestic 18th-century buildings, the Bourse (old Stock Exchange) and the Hôtel des Fermes (now housing the Musée des Douanes).

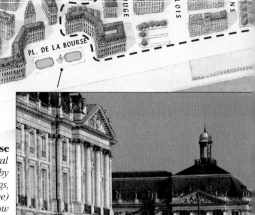

KEY

– – – Suggested route

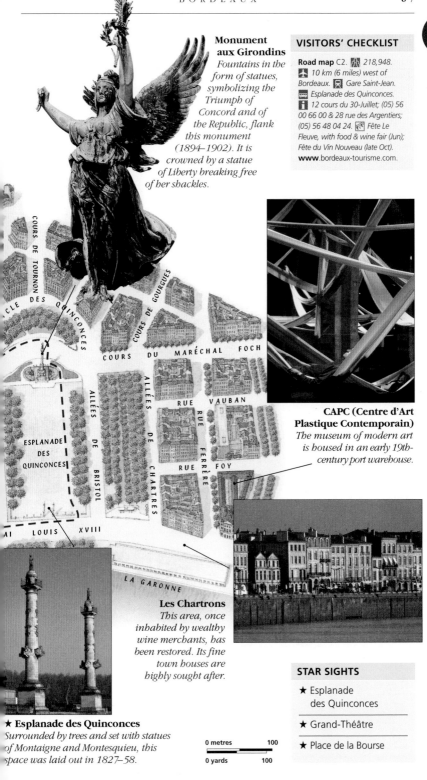

Monument aux Girondins
Fountains in the form of statues, symbolizing the Triumph of Concord and of the Republic, flank this monument (1894–1902). It is crowned by a statue of Liberty breaking free of her shackles.

VISITORS' CHECKLIST

Road map C2. 218,948. 10 km (6 miles) west of Bordeaux. Gare Saint-Jean. Esplanade des Quinconces. 12 cours du 30-Juillet; (05) 56 00 66 00 & 28 rue des Argentiers; (05) 56 48 04 24. Fête Le Fleuve, with food & wine fair (Jun); Fête du Vin Nouveau (late Oct). www.bordeaux-tourisme.com.

CAPC (Centre d'Art Plastique Contemporain)
The museum of modern art is housed in an early 19th-century port warehouse.

Les Chartrons
This area, once inhabited by wealthy wine merchants, has been restored. Its fine town houses are highly sought after.

★ Esplanade des Quinconces
Surrounded by trees and set with statues of Montaigne and Montesquieu, this space was laid out in 1827–58.

| 0 metres | 100 |
| 0 yards | 100 |

STAR SIGHTS

★ Esplanade des Quinconces

★ Grand-Théâtre

★ Place de la Bourse

Exploring Bordeaux

Since its restoration, carried out between 2000 and 2004, Bordeaux has revealed its many splendours: the richly decorated façades of its majestic buildings; the glorious Gothic churches that hint at its importance in medieval Europe; entire quarters that have been pedestrianized; and quays that offer long riverside walks. All these invite the visitor to explore the city's riches. Particularly impressive is the 18th-century Neo-Classical architecture, dating from a time when Bordeaux began to grow and prosper. The spacious squares, tree-lined avenues and elegant town houses all date from this time.

West door of Cathédrale Saint-André

🏛 Quartier Saint-Pierre

Located between the Garonne and the city centre, this quarter was enclosed by walls, which were demolished in the 18th century. Now restored, it is pleasant to explore on foot. What is now **place de la Bourse** was laid out by the Gabriels, a father-and-son team of architects, in 1729–55, when the square was known as place Royale. On its north side is the Bourse and on the south the Hôtel des Fermes, its upper storey set with columns on ornate pediments. Decorative carving covers the majestic façades here, with masks and ironwork on the balconies. In the centre of the square is the Fontaine des Trois-Grâces, erected in 1864 to replace a statue of Louis XV. Lined with restaurants and cafés, **place du Parlement**, formerly place du Marché-Royal, commissioned by Tourny in 1754, is a masterpiece of architectural harmony. Louis-XV town houses surround a paved courtyard, containing a neo-Rococo fountain that dates from 1867. On **place Saint-Pierre**, where an organic-food market is held on Thursdays, is the Église Saint-Pierre, built in the 14th–15th centuries and remodelled in the 19th.

🏛 Musée National des Douanes

1 place de la Bourse. **Tel** (05) 56 48 82 82. ⭕ Tue–Sun. ⚫ 25 Dec; 1 Jan. 🎨

Occupying a part of the Hôtel des Fermes that formerly served as a customs house, this museum, the only one of its kind in France, traces the history and work of French customs officers up to the present day. Exhibits include a fine painting by Monet, *La Cabane du Douanier, Effet d'Après-midi* (1882).

🏛 Porte Cailhau

Place du Palais. ⭕ Jun–Sep: daily pm.

This city gate offers good views of Pont de Pierre and the north bank of the river. The gate was built in 1495 to honour a victory won by the French king, Charles VIII, in Italy. It has both decorative features (small windows and a slated, conical roof) and defensive elements (a portcullis, machicolation and a crenellated gallery).

Fountain on place du Parlement

⛪ Cathédrale Saint-André

Place Pey-Berland. ⭕ daily.

A UNESCO World Heritage Site, this is the finest of all Bordeaux's churches. It was consecrated in 1096 by Pope Urban II, who had come to the city to preach in favour of the First Crusade. The nave, built in the 11th and 12th centuries, was altered in the 15th century. Depictions of the apostles, bishops and martyrs, and of the Last Judgment, adorn the west and north doors and the entrance to the southern wing of the transept (built in the 13th–14th centuries). The cathedral was restored in the 19th century, having been used to store animal feed during the Revolution.

🏛 Musée d'Aquitaine

20 cours Pasteur. **Tel** (05) 56 01 51 00. ⭕ Tue–Sun. ⚫ public hols.

Built in 1886, as the Faculty of Literature and Science, this building was converted into a museum in 1987. Its four floors display a large archeological collection. Among the prehistoric artifacts are the Venus of Laussel *(see p36)*. Gaulish items include an outstanding hoard of gold from Tayac, and Roman pieces include a bronze figure of Hercules *(see p38)*. Also on display

Carved frieze on the façade of the Musée d'Aquitaine

is a varied collection of pieces dating from the Middle Ages right up to the 19th century, including regional furniture and everyday objects. Another important aspect of the museum is its African and Oceanic collections.

🔲 Tour Pey-Berland

Tel (05) 56 81 26 25. ◻ Jun–Sep: daily; Oct–May: Tue–Sun. ⬤ 1 Jan, 1 May, 25 Dec. ▨

Built in the Flamboyant Gothic style (1440–46), this is the cathedral's bell tower. At the top sits a 19th-century statue of Notre-Dame-d'Aquitaine, which was regilded in 2002. There are fine views of the city from its two terraces.

🏛 Centre National Jean-Moulin

Place Jean Moulin. *Tel* (05) 56 79 66 00. ◻ Tue–Sun. ⬤ public hols. This centre, established in 1967, is devoted to the French

Grosse Cloche, vestige of Porte Saint-Éloi

Resistance, the deportation of France's Jews and the wartime role of the Free French.

🔲 Grosse Cloche

Rue Saint-James. This clock is the only surviving vestige of Porte Saint-Éloi, the city gate that was built in the ramparts in the 13th century. It was the belfry of the former city hall.

🔲 Palais Rohan

Place Pey-Berland. ▨ Wed. ▨ Dating from 1771–83, this was built as the residence of Archbishop Mériadec de Rohan. Since 1937, is has housed the city hall. The building consists of extensive living quarters, flanked by low wings set at right angles to enclose a courtyard. Features of particular note are the lavishly decorated dining-room and grand staircase.

BORDEAUX CITY CENTRE

Cathédrale Saint-André ⑨
Centre d'Art Plastique Contemporain (CAPC) ①
Centre National Jean-Moulin ⑬
Eglise Notre-Dame ③
Grand-Théâtre ④
Grosse Cloche ⑦
Monument aux Girondins ②
Musée d'Aquitaine ⑧
Musée des Arts Décoratifs ⑫
Musée des Beaux-Arts ⑪
Musée National des Douanes ⑤
Palais Rohan ⑩
Porte Cailhau ⑥

KEY

▨ Street-by-street map (pp66–7)

Key to Symbols see back flap

0 metres 800
0 yards 800

Grand-Théâtre

Victor Louis, architect of the Grand-Théâtre

The maréchal-duc de Richelieu, who was governor of Guyenne, commissioned Victor Louis (1731–1811) to design and build the Grand-Théâtre. A fine example of the Neo-Classical style, it was built between 1773 and 1780 on the site of a Gallo-Roman temple, known as the Piliers de Tutelle. Built to a rectangular plan 88m by 47m (290ft by 155ft), the building is surrounded by vaulted galleries and faced with 12 Corinthian columns. Above are stone statues of the nine Muses and the goddesses Juno, Venus and Minerva. The columned atrium, monumental staircase and auditorium within are remarkable. Restored in 1991, the auditorium, which is renowned for its acoustics, has been decorated in its original colours of blue, white and gold. The Grand Foyer, renamed the Salon Gérard Boireau, is a homogeneous example of the style of the Second Empire (1852–70).

★ Great Staircase
This extensively decorated feature inspired Garnier's design for the staircase at the Paris Opéra.

Grand Foyer

Atrium

Classical Statues
The façade is surmounted by statues of the goddesses Juno, Venus and Minerva, and the nine Muses, carved by Pierre-François Berruer (1733–1797).

★ Façade
The building is faced with 12 Corinthian columns. The arcaded galleries on either side once housed small shops.

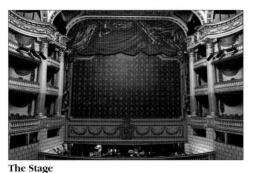

The Stage
Unusually large for the time it was built, the stage area takes up over a third of the theatre's interior.

VISITORS' CHECKLIST

Place de la Comédie.
Tel (05) 56 00 85 95.
Lines B and C. 10, 15, 29, 31, 53, 54, 55, 56, 58, shuttle.
for performances; for times of guided tours contact the tourist office.
www.opera-bordeaux.com

Dome
A painting by François Roganeau (1883–1974), executed in 1917, fills the dome. This detail shows The Allegory of the Garonne.

Crystal chandelier, with 400 lights

Ticket office

STAR FEATURES

★ Auditorium

★ Façade

★ Grand Staircase

★ Auditorium
Laid out to a horseshoe-shaped plan, the auditorium can seat 1,114 people. The majestic sweep of the three upper tiers is broken up by 12 ornate Classical columns. In 1871 it was used to house the National Assembly.

La Grèce sur les ruines de Missolonghi by Eugène Delacroix

🏛 Musée des Beaux-Arts

20 cours d'Albret. **Tel** *(05) 56 10 20 56.* ◯ *Mon, Wed–Sun.* ◉ *public hols.* 🖼

The north and south wings of the city hall, added to the building by Charles Burguet in 1878–81, now house this museum. Almost the entire history of Western art, from the Renaissance to the late 20th century, is covered by the collection on display. Represented are the Italian School, with works by Perugino and Titian; the Flemish School, with fine offerings by Breughel, Van Dyck and Rubens; Romantic painting including Delacroix and Corot; Impressionists, such as Boudin; and modern works, including those of Matisse and Kokoschka, as well as Bordeaux artists such as Redon and Marquet.

🏛 Musée des Arts Décoratifs

39 rue Bouffard. **Tel** *(05) 56 00 72 53.* ◯ *Mon, Wed–Sun (pm only).* ◉ *public hols.* 🖼

This museum is housed in the **Hôtel de Lalande**, a refined town house built by Étienne Laclotte in 1775–9. Several rooms evoke the opulence typical of Bordeaux town-house interiors in the 18th century. On display are paintings, miniatures, prints, sculpture, furniture, ceramics, metalwork and glass from the 18th and 19th centuries.

North of the centre

Although the Quartier des Chartrons and the Quartier Saint-Michel are now fairly industrial, some of the city's greatest religious buildings are here. Stylistically, they range from the Merovingian, as seen in the crypt of the Basilique Saint-Seurin, and the Romanesque, at the Église Sainte-Croix, to the Gothic, displayed by the Basilique Saint-Michel and the Église Sainte-Eulalie. There are also many fine examples of 18th-century architecture, including the handsome town houses along cours Xavier-Arnozan and the small Hôtel Labottière.

🏧 Quartier des Chartrons

This is the historic hub of Bordeaux's wine trade, which dates back to Roman times. Here the city's wealth was amassed and dynasties of wine merchants were established.

Shell-shaped dish by de Caranza

Maison Calvet is still an operative wine merchant's house, dating from 1818. Tours of the house offer a fascinating and aromatic insight into the history and techniques of the industry. The tour ends with a tasting and a chance to buy wines. The **Temple des Chartrons**, a Protestant church, is one the best examples of French Neo-Classical architecture. The **Halle des Chartrons** (market hall), built in 1869, is a highly successful combination of cast iron, glass and stone. The prestigious **cours Xavier-Arnozan**, also known as

Pavé des Chartrons, is lined with town houses built by wealthy wine merchants. Their Louis-XVI-style façades have overhanging balconies supported on stone columns. Since 1984 the **CAPC (Centre d'Art Plastique Contemporain)** has occupied a warehouse once used for imports from the colonies. On show here are works by Daniel Buren, Simon Hantaï and Sol LeWitt, and other present-generation artists, such as Peter Halley and Robert Combas.

The **Jardin Public**, once known as Jardin Royal, is a public park laid out by Gabriel. It was completed in 1756 but, a century later, having being ravaged during the French Revolution and Napoleon's Empire, it was relandscaped. A botanical garden, with 2,500 plant species, was also added. The **Muséum d'Histoire Naturelle** is housed in the Hôtel de Lisleferme, which was constructed by the architect Bonfin in 1770.

🏛 Maison Calvet

81 cours du Médoc. **Tel** *(05) 56 43 59 71.* ◯ *Jun–Oct: Tue–Sun.* 🖼

🏛 Temple des Chartrons

Rue Notre-Dame.

🏛 CAPC (Centre d'Art Plastique Contemporain)

Entrepôt Lainé, 7 rue Ferrère. **Tel** *(05) 56 00 81 50.* ◯ *Tue–Sun.* 🖼

🏛 Muséum d'Histoire Naturelle

5 place Bardineau. ◯ *Mon, Wed–Sun.* ◉ *public hols.* **Tel** *(05) 56 48 26 37.* 🖼

The old-world charm of a Bordeaux arcade, dating from the 1830s

For hotels and restaurants in this region see pp244–6 and pp260–61

West of the centre

The **Petit Hôtel Labottière** (1783–8) is a beautiful Neo-Classical town house with a courtyard and a garden. On the side facing the garden, the roof is faced by balusters. The late 2nd-century **Palais Gallien** is the only vestige of ancient Burdigala, as Bordeaux was known in Gallo-Roman times. About 130m (425ft) long and 110m (360ft) wide, this great amphitheatre could seat 15,000 people. Gutted by fire during the barbarian invasions of 276, it was partly destroyed during the Revolution.

The **Basilique Saint-Seurin** stands on place des Martyrs-de-la-Résistance. The west door has early 12th-century capitals and the 11th-century crypt contains several Merovingian tombs. Opposite is the **archeological crypt**, containing an impressive collection of 4th- to 18th-century tombs discovered during excavations in 1910. They include Gallo-Roman and Merovingian sarcophagi and amphorae that were used as tombs for children.

An arch of the Palais Gallien

🜊 **Petit Hôtel Labottière**
13 rue Saint-Laurent.
Tel (05) 56 48 44 10.
⬤ by appointment only.

🜊 **Palais Gallien**
Rue du Docteur-Albert-Barraud.
⬤ daily.

🛆 **Basilique Saint-Seurin**
Rue Jean-Burguet. ⬤ Tue–Sun.

🏛 **Archeological Crypt**
⬤ daily.

South of the centre

The Gothic **Église Sainte-Eulalie** was built in the 14th century and remodelled in the 19th. It contains artifacts from several churches and convents in Bordeaux. Opposite is the **Hôpital Saint-André**, built between 1824 and 1830 by Jean Burguet. Its huge cloister is surrounded by two-tiered arcaded galleries.

The **Porte d'Aquitaine**, in the form of a triumphal arch, is one of eight such gateways into the city. Dating from the 18th century, they replaced medieval postern gates. The Porte d'Aquitaine stands at the head of rue Sainte-Catherine, a pedestrianized thoroughfare and shopping precinct that, to the north leads to place de la Comédie, opposite the Grand-Théâtre *(see pp70–71)*.

The Romanesque **Église Sainte-Croix** stands in the restored quarter near the École des Beaux-Arts and Théâtre du Port-de-la-Lune (housed in a former sugar refinery). Its richly carved façade dates from the 12th century, although it was remodelled in the 19th. The hexagonal domes were added in the 13th century.

While the north bell tower is Romanesque, the south bell tower was added by Paul Abadie in 1860.

The **Basilique Saint-Michel**, on place Cantaloup, is in a colourful antiques dealers' district, where there is also a lively market on Mondays and Saturdays and a flea market on Sundays. Begun in the 14th century, the church was completed 200 years later

Basilique Saint-Seurin, extensively remodelled between the 12th and the 18th centuries

in the Flamboyant Gothic style. The Chapelle Saint-Jacques within was built for the use of Bordeaux's brotherhood of pilgrims. The belfry, 114m (374ft) high, is known as **La Flèche**. Dating from the 15th century, it was restored by Abadie in the 19th century and separated from the basilica. Beneath the belfry is a 15th-century crypt, which overlies the Carthusian monastery's former cemetery.

🛆 **Église Sainte-Croix**
⬤ daily.

🛆 **Basilique Saint-Michel**
⬤ daily pm; La Flèche: May–Sep.

MASKS OF STONE

Many of the façades of Bordeaux's houses are decorated with carved masks. While the earliest date from the 16th century, they are more typical of the 18th. On place de la Bourse, Mercury, god of trade, surveys the harbour traffic, while the bearded river gods glorify the confluence of the Dordogne and the Garonne, Ceres and Bacchus evoke the wealth that wine brings to the city, and the Zephyrs blow with all their strength. Gods, nymphs, satyrs and monsters wear expressions ranging from angry to brooding or mocking. In the streets round about, these faces take on an earthy wit. Quai Richelieu has faces with features verging on the grotesque, while a saucy pirate looks down from the front of Maison Francia in rue du Mirail.

Masks of Bordeaux

Tour of the Médoc ⑩

The Médoc vineyards produce some of the world's finest wines. The area is located around latitude 45° north and sits between the Gironde estuary and an extensive forest, with the Atlantic Ocean out to the west. It therefore enjoys a mild, humid climate that is ideal for vines. There is also a good mix of gravel, sand and clay soils. All this, combined with the expertise of local growers, accounts for the subtle wines created from traditional grape varieties, such as Cabernet-Sauvignon, Cabernet-Franc, Merlot and Petit-Verdot.

Château Mouton Rothschild ⑥
Made a *premier grand cru classé* in 1973, Château Mouton has been owned by the Rothschilds since 1853. Its wine cellars and museum are open to the public.

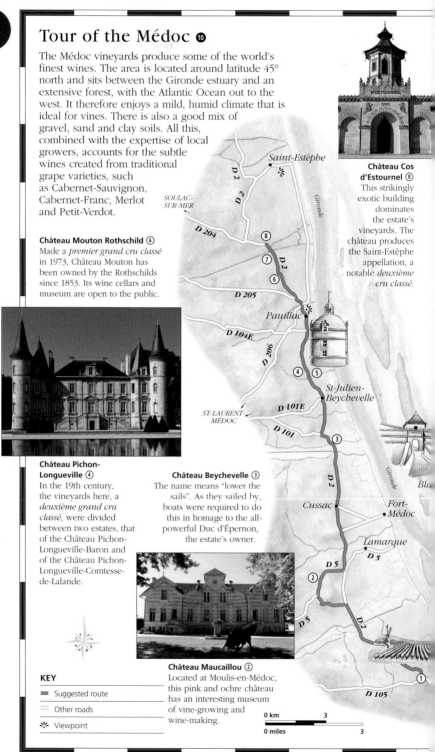

Château Cos d'Estournel ⑧
This strikingly exotic building dominates the estate's vineyards. The château produces the Saint-Estèphe appellation, a notable *deuxième cru classé*.

Château Pichon-Longueville ④
In the 19th century, the vineyards here, a *deuxième grand cru classé*, were divided between two estates, that of the Château Pichon-Longueville-Baron and of the Château Pichon-Longueville-Comtesse-de-Lalande.

Château Beychevelle ③
The name means "lower the sails". As they sailed by, boats were required to do this in homage to the all-powerful Duc d'Épernon, the estate's owner.

Château Maucaillou ②
Located at Moulis-en-Médoc, this pink and ochre château has an interesting museum of vine-growing and wine-making.

KEY

▪▪▪ Suggested route

═ Other roads

☼ Viewpoint

0 km　　　　3

0 miles　　　3

TIPS FOR DRIVERS

Tour length: 23 km (14 miles)
Stopping-off places: Château
Le Foulon (tel: (05) 56 58 20 18),
at Castelnau-le-Médoc, is a
pleasant guesthouse.
Château Guittot-Fellonneau (tel
(05) 57 88 47 81), at Macau, is
a farmhouse-inn that serves
local meals accompanied by
good-quality wine.

Château Lafite-Rothschild ⑦
Originating in the Middle Ages,
this château was rebuilt in the
18th century. Its wine cellars
were built by Ricardo Bofill.

Château Latour ⑤
This château dates from the 19th
century. The round tower that
looks out over the vineyards is
a vestige of the fortified building
that originally stood on the site.

Château Margaux ①
This stately Neo-Classical
château was built from
1810 to 1816 by Combes,
a pupil of Victor Louis,
the architect of the
Grand-Théâtre
in Bordeaux.

ORDEAUX

Façade of Château de Margaux, in a severely Neo-Classical style

Margaux ⑪

Road map C2. 🏚 *1,358*. **Wine
cellars** *Tel* (05) 57 88 83 83. ⬤ Mon–
Fri. ⬤ *public hols and during grape
harvest.* 📷 *book two weeks ahead.*

The vineyards around the
villages of Arsac, Cantenac,
Labarde, Margaux and Soussans
produce the wines officially
classed as Margaux. Over
this area of some 1,200 ha
(2,965 acres), vines grow on
the gravelly, pebbly soil of the
rolling hills. Château Margaux,
a *premier grand cru classé*,
produces a refined wine with
a fruity nose. Its attractive oak-
beamed cellars are open to
the public. The **Maison du Vin
et du Tourisme**, on the edge of
the small town of Margaux, is
an informative visitor centre.

🏛 Maison du Vin
et du Tourisme
7 place la Trémoille. *Tel* (05) 57 88
70 82. ⬤ *Jun–Sep: daily; varies out
of season so call ahead.*

Environs
About 25km (15 miles) north
of Bordeaux is the attractive
17th-century **Château d'Issan**.

At the weekend, the small cafés
in the little port of Macau serve
an assortment of locally caught
seafood, including shad, grey
mullet, plaice, eel, shrimps
and lamprey.

Moulis-en-Médoc ⑫

Road map C2. 🏚 *1,383*. ℹ *La
Verrerie, Pauillac (05) 56 59 03 08.*

This village has a 12th-
century Romanesque church
with a Gothic bell tower. The
capitals inside are carved with
naive depictions of wild
animals, monsters and scenes
from the Old Testament.
The **Maison du Vin de
Moulis** here organizes tours
of the châteaux within the
Médoc *appellation* area.
By taking the D5 northwards,
you will come to **Port de
Lamarque**, on the Gironde.
From here you can take a
ferry to Blaye *(see p76)*.

🏛 Maison du Vin de Moulis
Tel (05) 56 58 32 74. ⬤ *varies with
the season so call in advance.*

🚢 Port de Lamarque
Tel (05) 57 42 04 49.

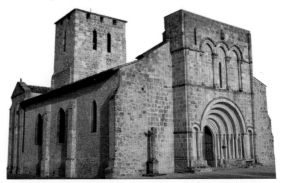

Fortifed Romanesque church at Moulis-en-Médoc, with a Gothic bell tower

Pediment of the Porte Royale at Fort-Médoc

Fort-Médoc ⑬

Road map C2. **ℹ** *16 avenue du Haut-Médoc, Fort-Cussac-Fort-Médoc; (05) 56 58 98 40.* **☀** *Jazz concerts (Jul).* ○ *daily.* ● *23 Dec–2 Jan.*

This fort was built by Vauban in the late 17th century and, together with the citadel at Blaye and Fort-Paté, it formed part of the Gironde estuary's defences. The Porte Royale, a gateway whose pediment is filled with a relief of the sun, symbolizing Louis XIV, leads through to a courtyard. Beyond are the surviving elements of the fort, which include the guardroom and the battery platform. Based on a rectangular plan, the building is set with four corner bastions. One of these, overlooking the Gironde, offers wide views of the estuary and opposite bank.

Environs

The **Château Lanessan**, 2km (1 mile) away, welcomes visitors to its wine cellars, where Haut-Médoc wines are matured. It also has a Musée du Cheval (a museum devoted to horses).

⚓ Château L anessan
Cussac-Fort-Médoc. **Tel** *(05) 56 58 94 80.* ○ *by arrangement.*

Pauillac ⑭

Road map B1. **👥** *5,404.* **🚌**
ℹ *La Verrerie (05) 56 59 03 08.*
☺ *Sat.* **☀** *Fête du Nautisme (May), Fête de l'Agneau de Pauillac (May), Fête du Vin et du Terroir (Jul), Marathon des Châteaux du Médoc (Sep).* **www**.pauillac-medoc.com

The marina here is a stopping-place on the Canal du Midi and also a family resort that is very popular in summer.

Pauillac, the capital of Médoc wine-making, is famous for its lamb, which is enjoyed all over France. The **Maison du Tourisme et du Vin** here sells local *grands crus* wines and organizes tours of the region's châteaux, with opportunities to meet the growers.

🏛 Maison du Tourisme et du Vin
Vinothèque La Verrerie. **Tel** *(05) 56 59 03 08.* **www**.pauillac-medoc.com ○ *daily.*

Environs

Some 8 km (5 miles) northwest of Pauillac is **Vertheuil**. The Abbaye des Prémontrés was founded here in the 11th century, but all that remains is an 18th-century building. The **Église Saint-Pierre**, which also dates from the 11th century, is a Romanesque church with a nave flanked by aisles. It has two bell towers, one dating from the 12th century. On the north side, the moulding round a restored doorway is carved with scenes from the life of Christ.

⛪ Église Saint-Pierre
Vertheuil. ○ *daily.* ● *Sun pm.*

Blaye ⑮

Road map C1. **👥** *4,924.*
🚌 🚢 *(for Lamarque).* **ℹ** *Allées Marine; (05) 57 42 12 09.* **☺** *Wed & Sat.* **☀** *Festival Musique et Théâtre (Jul–Aug); Chantiers de Blaye (Aug).*

Near the border with the Charente, Blaye is of interest chiefly for its citadel, built by Vauban in 1689 and set with star-shaped bastions. Overlooking the Gironde, the citadel offers breathtaking sunset views, especially from the Tour de l'Aiguillette. The views make it easy to under-stand why the Gironde estuary is so famous for its light.

Entry into Blaye, a village of low houses, covering just 18 ha (44 acres), is through Porte Royale (by car) or Porte Dauphine (on foot). In summer, it is filled with local craftsmen. North of the citadel is the medieval Château des Rudel, which is now a ruin.

The Manutention, a former prison next to Place d'Armes, houses the **Musée de la Boulangerie et Archéologie** as well as two exhibitions, **Estuaire Vivant** ("The Living Estuary") and **Blaye, 7,000 Ans d'Histoire**.

🏛 Musée de la Boulangerie et Archéologie
Manutention. **Tel** *(05) 57 42 39 42* (information from the Conservatoire de l'Estuaire, Place d'Armes). ○ *mid-Apr–Dec: daily pm.*

🏛 Estuaire Vivant
Manutention. ○ *daily pm.*

🏛 Blaye, 7,000 Ans d'Histoire
Manutention. ○ *daily pm.*

The citadal at Blaye, a fortress on the Gironde

Château du Bouilh, designed by Victor Louis, architect of the Grand-Théâtre in Bordeaux

Bourg-sur-Gironde ⑯

Road map C2. 🏛 *2,168.* 🚌
🏨 *Hôtel de la Jurade, place de la Libération; (05) 57 68 31 76.*
🅿 *Sun.* 🎭 *Foire du Troque-Sel (salt fair) (first weekend in Sep).*

Built from local limestone, Bourg was a fortified town in the Middle Ages. It once traded in salt from Charente, wines and locally quarried stone. Set on a steep slope, the town offers fine views over the river below and can only be visited on foot. Despite its name, Bourg is no longer in the Gironde but in the Dordogne *département*.

In the upper part of the town is the **Château de la Citadelle**. This elegant folly, built to an elongated plan and surrounded by formal gardens, was once the summer residence of the archbishops of Bordeaux. It now houses the **Musée Hippomobile**, a museum devoted to the horse-drawn carriage. The upper and lower town are separated by Porte Batailleyre, a 13th-century gate carved out of the surrounding rock.

Bourg is the birthplace of François Daleau (1845–1927), the prehistorian who discovered the decorated prehistoric cave, Grotte de Pair-non-Pair.

♣ Château de la Citadelle
Parc du Château 🅾 *daily.*

🏛 Musée Hippomobile
Tel (05) 57 68 23 57. 🅾 *Jul–Aug: daily; Sep–Oct & Mar–May: Sat–Sun.* 🅾 *Nov–Feb.* 🎟

Environs
A prehistoric cave, **Grotte de Pair-non-Pair**, is 4.5km (3 miles) east of Bourg on the D669. Discovered in 1881, its walls are covered with engravings. It is the only decorated cave in the Gironde open to the public. About 10km (6 miles) southeast of Bourg is **Château du Bouilh**, designed by Victor Louis.

♞ Grotte de Pair-non-Pair
Prignac-et-Marcamps. *Tel (05) 57 68 33 40.* 🅾 *Tue–Sun (book ahead).* 🅾 *public hols.* 🎟 🎟

♣ Château du Bouilh
Saint-André-de-Cubzac. *Tel (05) 57 43 06 59.* 🅾 *mid-Jun–Sep: Thu & Sat–Sun pm; mid-Jul–mid-Aug: daily.* 🎟 🎟

Libourne ⑰

Road map C2. 🏛 *22,457.* 🚆 🚌
🏨 *45 allée Robert Boulin; (05) 57 51 15 04.* 🅿 *Tue, Fri, Sun.* 🎭 *Fest'Arts (Aug).* **www**.libourne-tourisme.com

Lying at the confluence of the Isle and the Dordogne, this *bastide* town once depended on river trade for its wealth. Portions of the ramparts, as well as a gate, the Porte du Grand-Port, survive. The 15th-century town hall houses the **Musée des Beaux-Arts et d'Archéologie**.

🏛 Musée des Beaux-Arts et d'Archéologie
Place Abel-Surchamp. *Tel (05) 57 55 33 44.* 🅾 *Mon–Fri pm.*

Environs
The **Maison du Pays Fronsadais**, about 10km (6 miles) northwest of Libourne, documents the workings of the vineyards at Fronsac, which produce robust, full-bodied red wines.

To the north lie the vineyards of **Pomerol**. The fine wines that are produced here owe their smoothness to the iron oxides in the local soil. This is particularly true of Château Pétrus, the most well-known and most highly prized of them all.

At **Guîtres**, 15km (9 miles) north, is a large Romanesque abbey, dating from the 11th to the 15th centuries. At the **Musée Ferroviaire**, which has a small railway, visitors can relive the age of steam and diesel trains. The **Train Touristique de Guîtres** operates a steam train service that covers a 14 km (9 mile) circuit of the countryside between Guîtres and Marcenais and stops off at a pleasant rural café-restaurant. Visitors can also do a spot of wildlife-watching on a boat trip up the river Isle, or explore the town using the marked walks. There is also a wine *chai* (warehouse), where local wines can be tasted.

🏠 Maison du Pays Fronsadais
1 barrail-de-Tourenne, Saint-Germain-de-la-Rivière. *Tel (05) 57 84 86 86.* 🅾 *daily.*

⛪ Abbatiale de Guîtres
Guîtres. *Tel (05) 57 69 11 48.* 🅾 *Jul–Aug: daily.*

🏛 Musée Ferroviaire
Guîtres. *Tel (05) 57 69 11 48.* 🅾 *May–Oct: daily.*

🚂 Train Touristique de Guîtres
Guîtres. *Tel (05) 57 69 10 69.* 🅾 *May–Oct: Sun.* 🎟

Street-by-Street: Saint-Émilion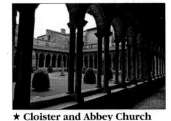

In the 8th century, a hermitage was set up by
Émilian, a monk from Vannes in Brittany, on
the northern slopes of the Dordogne valley.
Fortifications began to be built there in the
12th century, and throughout the Middle Ages
houses, chapels and monasteries were added.
The ochre-coloured stone of their walls and the
pinkish-red of their roof tiles make St-Emilion
a picturesque place. The town's architectural
heritage is almost without equal. Saint-Émilion's
alliegance oscillated during the Hundred Years'
War, but finally rested with the French, and it
was granted special privileges by Charles VII.

★ **Cloister and Abbey Church**
*The cloisters are 30m (98ft) square.
Built originally in the Romanesque
style, they were rebuilt in the
Gothic period.*

**Place de l'Église-
Monolithe**
*Once Place du Marché,
this square is lined with
restaurants. The original
Tree of Freedom, planted
in the centre during
the Revolution,
died and has
been replaced.*

★ **Bell Tower**
*One of the finest sights
in Saint-Émilion is the
bell tower of the
Église Monolithe.
It is the second-
highest in the
Gironde after
the spire of the
Église Saint-Michel
in Bordeaux.*

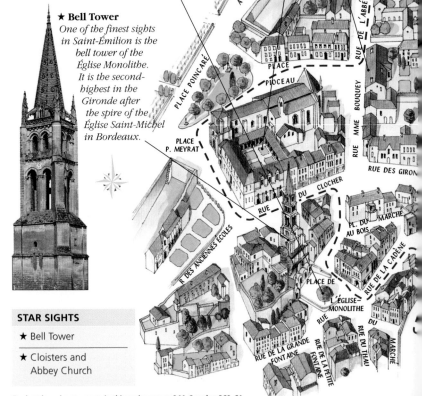

STAR SIGHTS

★ Bell Tower

★ Cloisters and
   Abbey Church

For hotels and restaurants in this region see pp244–6 and pp260–61

VISITORS' CHECKLIST

Road map C2. 🏘 *2,444.* 🚏
🚌 🛈 *Doyenné (Deanery), Place
des Créneaux (05) 57 55 28 28).*
🚗 *Sun.* 🎭 *Grandes Heures
de Saint-Émilion (Mar–Dec) ;
Jurade (third Sun in Jun and Sep).*
www.saint-emilion-
tourisme.com

Rooftops of Saint-Émilion, with the bell tower of the Église Monolithe

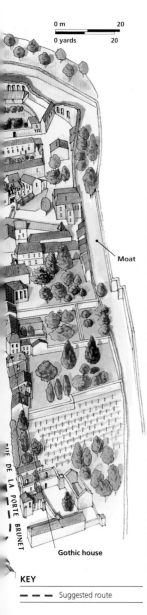

Moat

CITE DE LA PORTE BRUNET

Gothic house

KEY

- - - Suggested route

Exploring Saint-Émilion

The town can only be visited on
foot, along steep, narrow **paved
streets** known as *tertres* and
small **flights of steps** known
as *escalettes*, which sometimes
offer striking perspectives.
Approaching the town by the
D243, to the north, visitors will
see its great **ramparts**, the
remains of the first Dominican
monastery that was built here.

🔓 Église Monolithe
Place de l'Église-Monolithe. 🖼
through the tourist office, pm daily.
This church sits at the heart of
the town in the **place de
l'Église-Monolithe**,
with its ancient
covered market and
many restaurants. A
troglodyte building, it
was dug directly out
of the surrounding
limestone rock
between the 9th and
13th centuries, and is
unique in Europe.
With a nave 20m
(66ft) high and
decorated with relief
carvings, it has a 14th-century
Gothic doorway with a
tympanum containing
depictions of the Last Judgment
and the Resurrection of the
Dead. In 2001, excavations
brought to light drainpipes
that the monks had installed
to channel away rainwater.

🏛 Bell Tower of the Église Monolithe
Opposite the tourist office. 🕐 *daily.*
The church's tall bell tower
rises 133m (436ft) above
place du Marché. There are
breathtaking views of Saint-
Émilion and its surrounding
vineyards from the top.

🏛 Catacombs
Place de l'Église-Monolithe. 🖼
through the tourist office, daily.
Beyond the entrance to
the Église Monolithe is an
underground passage, leading
to a space containing several
burial niches, dug directly into
the rock. Its dome above
forms the base of a well
whose walls enclose a spiral
staircase. Archaeologists have
recently shown that these
catacombs may have been
originally used as a
funerary chapel.

🔓 Chapelle de la Trinité
Place de l'Église-
Monolithe.
🖼 *through the tourist
office, daily.*
The Chapelle de la
Trinité, a Gothic
chapel built in the
13th century, has
an apse with four-
arched ribbed
vaulting and
frescoes.

St John the Baptist

🏛 Ermitage de Saint-Émilion
Place de l'Église-Monolithe. 🖼
through the tourist office, daily.
The Ermitage de Saint-Émilion
is supposed to be where the
monk Émilian spent his days.
The spring water that flows
from the rock nearby is said
to have therapeutic powers.

🏛 Rue de la Cadène
From Place de l'Église-
Monolithe, rue de la Cadène
leads to **Porte de la Cadène**,
once the access point between
the upper and the lower
town. A 15th-century wooden
house is built onto it.

Tour du Roy in Saint-Émilion, where
the Jurade takes place

🏠 Abbey Church and Cloisters

Entrance to church off ave de Verdun,
to cloisters via tourist office. ☐ *daily.*
The church's original 12th-
century nave, in the
Romanesque style, has
Byzantine-style domes
supported by stone pillars.
Traces of frescoes remain,
including an image of the
Madonna and the martyrdom
of St Catherine. The choir
dates from a later phase of
construction in the 14th
century. Near the vestry door
is a statue of St Valéry, who
local vine-growers consider
their patron saint. The cloister
dates from the 14th century.

♣ Château du Roi

☐ *Apr–Nov: daily; Dec–Mar: Sat,*
Sun & school hols. ● *Jan.* 🖼
A symbol of royal power in
Saint-Émilion, this fortress
was built in the 13th century.
The Fêtes de la Jurade (a
committee of wine tasters that
release Saint-Émilion wine for
global export), takes place at
the top of the keep, the **Tour
du Roy** *(see p34).*

🏰 Ramparts

Surrounded by a dry moat,
the ramparts encircled the
upper part of the town. They
were pierced by six gates.
The Romanesque **Porte
Brunet**, on the southeastern
side, the **Tour du Guetteur**, to
the south, and **L'Éperon**,
a lookout tower at **Porte
Bouqueyre**, still stand.

Vineyards of Saint-Émilion ⑲

The vineyards of Saint-Émilion and its surrounding
villages enjoy an exceptionally favourable climate and
have exceptionally good vine-growing soil. Since 1289,
the villages around the town have fallen under Saint-
Émilion's jurisdiction, and in 1999 the whole was
declared a World Heritage Site. This hilly terrain,
covering 7,800ha (1,900 acres), is dotted with
picturesque villages and crossed by narrow roads
that wind between vineyards. With colours that
change with the seasons, it is strikingly beautiful.
The Saint-Émilion appellation consists of 74 grands
crus classés, the most famous of which are Ausone
(after Ausonius, the 4th-century Gallo-Roman consul
and poet) and Cheval Blanc.

Saint-Laurent-des-Combes ⑦
The village nestles in a cluster
of wooded valleys, or coombs,
which gave it its name. The
Romanesque church here
is set on the edge of
the plateau.

LIBOURNE

**Saint-Sulpice-
de-Faleyrens** ⑥
At Pierrefitte, near the
village, is a prehistoric
menhir. Standing 5m
(16ft) high, it is made
of limestone, widely
found on the Saint-
Émilion plateau.

St-Martin

D 243

D 670

D 19

⑥ *D 19E*

D 122

D 19

D 122

D 936

BORDEAUX

Dordogne

Vignonet ⑤
The village's economy
is based entirely on vine-
growing, with vineyards
right up to the banks of
the Dordogne. The
village church is in the
Romanesque style, but
was enlarged in
the 18th century.

Saint-Christophe-des-Bardes ①
Saint-Christophe-des-Bardes has a Romanesque church with a 12th-century doorway. At the top of the hill stands Château Laroque *(left)*, a *grand cru classé*.

Saint-Hippolyte ②
A twisting road leads up from the Dordogne valley to Saint-Hippolyte, a village with a 16th–18th-century château and a Romanesque church, set in the middle of vineyards. The views from here are spectacular.

Saint-Étienne-de-Lisse ③
At the heart of this charming village is a 12th-century church in the shape of a Latin cross. Above the village stands the Château de Preyssac, built by the English in the 15th century and remodelled in the 18th century.

Saint-Pey-d'Armens ④
Spread out on either side of the road from Libourne to Castillon, this small town is named after St Peter (*Sent Pey* in Gascon), to whom its church is dedicated.

0 km   1
0 miles   1

KEY

 Suggested route
Other roads
Viewpoint

NOTES FOR DRIVERS

Tour length: 26km (16 miles)
Stopping-off places: brochures giving information on where to stay, châteaux open to the public, and wine-tasting are available from the tourist office at Saint-Émilion (see p78).

Entre-deux-Mers, between the Dordogne and the Garonne, ideal for watersports and relaxation

Entre-deux-Mers ⑳

Road map C2. ⓘ *4 Rue Issartier, Monségur; (05) 56 61 82 73.* 🚍 *Sun am.* www.entredeuxmers.com

In spite of its name, the area known as Entre-deux-Mers ("Between Two Seas") lies in fact between two rivers, the Dordogne and the Garonne. It consists of a large plateau cut by small valleys that are covered with meadows, fields and woodland. Human settlement here goes back far into prehistory. Entre-deux-Mers also boasts a rich heritage of *bastide* towns, Romanesque churches and fortified mills.

Vayres, set high above the Dordogne, is the gateway to the region. The 13th–17th-century **Château de Vayres** was owned by Henri IV. Entre-deux-Mers' vineyards cover 1,500ha (3,700 acres), with 240 winegrowers producing a fruity dry white wine. Visitors can enjoy tastings at the **Maison des Vins de l'Entre-deux-Mers**.

🏠 Maison des Vins de l'Entre-deux-Mers
4 rue de l'Abbaye, La Sauve.
Tel (05) 57 34 32 12.
www.vins-entre-deux-mers.com

♣ Château de Vayres
Tel (05) 57 84 96 58. ◯ *Jul–mid-Sep: pm daily.* ◯ *Easter–Oct: Sun & public hols.* 🖼

Capital at La Sauve-Majeure

La Sauve-Majeure ㉑

Road map C2. ⓘ *La Gare, Boulevard Victor-Hugo, Créon (05) 56 23 23 00.*

The Benedictine **abbey** of La Sauve-Majeure was founded by Gérard de Corbie in 1079, in an area that the monks gradually cleared of trees. Located on the pilgrim route to Santiago de Compostela, the abbey became a dynamic centre of religion and trade, and counted 70 priories in its sphere of influence. Reduced to ruins by wars and the unrest during the French Revolution, the abbey has undergone several phases of restoration since 1952, and was made a World Heritage Site in 1988.

The abbey's majestic Romanesque and Gothic ruins stand in beautiful, mostly open countryside. The choir has Romanesque capitals carved with strikingly expressive biblical scenes. Next to the church are the remains of the 13th-century cloister, the chapter room and the refectory. A museum displays pieces found during excavations of the abbey.

Fine 13th-century frescos can be seen in The Église Saint-Pierre, in the village.

🏠 Abbey
Tel (05) 56 23 01 55. ◯ *Jun–Sep: daily; Oct–May: Tue–Sun.* 🖼

Environs
At **Sadirac**, 10km (6 miles) west of La Sauve, is **Oh! Légumes Oubliés** (Oh! Forgotten Vegetables), a farm-park where neglected delicacies such as nettles and Jerusalem and Chinese artichokes are grown.

The **Maison de la Poterie** here displays a range of pottery, made in a style that has been traditional in Sadirac since antiquity.

🥬 Oh! Légumes Oubliés
Château de Belloc, Sadirac.
Tel (05) 56 30 62 00.
◯ *Mar–mid-Sep: daily, pm.* 🖼
www.ohlegumesoublies.com

🏛 Maison de la Poterie
Tel (05) 56 30 60 03. ◯ *call ahead for opening times.* 🖼

The ruined abbey at La Sauve-Majeure

Ramparts at Castillon-la-Bataille

Castillon-la-Bataille ㉒

Road map C2. 🏠 *3,162.* 🚻 *Place Marcel-Paul (05) 57 40 27 58.* 🚉 🚌 🛇 *Mon.* 🎪 *Bataille de Castillon (mid-Jul–mid-Aug: Fri–Sat).*

Castillon-la-Bataille is named after the decisive battle fought between the French and the English on the Plaine de Colly in July 1453. General Talbot was killed by Charles VII's troops, under the command of the Bureau brothers, and his 8,000-strong army was decimated. This defeat of the English marked the end of the Hundred Years' War and led to Aquitaine and the southwest being restored to the French crown.

Vestiges of this eventful past include the town's 11th–12th-century gate, the Porte de Fer, a 17th–18th-century Baroque church and the Église Saint-Symphorien. The town hall, a former inn in the form of a rotunda, was built in 1779 with funds provided by Maréchal de Turenne.

The Côtes-de-Castillon wine *appellation*, created in 1989, covers 3,000ha (7,400 acres) of vineyards and includes about 350 vine growers. It has its own **Maison du Vin**.

🍷 **Maison du Vin des Côtes-de-Castillon**
6 allées de la République.
Tel (05) 57 40 00 88.

Environs
At **Petit-Palais-et-Cornemps**, 17km (10 miles) north of Castillon, is the Église Saint-Pierre. It is located just behind the cemetery and its façade is one of the best examples of Romanesque architecture in southwestern France. It has three superimposed arcatures supported by four sets of double columns. The doorway has spectacular carvings of lions and human figures, including a Spinario (a boy removing a thorn from his foot), based on the famous Roman statue.

Rauzan ㉓

Road map C2. 🏠 *1,055.* 🚌 🚻 *12 rue Chapelle (05) 57 84 03 88.* 🛍 *Sat.*

The castle in its present form was built by the Plantagenets in the 14th century. Restored in Gothic style after the Hundred Years' War, it then passed to the Durfort de Duras family. It was acquired by the municipal authorites of Rauzan in 1900. Built on a limestone plateau, the castle still has some impressive features, such as the keep, the main living quarters and central tower. Access is over a bridge that leads to a massive gateway. The top of the keep, which is 30m (98ft) high, offers visitors a wide panorama of the surrounding countryside.

The **Grotte Célestine**, an underground river discovered in about 1845, is open to visitors. Boots, protective clothing and helmets with headlamps must be worn and are provided.

♣ **Castle**
🛇 *daily.* ● *Sep–Jun: Mon.* 🎫
⋔ **Grotte Célestine**
Tel (05) 57 84 08 69. 🛇 *daily.*
● *Sep–Jun: Mon.* 🎫

Blasimon ㉔

Road map C2. 🏠 *725.* 🚻 *Mairie (05) 56 71 52 12.*

Founded in 1273, Blasimon became a *bastide* town in 1322 on the orders of Edward II of England, when the area was under his rule.

Nestling in a small wooded valley washed by the Gamage river is Blasimon's stately **Benedictine abbey**. Built in the 12th and 13th centuries, it was owned by the abbey of La Sauve-Majeure. The two-tier façade looks particularly beautiful at sunset, when it is bathed in golden light. The doorway and the arches that frame it are decorated with some of the most delicate of all Romanesque carvings in the Gironde. Some of the monastery buildings nearby are now in ruins.

On Wednesdays in July and August, a market takes place here, with local craft items and locally grown produce.

🔒 **Benedictine Abbey**
Quai Pascal Elissalt. 🛇 *Inner courtyard: all year.*

The abbey at Blasimon, set in a small valley washed by the Gamage river

A medieval house with a corner tower, now Sainte-Foy's tourist office

Sainte-Foy-la-Grande 25

Road map D2. 🏠 *2,893*. 🚊
Saint-Jean-de-Luz. 🔢 *102 rue de la République; (05) 57 46 03 00.*
🛋 *Sat.*

This 13th-century *bastide* town on the banks of the Dordogne was founded by Alphonse of Poitiers, brother of Louis IX. After 1271, it stood in English territory, but was retaken by the French in 1453. In the 16th century, when it had become a major centre of trade, Sainte-Foix was one of most dynamic of all Huguenot towns.

Of the medieval town, only four towers survive, which have been converted into houses. There are also several half-timbered dwellings from the 15th–17th centuries, with towers or carved window surrounds, and a number of fine 18th-century town houses.

The tourist office includes the **Musée Charles-Nardin**, a small museum devoted to prehistory and archaeology.

Sainte-Foy-la-Grande is the birthplace of Élisée Reclus (1830–1905), pioneer of modern geography and ecology and author of the great 19-volume *Géographie Universelle*, and of the art historian Élie Faure (1873–1937).

At Port-Sainte-Foy, on the opposite bank of the river, is the **Musée de la Batellerie**. Housed in the Maison du Fleuve, this fascinating museum of river craft has models of *gabares*, wide flat-bottomed boats that sailed down the river as far as the Atlantic. Films are also shown here.

🏛 **Musée Charles-Nardin**
Tourist office. ◯ *Mon–Sat.*

🏛 **Musée de la Batellerie**
Maison du Fleuve. **Tel** *(05) 53 61 30 50.* ◯ *Jun–Sep: Tue–Sun pm; Oct–May: by appointment only* ✍

Sauveterre-de-Guyenne 26

Road map C2. 🏠 *1,821*. 🚌
🔢 *2 rue Saint-Romain; (05) 56 71 53 45.* 🛋 *Tue (since 1530)*
🎭 *Fête de la Vigne et de la Gastronomie (last weekend in Jul).*

In 1283, Edward VII, king of England, founded the *bastide* town of Selva-Terra. Later known as Sauveterre, it stood on the site of Athala, a small town founded in the 9th century. With its strategic location at the junction of roads running between Libourne and La Réole, and between Bordeaux and Duras, Sauveterre was long an object of dispute between the French and English, until it finally fell to the French in 1451. Sited at the heart of Entre-deux-Mers *(see p82)*, the town no longer has its ramparts, which were destroyed in the early 19th century, though the four gates at the corners of the town remain. A vestige of Sauveterre's days as a defensive town is Tour Saubotte, on its west side, a tower with arrow-slits and a rampart walk.

Environs
Castelviel, situated 4km (2 miles) southwest of Sauveterre, has a church with a beautiful Romanesque doorway. The barrel vaulting is decorated with carvings of allegorical figures of the Virtues and Vices.

About 7km (4 miles) south-west is **Castelmoron-d'Albret**. With 62 inhabitants, this is the smallest village in France.

One of Sauveterre-de-Guyenne's four medieval gates

This former seneschal town of the House of Albret is set on a rocky outcrop with sheer cliffs 80m (260ft) high. As it was also surrounded by walls, it could not expand.

Abbaye de Saint-Ferme ②⑦

Road map C2. ⚑ 364. ⓘ *Place de l'Abbaye (05) 56 61 69 92.*

The great Abbaye de Saint-Ferme, which seems almost to overwhelm the town, was founded in the 11th century. Being near the Dropt, the river marking the border between French and English territory, it was fortified. This wealthy abbey was run by enterprising monks, who took in pilgrims on the road to Santiago de Compostela. It was sacked during the Hundred Years' War (1337–1453) and again during the Wars of Religion (1562–1598).

The 12th-century **abbey church** is crowned by a dome, the earliest Gothic-style one in the Gironde. Its Romanesque capitals have magnificent carvings of Daniel in the Lions' Den and other biblical scenes.

Monastery buildings now house the town hall and a small **museum**, with exhibits relating to the abbey, and also a 3rd-century hoard of 1,300 Roman coins that were discovered in 1986.

🔒 Abbey church and monastery
Tel (05) 56 61 69 92. ☐ *Jun–Sep: Tue–Sat pm only; Oct–May: Tue–Fri pm only.* 🅿 ▮

🏛 Musée de l'Abbaye
Details and opening times as for the abbey church and monastery buildings.

Monségur ②⑧

Road map C2. ⚑ 1,454. ▦ ⓘ *33 rue des Victimes-du-3-Août-1944; (05) 56 61 89 40.* 🅿 *Fri.* 🎪 *Foire au Gras (second Sun in Dec and Feb).*

This *bastide* town was founded in 1265 by a charter granted by Eleanor of Provence, wife of Henry III of England (who was also Duc d'Aquitaine). It was built on a promontory overlooking the valley of the river Dropt ("Monségur" means "hill of safety"). The surviving medieval buildings include some half-timbered houses, a narrow alley known as the Ruelle du Souley, and a Gothic tower, the Tour du Gouverneur. In the northeast corner of the arcaded square stands the Église Notre-Dame, a late Gothic building that was restored in the 19th century.

The cast-iron and glass market hall dates from the late 19th century. It was large enough to store around 700 to 800 tonnes of *pruneaux d'Agen,* the famous local prunes (*see p153*). Today it is the setting for two weekly markets and various festivals.

La Réole ②⑨

Road map C2. ⚑ 4,340. ▦ ▦ ⓘ *Place Richard Coeur de Lion (05) 56 61 13 55.* 🅿 *Wed, Sat, Sun.* 🎪 *Festival VivaCité (Jul, every even-numbered year, along with the Festival International de Folklore).*

Place du Marché and Église Notre-Dame in Monségur

Because of its strategic location on the banks of the Garonne, not far from the opening of the Dropt valley, this ancient walled town grew rich in the Middle Ages.

The town hall, founded by Richard the Lionheart in about 1200 and superbly well restored, is one of the oldest in France. The 13th-century Château des Quat'Sos is now privately owned.

The town's Benedictine priory is now home to municipal offices. The grille over the central doorway of this jewel of 18th-century architecture was made by the master ironworker Blaise Charlut, who also made the banister of the inner staircase. The building is fronted by an elegant stone double staircase. The Église Saint-Pierre has a Romanesque apse and Gothic vaulting, which was rebuilt during the 17th century.

A signposted walk around the town, with explanatory boards, lets visitors explore its architectural heritage. The town's ramparts were dismantled in 1629 by order of Cardinal Richelieu, but some remains can still be seen, such as the Porte de Sault de Piis with its staircase leading from the quays up to the priory. The suspension bridge that links the town centre to the bank of the Garonne river was designed by Gustav Eiffel when he was still a little known public servant.

Double stairway of the priory at La Réole

Château de Roquetaillade ③

Angel in the Pink Room

Set in extensive parkland full of centuries-old trees, this is one of the most astonishing castles in the Gironde. It perches high over a series of troglodyte caves, a perfect position for striking at would-be invaders. The castle consists of two main parts: the 12th-century Château-Vieux (Old Castle), with its fortified gatehouse, guardroom and keep; and the 14th-century Château-Neuf (New Castle), built by Cardinal Gaillard de La Mothe, nephew of Pope Clement V, in 1306, with the permission of King Edward I of England (then ruler of Aquitaine). Still owned by the Cardinal's family, it boasts six towers and an impressive central keep. In the 19th century, Viollet-le-Duc, the great French exponent of Neo-Gothic architecture, restored the castle, turning it into a highly romanticized medieval jewel.

Monumental Fireplace
This is in the Synod Room, where Pope Clement V held meetings.

★ Pink Room
Like the chapel, the Green Room and the dining room (formerly a stable and barn), this was completely overhauled by Viollet-le-Duc. The decoration and furniture here have been classified as historic monuments.

Underground passage

Entrance

Drawbridge

VIOLLET-LE-DUC, FATHER OF NEO-GOTHIC

The Mauvesin family, who had inherited the castle in 1864, commissioned Eugène Viollet-le-Duc (1814–79) to restore Roquetaillade. This famous architect had already shown his enthusiasm for Gothic styling by restoring medieval buildings in Carcassonne and Vézelay, as well as Notre-Dame-de-Paris and Pierrefonds. Work on Roquetaillade began in 1865, when Viollet-le-Duc started on the exterior. He opened out the ground floor, installed the drawbridge, and

Viollet-le-Duc

created the Grand Staircase and dining room. The Green Room and the Pink Room were decorated with his colleague Edmond Duthoit (1837–89). The castle's decoration, in a style that anticipates Art Nouveau, was never finished.

STAR FEATURES

★ Grand Staircase

★ Pink Room

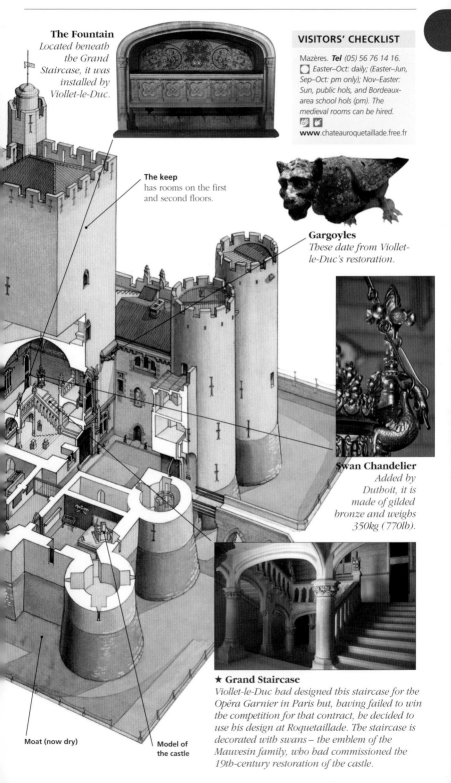

The Fountain
Located beneath the Grand Staircase, it was installed by Viollet-le-Duc.

VISITORS' CHECKLIST

Mazères. **Tel** (05) 56 76 14 16.
☐ *Easter–Oct: daily; (Easter–Jun, Sep–Oct: pm only); Nov–Easter: Sun, public hols, and Bordeaux-area school hols (pm). The medieval rooms can be hired.*
www.chateauroquetaillade.free.fr

The keep
has rooms on the first and second floors.

Gargoyles
These date from Viollet-le-Duc's restoration.

Swan Chandelier
Added by Duthoit, it is made of gilded bronze and weighs 350kg (770lb).

Moat (now dry)

Model of the castle

★ **Grand Staircase**
Viollet-le-Duc had designed this staircase for the Opéra Garnier in Paris but, having failed to win the competition for that contract, he decided to use his design at Roquetaillade. The staircase is decorated with swans – the emblem of the Mauvesin family, who had commissioned the 19th-century restoration of the castle.

Restored 14th-century frescoes in the church at Saint-Macaire

Saint-Macaire ③

Road map C2. 👥 *1,541.* 🚌 ℹ️ *8 rue du Canton (05) 56 63 32 14.* 🗓 *Thu.* 🎭 *Les Médiévales (Jul–Aug).*

This medieval village, on the edge of the Bordeaux region, grew rich from river trade. It boasts some attractive buildings in ochre-coloured limestone. The priory church of Saint-Sauveur, in the form of a Latin cross, contains 14th-century frescoes, as well as a gilded wooden statue of the Madonna and Child. Place du Mercadiou, the ancient market square, is lined with fine 15th- and 16th-century merchants' houses. In summer, the village hosts Les Médiévales, with plays and concerts.

Environs
About 7.5km (5 miles) northeast of Saint-Macaire, on the D672, is the wine-producing **Château Malromé**, built in the 14th–16th centuries. It was the home of the artist Henri de Toulouse-Lautrec, who died there in September 1901. He is buried in the cemetery at **Verdelais**, 3km (2 miles) north of Malromé. The inside of the château is not open to the public. About 3km (2 miles) to the northwest is

Saint-Maixant. The **Centre François-Mauriac** here is devoted to the life and work of this French author (1883–1970) and Nobel laureate.

♠ Château Malromé
Saint-André-du-Bois. **Tel** *(05) 56 76 44 92.* ⭕ *only open for wine business.* **www**.malrome.com

🏛 Centre François-Mauriac
Domaine de Malagar, Saint-Maixant. **Tel** *(05) 57 98 17 16.* ⭕ *Jun–Sep: Mon, Wed–Sun; Oct–May: Wed–Sun.* 📷 💺
www.malagar.asso.fr

Cadillac ③

Road map C2. 👥 *2,532.* 🚌 ℹ️ *9 place de la Libération (05) 56 62 12 92.* 🗓 *Sat.*

Set on the banks of the Garonne, the *bastide* town of Cadillac was established in 1280 to halt the progress of French troops. A gate, the Porte de la Mer, is a reminder of those warlike times.

The town is dominated by the **Château des Ducs d'Épernon**. It was founded in 1599 by one of Henri III's favourites, who demolished the medieval fortress that stood on the site and built a sumptuous residence. Notable features of the interior include the decorated ceiling and eight monumental chimneypieces.

The building was looted in French Revolution, then in 1818 it served as a women's prison. From 1890 to 1952, it was used as a school for young offenders.

♠ Château des Ducs d'Épernon
Tel *(05) 56 62 69 58.* ⭕ *Jun–Sep: daily; Oct–May: Tue–Sun.* 📷 💺

Environs
Rions, 4.5 km (3 miles) north of Cadillac on the D10, is a small town of Gallo-Roman origin and with medieval fortifications. About 11km (7 miles) northwest on the D10 is the impressive **Forteresse de Langoiran**.

♠ Forteresse de Langoiran
Tel *(05) 56 67 12 00.* ⭕ *Jul–Aug: daily; out of season: Sat–Sun.* 📷 💺

La Brède ③

Road map C2. 👥 *3,000.* ℹ️ *3 avenue Charles-de-Gaulle (05) 56 78 47 72.*

A wide avenue leads up to the **Château de La Brède**, where Montesquieu was born and lived. This rather austere Gothic building is surrounded by a man-made lake and moats. While the keep dates from the 13th century, the circular

Château de La Brède, birthplace and residence of Charles de Montesquieu

towers, chapel and other buildings date from the 15th century. Inside, Montesquieu's bedroom/study has been preserved. It was here that he wrote *The Spirit of Laws*. His great library, with a barrel-vaulted ceiling, holds 7,000 books. The landscaped grounds in which the château stands were laid out by Montesquieu after a visit to England.

♣ Château de la Brède
Tel (05) 56 20 20 49. ☐ *Jul–Sep: Mon, Wed–Sun; Apr–Jun, Oct–11 Nov: Sat–Sun & public hols; Dec–Mar: pm only.* 🖼 🖼

MONTESQUIEU (1689–1755)

Charles-Louis de Secondat, later Baron de La Brède et de Montesquieu, was born in La Brède in 1689. He became a lawyer but also had a keen interest in science. In 1721, his *Persian Letters*, a political satire on the reign of Louis XIV and a brilliant critique of social mores, were published in Amsterdam, bringing him lasting fame. Elected president of the Parlement de Bordeaux, he also kept in touch with Parisian literary circles. He travelled widely, drawing on his observations to write *The Spirit of Laws* (1748), which laid the foundations of political science.

Charles de Montesquieu

An intellectual, a landowner, and a tireless promoter of the merits of Bordeaux wines, he died in Paris in 1755.

Graves ㉞

Road map C2.

This area stretches along the south bank of the Garonne, south of Bordeaux on the Pessac and Léognan side. The Graves is the oldest wine-produding area in the Bordeaux region. The soil here is gravelly *(graveleux)*, hence its name. There are no fewer than 350 vine-growing estates in the Graves. Both red and white wines are produced, sometimes on the same estate, as at **Château Haut-Brion**. The Graves *appellation* covers an area of 3,700ha (9,000 acres), which produce about 18,200,000 litres of wine a year.

Podensac, a major port on the Garonne in the 18th century, has some fine houses of this period. *Lillet*, a mixture of wine, fruit liqueur and cinchona bark *(see p258)*, is the traditional aperitif here.

The town's **Maison des Vins de Graves** illustrates the history of local wine-making. Podensac is also one of the best places to see the steep wave *(mascaret)* that sweeps up the Gironde estuary with each incoming tide.

At **Portets**, in the heart of the Graves, stands Château Langueloup. Its vast 19th-century wine cellars have devices that seem impressively sophisticated for their time. There is also a **Musée de la Vigne et du Vin** here.

♣ Château Haut-Brion
Tel (05) 56 00 29 30. ☐ *by prior arrangement.* **www**.haut-brion.com

☐ Maison des Vins de Graves
61 cours du Maréchal-Foch, Podensac. *Tel* (05) 56 27 09 25. ☐ *May–Oct: daily; Nov–Apr: Mon–Fri.* **www**.vins-graves.com

🏛 Musée de la Vigne et du Vin
2–4 rue de la Liberté, Portets. *Tel* (05) 56 67 18 11. ☐ *call ahead.*

Altarpiece in the church at Barsac

Barsac ㉟

Road map C2. 🏛 1 981. ▦
🔲 1 allée Jean-Jaurès, Langon (05) 56 63 68 00.

From the 18th century, Barsac was an important centre of trade. It owed its wealth not only to wine, but also to the local limestone that was used for building throughout the Bordeaux area. The church, which is dedicated to St Vincent, patron saint of Gironde vine-growers, was rebuilt in the 18th century by the architect who designed the Château de Malle *(see p90)*. The Baroque interior features an altarpiece by Vernet and an organ loft by Mollié.

The Barsac *appellation* applies to several châteaux, including Climens and Coutet, *premiers crus classés*.

☐ Maison des Vins de Barsac
Place de l'Église. *Tel* (05) 56 27 15 44.

Château-Olivier at Léognan, in the Graves area

The central pavilion of the Château de Malle, in the Louis XIV style, and one of the wings

Château de Malle ③⑥

Road map C2. Preignac.
Tel (05) 56 62 36 86. ☐ Apr–Oct:
daily pm. 🌐
www.chateau-de-malle.fr

Encircled by the A62, the RN113 and the Bordeaux-to-Langon railway line, this charming residence was built in the 17th century for Jacques de Malle, a magistrate from Bordeaux. The original parts of the château include the main building and its two wings, which are set at right angles to it, each ending in a circular tower. There is also a two-storey central pavilion, which dates from the 18th century. The balustraded terrace leads to an Italian-style garden, which has an open-air theatre and many stone statues.

The interior contains fine antique furniture and a curious collection of 17th-century trompe l'œil silhouettes that served as "extras" in theatrical productions.

Unusually, the château's vineyards produce two types of wine: fine, top-grade, sweet *cru classé* Sauternes, as well as more basic Graves.

Sauternais ③⑦

Road map C2/C3. 🚉 601. 🚌
🛈 11 rue Principale, Sauternes
(05) 56 76 69 13 (May–Sep).

Lying along the south bank of the Garonne, 40km (25 miles) southeast of Bordeaux, the Sauternais area has a mix of siliceous, limestone and gravelly soil. The Ciron river, which flows through the area, gives it a favourable climate. The Sauternais is also dotted with prestigious châteaux, the most famous of which is undoubtedly the **Château d'Yquem**. Rated *premier cru supérieur*, the Sauternes produced there are some of the finest and most expensive wines in the world. Dating from the 15th century, Yquem is also one of the oldest wine estates in the area. Its vineyards cover about 100ha (250 acres).

The Sauternes *appellation* covers five villages: Sauternes, Bommes, Fargues, Preignac and Barsac. These *grands crus* can be tasted and purchased at the **Maison des Vins de Sauternes**.

🍷 **Château d'Yquem**
Tel (05) 57 98 07 07. **Wine cellars**
☐ send a written request. 🍷 Aug.

🛈 **Maison des Vins de Sauternes**
14 place de la Mairie, Sauternes.
Tel (05) 56 76 69 83. ☐ daily.

Environs
About 4.5km (3 miles) west of Sauternes, is the fortress at **Budos**, one of Pope Clement V's castles, built in 1308. Ruins of another of his castles lie at **Fargues**, 5km (3 miles) east.

Villandraut ③⑧

Road map C3. 🚉 826. 🚌
🛈 Place du Général-de-Gaulle ;
(05) 56 25 31 39. 🛒 Thu.

The impressive **château** here was built in 1305, both as a residential palace and for defensive purposes, on the orders of Pope Clement V *(see p39)*, who was born in Villandraut. A huge building with an interior courtyard, it was – like the Château de Roquetaillade *(see pp86–7)* – defended by a rectangular line of ramparts set with six

---

SAUTERNES

The grapes used for Sauternes must have been infected by a form of the fungus, *Botrytis cinerea*, known as noble rot. This causes them to shrivel and have a very high sugar content, which accounts for the sweetness of the wines. The Sauternes grape harvest is a long and painstaking process, in which every single grape is picked by hand. After fermentation, the wine matures in barrels for two years, before being bottled. Sauternes is served well chilled, but it is not only a dessert wine. It can also be enjoyed as an aperitif, or sipped with foie gras or Roquefort cheese.

Barrels of Sauternes, left for two years to mature

---

towers. From the top of these, there are fine views of the surrounding landscape.

♣ Château de Villandraut
Tel (05) 56 25 87 57. ◯ Feb–Nov: varies so call first. ◉ Dec–Jan. 🗐 📷

Environs
Saint-Symphorien, 10km (6 miles) to the west is the village where the writer François Mauriac spent his childhood. It was the inspiration for *Thérèse Desqueyroux*.

Château de Cazeneuve ㊴

See pp92–3.

Uzeste ㊵

Road map C3. 🏘 417. 🖽 *Place du Général-de-Gaulle, Villandraut (05) 56 25 31 39.* 🎵 *Festival d'Uzeste (Aug).*

Consecrated in 1313 on the orders of Pope Clement V *(see p39)*, the **Collégiale d'Uzeste** is one of the Gironde's finest Gothic buildings. Large in relation to the size of the village, this abbey church was probably built to house the Pope's tomb (sited in the choir). The bell tower, in

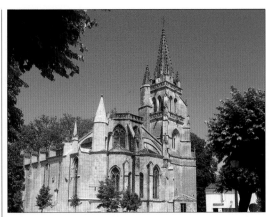

The imposing Collégiale d'Uzeste

the Flamboyant Gothic style, stands at the east end.

🛈 Collégiale d'Uzeste
◯ Easter–Oct: daily. 🗐 📷

Bazas ㊶

Road map C3. 🏘 4,788. ▭ 🖽 *Place de la Cathédrale (05) 56 25 25 84.* 🛒 *Sat.* 🎵 *Fête des Bœufs Gras (Thu before the Feb carnival).* **www**.ville-bazas.fr

Founded over 2,000 years ago, as the capital of the Roman province of Vasates, the town of Bazas later became a bishopric on the pilgrim route to Santiago de Compostela. Its magnificent

The cathedral at Bazas, a World Heritage Site

Gothic cathedral was built between the 13th and 17th centuries, and has been recently restored. Particularly striking are the beautiful rose window and a triple Gothic doorway embellished with intricate carvings, both dating from the 13th century. Behind this majestic building lie the chapterhouse gardens.

Place de la Cathédrale is a gently sloping square on which a colourful market has been held for centuries. It is lined with arcaded 16th-and 17th-century houses, which have finely decorated façades.

The **Musée de Bazas** is devoted to the archeology and history of the town. The **Apothicairerie de l'Hôpital Saint-Antoine** contains a fine collection of pottery and glassware. A waymarked walk allows visitors to explore the town's picturesque old streets.

🏛 Musée de Bazas
Tel (05) 56 25 25 84. ◯ by appointment only. 📷

🏛 Apothicairerie de l'Hôpital Saint-Antoine
Tel (05) 56 25 25 84. ◯ call for details.

Environs
The town of **Captieux** 17km (10 miles) south of Bazas, lies on the migration route of cranes travelling south from Scandinavia to Spain. For information about these birds, contact the Ligue de Protection des Oiseaux Aquitaine in Bègles (tel (05) 56 91 33 81).

Château de Cazeneuve ㊴

Set high above the deep, picturesque gorge carved by the Ciron river, the castle is fronted by 50ha (120 acres) of wooded parkland. Although this elegant building has a unified look, its appearance today is the result of several successive phases of building. The castle grew out of a simple keep built on a motte in the 11th century. Three hundred years later it had become a fortress and in the 17th century it was converted into a sumptuous residence. The buildings, which are still inhabited, are arranged round the main courtyard. An extensive tour takes visitors through the castle's various stage of development and brings to life famous visitors and inhabitants, including Henri IV of France, who owned it, his queen, Margaret, and the dukes of Albret.

The castle, set high above the gorge of the Ciron river

The chapel
Light streams into this large, vaulted space through the seven windows. The nave is flanked by aisles.

The cellars
Dating from the Middle Ages, they are stacked with barrels of highly prized Bordeaux wines.

Merovingian tombs

The lower courtyard
leads to the pool and to the medieval wine cellars.

STAR FEATURES

★ Queen Margaret's Drawing Room

★ Henri IV's Bedroom

★ Henri IV's Bedroom
This contains a kneehole desk and a Louis XIV-style walnut wardrobe. The foot of the bed is inscribed with an H (for Henri) and two opposed Fs (for the alliance of France and Navarre).

VISITORS' CHECKLIST

Road map C3. Préchac.
***Tel** (05) 56 25 48 16.* ☐ *June–Sep: daily pm; Easter–May, Oct: Sat–Sun & public hols pm.* **Visitor reception, wine-tasting on request.**
www.chateaudecazeneuve.com

Study

Queen Margaret's Bedroom
The room is hung with a fine Aubusson carpet and has an imposing Louis XIII-style wardrobe.

★ Queen Margaret's Drawing Room
This has a fine Renaissance chimneypiece and furniture mostly in the Louis XV style.

Troglodytic caves

QUEEN MARGARET'S TURBULENT LOVE LIFE

In 1572, Henry III of Navarre, the future Henri IV of France, inherited the Château de Cazeneuve and married Margaret of France, Duchesse de Valois (1553–1615). An intelligent and cultivated woman, she was the daughter of Henri II and Catherine de Médicis. Margaret was unable to bear Henri an heir and in 1583, waiting for their marriage to be annulled, he banished his wife to Cazeneuve. This did not prevent Margaret from leading a frivolous life and, tiring of her excesses, Henri finally incarcerated her in the Château d'Usson, in Auvergne, where she remained for 18 years (1587–1605) and where she wrote her *Poems* and *Memoirs*. She later returned to Paris, where she died in 1615.

Portrait of Queen Margaret

PÉRIGORD AND QUERCY

From the deep, narrow gorges of the Vézère to the fertile plains of the wide Dordogne valley, and from the panoramic Cingle de Trémolat to the dense woodland on the edge of the Limousin, the Périgord is a land of contrasts. This varied landscape is also dotted with painted caves, medieval villages and massive castles, traces of human activity that date back to prehistoric times.

Périgord-Quercy stretches across two *départements*, the Lot and the Dordogne – the latter being the third-largest in France, after its Aquitanian neighbours the Landes and the Gironde. The mix of landscapes that make up this region offer something for everyone: to the north, meadows and forests, merging into those of neighbouring Limousin; to the east, rugged limestone plateaux; to the south, vineyards, running down almost seamlessly into those of Bordeaux; and to the west, flatter land, bathed by the pearly coastal light flowing in from the Charentais. Across all of these areas, humans have left their mark, a legacy going back to prehistoric times. The Vézère valley caves, the Gallo-Roman museum in Périgueux, the great castle at Castelnaud that witnessed the Hundred Years' War, the many medieval *bastide* towns, and Sarlat's Renaissance town houses are just a few aspects of a heritage that covers around two-and-half million years. From troglodytic cliff-dwellings and fortress towers set high on rocky spurs, to watermills that straddle rivers, and a string of Romanesque churches built in the local ochre sandstone, the architecture sits in perfect harmony with the scenery of this multifaceted yet unified region.

Geese in the Périgord, raised for the production of foie gras

◁ Château de Belcastel, between Souillac and Lacave

Exploring Périgord and Quercy

Most of the region lies within the département of the Dordogne, the capital of which is Périgueux, set on the banks of the Isle river. The Dordogne divides into four distinct areas. The Périgord Blanc (White Périgord) consists of limestone plateaus, stretching across the centre of the Isle valley, the Vern valley to the east and Forêt de la Double to the west. The Périgord Vert (Green Périgord) covers the north of the *département*, from Ribérac to Hautefort. The picturesque Périgord Noir (Black Périgord) consists of the Vézère and Dordogne valleys, as far as Sarlat and the border with Quercy. And in the southwest is the Périgord Pourpre (Purple Périgord), covered in vineyards and dotted with the *bastide* towns of the Bergerac area.

GETTING AROUND

From Bergerac, which has an international airport, there is a connecting train service to the TGV (high-speed train) at Bordeaux. The railway links Périgueux and Bergerac with Sarlat, Bordeaux and Limoges. The A89 connects Périgueux with Bordeaux from Mussidan. In the opposite direction, the A89 will soon run as far as Brive-la-Gaillarde. The N89 runs through the Périgord from east to west, and the N21 from north to south. The Périgord is served by a network of roads that run along the main valleys. In Quercy, the A20 links Brive and Cahors, and the N140 provides access to Rocamadour and Padirac from Figeac. There is a bus service between Périgueux and Bergerac, and buses also run between the main towns of the Dordogne.

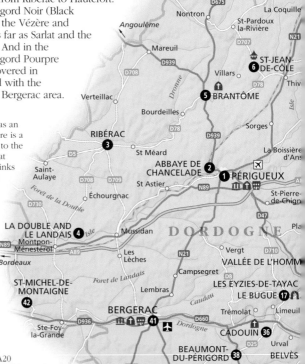

Jardins de l'Imaginaire at Terrasson-Lavilledieu

KEY

- Motorway
- Dual carriageway
- Main road
- Minor road
- Main railway
- Minor railway
- Regional border

A steep, narrow street in
Saint-Cirq-Lapopie

THE REGION AT A GLANCE

Half-timbered turret at
Autoire, in Quercy

Map labels

ÉZÈRE
LLEY ❽
Génis

CHÂTEAU DE
HAUTEFORT ❼
St-Rabier
enon

ÉZÈRE
LLEY ⓾
TERRASSON-
LAVILLEDIEU ❾
ST-AMAND-
DE-COLY ⓫
ASCAUX ⓭
-LÉON-SUR-
ÉZÈRE
Thonac
Salignac
Brive-la-
Gaillarde
MARTEL ㉑
Carennac
CASTELNAU-
BRETENOUX ㉓
EYRIGNAC ⓯
SARLAT ⓲
NAC
SOUILLAC ⓴
PADIRAC ㉒
Autoire
ST-CÉRÉ ㉕
DORDOGNE VALLEY ⓳
ROCAMADOUR ㉔
CASTELNAUD ❸
Domme
Payrac
Gramat
Lacapelle-
Marival
GOURDON ㉜
Le Basstit
Salviac
Causses de Gramat
ASSIER ㉖
efranche-
Périgord
Lamothe-
Cassel
LOT
Grèzes
FIGEAC ㉗
Capdenac-
le-Haut
Frayssinet-le-Gélat
Catus
Espagnac-
Ste-Eulalie
Aurillac
Rodez
Puy-l'Evêque
Caillac
Cabrerets
PECH-MERLE ㉙
VINEYARDS
OF CAHORS ㉛
CAHORS ㉚
Bouziès
Cajarc
ST-CIRQ-LAPOPIE ㉘
Montcuq
Limogne-
en-Quercy
Lalbenque
Castelnau-
Montratier
Montauban

SEE ALSO

- **Where to Stay** pp246–8

- **Where to Eat** pp262–3

0 km　　　10

0 miles　　　10

Street-by-Street: Périgueux ❶

The ancient centre of Périgueux is one of
the largest urban conservation areas in
France. A programme of restoration, which
began in 1970, has brought to life the narrow
streets that run from the boulevards of the
upper town down to the banks of the river
Isle, and from the Mataguerre to the Plantier
districts. Around the cathedral is the city's
pleasant, pedestrianized, medieval area.
Place de la Mairie, place du Coderc and
place de la Clautre buzz with activity on
market days. Place Saint-Louis, not far from
rue Limogeanne, and the alleys leading off
place de la Vertu make for a pleasant stroll.

Rue Limogeanne, the city's main pedestrian
thoroughfare, with shops and Renaissance houses

★ Place Saint-Louis
*The finest building on this
square is Maison du Pâtissier,
or Maison Tenant. This
restored 14th-century
town house is an
important example of
Renaissance building
in the town. The
door was added in
the 16th century.
Its pediment bears
an inscription
in Latin.*

RUE VOLTAIRE
RUE LIMOGEANNE
PLACE SAINT-LOUIS
RUE ÉGUILLERIE
RUE MALESHERBE
RUE DE LA SAGESSE
RUE DES CHAINES
PLACE DU CODERC
PLACE DE L'HÔTEL DE VILLE
RUE DU SERMENT
RUE SAINIÈRE
PLACE LA CLAU

Hôtel La Joubertie
*The town house at 1 rue de la Sagesse has
a magnificent Renaissance staircase with
coffered vaulting and columns whose
capitals are carved with fantasy animals.*

Hôtel
de Ville

Hôtel Estignard
is a town house
built in the reign
of François I
(1515–1547).

Place du Coderc
*Périgueux's colourful
market stalls fill this
square, near the Hôtel
de Ville (town hall).*

KEY

– – – Suggested route

Logis Saint-Front or Hôtel Gamenson

This building, at 7 rue de la Constitution consists of two 15th-century houses, a 16th-century half-timbered wing and a staircase tower, arranged in a square shape.

Freemasons' Hall

The original masonic symbols on this 1869 building were restored in 1987, having been destroyed under the Vichy government 1940–1944).

VISITORS' CHECKLIST

Road map D1. 32,294. 26 place Francheville (05) 53 53 10 63. Great Market: Wed & Sat am; foie gras market: mid-Nov–Mar. Mimos (Festival of Mime) (early Aug); Sinfonia (Sep); Salon International du Livre Gourmand (Nov, even years).

0   20 m

0   20 yards

★ Quayside Houses
These Renaissance buildings include the 17th-century Hôtel Salleton, the 15th-century Maison des Consuls (or Maison Cayla), with its Gothic dormer windows, and Maison Lambert, with its coffered ceilings and carved pilasters.

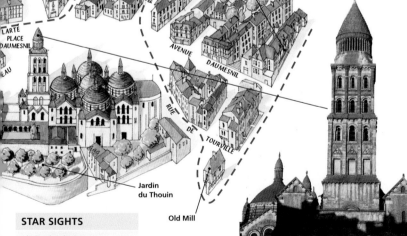

Jardin du Thouin

Old Mill

STAR SIGHTS

★ Cathédrale Saint-Front

★ Place Saint-Louis

★ Quayside Houses

★ Cathédrale Saint-Front
The original roman church was destroyed by fire in 1120, and rebuilt in the form of a Greek cross, like St Mark's in Venice. The plainness of the interior emphasizes its fine proportions. The domes, supported by columns, are 38m (125ft) high and 25m (82ft) across.

Exploring Périgueux

Musée du Périgord

The modern city of Périgueux sits on the site of ancient Vesunna. Founded in about 16 BC, this Gallo-Roman settlement fell into a decline from around the 4th century onward. During the Middle Ages, a new community sprang up, concentrated around the present Église de la Cité and the Château Barrière, but it was largely overshadowed in importance by Le Puy-Saint-Front to the north, which thrived by serving the needs of pilgrims on the road to Santiago de Compostela. After years of hostility between the two towns, peace was finally made in 1240. During the Renaissance, Périgueux began to grow, spreading out from the area around the cathedral, which remains the hub of the city to this day.

Remains of the Roman amphitheatre in Jardin des Arènes

⛩ Vesunna
Parc de Vésone. **Tel** (05) 53 53 00 92. ⬤ Jan, Christmas and out of season: Mon. 🖼️
This museum is named after the ancient city that occupied the site of modern Perigueux. The artworks and everyday objects on show give an insight into daily life in Gallo-Roman times. A building by the architect Jean Nouvel

(1945–) covers the remains of a Roman house discovered in 1959. Nearby is the imposing **Tour de Vésone**. Some 24m (80ft) high and with an internal diameter of 17m (56ft), it gives an idea of the size of the temple, long gone, of which it formed part. The Jardin des Arènes contains the remains of an amphitheatre that held 20,000 spectators.

♣ Château Barrière
Rue de Turenne, outside only.
For centuries this 12th-century castle served as a fortress for the aristocratic families of the Périgord. It was remodelled in the 15th century and came under attack from Protestant forces in 1575, during the Wars of Religion. The oldest

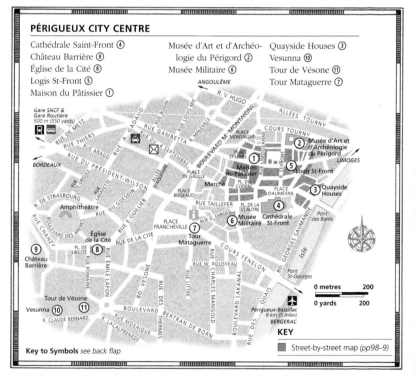

PÉRIGUEUX CITY CENTRE

Cathédrale Saint-Front ④
Château Barrière ⑨
Église de la Cité ⑧
Logis St-Front ⑤
Maison du Pâtissier ①

Musée d'Art et d'Archéo-logie du Périgord ②
Musée Militaire ⑥

Quayside Houses ③
Vesunna ⑩
Tour de Vésone ⑪
Tour Mataguerre ⑦

Key to Symbols see back flap

KEY

▣ Street-by-street map (pp98–9)

parts – a Gallo-Roman wall and keep – can be seen at the rear. The elegant five-tiered tower and residential quarters date from the Renaissance.

🔒 Cathédrale Saint-Front
Place de la Clautre.
The Byzantine-Romanesque elements of Saint-Front, a cathedral since 1669, were added by Paul Abadie, later architect of the Sacré-Cœur in Paris. He added the five domes and installed 12 small steeples. The interior has a magnificent 17th-century Baroque altarpiece and Stations of the Cross by Jacques-Émile Lafon. The remains of the old bell tower are kept in the cloisters. In summer, organ recitals are given, on the 1869 organ.

🔒 Église de la Cité
Place de la Cité.
Périgueux's first cathedral, the Romanesque, single-nave Église Saint-Étienne-de-la-Cité, was built in the 11th century and remodelled in the 17th, when it also lost its cathedral status. It still has two of its four original domes.

🏯 Tour Mataguerre
Place Francheville. *Tel* (05) 53 53 10 63. 🖼
Of the 28 towers that once surrounded Le Puy-Saint-Front, only this one still stands. The tourist office next door organizes tours of this vestige of the fortifications that encircled the city from the

The 15th-century Tour Mataguerre, a vestige of the city's ramparts

A Soul in Heaven (1878) by W A Bouguereau, Musée du Périgord

12th to the 19th centuries. The top of the tower offers a breathtaking view of Périgueux.
Some of oldest buildings in the city can be found nearby. Among them are the 12th-century Maison des Dames de la Foi, at 4–6 rue des Farges.

🏛 Musée d'Art et d'Archéologie du Périgord
22 cours Tourny. *Tel* (05) 53 06 40 70. ◐ Wed–Mon (Sat–Sun: pm only). ◉ public hols. 🖼
This museum, which in some respects resembles a cabinet of curiosities, holds a large and fascinating prehistoric collection. This includes the world's most complete Neanderthal skeleton, found at Régourdou. In addition, beautiful glass, mosaics and earthenware from ancient Vessuna, as well as artifacts from Africa and Oceania, can be seen, along with a display of local paintings, scultpures and pottery, bequeathed by Étienne Hajdu (1907–96) Regular temporary exhibitions are also held here.

🏛 Musée Militaire
32 rue des Farges. *Tel* (05) 53 53 47 36. ◐ Mon–Sat. 🖼
There are around 13,000 exhibits here, in the oldest museum of military history in France. One room houses a moving series of drawings made in the trenches during World War I by Gilbert-Privat (1892–1965), winner of the Prix de Rome. The colonial and World War II collections, as well as medals, insignia and other wartime memorabilia, help serve as a reminder of the sacrifice of those who fought, and of the need to preserve the peace.

Environs
Sorges, northeast of Périgueux, is the Périgord's truffle capital. The **Écomusée de la Truffe** has displays showing how truffles grow, the methods of finding them, and details of some spectacularly large examples.

🏛 Écomusée de la Truffe
Sorges. *Tel* (05) 53 05 90 11. ◉ 4 Oct–13 Jun: Mon. 🖼

TRUFFLES
The Périgordian truffle, *Tuber melanosporum,* is a highly prized delicacy that, for gourmets, is almost worth its weight in gold. An ingredient of many local specialities, this subterranean fungus is now scarce. In 1870, Sorge's limestone plateau alone produced 6 tonnes of truffles a year, which equals the yield obtained today from the whole of the Dordogne. The main truffle market takes place at Sainte-Alvère, in the Bergerac region. The going price is usually 600 per kilogram (about £400 per lb).

A dry-stone truffle-hunter's hut, at the Écomusée de Sorges

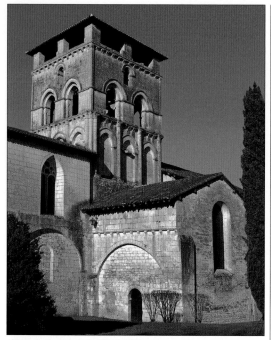

Abbaye de Chancelade, built in the 12th century

Abbaye de Chancelade **②**

Road map D1. 🏠 *3,999.* 🚉
🚌 *Périgueux.* 🏢 *26 place Francheville, Périgueux (05) 53 53 10 63.* ⏰ *daily (access to the exterior only).*

Set in the Beauronne valley, the Augustinian Abbaye de Chancelade was founded in the 12th century, and became an important centre of intellectual life. Having survived the Hundred Years' War and the Wars of Religion, it once again became influential in the 17th century. It is one of the few religious buildings of the period to have been partly preserved, with a wash-house, stables, workshops and a mill.

Environs
From the abbey, a marked 14-km (9-mile) long path through woods leads to the old village of **Les Maines**, with a view of the former Templar house at Les Andrivaux.
The **Prieuré de Merlande**, 4km (3 miles) northeast of Chancelade is a priory founded by monks from Chancelade.

Ribérac **③**

Road map D1. 🏠 *4,000.*
🚉 *Périgueux.* 🏢 *Place du Général-de-Gaulle (05) 53 90 03 10.* ⏰ *Fri.*
🎪 *Festival Musique et Paroles (Jul).*

Birthplace of 12th-century troubadour Arnaud Daniel, Ribérac is a town where you are just as likely to hear English as Occitan at Friday's market, because of the large number of English expatriates living in nearby villages. The abbey church, built in the 12th century with later additions, has 17th-century paintings and a dome above the choir.

Many Romanesque domed churches are dotted around Ribérac: the church at **Siorac-de-Ribérac**, fortified in the 14th century, contains an interesting 18th-century painted and gilded wooden statue; the church at **Grand-Brassac** has a splendid carved doorway as well as three domes supported on stone columns; and the church at **Saint-Privat-des-Prés**, an architectural jewel, has a circular arch with ornate moulding over the entrance.

Environs
30km (19 miles) northwest of Ribéra are the **Tourbières de Vendoire**, peat bogs where visitors can see extraordinary water-filled plant fossils.
The **Château de Mareuil**, 30km (19 miles) north of Ribérac, is the only medieval fortress to be built on a plain. It was once owned by the Talleyrand family, and still has 12th-century towers and ramparts, a 15th-century keep with living quarters and a Flamboyant Gothic chapel.

🔖 **Tourbières de Vendoire**
Tel (05) 53 90 79 56. ⏰ *May–Sep: daily; Oct–Apr: appointment only.* 📷

⛪ **Château de Mareuil**
At junction of D939 & D708. *Tel (05) 53 60 99 85.* ⏰ *Jul–Aug: daily (not Sun am); Sep–Jun: Sun pm.* 📷 📷

La Double and Le Landais **④**

Road map D2. Between Montpon and Ribérac, via the D708.

The stunning, wild, marshy countryside here is covered with areas of dense forest,

The village of Grand-Brassac and its church, near Ribérac

The covered market and castle at Saint-Jean-de-Côle

dotted with ponds and clearings. At the **Ferme du Parcot** visitors can see local houses made with cob-filled wooden frames. **Saint-Aulaye** is a village known for its church, Cognac museum and a riverside beach along the Dronne. At nearby **La Latière**, a well-attended cattle market has been held since the Middle Ages.

🌿 **Ferme du Parcot**
On the Saint-Astier road, Échourgnac. **Tel** (05) 53 81 99 28. ⬤ May, Jun & Sep: Sun pm; Jul–Aug: Tue–Sun pm. 🎫

Brantôme ❺

Road map D1. 🏛 2,075. 🚉 Périgueux. 🚌 Boulevard Charlemagne; (05) 53 05 80 52. 🚃 Fri am.

The town of Brantôme sits on an island, encircled by a loop of the river Dronne. Its buildings cluster around the 9th-century Benedictine **abbey**. The bell tower, dating from the 11th century, is one of the oldest in France. A 16th-century bridge links the abbey to its gardens. Close by is the Grotte du Jugement Dernier, a cave with a 15th-century carved relief of the Last Judgment.

🏛 **Abbey**
Tel (05) 53 05 80 63. ⬤ Jan & Apr–June: Tue. 🎫 📷

Environs
10.5km (6 miles) southwest of Brantôme is the 13th-century **Château de Bourdeilles**. It has an octagonal keep and later Renaissance buildings and ramparts.

The 16th-century **Château de Puyguilhem**, 10km (6 miles) northeast of Brantôme, has an elegant main house, towers, dormer windows and battlements. The château's interiors are also exceptionally fine.

The **Grotte de Villars**, 15km (9 miles) northeast of Brantôme, is a network of caves with 13km (8 miles) of galleries, filled with fascinating rock formations and some prehistoric paintings.

Brantôme, "the Venice of the Périgord"

🏰 **Château de Bourdeilles**
Tel (05) 53 03 73 36. ⬤ Jan–Apr: Tue.

🏰 **Château de Puyguilhem**
Villars. **Tel** (05) 53 54 82 18. ⬤ Jan–Apr: Mon.

🏛 **Grotte de Villars**
Tel (05) 53 54 82 36. ⬤ Apr–Oct: daily. 🎫 📷 www.grotte-villars.com

Saint-Jean-de-Côle ❻

Road map D1. 🏛 340. 🚉 Thiviers. 🚌 Rue du Château (05) 53 62 14 15. 🎉 Floralies (late Apr or early May).

Classed as one of France's prettiest villages, Saint-Jean-de-Côle sits on the banks of the river Côle. Its focal point is a late 11th-century priory, torched by the English during the Hundred Years' War and looted by Protestants in 1569, during the Wars of Religion. It was rebuilt in the 17th century. The 12th-century Byzantine-Romanesque church has a very unusual plan: it forms a semicircle around the apse. Wooden carvings in the choir date from the 18th century.

The medieval bridge and the rue du Fond-du-Bourg, lined with 14th-century half-timbered houses, add to the village's picturesque appeal. The 12th-century Château de la Marthonie, on place Saint-Jean, was rebuilt in the 15th century and enlarged in the 17th.

Environs
The **Château de Jumilhac**, 20km (12 miles) northeast of Saint-Jean-de-Côle, is a 13th-century castle. A magnificent roof set with pepperpot towers and skylights was added in 1600. The outbuildings and ramparts were demolished in the 17th century to make room for luxurious reception areas, including a drawing room based on that at Versailles, and a magnificent Louis XIII-style staircase.

🏰 **Château de Jumilhac**
Jumilhac. **Tel** (05) 53 52 42 97. ⬤ Jun–Sep: daily; Oct–Nov & Mar–May: daily; Nov–Mar: Sun pm. 🎫 📷

Château de Hautefort ❼

Closely associated with the warrior-troubadour Bertran de Born, Hautefort was originally a medieval fortress. The imposing residence that later replaced it was built for the Marquis de Hautefort, who envisaged a classic building in the style of a Loire Valley château. Work began in 1630, to plans by Nicolas Rambourg, and was completed in 1670. A drawbridge leads through to the courtyard and main building, with an arcaded gallery and steep slate roof. Baron and Baronne de Bastard began restoring the main building in the 1920s, but this was brought to an abrupt end by a fire in August 1968. All that was saved were the 16th-century tapestries. Photographs showing the devastation of the fire are on view in the 14th-century Tour de Bretagne, the only surviving medieval part of the castle. Further phases of restoration were completed in 1995 and 2005.

★ Grand Staircase
This curves back on itself to lead to the upper floor.

The master bedroom is decorated with wood carvings and filled with antique furniture.

The roof structure of the Tour de Bretagne dates from 1678.

The large drawing room is hung with Brussels tapestries. Monumental wooden chimneypieces fill each end of the room.

The village of Hautefort, with its imposing château above

STAR FEATURES

★ Chapel

★ Grand Staircase

★ **The Chapel**
The ceiling, a trompe l'oeil coffered dome, looks down on a simple clay floor.

The terrace was rearranged in the 1930s. Box and yew have been clipped into dome shapes to echo the outline of the château and its slate-roofed towers. This formal garden is laid out to give the shape of a gushing fountain, when viewed from above,

The formal gardens are best seen from above, particularly from the main courtyard, which also commands a view of the village on its southern side.

Auvézère Valley 8

Road map E1. 🚉 *Périgueux.*
ℹ️ *Place du Marquis, Hautefort (05) 53 50 40 27. Or 4 place Thomas-Robert-Bugeaud, Lanouaille (05) 53 62 17 82.* 🎪 *Fête de la Noix (Nailhac), Festival du Pays d'Ans (Jan).*

This valley contains several interesting sights. The **Chapelle d'Auberoche**, with its traditional Périgordian-tile roof, perches high on a cliff, offering dramatic views. Moving upriver, the Blâme cascades dramatically into the Auvézère at **La Boissière d'Ans**. Commanding views of the Loue and Auvézère valleys can also be had from the **Colline de Saint-Raphaël**. Two massive columns, in front of the church here, are the remains of a Benedictine priory. **Génis** is also set high up, on a granite plateau, looking down on the gorges of the river Dalon. Upstream from here is an old mill, the **Moulin du Pervendoux**, beyond which are rapids and the **Cascade du Saut-Ruban**. A path (GR 646) leads down to this waterfall from the **Église de Saint-Mesmin**. At Le Puy-des-Âges, set on a quartz-rich spur, is the little chapel of **Notre-Dame-de-Partout**, filled with votive offerings. The hill-top château close to **Savignac-Lédrier**, looks down on a 17th-century forge, while at **Payzac** is the former Vaux papermill. Round about, oval, stone barns that were originally thatched, lie dotted across the landscape.

THE TROUBADOUR OF HAUTEFORT

Bertran de Born (c.1150–1215), Viscount of Hautefort, is a legendary figure in the Pay d'Oc. Over 40 of his poem-songs survive, many on the theme of courtly love, but some are of a political and warlike nature. On several occasions, he fought both his brother and the English monarchy (then Dukes of Aquitaine) for ownership of Hautefort. This belligerent

Miniature of Bertran de Born on horseback

stance led some to blame him for the conflict between England and France at the time. For this, Dante, in the *Inferno*, portrays him as a sower of discord and places him in hell. He ended his life as a monk at the Abbaye du Dalon.

The Auvézère valley, an unspoilt area of hills, woods and pasture

Jardins de l'Imaginaire, on the Vézère river at Terrasson-Lavilledieu

Terrasson-Lavilledieu ❾

Road map E2. On the N89.
🏠 *6,700.* 🚉 🚌 🛈 *Rue Jean-Rouby (05) 53 50 37 56.* 🛒 *Thu am.*
🎭 *Les Chemins de l'Imaginaire (Jul).*

At the head of the Vézère valley, which leads down into the Périgord, the town of Terrasson-Lavilledieu grew up around a Merovingian abbey. The Pont Vieux, the town's old stone bridge, dates back to the 12th century, but was damaged during the Hundred Years' War and largely rebuilt in the late 15th century, as were the church and the monastery. Terrasson was also a strategic town during the 16th-century Wars of Religion and also opposed the French Revolution.

The **Jardins de l'Imaginaire**, overlook the old town. These 6ha (15 acres) include a rose garden, a sacred wood, a water garden, a belvedere and scattered springs, all designed around historical and mythological themes.

🌷 **Jardins de l'Imaginaire**
🛈 *Place du Foirail*
(05) 53 50 86 82.
🕐 *Apr–mid-Oct.* 🎟️ 🖼️

Vézère Valley ❿

Road map E2. 🚉 *Périgueux.*
🚌 *Les Eyzies.* 🛈 *19 Rue de la Préhistoire, Les Eyzies (05) 53 06 97 05.* 🎭 *Festival du Périgord Noir (Jul–Aug), Festival du Folklore International (Montignac, Jul)*

The valley is dotted with picturesque small towns. **Condat-sur-Vézère**, once a Templar town, stands at the confluence of the Vézère and the Coly. It has a Romanesque church and a castle with a square tower. **Fanlac** clusters round its church and bell tower. The town was the setting for *Jacquou le Croquant*, the film of the novel by Eugène Le Roy. The backdrop to the story was the Forêt Barade and **Château de l'Herm**, nearby. Set in woodland, these highly atmospheric ruins include a polygonal tower with a Gothic doorway that leads to a spiral staircase.

Rouffignac was almost totally destroyed during World War II, athough the church, with a beautiful Renaissance doorway, was spared. Nearby is the **Grotte de Rouffignac**, inhabited around 10,000 BC and open to visitors since the 16th century. A little train takes visitors down 8km (5 miles) of tunnels, which are covered with paintings and engravings, including 158 depictions of mammoths.

At **Plazac**, the 12th-century keep was converted into a Romanesque church with square belfry and adjoining cemetery. The village of **Saint-Geniès** is filled with attractive ochre sandstone houses. The village also has a 15th-century church and a 17th-century château. The Gothic chapel at Le Cheylard, just outside the village, is decorated with 14th-century biblical scenes. The château at **Salignac**, once a walled fortress, is now an elegant residence with a tiled roof. The 16th–17th-century Manoir de la Cipière at **Saint-Crépin** is worth a detour.

Crossing the Beune, the road leads from **Tamniès**, above a lake, to **Marquay**, a village with a fortified Romanesque church. Further on is the **Château de Commarque**, which lies in a valley that has

---

TIBETAN LAMAS IN THE PÉRIGORD

In 1977, a hillside close to the village of Le Moustier, near Saint-Léon-sur-Vézère, was chosen by a group of Tibetan Buddhists, under the leadership of HH Dudjom Rinpoche, as the site of a new spiritual community. The emphasis at **Laugeral**, as it was called, is on meditation and the study of the teachings of the Nyingma school of Buddhism by groups of residential students. Anyone, however, is welcome to visit, as long as they come in a spirit of peace. The Dalai Lama is among many distinguished visitors to this unique place.

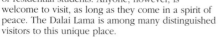

The stupa at the Dhagpo centre

---

been settled since prehistoric times. The castle, partly in ruins, has a 4th-century church. The walk to the keep offers a fine view of the **Château de Laussel**. *Bories*, Périgordian dry-stone circular huts, can be seen around **Sireuil**. A group of these at Bénivès, the **Cabanes du Breuil**, form part of an open-air museum.

Set in woodland, the **Château de Puymartin** is almost completely hidden by trees. It was built in the late 13th century, rebuilt in the 15th and restored around 1890. It contains period furniture, tapestries and paintings, including mythological scenes on some ceilings and walls.

⛪ **Château de l'Herm**
Via the D31, Rouffignac-St-Cernin-de Reilhac. **Tel** (05) 53 05 46 61. ☐ Apr–11 Nov: daily. ☑ by arrangement. ▨

♪ **Grotte de Rouffignac**
Via the D32, Rouffignac-St-Cernin-de Reilhac. **Tel** (05) 53 05 41 71. ☐ Apr–1 Nov: daily. ☑ ▨

⛪ **Château de Commarque**
On the D48, Sireuil. **Tel** (05) 53 59 00 25. ☐ Apr–Sep: daily. ☑ ▨

⌂ **Cabanes du Breuil**
Via the D47, Saint-André-d'Allas. **Tel** (06) 80 72 38 59. ☐ Mar–mid-Nov: daily; mid-Nov–Feb: Sat & Sun.

⛪ **Château de Puymartin**
On the D47, Marquay. **Tel** (05) 53 59 29 97. ☐ Apr–Oct: daily. ☑ ▨

Traditional Périgordian circular huts at Le Breuil, with dry-stone walls

Saint-Amand-de-Coly ⓫

Road map E2. Off the D704 or D62. ▨ 362. ▮ Maison du Patrimoine (05) 53 51 47 85. ☑ church.

Originally part of a Romanesque abbey founded in the 7th century, the massive, fortified **church** here, with a nave 48m (158ft) long, still has defensive elements. Built on the plan of a Latin cross, it is enclosed by 300m (985ft) of walls. Its 30-m (98-ft) high belfry-keep is

The Romanesque church at Saint-Léon-sur-Vézère

crowned by a garrison. The nave is lit by a stained-glass window set above the three-arched doorway. The floor of the beautifully empty interior slopes gently down towards the choir.

Concerts of classical music forming part of the Festival du Périgord Noir *(see p33)* take place in this church and in those of Saint-Léon-sur-Vézère and Auriac. These Romanesque churches provide both a magical setting and fine acoustics.

Saint-Léon-sur-Vézère ⓬

Road map E2. On the D706. ▨ 422. ▮ Place Bertran-de-Born, Montignac (05) 53 51 82 60. ▨ Wed & Sat.

The 11th-century church here is one of the oldest in the Périgord. Its interior is decorated with frescoes, from the 12th to 17th centuries.

The beautifully restored 14th–17th century Château de Chabans has fine stained glass, tapestries and furniture, but is no longer open to the public.

Nearby, at Le Moustier, is a Buddhist centre, **Laugeral**. Founded in 1977, this retreat offers meditation and study, and daily practice for followers.

⌂ **Laugeral** Saint-Léon-sur-Vézère. **Tel** (05) 53 70 75. ☐ daily. Students by prior appointment.

The imposing church at Saint-Amand-de-Coly

Lascaux
ıx II ®

trive & Sarlat.

place Bertran-de-Born, Montignac
(05) 53 51 82 60 or (05) 53 05 65 65.
Jun–Sep: daily; Apr–May &
Oct–Dec: Tue–Sun. Jan, early Feb.
www.culture.gouv.fr/
culture/arcnat/lauscaux.fr

The cave that became
known as the "Sistine
Chapel of prehistory" was
discovered on 12 September
1940 by four young boys
who were out walking. Its
paintings, which date from
around 18,000 BC, provide a
glimpse of that remote age.
It is now known that the cave
was never inhabited, and
the precise meaning of the
images on its walls remains
unclear. The prehistoric artists
who created them used the
relief of the cave walls to
help breathe a sense of life
into their depictions of bulls,
deer, horses and ibexes that
cover every surface from
floor to ceiling.

The cave rapidly became a
major attraction, drawing in
thousands of visitors. But
this influx also allowed in a
number of harmful micro-
organisms, which caused the
paintings to deteriorate. It
was therefore decided to
close the cave in 1963. The
local authority then went

about creating an exact
replica, just 200m (700ft)
from the original, close to
the town of Montignac.

Lascaux II, a remarkable feat
of scientific accuracy and
artistic skill, opened in 1983.
Executed by an artist using
the same techniques and
materials as her distant
ancestors, the paintings are
an accurate reconstruction of
the originals, around 70 per
cent of which have been
replicated on the walls of
two main cavities, the
Diverticule Axial (Central
Passage) and the Salle des
Taureaux (Hall of Bulls).

Montignac itself, is also
worth a visit. A bustling town,
it contains a number of fine
14th–16th century houses.

Environs
At Thonac, 10km (6 miles)
to the southwest of Lascaux,
is the **Château de Losse**, an
elegant residence built in
1576 on the ruins of the town's
medieval fortress. It was once
the residence of Jean II de
Losse, the private tutor of Henri
IV. The 14th-century Tour de
l'Éperon stands on the ramparts
and a fortified gatehouse
guards the fixed bridge that
leads to the main courtyard. A
range of interesting 15th- and
17th-century furniture fills the
building's Renaissance-style
interior. Nearby is the **Tour de**

The 16th-century Château de Losse,
near Lascaux

la Vermondie. According to
legend, this 13th-century
leaning tower was built at this
angle in order to make it
possible for the young girl
who was imprisoned there to
lean out and kiss her fiancé
as he passed by.

♣ **Château de Losse**
Thonac. **Tel** (05) 53 50 80 08.
Easter–Sep: daily.
part of the tour.

Vallée
de l'Homme ®

Road map E2.On the D706,
between Montignac and Les Eyzies.

This section of the Vézère
valley, also known as the
Vallée de l'Homme (Valley of
Man), contains a very large
number of prehistoric sites.

🏛 Le Thot, Espace
Cro-Magnon
Thonac. **Tel** (05) 53 50 70 44. Jan;
12 Nov–Dec & Feb–Mar: Mon.
The animal park at Le Thot
contains species descended
from the wild creatures that
inhabited the region in the
Upper Palaeolithic period,
and whose likenesses can be
seen on the walls of the
prehistoric caves at Lascaux.
Among them are reindeer,
aurochs (long-horn African
cattle) and Przewalski's
horses. There are also models
of extinct species, such as
mammoths and woolly rhinos.

The museum features the
re-creation of a prehistoric
cave, showing methods used

Horses and deer, some of the animals depicted at the Grottes de Lascaux

A mammoth hunt, one of several reconstructions of prehistoric scenes at Préhisto Parc, Vallée de l'Homme

for painting and engraving the walls. An exhibition area and auditorium tells the story of Lascaux II. Four facsimiles of paintings that are not on view at Lascaux II are displayed here. They depict human figures, deer, a cow, horses and bison.

🏛 Préhisto Parc

Tursac. *Tel (05) 53 50 73 19.*
☐ *15 Feb–11 Nov: daily.* 🖼 ♿
With reconstructions of daily life in prehistoric times, the family-oriented Préhisto Parc takes visitors on a journey through time, from Neanderthal to Cro-Magnon Man. Flint-knapping, spear-throwing, cave painting and fire-making workshops give visitors a direct insight into prehistoric skills.

⌂ Village de la Madeleine

Tursac. *Tel (05) 53 46 36 88.*
☐ *daily.*
The rock shelter at La Madeleine gave its name to the Magdalenian society of hunter-gatherers that lived in the area from around 18,000–10,000 BC. Excavations at this site brought to light a large array of pieces, including a fragment of engraved mammoth ivory. A child's grave, decorated with shells and red ochre, was also discovered here.

From the 8th century, the troglodytic village, cut into the cliff-face over the Vézère, was used as a place of safety.

⌂ La Roque-Saint-Christophe

Peyzac-Le Moustier. *Tel (05) 53 50 70 45.* **wwww**.roque-st-christophe.com ☐ *daily.* 🖼 🖼
This sheer rockface above the Vézère is 80m (260ft) high and 1km (0.5 mile) long. It has been inhabited since prehistoric times. The troglodytic fort and town carved in the rock here dates from the 10th century, but additions were made throughout the Middle Ages to increase security. This natural fortress could hold over 1,000 people. Flat, terrace-like areas offer good views out over the valley. A reconstruction of a medieval building site gives a glimpse into the daily life of the period.

Château de Belcayre, between Thonac and Sergeac

🏕 Sergeac

ℹ *Place Bertran-de-Born, Montignac (05) 53 51 82 60.*
A 15th-century carved cross stands at the entrance to the village, which was the Knights Templar's main base in the Périgord. Near the commander's residence, a house dating from the 14th–15th centuries, is a fortified church roofed with traditional Périgordian tiles. The museum here has a famous jewellery collection.

Not far from Sergeac is the small valley of **Castel-Merle**, with rock-shelters that were inhabited from the Palaeolithic period to the Iron Age. Between Thonac and Sergac is the splendid Château de Blecayre.

⌂ Grottes du Roc de Cazelle

Beyond Les Eyzies, on the D47 to Sarlat. *Tel (05) 53 59 46 09.*
☐ *daily.* 🖼 🖼
The exhibiton at Roc de Cazelle, one of the many rock-shelters in this area, tells the story of the human habitation of these caves from Upper Palaeolithic times to 1966. The tour includes the reconstruction of scenes from the daily life of the early hunter-gatherers to that of farmers in the 20th century. Other displays show how the rock was made habitable, how a fort was built and houses here were cut out of the living rock.

Gardens of the Manoir d'Eyrignac ⓯

First laid out in the 18th century, the gardens of this manor house form a cool oasis of greenery amidst the dry, rocky limestone of the Périgord Noir. Watered by seven springs, they were made over in the Romantic style in the 19th century, but within 100 years had fallen into such neglect that it took the owners, Gilles Sermadiras and later his son, nearly 40 years to restore them to their full glory. They finally opened to the public in 1987. Today, the gardens are a mix of the more formal French and wilder-looking Italian styles, with rolling lawns and a mass of mature trees and shrubs, such as box, yew, hornbeam and cypress. The French garden, a masterpiece of symmetry and order, with topiary and carefully arranged parterres, stands in stark contrast to the more irregular, "jigsaw" of the Italian garden. There are also many surprises to delight the visitor, such as secret nooks and unexpected vistas.

Stonework and greenery sit together in perfect harmony

Restaurant
Côté Jardin

Red lacquer
Chinese pagoda

★ **Hornbeam Walk**
Running parallel with the urn-lined walk, this long, grassy, hornbeam-lined avenue is a geometric masterpiece in a palette of harmonious greens. The meticulously trimmed yew and hornbeam create an impressive perspective.

English Arcade
Covered in vegetation that casts subtle patterns of light and shade, this walkway leads from the pavilion, beside the Hornbeam Walk, to a sandy courtyard fronting the manor house.

STAR FEATURES

★ French Garden

★ Hornbeam Walk

White Garden
Planted only with white roses, this consists of parterres running along wide, straight avenues. In early summer the flowers fill the air with a delicate scent.

VISITORS' CHECKLIST

Road map E2. On the D60.
Salignac. 1,123 Souillac
and Brive-la-Gaillarde.
Tel (05) 53 28 99 71. daily.
www.eyrignac.com
contact@eyrignac.com

The Pools
Laid out in a geometric pattern, five pools complement the rose garden. The large central pool is surrounded by fountains.

The "enchanted terrace",
with the rose garden behind,
offers a fine view of the
manor house and the
paddock, and of the formal
French garden below.

★ French Garden
The terrace, which is laid out with flower-filled parterres, is fronted by a sandy courtyard and a small pond. This garden consists of symmetrical box-tree arabesques and an immaculate lawn.

The manor house
was built in 1653

Les Eyzies-de-Tayac ⑯

At the heart of the Vézère valley, with its prehistoric painted caves and rock-shelters, sits the village of Les Eyzies. Known as "the capital of prehistory", it stretches out along the foot of ochre-coloured cliffs that bear traces of some of the earliest human settlements. The exhibits in the recently enlarged museum cover most of what is known about early man, and would make an ideal preliminary to any visit to the nearby painted caves. A 12th-century, fortified church in Tayac, the hamlet beside Les Eyzies, is also worth a visit.

🏛 Musée National de la Préhistoire

Tel (05) 53 06 45 45. ☐ daily. 📧 Sep–Jun: Tue. 📷 📹
The museum's collections, which consist mostly of finds from the Vézère valley, include stone tools, burial artifacts, bones of prehistoric animals, ornaments, small sculptures and engravings. The terrace commands impressive views of the valley.

🏠 Abri Pataud

Tel (05) 53 06 92 46. ☐ Jul–Aug: daily; out of season call in advance. 📷 📹
The walls of this engraved rock-shelter contain traces of around 40 encampments dating from 35,000 to 20,000 BC, covering the Aurignacian, Gravettian and Solutrean periods. Just below this is another rock-shelter, its ceiling decorated with a splendid relief of an oryx (Solutrean, 17,000 BC). The museum displays finds from the site and gives details of the archaeological excavations that have been carried out here to date.

🏠 Abri du Cap Blanc

Marquay. **Tel** (05) 53 06 86 00. ☐ Apr–Oct: Sun–Fri. 📷 📹
More than 15,000 years ago, prehistoric people carved representations of horses, bisons and reindeer on the wall of this rock-shelter. A small display sheds light on daily life during the Magdalenian period, as well as the art that typifies it.

🏠 Le Moustier, La Micoque and La Ferrassie

Tel (05) 53 06 86 00. ☐ summer; prior booking essential. 📷 📹
The rock-shelter at Le Moustier, where a Neanderthal skeleton was discovered, gave its name to the Mousterian culture (80,000–30,000 BC). La Micoque, the oldest site in the Dordogne, was inhabited from 300, 000 BC. The rock-shelter of La Ferrassie, inhabited from 40,000 to 25,000 BC, contained Neanderthal burials. Excavations here also uncovered engraved stone slabs from the Aurignacian period. These are the earliest-known examples of prehistoric art in the Vézère valley.

Primitive Man, Musée de la Préhistoire

🏠 Abri de Laugerie Haute

Tel (05) 53 06 86 00. 📧 Sat & public hols. 📷 prior booking essential. 📹
This huge rock-shelter was inhabited from 22,000 to 12,000 BC. It was abandoned when the ceiling fell in. Flint and bone tools, as well as a large number of harpoons, were discovered here.

🏠 Abri du Poisson

Tel (05) 53 06 86 00. 📧 Sat & public hols. 📷 prior booking essential. 📹
This small rock-shelter in the valley of the Gorge d'Enfer is named after the relief of a fish that was discovered here. It is of a salmon, 1m (3ft) long, carved in about 25,000 BC.

🏠 Grotte des Combarelles

Tel (05) 53 06 86 00. 📧 Sat & public hols. 📷 prior booking essential. 📹
This cave, used during the Magdalenian period (around 15,000 BC), has some 600 engravings and drawings of horses, reindeer, mammoths and woolly rhinoceros, as well as anthropomorphic figures.

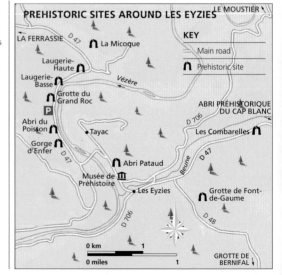

PREHISTORIC SITES AROUND LES EYZIES

LE MOUSTIER
LA FERRASSIE D 47   La Micoque
Laugerie-Haute 🏠
Laugerie-Basse 🏠   Vézère
Grotte du Grand Roc 🏠
P
Abri du Poisson 🏠   ● Tayac
Gorge d'Enfer 🏠 D 47
Musée de Préhistoire 🏛
🏠 Abri Pataud
● Les Eyzies

KEY
═══ Main road
🏠 Prehistoric site

ABRI PRÉHISTORIQUE DU CAP BLANC
D 706
Les Combarelles 🏠
D 47   Beune
Grotte de Font-de-Gaume 🏠
D 706   D 48
0 km   1
0 miles   1
GROTTE DE BERNIFAL

Drawing of a deer in the Grotte de Font-de-Gaume

⋔ Grotte de Font-de-Gaume
Tel (05) 53 06 86 00. ◯ *daily.* ✎ *prior booking essential.* ♿

The walls of this cave are covered with magnificent multicoloured paintings dating from the Magdalenian period. It also has drawings and engravings of almost 200 animals, including 82 bisons.

⋔ Grotte de Bernifal
Meyrals. *Tel* (05) 53 29 66 39. ◯ *Jun–Sep: daily.* ✎ ♿

This small cave is reached by walking up through an atmospheric woodland. By torchlight, visitors can see about 100 representations of mammoths and human figures, and signs and symbols, dating from the Magdalenian period.

⋔ Abri de Laugerie Basse
Tel (05) 53 06 92 70. www. grandroc.com ◯ *Feb–mid-Nov & Christmas period: daily.* ✎ ♿ *special price ticket when combined with a visit to Grand Roc.*

This rock-shelter, from the Magdalenian period, contains displays on the life of Cro-Magnon people, covering the the tools they made, what they ate, their hunting methods and their artistic skills. Some pieces are replicas because the originals have been taken to other museums around the world. The earliest female figure to be discovered in France, known as the Venus Impudique (Shameless Venus), was found here in 1864 by Marquis Paul de Vibraye.

⋔ Grotte du Grand Roc
Tel (05) 53 06 92 70. www. grandroc.com ◯ *Feb–mid-Nov & Christmas period: daily.* ✎ ♿ *special price ticket when combined with a visit to Abri de Laugerie Basse.*

Lit to reveal its wonders, this cave contains fantastic mineral formations, including stalagmites, stalactites and an assortment of rather weird shapes, some of which are hollow. One of the most amazing forms a cross.

Le Bugue-sur-Vézère ⓱

Road map E2. On the D710. ⊞ *Agen, Périgueux.* 🚶 *2,825.* 🛈 *Porte de la Vézère* (05) 53 07 20 48. 🚌 *Tue & Sat.*

An important tourist centre, this sizeable town offers a variety of attractions, from the **Aquarium du Périgord Noir**, with 6,000 fish, to the **Village du Bournat**, where scenes of rural life in the Périgord in times gone by are re-created in a large open-air museum.

🐟 Aquarium du Périgord Noir
Tel (05) 53 07 10 74. ◯ *mid-Feb–mid-Nov: daily.* ♿ ♿

🏛 Village du Bournat
Tel (05) 53 08 41 99. ◯ *mid-Feb–mid-Nov.* ✎ ♿

⋔ Grotte de Bara-Bahau
Le Bugue. *Tel* (05) 53 07 44 58. ◯ *daily.* ⬤ *Jan.* ✎ ♿

This cave has a large gallery of unusual rock formations. This leads to a cavity that has been decorated with engravings of bears, horses and bison, as well as hands, a phallus and other symbols.

Son et lumière inside a chasm in the Gouffre de Proumeyssac

The Grand Roc at Les Eyzies, on the banks of the Vézère

🗻 Gouffre de Proumeyssac
4km (2.5 miles) from Le Bugue, on road to Audrix. *Tel* (05) 53 07 27 47. ◯ *daily.* ⬤ *Jan.* ✎ ♿

The cathedral-like domed interior of this cave contains mineral formations in a huge variety of shapes. There is also a fascinating display on geological formations. By prior arrangement, visitors can descend into the chasm in a cradle suspended on cables, as the first people to explore this cave would have done.

Environs
At the confluence of the Vézère and the Dordogne, 5km (3 miles) southwest of Le Bugue, is the village of **Limeuil**. It has a pleasant riverside beach and many craftsmen's workshops. Narrow streets lead up to the grounds of the château and an arboretum. Thomas à Becket once visited the elegantly proportioned Chapelle Saint-Martin here.

At Le Buisson de Cadouin, 10km (6 miles) south of Le Bugue, are the **Grottes de Maxange**. Found in 2000, these caves contain extraordinary rock formations.

⋔ Grottes de Maxange
Le Buisson de Cadouin. *Tel* (05) 53 23 42 80. ◯ *Easter-Oct: daily.* ✎ ♿

Street-by-Street: Sarlat ⑱

Nestling at the foot of a cluster of *pechs* (small hills), Sarlat has undergone extensive restoration, returning its narrow streets and courtyards to their original splendour. A number of houses here consist of a medieval ground floor with Renaissance floors above. This centre of trade on the road to Santiago de Compostela grew rapidly in the 13th century, and again in the mid-15th century, when its splendid Renaissance houses were built. Rue de la République, laid out in the 19th century and nicknamed "La Traverse", runs between the picturesque medieval district and the town's other ancient streets. Although Sarlat's restored quarter is an architectural jewel, the town's truffle and fois gras fairs also attracts visitors.

Rue des Consuls
Fine 15th- to 17th-century houses line this street.

Place aux Oies
This square (Goose Square) was once the venue of Sarlat's live fowl market. This is commemorated by bronze statues of geese by Lalanne. It contains two fine Renaissance buildings: the turreted Hôtel de Vassal, and the Hôtel Chassaing.

★ Place de la Liberté
The hub of Sarlat, this square is lined with picturesque 16th- and 18th-century houses that have featured in a number of films. The Église Sainte-Marie, in the background, was restored by the architect Jean Nouvel (1945–), and is now a covered market.

STAR SIGHTS

★ Maison de La Boétie

★ Place de la Liberté

0 metres 50
0 yards 50

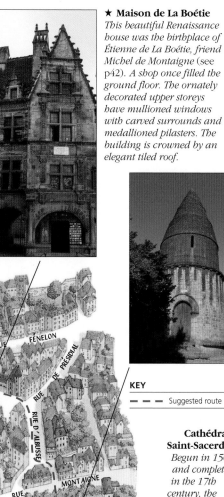

★ Maison de La Boétie
This beautiful Renaissance house was the birthplace of Étienne de La Boétie, friend Michel de Montaigne (see p42). A shop once filled the ground floor. The ornately decorated upper storeys have mullioned windows with carved surrounds and medallioned pilasters. The building is crowned by an elegant tiled roof.

Lanterne des Morts
Constructed in the 12th century to commemorate St Bernard's visit to Sarlat, this tower offers a fine view of the apse and bell tower of the church.

KEY

– – – Suggested route

Cathédrale Saint-Sacerdos
Begun in 1504 and completed in the 17th century, the cathedral lacks stylistic unity. A notable feature of the interior is the overhanging organ loft of 1770.

Chapelle des Pénitents Bleus is the only surviving element of an earlier Romanesque abbey church.

Bishop's Palace
This building has fine Gothic and Renaissance windows and an upper gallery. It now houses the tourist office, which puts on excellent summer exhibitions.

Exploring Sarlat

In summer, when it is closed to traffic, the heart of Sarlat's old town, with its many architectural jewels, is pleasant to explore on foot. On place de la Liberté is the Hôtel de Maleville (or Hôtel de Vienne), a town house in a combination of French and Italian Renaissance styles. Passage Henri-de-Ségogne, in the restored quarter of the town, is lined with 13th-, 15th- and 16th-century half-timbered corbelled houses with tiled roofs.

🏛 Cathédrale Saint-Sacerdos

The cathedral was rebuilt in the 16th and 17th centuries on the site of an early Romanesque abbey church. The interior is arranged around a nave with four ribbed-vaulted sections. A stroll in the vicinity of the cathedral takes in the

Traditional Périgordian tiled roofs on houses in Sarlat's old quarter

Cour des Fontaines and the Chapelle des Pénitents Bleus, the remains of the old cloister, and the Jardin des Enfeus, a former cemetery with burial niches carved into the wall. The purpose of the 12th-century Lanterne des Morts (Lantern of the Dead), in which a lamp could be lit, is still unclear.

🏛 Eastern Sarlat

The former **Présidial**, in rue Landry, was the seat of the law courts in the 17th century. The façade has a low arch with a loggia, containing a lantern, above. On either side of the **town hall** are 15th- and 17th-century gabled houses. On

---

Dordogne Valley ⓭

Several fine châteaux line this stretch of the Dordogne. They can be admired from the river – in a canoe or *gabare* (local river craft) – or from the road. The hills all around offer extensive views of the landscape. From the esplanade at Domme, the loop in the river at Montfort is a stunning sight. With reflections of sky and sunlight, the river winds like a silver ribbon through cultivated land.

Château de Beynac ⑤

Following the river beyond the attractive village of Envaux, the narrow road sweeps across the plain, bringing into view the imposing Château de Beynac *(see p132)*. From here it is possible to see for miles in all directions.

BERGERAC

St-Vincent-de-Cosse

Allas-les-Mines

Envaux

Dordogne

D 703

D 50

D 53

D 50

D 5

6

Château des Milandes ⑥

Built in 1489 and remodelled in the 19th century, the château was once owned by Josephine Baker (1906–75), the singer, dancer, entertainer and philanthropist. Part of the tour of the castle is devoted to her life. Displays of medieval falconry take place in the gardens, against the backdrop of this Renaissance-style setting.

TIPS FOR DRIVERS

Road map: E2.
Tour length: 37km (23 miles).
Stopping-off places: There are farmhouse-inns and restaurants along the way. Information is available at Sarlat: (05) 53 31 45 45.

0 km   2

0 miles   2

Château de Castelnaud ⑦

(see pp134–5) Perched on a cliff above the Dordogne river, the château is visible for miles across the countryside.

rue Fénelon, opposite the alley leading to the 16th-century Hôtel de Gérard, is a doorway framed by four columns decorated with fleur-de-lis. It was once the town hall entrance.

Place de la Liberté
The 15th-century **Hôtel de Gisson**, with tiled roof, is the hub of Sarlat's summer drama festival. Gargoyles stare down from on the bell tower of the **Église Sainte-Marie**, now a covered market.

Rue des Consuls
This street is lined with fine town houses. Among them are the Hôtel Plamon, dating from the 14th to the 17th centuries,

Sarlat's old town, ideal for an evening stroll

and **Hôtel de Mirandol**, near the Fontaine Sainte-Marie. Beyond the arch is the **Hôtel Tapinois de Bétou** with its 17th-century wooden staircase.

Western Sarlat
Half-timbered houses line **rue des Armes**, and can be seen from the ramparts. The **Chapelle des Pénitents Blancs** is the remains of a 17th-century convent. Further on is the former **Abbaye Sainte-Claire**, also from the 17th century.

Environs
18km (11 miles) southeast of Sarlat is **Château de Fénelon**. The theologian and philosopher François de Salignac de la Mothe Fénelon (1651–1715) was born here.

Château de Fénelon
Sainte-Mondane. **Tel** (05) 53 29 81 45. ☐ Call ahead. 🏛 🎦

Parc de Marqueyssac ④
The 6km (4 miles) of footpaths that wind through these 22ha (54 acres) of parkland, lead to a stunning belvedere. Fine views can be had, all long this walk, of the many villages and châteaux that dot the surrounding landscape. There are 150,000 finely clipped box trees and cypresses planted here.

Cingle de Monfort ①
A canoe ride along this loop in the river offers good views of the Château de Monfort.

Domme ②
Porte des Tours is marked with graffiti made by Knights Templar who were imprisoned here. On place de la Halle is the 15th–16th-century governor's house and the church, with a belfry. A tunnel from the church leads to caves with stalactites and stalagmites.

La Roque-Gageac ③
This village's ochre-coloured houses spread out down to the riverbank. Not far from the church, with its single-wall belfry, and the graceful Manoir de Tarde, is a garden of exotic plants. High on the cliffs stands a troglodytic fort. The steep walk up to it is rewarded by a view of the valley, 40m (130ft) below.

KEY

▬ Suggested route

= Other roads

✼ Viewpoint

Map labels: SARLAT, Fayrac, Montfort, Vitrac, Dordogne, Cénac-et-St-Julien, D 57, D 703, D 46, D 55, D 50, D 46E, D 704

Souillac ⑳

Road map E2. A20 Paris–Toulouse.
🏠 *3,468.* 🚆 *Souillac.*
ℹ️ *Boulevard Louis-Jean-Malvy
(05) 65 37 81 56.* 🍽️ *Fri am.*
🎭 *Festival de Jazz (Jul) ; Festival du
Mime Automate (Aug); Musicales
de Souillac (Jul).*

The town of Souillac lies
between the Dordogne and
the Borrèze, in Haut-Quercy.
It grew up around a
Benedictine monastery that
was founded around 655 and
that became an abbey in the
16th century. Souillac's
influence extended to 150
priories in the area, but it
later became a centre of
trade, with goods arriving
by barge until the
installation of the railway
in the 19th century.

The **Église Sainte-Marie**,
the town's abbey church,
was built in the 11th and
12th centuries. Laid out
on the plan of a Latin cross
and crowned with three
domes raised on stone
pillars, it is in a splendidly
pure Byzantine-
Romanesque style inspired by
the church of Haghia Sophia
in Istanbul. Two notable
features of the church are the
doorway, which was reversed
in the 17th century so as to
face inwards, and the 12th-
century carvings. These
include a column showing
animals and humans
locked in fierce
combat. The
Prophet Isaiah is
depicted with
unusual
vigour.

**Musée de
l'Automate**

The tourist office occupies a
deconsecrated church, the
Église Saint-Martin, which has
a damaged belfry and Gothic
vaulting. Art exhibitions are
also held here. The town
centre is pleasant to explore
on foot, particularly along
rue des Oules and rue des
Craquelins and in place
Roucou and place Benetou.

With 3,000 exhibits, the
Musée de l'Automate, set up
in 1988 in the abbey gardens,
is the largest of its kind in
Europe. The 19th- and 20th-
century collections come mostly
from the Roullet-Decamps
workshops, which began
making automata in 1865.
The exhibits, which include
a woman powdering her
face, a jazz-
band and a
snake charmer,
are very expressive,
their movements
controlled by finely tuned
mechanisms. Designed
in collaboration with the
Cité des Sciences et de
l'Industrie in Paris, the
section devoted to
robots uses state-of-
the-art technology.

🏛️ **Musée de l'Automate**
Place de l'Abbaye. **Tel** (05) 65 37
07 07. 🌐 *Jan–Mar & Nov–Dec:
Mon–Tue am; Apr–May & Oct: Mon.*
📷 ♿

Environs
11km (7 miles) southeast of
Souillac are the **Grottes de
Lacave**, caves that were
discovered in 1902. Riding on a
small train, then taking a lift,
visitors travel along 1.6km (1
mile) of galleries and through a
dozen caverns. The sheer
variety of weird shapes
formed by its stalactites and
stalagmites, including some
that suggest fantastic animals,
makes this the most impressive
of all such caves in France.

🔦 **Grottes de Lacave**
Tel (05) 65 37 87 03. 🌐 *mid-Mar–
Oct: daily.* 📷 ♿ **www.**
grotte-de-lacave.com

Martel ㉑

Road map E2. On the RN140, near
the A20. 🏠 *462.* 🚆 *Quatre-Routes.*
ℹ️ *Palais de la Raymondie, Place des
Consuls; (05) 65 37 43 44.* 🍽️ *Wed
& Sat, am.*

Once the seat of the
Vicomte de Turenne,
Martel has seven towers,
including the bell tower of
its fortified Gothic church,
which is pierced with arrow
slits. Visitors can also see the
remains of the 12th–14th-
century ramparts, the
13th–14th-century Palais de
la Raymondie – which houses
a museum of early history,
including Gallo-Roman
artifacts – and the 18th-
century covered market.
As well as the regular
twice-weekly
markets, a truffle
market is held
here in winter.

The carved tympanum over the doorway of the Église Sainte-Marie in Souillac

Boat trips on the lake at the bottom of the Gouffre de Padirac

Environs

7km (4 miles) south of Martel on the N140 is the pre-Romanesque church at **Creysse**. It is unusual in having two identical apses against the straight wall of its east end. The nave follows the rocky spur's convex shape. The church's interior is not open to the public. The village, which has attractive houses roofed in various styles, lies between the course of the Dordogne and walnut orchards.

From 1681 to 1695, Fénelon was prior of the fortified monastery at **Carennac**, 18km (11 miles) southeast of Martel via the D103, then the D20. All that remains of the mona-stery are the dean's residence, now a local tourist office, the church, with an arresting depiction of the Last Judgment in the tympanum, and the cloister and chapter room. The village, opposite the Île de la Calypso, an island in the river, is dotted with interesting old houses.

With its lofty setting, the village of **Loubressac**, 20km (12 miles) southeast of Martel, offers a wide view of the Cère, Bave and Dordogne valleys. From here the Château de Castelnau, Saint-Céré and the towers of Saint-Laurent can be seen. Inside the ramparts, narrow streets wind between the ochre-coloured houses, some of which are covered with cascades of flowers.

Autoire, a village 25km (15 miles) southeast of Martel, is best approached from the crest of the limestone plateau above the waterfall that crashes down for a sheer 40m (130ft). Flanked by majestic cliffs, here the rustic architecture of Quercy rubs shoulders with grand manor houses. The pattern created by the rooftops with their dormer windows, dovecotes, chimneys, finials and turrets creates an almost mosaic-like effect. It is easy to explore the village on foot, taking in the Chapelle Saint-Roch and the Château des Anglais, which was reduced to ruins during the Hundred Years' War (1337–1453).

Gouffre de Padirac ㉒

Road map F2. 🚆 Rocamadour-Padirac. 🚌 Brive–Toulouse. **Tel** (05) 65 33 64 56. 🕐 Apr–Oct. 🖼 🅿 **www**.gouffre-de-padirac.com

Detail of the porch at Carennac

Viewed from above, the huge opening in the earth, that forms the entrance to this series of underground caverns, seems almost to be attempting to swallow up the sky. Discovered in 1889, the tunnels inside this geological curiosity were formed at least 1 million years ago, although the gaping hole in the ground that has made them accessible was probably created just 10,000 years ago. Reaching down to about 100m (230ft), the caves have a steady temperature of around 13°C (55°F). Tours consists of a 400-m (440-yd) walk and a 500-m (550-yd) boat ride. Some 10m (33ft) beneath the ground, under the 94-m (300-ft) Great Dome is a spectacular group of giant stalagmites. Beyond this lies a lake, fed solely by water filtering through the rock, that sits "suspended" some 27m (89ft) above the level of an underground river. There are also a further 9km (6 miles) of tunnels that are not generally open to visitors.

Castelnau-Bretenoux ㉓

Road map F2. On the D803. **Tel** (05) 65 10 98 00. 🕐 daily. 🔵 Sep–Jun: Tue. 🖼

With a square keep and seigneurial quarters, this château is a resolutely defensive building. It was founded in the 12th century by the barons of Castelnau, and clear traces of its military past can still be seen in its elegant outline. Remodelled in the 16th and 17th centuries, then abandoned in the 18th, the castle was restored in the late 19th century, with funds provided by Jean Mouliérat, the famous tenor. It now contains a fine collection of paintings and furniture.

The impressive fortress of Castelnau-Bretenoux, a fine example of military architecture

Rocamadour ㉔

Black Virgin and Child

Sitting on a rocky plateau high above the Alzou valley, Rocamadour looks as if it is carved straight out of the limestone rock face. The best views are to be had from the nearby hamlet of L'Hospitalet. The village became one of the most famous centres of pilgrimage in France because of the 12th-century statue of the Black Virgin and Child in the Chapelle Notre-Dame that was believed to have miraculous powers. An account dating from 1172 describes the 126 miracles granted by the Madonna, who is still honoured on 8 September each year during the Semaine Mariale (Marian Week). Also, in 1166, an ancient grave was discovered containing an undecayed body, said to be that of the early Christian hermit St Amadour.

The castle was built against the 14th-century ramparts that defended the shrine from the west.

Chapelle Saint-Michel
The chapel is decorated with beautiful 12th-century frescoes.

Crypte de Saint Amadour is named after the hermit whose reliquary it contains. Pilgrims came here to venerate the saint.

Great Stairway
This broad flight of steps links the village with the shrines. Pilgrims would climb these on their knees, saying their rosaries as they went.

Chapelle Saint-Jean-Baptiste faces the fine Gothic portal of the Basilica Saint-Sauveur.

Basilique Saint-Sauveur, a late 12th-century sanctuary, backs on to the bare rock face.

Chapelle Sainte-Anne, from the 13th century, has a fine 17th-century gilded altarpiece.

Ramparts

Cross of Jerusalem

VISITORS' CHECKLIST

Road map E2. 🚗 630.
🚉 Rocamadour. ℹ️ At L'Hospitalet and in Rocamadour's medieval centre (05) 65 33 22 00. **www**.rocamadour.com
🎭 Les Éclectiques (mid-Jul); torchlit procession (14 Aug); Semaine Mariale (devoted to the Black Madonna; mid-Sep).

View of the village
Rocamadour, which almost seems to sprout up from the base of the cliff, is at its most breathtaking at sunrise.

Chapelle Saint-Blaise

The Village
The 13th-century Porte du Figuier, on the pilgrims' route, leads to the main street, which is now filled with souvenir shops.

Chapelle Notre-Dame
The remains of St Amadour were found under the floor in front of the chapel. On the altar is the statue of the miraculous Black Virgin and Child.

Exploring Rocamadour

The views from the ramparts of this fortified town are truly breathtaking. Pilgrims climbing on their knees up the 216 steps of the Great Stairway to the shrines could stop at the resting places along the way and gaze for miles across the Alzou valley below. By the 13th century, thousands of them were flocking to Rocamadour every year. The town was pillaged by the English during the Hundred Years' War and desecrated during the Wars of Religion in the 16th century, but the Black Virgin and her miraculous bell survived. Pilgrimages ceased with the Revolution of 1789, but resumed in the 19th century, when the shrine was rehabilitated.

🏛 Grand'Rue
The Voie Sainte (Sacred Way), used by pilgrims, runs from the hamlet of L'Hospitalet and joins Grand'Rue at the 13th-century Porte du Figuier, one of the eight surviving fortified gates that controlled entry into the town. The 15th-century town hall, in rue de la Couronnerie, close by, has a huge tapestry by Jean Lurçat (1892-1966), which he gave to the town in 1960. It was entirely sewn by hand at Aubusson, and depicts the flora and fauna of the region.

🔒 Chapelle Notre-Dame
This Flamboyant Gothic chapel was built in about 1476 on the site in the cliff face that the hermit St Amadour is thought to have inhabited. The object of pilgrimage here is the Black Virgin and Child,

a 12th-century walnut statue, 69cm (27in) high, covered with silver leaf blackened by candle smoke. According to popular belief, the 9th-century bell above her rang spontaneously whenever the Virgin saved a sailor in peril at sea.

🔒 Shrine
Built into the cliff, the shrine consists of seven churches and chapels. While services are held in the Basilique Saint-Sauveur, Chapelle Saint-Blaise is for silent prayer. This Romanesque ensemble was altered in the 19th century.

Painted wooden pietà

🏛 Chemin de Croix
There are plans to restore this pathway. With its 14 Stations of the Cross, it winds through woodland and leads to the Cross of Jerusalem.

♜ Ramparts
Tel *(05) 65 33 23 23.* ☐ *daily.* 🎫
These are all that remain of the 14th-century fortress which once defended the town and its shrine. The ramparts command extensive views of Rocamadour and the valley below.

⛰ Grottes des Merveilles
Tel *(05) 65 33 67 92.* ☐ *Easter–Oct: daily.* 🎫 🎫
www.grotte-des-merveilles.com
This cave, discovered in 1920, contains a mass of stalactites and stalagmites, and its walls are decorated with paintings that date from the Upper Palaeo-lithic era. Among the 22 images, which are mostly of animals, including horses and deer, are the outlines of six human hands.

🐒 Forêt des Singes
Tel *(05) 65 33 62 72.*
☐ *Apr–11 Nov: daily.* 🎫
This animal park is home to 130 macaques, who roam over its 10ha (25 acres) of woodland. These monkeys, native to the high plateaus of Africa, are endangered.

The crypt of St Amadour, built into the rock face

🦅 Rocher des Aigles

Tel (05) 65 33 65 45. ☐ *Apr–Oct: daily.* 🗒 🛠

Dedicated to breeding birds of prey, this centre has about 100 from all over the world. Visitors can see displays of falconry here.

🏛 Préhistologia

Lacave. *Tel* (05) 65 32 28 28. ☐ *Apr–May: Sun & public hols; Jun–Aug: daily; Sep–mid-Nov: daily pm.* 🗒 **www**.prehistologia.com

The largest dinosaur park in Europe traces the evolution of the species, from the Big Bang to neolithic times.

Saint-Céré ㉕

Road map F2. On the D803/D673. 👥 3,760. 🚌 *Bretenoux.* 🏠 *Place de la République* (05) 65 38 11 85. 🛒 *Sat am.* 🎭 *Festival Lyrique (late Jul–early Aug).*

Saint-Céré grew thanks to the traffic of pilgrims visiting the tomb of St Spérie, which stands here. In the 12th century craftsmen settled and markets were established. The town suffered as a result of epidemics and wars, but regained some of its splendour in the 17th century.

Remains of past prosperity can be seen in rue du Mazel, with the 15th-century Hôtel d'Auzier and the 17th-century Maison Queyssac, and in impasse Lagarouste, with its half-timbered corbelled houses. Hôtel d'Ambert, in rue Saint-Cyr, has turrets and a Renaissance doorway. Rue Paramelle leads to Maison Longueval, a 15th-century turreted house, and the 15th-century Hôtel de Puymule, in the Flamboyant Gothic style. The church contains an 18th-century marble altarpiece and has a Carolingian crypt. On a plateau above the town are the Tours de Saint-Laurent, a 13th- and a 15th-century keep, all that remains of the castle. In 1945, they were acquired by Jean Lurçat (1882–1966), the painter and tapestry maker, and are now a **museum-workshop**. There are also many artists' and craftsmen's studios in Saint-Céré itself.

A tapestry by Jean Lurçat, with colourful and innovative motifs

🏛 Atelier-Musée Jean-Lurçat

Tel (05) 65 38 28 21. ☐ *Easter; 14 Jul–Sep.* 🗒

Environs

The **Château de Montal**, 2km (1 mile) from Saint-Céré, was stripped of its finest architectural elements in the 19th century. However, thanks to the work of Maurice Fenaille (1855-1937), the castle's 16th- and 17th-century tapestries and furniture have been restored to their original setting. The 15th-century circular towers frame a beautiful Renaissance court-yard with a double staircase. A 17th-century Aubusson tapestry hangs in the guardroom. The upper floor rooms have ceilings with exposed beams.

♣ Château de Montal

Saint-Jean Lespinasse. *Tel* (05) 65 38 13 72. ☐ *Easter–Oct.* ● *Mon, Tue.* 🗒 🗒

16th-century dovecote built by Galiot, lord of the manor of Assier

Assier ㉖

Road map F2. 🚂 533. 🚌 *Brive–Toulouse.* 🏠 *Causse valley* (05) 65 40 50 60.

The remains of the **Château d'Assier** show that this was a Renaissance palace on a par with the finest châteaux of the Loire. It was built by Jacques Galiot de Genouillac (1465–1546), an artillery commander under Louis XII and François I. Of the building completed in 1535, only the entrance wing, with a spectacular portico door-way, survives. The decoration consisted of mythological and classical scenes, Renaissance figures and military emblems. The carved staircase is the finest feature of the interior.

The church contains an effigy of Galiot and a curious relief on the exterior refers to the art of warfare. Uniquely in France, the dome over the burial chapel has triple groined vaulting that forms an elaborate star pattern.

♣ Château d'Assier

Tel (05) 65 40 40 99. ☐ *daily.* ● *Sep–Jun: Tue.* 🗒 🗒

Environs

The 16th-century **dovecote** on the Lacapelle-Marival road stands 11m (36ft) high and holds 2,300 nesting chambers. The birds enter and exit via the open lantern on top.

Near the village are two dolmens known as the **Table de Roux** and **Bois des Bœufs**. There are 11 of these burial chambers, dating from around 1,500 BC, in the vicinity.

Figeac ⓝ

The town of Figeac, which sits clustered around its 9th-century abbey, grew and prospered as the result of trade. By the 12th century, its growing wealth enabled many inhabitants to build fine houses here. Fortified in the 14th century, the town still has a medieval appearance, reflecting its past importance.

Enlarged replica of the Rosetta Stone, on Place des Écritures

Exploring Figeac

Figeac's most prosperous period stretched from the 12th to the 14th century, and the town boasts exceptionally fine houses from this time. Built of stone and wood, they usually have an *aula* (main living room) on the upper floor, with shops fronted by arcades opening onto the street below. Windows were decorated with finely executed Romanesque carving. Many more fine houses were built in the 15th and 16th centuries, with a *solelho* (open granary) on the top floor. Examples are on place Gaillardy.

Houses were still being built in the medieval style during the Renaissance, but many also had elements such as turrets, arcaded courtyards, spiral staircases and mullioned windows set in an orderly way into the façade. The town houses of the 18th century have monumental staircases. With this rich architectural heritage, Figeac offers a complete panorama of local urban architecture from the 12th century to the present day.

🏛 Hôtel de la Monnaie

Place Vival. **Museum and tourist office Tel** (05) 65 34 06 25. ⬜ *daily.* ⬤ *Oct–Apr: Sun; May–Jun & Sep: Sun pm.* 🈺

Although the Ortabadial quarter was partly demolished to make way for place Vival, this 13th-century town house survived. A fine example of a grand Renaissance residence, it has an arcaded ground floor and gemelled windows. It is now the tourist office and the Musée du Vieux Figeac. A star exhibit here is the carved walnut doorway of the former Hôtel de Sully.

Ibis, Musée Champollion

🛈 Abbatiale Saint-Sauveur

Tel (05) 65 34 11 63. This church is one of the surviving elements of the abbey around which the town grew. The 13th-century chapter room is now the Chapelle Notre-Dame-de-la-Pitié. It is decorated with 17th-century painted panels.

🏛 Place Champollion

With place Carnot, this is one of Figeac's two main squares. Formerly place de l'Avoine, it is surrounded by medieval houses. Maison du Griffon, at no. 4, dates from the 12th century and has carved Romanesque decoration. The 14th-century Gothic house at no. 5 has a stone *solelho*.

🏛 Musée Champollion

4 rue des Frères-Champollion. *Tel* (05) 65 50 31 08. ⬜ *Apr–Jun & Sep: Tue–Sun; Jul & Aug: daily; Oct: Wed–Sun.* 🈺 🉑

The museum is in the house where Jean-François Champollion (1790–1832), the great Egyptologist, was born. Dating from the 13th and 14th centuries, it is due to reopen in 2007, with displays on the life of the man who deciphered the Rosetta Stone, revealing the meaning of Egyptian hieroglyphics.

View of Figeac from Église Notre-Dame-du-Puy

VISITORS' CHECKLIST

Road map F2. 🏯 9,554. 📮
ℹ️ *Hôtel de la Monnaie,
place Vival (05) 65 34 06 25.*
📅 *Sat.* 🎭 *Festival Théâtral (late
Jul–early Aug); Rencontres
Musicales (Aug).*

🏛 Place des Écritures

This unusual area was laid
out by Joseph Kosuth
(1945–), a pioneer of
conceptual art. Part of his
permanent installation here
features an enlarged replica
of the Rosetta Stone.

🏛 Hôtel de Colomb

5 rue de Colomb. **Tel** (05) 65 50
05 40. ◯ *10 Jul–19 Sep: daily;
Apr–9 Jul & 20 Sep–Oct: Tue–Sun pm.*
With a restrained façade and
a highly decorated staircase,
this town house is typical of
the 17th-century. It contains a
permanent exhibition on
Figeac's history and heritage.

🏛 Medieval Buildings

Many other buildings in
Figeac are worth a view. They
include the Hôtel Galiot de
Genouillac, with a fine spiral
staircase; the 14th-century
Palais Balène, arranged round
an interior courtyard; the
Hôtel d'Auglanat, with a turret
on one of its outer corners
and a 14th-century decorated
doorway; and the Église
Notre-Dame-du-Puy, whose
13th-century apse was altered
in the 17th century, when a
monumental altarpiece of the
Madonna was installed.

Environs

Capdenac-le-Haut, 5km (3
miles) southeast of Figeac, looks
down over the Lot. From the
esplanade, it is easy to see the
strategic importance of this
naturally fortified site. The
ramparts, keep and former
consul's house form a pleasant
walk. The Fontaine des Anglais
is carved directly into the rock.

The village of **Espagnac-
Sainte-Eulalie**, about 20km
(12 miles) west of Figeac,
nestles in a bend in the Célé
river. It developed around a
12th-century priory. The Église
Notre-Dame, which dates
from the 13th century, has a
half-timbered bell tower.

Saint-Cirq Lapopie ㉘

Road map E3. 🏯 170. ℹ️ *Place du
Sombral (05) 65 31 29 06.*

Its exceptionally picturesque
location and ensemble of
attractive buildings make
Saint-Cirq-Lapopie one of the
jewels of the Lot valley. Rising
in tiers up the limestone cliff-
face, it sits some 100m (300ft)
above the river. Along its
narrow streets are small
courtyards and attractive
13th- and 15th-century stone
and wooden houses. In the
lower village, a 13th-century
gate, Porte de la Pélissaria (or
Porte de Rocamadour) opens
on to Grand'Rue, where the
medieval village begins. Places
of note include **place du
Carol**, with a belvedere-
dovecote, where the painter
Henri Martin (1860–1943)
lived; the 13th-century Maison
Vinot; the 14th-century
**Maison Médiévale Daura;
Maison Breton**, once owned
by the Surrealist writer André
Breton (1896–1966); Maison
Bessac with double corbelling;

place du Sombral with
the 15th-century **Maison
Larroque** and **Maison
Rignault**, which houses the
Musée Rignault; and **Maison
de la Fourdonne**, which
contains the Musée de la
Mémoire du Village. Near the
ruined castle, stands a late
16th-century fortified **church**.

The economy of the village,
which had 1,500 inhabitants
during the Middle Ages, was
based on manufacturing, with
craftsmen's workshops under
the arcades along rue de la
Pélissaria and rue de la
Peyrolerie. Today, the work of
robinetaïres, specialist wood-
turners who make taps for the
Cahors wine barrels, is a craft
peculiar to Saint-Cirq-Lapopie.

Environs

From **Bouziès**, 5km (3 miles)
from Saint-Cirq-Lapopie, visitors
can take a boat ride on the Lot
(information: (05) 65 35 98 88).

Cajarc, 15km (9 miles) east
of Saint-Cirq-Lapopie, is a
village with narrow medieval
streets and fine houses around
Maison de l'Hébrardie, a 13th-
century former castle.

The fortified church at Saint-Cirq-Lapopie

Grotte du Pech-Merle ㉙

To visit this cave is literally to tread in the footsteps of early *Homo sapiens,* entering a mysterious and magical world. About 60 million year ago, a gallery was carved out 50m (165ft) below the surface by an underground river. This dank space, full of extraordinary natural rock formations, consists of seven caverns that contain hundreds of paintings, drawings and engravings of animals, human figures and abstract symbols. Unique to Pech-Merle is the way in which these prehistoric images have been combined with the geological features of the cave. The drawings were executed in charcoal, iron oxide and manganese dioxide. Because it was blocked up by a rockfall around 10,000 years ago, at the end of the Ice Age, the cave remained intact until its discovery in 1922.

Gallery at Pech-Merle, created by an underground river

Roots of an oak tree

Cave entrance

Modern stairway

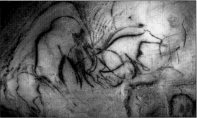

Black Frieze
The cavern known as the Chapel of the Mammoths contains depictions of 11 mammoths, 5 bisons, 4 horses and 4 aurochs (cattle) and clusters of red spots.

Chamber closed to the public

Bear hollow

Le Combel
The fossilized bones of bears, hyenas, horses, bison and deer discovered in the cave are displayed in Le Combel area.

Frieze of the Spotted Horses
In this 4-m (13-ft) long frieze, the artist has used the unevennesses of the cave wall to give a three - dimensional effect to the paintings. The main subjects are two black horses, back to back, a fish drawn in red, 252 spots and the negative prints of six human hands.

Hall of the Discs
*In this cavity, the calcite from the limestone has crystallized
in concentric circles, which look like large discs.*

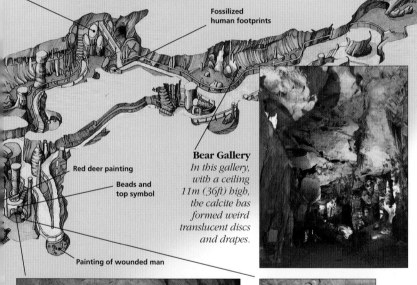

**Fossilized
human footprints**

Bear Gallery
*In this gallery,
with a ceiling
11m (36ft) high,
the calcite has
formed weird
translucent discs
and drapes.*

Red deer painting

**Beads and
top symbol**

Painting of wounded man

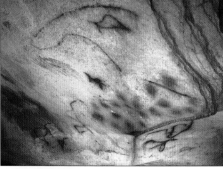

Frieze of the Bison-Women
*This small frieze, on the underside of an over-
hanging rock in the cavern with the Ceiling
of the Hieroglyphs, shows a mammoth and
stylized female shapes drawn in red.*

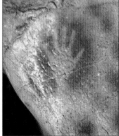

Negative Handprint
*Handprints, believed by some
archeologists to be those of
women, are a rare motif in
cave art. To spray the paint
onto the wall, the artist
is thought to have spat it out
of his or her mouth.*

Cahors ⑳

Arms of Cahors

The origins of Cahors, encircled by a loop in the river Lot, go back to the 1st century BC. Evidence of this ancient past can be seen in the ruins of the Gallo-Roman baths, now known as the Arc de Diane. In the 13th century, trade brought prosperity leading to the creation of the town's elegant mercantile sector (now rue du Château-du-Roi). The fortifications date from the 14th century and include the ramparts, set with 11 towers and two gatehouses. Three fortified bridges, including the Pont Valentré, span the river. In the 19th century, Cahors began to spread out from this medieval core. This was when boulevard Gambetta, with the town hall, theatre and law courts, was built, and the quayside, walks and gardens were laid out.

Maison Henri-IV, with exquisite Renaissance decoration

Pont Valentré, one of the most beautiful medieval bridges in Europe

🚩 Vieille Ville

Starting from the tourist office, and walking along rue du Dr-Bergounioux, rue de Lastié, rue Saint-Urcisse, place Saint-James, rue de la Chantrerie, the Daurade quarter and the cathedral quarter, visitors will see decorated courtyards, half-timbered houses with brick overhangs and houses with carved façades. Typical of the Renaissance is a form of decoration consisting of branches, roses and suns; particularly fine examples can be seen on the doors and chimneypieces of **Maison Henri-IV**, at Collège Pélegry and Hôtel d'Alamand. In the 16th century, windows were decorated in the Italian style, and in the 17th century many town houses with ornate doorways were built. Tour Jean-XXII, to the north, is all that remains of Palais Duèze,

once owned by the Pope's brother. The **Musée de la Résistance, de la Déportation et de la Libération** is also worth a visit.

🏛 Musée de la Résistance
Place Bessières. **Tel** (05) 65 22 14 25.
⏰ pm. ◐ 1 Jan, 1 May, 25 Dec

🚩 Pont Valentré

Built in the 14th century and never attacked, this impresssive fortified bridge has six Gothic spans with chamfered piers. Its three fortified towers command views over the Lot from a height of 40m (130ft). Standing as the symbol of Cahors, it was restored in 1879 by Paul Gout and is the best preserved medieval bridge in Europe. It is visible from the Terrasses Valentré (Allée des Soupirs), the Fontaine des Chartreux, and the heights of Croix Magne.

🔒 Cathédrale Saint-Étienne

A stopping-place on the pilgrim route to Compostela, the cathedral underwent several phases of construction from the 11th to the 17th centuries, and was restored in the 19th century. The result is a harmonious mix of styles. The nave, 20m (66ft) wide, is the oldest part of the building. Above it are two great domes, 16m (52ft)

A DEVILISH TALE

Pont Valentré took almost 50 years to build. According to a legend that grew up around it, the architect asked the Devil to help him complete this feat of civil engineering, in return for his soul. To escape the agreement, he tried to dupe the Devil, who took his revenge: each night the last stone to be laid in the central tower would mysteriously fall, to be replaced the next day. In 1879, while restoring the bridge, Paul Gout, the architect, immortalized this tale by setting a carving of the Devil on the central tower, now known as the Tour du Diable (Devil's Tower).

Sculpture on the Tour du Diable

Portrait of Léon Gambetta, Musée Henri-Martin

across. The Romanesque north doorway, with 12th-century tympanum, is as elaborate as those at Moissac and Souillac. The choir is in a southern Gothic style. The square in front of the cathedral was laid out on place Chapou in the 14th century, when the cathedral acquired a new façade. The cloister, a Flamboyant Gothic masterpiece, dates from 1506.

🏛 Musée Henri-Martin

792 rue Émile-Zola. *Tel (05) 65 20 88 66.* ⬜ *Wed–Mon: daily.* ⬤ *Sun am, 25 Dec, 1 Jan.* 🈂

This museum in Parc Tassart is housed in the former bishop's palace, which dates from the 17th century. Founded in 1833, it contains about 18,000 exhibits, ranging from archaeological artifacts and coins to ethnographic pieces and fine art.

Among its collections are paintings by the Surrealist artist Henri Martin (1860–1943), sketches by Courbet and Corot, and paintings by Dufy and Lurçat. A section is devoted to Léon Gambetta (1838–1882), father of the French Republic, who was born in Cahors. The display contains 3,000 documents relating to his public life.

Temporary exhibitions may be in place, while restoration work is being carried out.

Painting by Henri Martin, Musée Henri-Martin

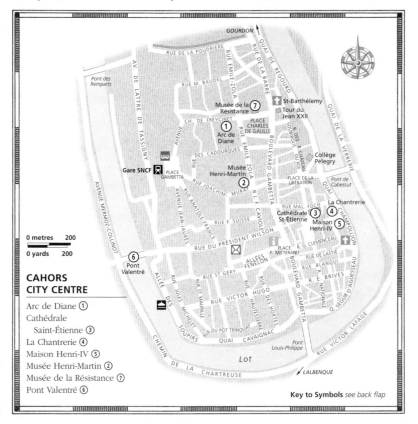

CAHORS CITY CENTRE

Arc de Diane ①
Cathédrale
  Saint-Étienne ③
La Chantrerie ④
Maison Henri-IV ⑤
Musée Henri-Martin ②
Musée de la Résistance ⑦
Pont Valentré ⑥

0 metres 200
0 yards 200

Key to Symbols *see back flap*

🏛 La Chantrerie

35 rue de la Chantrerie. **Tel** *(05) 65 23 99 70.* ☐ *Jul–Aug: Tue–Sat.*

Laid out in what was once a washhouse, the **Musée du Vin et de la Truffe** at La Chantrerie provides an overview of local delicacies. The workings of seven of the area's wine-producing châteaux are explained, along with displays of wine-making equipment. There is also an exhibit on Kagor, a sweet wine made in the Crimea. This historic 14th-century building also contains a re-creation of the interior of a medieval merchant's house, and on the upper floor there are regular temporary exhibitions.

Environs

The village of **Lalbenque**, 15km (9 miles) southeast of Cahors, is renowned for its truffle market, which takes

Église Saint-Pierre at Gourdon

place on Tuesday afternoons from December to March, and for many festivities celebrating this "black diamond". The Lot produces 3–10 tonnes of truffles a year. Almost all of Quercy's harvest of black truffles comes from the countryside around Lalbenque.

Gourdon ❷

Road map E2. On the D704. 🏘 *4,876.* 🚉 ℹ *24 rue du Majou (05) 65 27 52 50.* 🛒 *Tue & Sat: am (& Thu am Jul–Aug).* 🎭 *Les Médiévales (1st weekend in Aug).*

The town of Gourdon, which comes to life on market days, is the capital of Bouriane. In the 16th century it grew rich from its weaving industry. The medieval heart of the town has a 13th-century fortified gate and some fine houses, including the Maison du Sénéchal, Maison Cavaignac and Maison d'Anglars. Two particularly picturesque streets are rue du Majou, which was filled with drapers' shops in the Middle Ages, and rue Zig-Zag. The

---

Vineyards of Cahors ❸

The vineyards around Cahors are among the oldest in Europe. Since the Middle Ages, Cahors wine has been noted for its excellent ageing properties, which stem from the high quality vine-growing soil on the limestone plateau of the Causse. Vineyards stretch out for 60km (35 miles) on either side of the Lot river, mainly in the valley below the city. While an exploration of the region offers many opportunities for wine-tasting, the countryside itself provides a visual feast.

Montcabrier ①

This *bastide* town, established in the Thèze valley by Philip the Fair in 1298, has houses with magnificent façades and corbelled corner-tiles.

Duravel ②

The village grew up around an 11th-century priory. The Romanesque church here contains a sarcophagus with the remains of three saints. The square pre-Romanesque crypt beneath the nave is crowded with pillars and columns that support the roof.

Puy-l'Évêque ③

From the quayside, where there was once a river port, to place de la Truffière, a vantage point with expansive views, the narrow streets of the village wind around medieval houses, passing the massive 13th-century keep and a fortified church, Église Saint-Sauveur, dating from the 14th century.

Église Saint-Pierre, a Gothic church with asymmetrical towers, has some splendid 16th-century stained-glass windows and Baroque wood carvings. The town is dotted with other religious buildings. Among them are the Église des Cordeliers, built in the 13th century and altered in the 19th, Chapelle Notre-Dame-des-Neiges, Église Saint-Siméon and Chapelle du Majou. The medieval castle was destroyed in the 18th century, but the esplanade that fronted it remains and offers good views of the Bouriane river.

Environs
The **Grottes de Cougnac**, 3km (2 miles) from Gourdon on the D17, are full of stalactites and stalagmites, and other interesting rock formations, which look magical when lit up. The Cro-Magnon people, who used the cave 25,000 to 14,000 years ago, decorated some walls with paintings of moufflon (wild sheep), human figures and symbols.

Grottes de Cougnac
Tel (05) 65 41 47 54.
Easter–Oct: daily.

The team of speleologists who discovered the Grottes de Cougnac

Luzech ⑥
In the shadow of the imposing 12th-century keep, this ancient Cathar fiefdom became one of Quercy's four baronies. A walk around the peninsula leads to the Chapelle Notre-Dame-de-l'Île, a 16th-century chapel. Maison des Consuls, built in the 12th century, houses an archeological museum.

TIPS FOR DRIVERS

Road map: E3.
Tour length: 70km (43 miles).
Stopping-off places: Two good places to stop are Parnac, where you can sample the local wine at the Cave Coopérative du Vignoble de Cahors (Les Côtes d'Olt) (05 65 30 71 86) in summer, and the Musée du Vin et de la Truffe, at La Chantrerie.

Caillac ⑦
Thre are several châteaux here: Laroque (13th–15th century), Langle (16th century) and Lagrézette, a Renaissance château.

Mercuès ⑧
The Château de Mercuès was once the summer residence of the bishops of Cahors. It is now a hotel.

Bélaye ④
From this village there are stunning views of the Lot valley and Cahors vineyards. In the village are the remains of a bishop's castle and a 15th-century fortified church with a 17th-century altarpiece.

Albas ⑤
Once a fort, Albas overlooks the Lot from a clifftop. The bishops of Cahors resided here in the Middle Ages. The turret of the 18th-century École des Mirepoises stands out amongst the knot of narrow streets.

0 km 3
0 miles 3

KEY
— Suggested route
= Other roads
☆ Viewpoint

Castelnaud 🐾

See pp134–5.

Beynac 🐾

Road map E2. On the D703.
🚶 *516.* 🚉 *Sarlat.* 🚏 *La Balme
(05) 53 29 43 08.*
www.perigordnoir.info

Beynac, which clings dramatically to a steep cliff-face, has attracted a clutch of artists and writers, including Camille Pissarro (1830–1903), Henry Miller (1891–1980) and the poet Paul Éluard (1895–1952), who spent the last years of his life here. The village is still filled with the artists' studios. The narrow street from the lower village up to the castle passes several ancient houses and offers expansive views.

Perched on a rock 150m (490ft) above the river, **Château de Beynac** is visible from afar. The seat of one of the Périgord's four baronies, it occupies a strategic position, like its rival, Castelnaud. The castle repeatedly came under attack during the Hundred Years' War and again during the Wars of Religion in the 16th century. Restoration work began in 1961.

Entry is across a double moat and through a double line of ramparts. The 13th-century keep is flanked by the main building, dating from the same period but remodelled in the 16th century, and another building dating from the 14th and 17th centuries. The great hall, with vaulted ceiling, has a Renaissance chimneypiece. The castle's owner is still

The village of Belvès, on the site of an ancient hill fort

painstakingly restoring the building to evoke life as it was lived here in the past. The exquisite 12th-century chapel, now a parish church, is roofed with traditional Périgordian tiles.

The **Parc Archéologique** at the foot of the castle features the reconstruction of a Bronze Age settlement, creating a vivid impression of the food, clothing, houses and farms of that time. There are also workshops giving visitors an insight into life in the Neolithic period and the Iron Age.

⚓ Château de Beynac
Tel *(05) 53 29 50 40.* ⬜ *daily.*
🗓 *except mid-Nov–mid-Mar.* ♿

⛪ Parc Archéologique
Tel *(05) 53 29 51 28.* ⬜ *Jul–Aug.*
🗓 ♿

Environs
The delightful, adjoining hamlet of **Cazenac** has a 15th-century church. A walk along the road, running down to the left of it, offers a stunning panorama of the valley below, with the Château de Beynac in the distance.

Belvès 🐾

Road map D2. On the D710.
🚶 *1,431.* 🚉 🚏 *1 rue des Filhols
(05) 53 29 10 20.* **www**.
perigord.com/ belves
🍴 *Sat am.* 🎿 *Les 100km du Périgord Noir (ultra-marathon race, last Sat in Apr); Festival Bach (Jul–Aug); Fête Médiévale (first Sun in Aug).*

Set on a hilltop, this village was a fort in the 11th century. Its medieval heart centres on the castle and place d'Armes, where there is a 15th-century covered market. Nearby is the 13th-century Hôtel Bontemps, with a Renaissance façade. The town has seven towers, some of them bell towers. These include one from the 15th-century, the 11th-century keep (known as Tour de l'Auditeur) and the Tour des Frères. Église Notre-Dame, with its Flamboyant Gothic doorway, is all that remains of Belvès's abbey. The troglodytic dwellings cut into the village's medieval fortifications were in use from the 13th to the 18th century.

Château de Beynac, perched high above the Dordogne

Environs

About 8km (5 miles) west, on the edge of the Forêt de la Bessède, lies the attractive village of **Urval**. It has a 13th–14th-century communal oven, a rare vestige of medieval village life. Close by is an 11th–12th century fortified Romanesque church.

Cadouin ㊱

Road map D2. 🚶 2,115. 🚉
🛈 *Place du Général-de-Gaulle, Le Buisson (05) 53 22 06 09.* 🛒 *Wed am.*

The village grew up round the 12th-century Cistercian **Abbaye de Cadouin** (a World Heritage Site), on the pilgrim route to Compostela. Until 1932 what was believed to be the Holy Shroud was kept here, and the village grew wealthy from the pilgrims who flocked to this sacred relic. Behind the abbey's imposing buttressed façade is the cloister, built in the 15th and 16th centuries in a mixture of Flamboyant Gothic and Renaissance styles. The carved finials and images, of both biblical and secular subjects, are a masterpiece of stone carving. In the cloister garden stands a tall, pagoda-like bell tower.

🔒 Abbaye de Cadouin
Tel *(05) 53 63 36 28.* 🕐 *Jun–Sep: daily; at other times, call ahead.* 📷 📷

The covered market in Cadouin

Environs

Trémolat, 10km (6 miles) northwest of Cadouin, was the location where Claude Chabrol shot his film *Le Boucher*. From the belvedere, there are stunning views of the Cingle de Trémolat (the great loop in the Dordogne), and of the fertile plain. The

Monpazier, one of the best-preserved *bastide* towns in France

fortified church, with its keeplike bell tower, is arrestingly austere. The village also has some interesting, fine houses, dating from the 12th to the 18th centuries.

Monpazier ㊲

Road map D2. On the D660. 🚶 523. 🚉 *Belvès.* 🛈 *Place des Cornières (05) 53 22 68 59.* 🛒 *Thu am.*

Monpazier is a classic *bastide* town. With a grid of streets and alleyways within its ramparts, it is also one of the most attractive in southwest France. Founded in 1284 by Edward I, king of England, Monpazier has remained almost unchanged for 800 years, although only three of its original six fortified gates still stand. It has been used as a medieval location for several films. Its picturesque central square is lined with arcades that are filled with shops. The square also has a 16th-century covered market,

which still contains some antique grain measures. Monpazier is the birthplace of the writer and explorer Jean Galmot (1879–1928).

Environs

17km (10 miles) southeast of Monpazier, lies **Villefranche-du-Périgord**, a *bastide* town, established in 1261 at the meeting point of the Périgord, Quercy and Agenais. Every autumn, it hosts a famous *cèpes* (boletus) market. This takes place in the town's covered market area, which still has antique grain measures. Attractive arcaded houses stand opposite this market. The oak forests nearby are a pleasant place to take a walk.

A few kilometres further along the D57 lies **Besse**, a village with a splendid fortified church. The single-walled bell tower has an 11th-century doorway, with three archivolts that are covered with carvings of mythological animals.

Château de Castelnaud ❸

Spread out between its castle and the banks of the river, the village of Castelnaud sits at the intersection of the Dordogne and Céou valleys. In the 13th century, a Cathar lord, Bernard de Casnac, fought Simon de Montfort for control of the castle, which was destroyed by fire but quickly rebuilt. Because the Caumont family, lords of Castelnaud during the Hundred Years' War, sided with the English, the French laid siege to the castle in 1442. During the Wars of Religion in the mid-16th century, Geoffroy de Vivans, a Huguenot, gained control. Abandoned during the French Revolution, the castle gradually fell into ruin. It was bought in 1966 and classed as a historic monument. Restoration work continued until 1998. It is now open to the public.

Château de Castelnaud, on a cliff overlooking the village

The artillery tower has three floors with embrasures, a falconet (light cannon), a bronze hackbut, veuglaires (small cannon) and two organ guns (mounted on wheels).

The curtain wall has a rampart walk, and is pierced by arrow slits. It overlooks the upper courtyard at the foot of the keep.

★ Barbican
Pierced with gun-holes on two levels, the barbican defended the castle entrance. The 15th-century bombard opposite could project cannonballs weighing over 100kg (220lb), but only one per hour, as it had to cool before being reloaded.

★ Armoury
Decorated daggers, swords, helmets, crossbows, shields and other weapons, such as flails, maces and battle-axes, are displayed in the armoury. It also contains an interesting collection of halberds.

STAR FEATURES

★ Armoury

★ Barbican

★ Panorama

For hotels and restaurants in this region see pp246–8 and pp262–3

The inner courtyard
Sited at the foot of the keep, this contains a 46-m (150-ft) well and a cistern where rain water was collected.

VISITORS' CHECKLIST

Road map E2. On the D57, 15km (9 miles) from Sarlat. **Tel** (05) 53 31 30 00. www.castelnaud.com
⬛ daily. 🅿️ 📷 in summer. History tour, including heritage workshops, by arrangement; medieval shows & late evening tours for groups.

The outer courtyard, defended by a low wall and two semicircular towers, was a place of refuge for the villagers in times of danger. The courtyard also contained the forge, the oven, the stables and craftsmen's workshops.

Small catapults worked on the principle of the sling. They could project stones weighing 5–15kg (11–33lb) over distances of up to 60m (300ft), at a rate of two per minute.

★ Panorama
The castle's strategic position was one of its defences. With wide views of the valley, it controlled all local communication routes. Beynac, Marqueyssac and La Roque-Gageac can all be seen from here.

Catapults were used mostly to repel attacks. As deterrents, they were positioned to be visible, so as to intimidate the enemy.

WAR IN THE MIDDLE AGES

The Battle of Crécy, fought between the French and the English on 26 August 1346

A formidable arsenal of weapons was developed in the Middle Ages. It included the falconet (a light cannon), the bombard (a stone-hurling contraption) and the arquebus (a long-barrelled gun on a tripod). Various types of catapult were used, often as deterrents that were wheeled out simply to intimidate the enemy. Battles in the 15th century were fought with quite small forces: the cavalry backed up by infantry with knives and lances. From the 16th century, armies were professionally trained and led.

The fortified church at Beaumont-du-Périgord, dominating the village

Beaumont-du-Périgord ⚅

Road map D2. On the D25 from Le Buisson. 🏛 *1,150.* 🚉 *Le Buisson-de-Cadouin.* ℹ *Place Centrale (05) 53 22 39 12).* 🛒 *Tue & Sat am.*

Since its foundation in 1272, Beaumont, a *bastide* town built by the English, has undergone much alteration. Of the 16 gates that once formed part of its fortifications, only one, the Porte de Luzier, remains, forming the present entrance into the town. The central square was remodelled in the 18th century and the covered market no longer exists. There are some fine 13th-, 14th- and 15th-century houses, particularly in rue Romieu and rue Vidal. The town's architectural jewel is its impressive fortified church, the Église Saint-Laurent-et-Saint-Front. One of the finest in southwest France, this huge, severely plain church is in a military Gothic style, with four belfry-like towers, linked by a wall-walk. The church

was built from 1280 to 1330 and formed part of the town's defences. The doorway is decorated with a frieze filled with grimacing figures.

Environs
The medieval village of **Saint-Avit-Sénieur**, 5km (3 miles) east of Beaumont, is visible from afar due to its church. This Romanesque structure was fortified in the 14th century, and a wall-walk connects its two towers.

Some 10km (6 miles) east of Beaumont lies the village of **Montferrand-du-Périgord**. It has a splendid 16th-century covered market and the ruins of a castle with a 12th-century keep.

The **Château de Lanquais**, 10km (6 miles) northwest of Beaumont, has a 15th-century circular tower and polygonal staircase tower, as well as residential quarters dating from the 16th and 17th centuries.

⚜ **Château de Lanquais**
Tel (05) 53 61 24 24. ⬤ *Apr–Oct:* daily. ⬤ *Nov–Easter: Tue.* 📷 🖼

Biron ⚆

Road map D2. 🏛 *141.* ℹ *Place des Cornières, Montpazier (05) 53 22 68 59.*

Once the seat of one of Périgord's four baronies, the massive **Château de Biron** straddles the border between the Périgord and the Agenais. With a 12th-century keep, Renaissance living quarters, a Gothic chapel and a small 14th-century manor house, decorated with 16th-century frescoes, it embodies a stunning medley of architectural styles spanning the 12th to the 18th centuries.

Having given asylum to Cathars in 1211, the castle was besieged by Simon de Montfort, and it changed allegiance countless times during the Hundred Years' War, suffering attack and damage as a result. It was largely rebuilt during the Renaissance and now towers over the village of Biron, which has some fine houses around its covered market.

⚜ **Château de Biron**
Tel (05) 53 63 13 39. ⬤ *Jun–Sep:* daily; out of season: call.
www.semitour.com 📷 🖼

Eymet ⚇

Road map D2. 23km (14 miles) from Bergerac on the D933. 🏛 *2,552.* 🚉 *Bergerac.* ℹ *Place des Arcades (05) 53 23 74 95.*

This *bastide* town, built in the Dropt valley in 1270, retains its original square layout. Gargoyles look down from the

The Château de Biron, on the border between the Périgord and Agenais

For hotels and restaurants in this region see pp246–8 and pp262–3

The 16th-century library-tower, all that remains of the Château de Montaigne

Bergerac ❹

See pp138–9.

Saint-Michel-de-Montaigne ❷

Road map C2. 47km (29 miles) from Bergerac on the D936. 312. Bourg (05) 53 73 29 62.

The Romanesque church here has a doorway with columns and four intricately moulded arches. The interior features carved 17th-century furniture and the Stations of the Cross by the artist Gilbert Privat (1892–1969).

Of the château where Montaigne lived, only the 16th-century **tower**, where he had his library and where he wrote, remains. The beams of his study, on the top floor, are inscribed with 57 Greek and Latin sentences and maxims, that represent the Epicurean, Stoic and sceptic ideas that influenced Montaigne. The views from the terrace stretch out over the Lidoire valley.

⌂ Tower
Tel (05) 53 58 63 93. Jan & Mon–Tue.

Environs
About 44km (27 miles) from Bergerac on the D936 to Castillon-la-Bataille, is the village of **Montcaret**. The Romanesque church here has capitals that may have been taken from an earlier Gallo-Roman building. Nearby are the remains of a large Gallo-Roman villa, discovered in 1827. It has fine mosaic flooring, an inner courtyard lined with columns, a 60-sq-m (645-sq-ft) main room with a triple apse, a pool with mosaics of aquatic subjects and baths with a sophisticated heating system. The quality and detail of workmanship suggest that this was a place of luxury. It was built in the 1st century and rebuilt in the 4th. Evidence suggests that the site has been inhabited since antiquity.

13th-century keep, and the 15th- and 16th-century houses have turrets with mullioned windows. A 17th-century fountain sits in the main square. Once an English stronghold, Eymet now has a large British expatriate community.

Environs
Some 20km (12 miles) northeast of Eymet is the medieval village of **Issigeac**, with a spiral layout and 13th-century ramparts. The 15th–16th-century Gothic church, with a bell tower over its entrance, stands on the site of a priory. The former bishop's palace, its two pavilions set with corbelled turrets, is now the town hall, while the former tithe barn now houses a tourist office. The main street is lined with fine houses, one of which has 14th-century carved beams.

Arcades in the bastide town of Eymet

MONTAIGNE THE HUMANIST

Montaigne

Michel Eyquem de Montaigne was born at the Château de Montaigne in 1533. He studied law and in 1557 became a councillor in Périgueux, then at the Parlement de Bordeaux. From 1572 to 1580, with the Wars of Religion raging around him, he began to consider the nature of human happiness and worked on his famous *Essays*. He led a rather secluded life, but maintained links with powerful people. Elected mayor of Bordeaux in 1581, he led the city with great diplomacy at a time when it was torn between Catholics and Protestants, then hit by plague. He died in 1592.

Bergerac

Bergerac was held alternately by the French and the English during the Hundred Years' War, and later became a stronghold of the Protestant faith. Set on the banks of the Dordogne, it developed as a centre of trade, a stopping point for *gabares* (traditional wooden barges) carrying wood, blocks of stone, paper milled in Couze, wines, locally grown walnuts and chestnuts and other goods between the Périgord and the port at Bordeaux. This Huguenot town once had several harbours of its own. In the 18th century, some 15,000 tonnes of goods and around 1,500 boats passed through every year. The present quayside was built as late as 1838, but was rendered obsolete by the arrival of the railway in the late 19th century. Today *gabares* still set off daily from quai Salvette, although they now carry a cargo of visitors on scenic trips up and down the Dordogne river.

Faïence de Bergerac

Restaurant in a pedestrianized street in Bergerac's Vieille Ville

🏛 Vieille Ville

The old, half-timbered houses of master-boatmen line place de la Mirpe, where there is a **statue of Cyrano de Bergerac**, Edmond Rostand's long-nosed hero *(see p200)*. Rue Saint-Clar is lined with corbelled houses, with cob, brick and half-timbered walls. Place Pélissière, in a recently restored area of the town, is named after the skinners, whose workshops once stood there. With the Église Saint-Jacques and Fontaine Font-Ronde, once a public wash house, it forms a picturesque enclave. Place Pélissière is the setting for another statue of Cyrano de Bergerac, which was erected in 2005. Rue Saint-James has

Statue of Cyrano

several interesting houses, including an 18th-century town house, with a shop on the ground floor and bosses on its façade, a 16th-century house with mullioned windows, and 17th- and 18th-century half-timbered houses. Rue des Fontaines has two **medieval houses**.

🏛 Église Saint-Jacques

Place Pélissière.
This 12th-century chapel on the pilgrim route to Compostela, was enlarged in the 13th century, when it became the medieval town's church, with a single-wall belfry. It was later remodelled on several occasions, the nave being completely rebuilt in the 18th century. The Neo-

Gothic organ, built by Aristide Cavaillé-Coll in 1870, is listed as a historic monument.

🏛 Musée Costi

Access via the inner courtyard of place de la Petite-Mission. **Tel** *(05) 53 63 04 13.* ⬜ *by prior arrangement.* 🖼
Opened in June 2003, the museum fills two cellars of the Presbytère Saint-Jacques. It contains works donated by Costi, a sculptor born in 1906 and who studied under Antoine Bourdelle. They consist of 52 bronzes and seven plaster casts, made between 1926 and 1973.

🏛 Maison des Vins-Cloître des Récollets

1 rue des Récollets. **Tel** *(05) 53 63 57 55.* ⬜ *mid-Jun–mid-Sep: daily; mid-Sep–mid-Jun: Tue–Sat.* 🏛 *Jan.*
The Cloître des Récollets was built in 1630 on the site of the former gardens of the Château de Bergerac. The 16th- and 18th-century galleries look on to the courtyard. For a time the chapel served as a free-mason's hall. It now houses the Maison des Vins de Bergerac, which regulates local wine production and offers tastings. The starting point for the "Route des Vins" is available at the tourist office.

🏛 Musée du Vin et de la Batellerie

5 rue des Conférences. **Tel** *(05) 53 57 80 92.* ⬜ *Tue–Fri, Sat am & mid-Mar–mid-Nov: Sun pm.* 🖼
This museum is devoted to the history of river shipping

BERGERAC WINES

Bergerac wines were highly thought-of in England during the Hundred Years' War, and in Holland when the town was a Protestant stronghold, but their renown goes back as far as the 13th century. Today there are 12,400ha (306,400 acres) of vineyards in the area, with 13 *appellations*, for red, rosé, and both dry and sweet white wines, including the famous Monbazillac: morning mists and autumn sunshine nurture the *pourriture noble* mould, giving the grapes their extra sweetness. For information on local wine routes, contact the Conseil Inter-professionnel des Vins de la Région de Bergerac (CIVRB): (05) 53 63 57 57, www.vins-bergerac.fr

Bottle of Monbazillac wine

The Cloître des Récollets, now home to the Maison des Vins

and the local wine trade. The displays include a wide variety of artifacts, models, documents, photographs, and archive materials that have been donated by boat-owning and wine-producing families in the area.

🏛 Musée d'Intérêt National du Tabac

Maison Peyrarède, place du Feu. **Tel** (05) 53 63 04 13. ● Sun am, Mon; mid-Nov–mid-Mar: Sat–Sun . ♦ ♦ Created in 1950 by the Direction des Musées de France, this museum occupies

Maison Peyrarède, a town house built in 1604 and restored in 1982. The only one of its kind in Europe, the museum traces the history of tobacco over 3,000 years. Its collections illustrate the earliest use of the plant, its spread throughout the world and the ways in which it was smoked, and tackles the anti-smoking lobby. Various smoking implements, with details of their manufacture, are shown. The importance of tobacco-growing in the Dordogne valley is also highlighted.

BERGERAC TOWN CENTRE

Église Saint-Jacques ①
Maison des Vins-
   Cloître des Récollets ⑤
Medieval houses ⑥
Musée Costi ②
Musée d'Intérêt National
   du Tabac ⑦
Musée du Vin et
   de la Batellerie ③
Quai Salvette ⑧
Statue of Cyrano ④

0 metres   200
0 yards   200

Key to Symbols see back flap

LOT-ET-GARONNE

The 19th-century French novelist, Stendhal, likened the sunny, undulating landscape of the Lot-et-Garonne to that of Tuscany. This prosperous and mostly agricultural area also has a rich architectural heritage that reflects its eventful history. Castles, Romanesque churches, bastide towns and picturesque villages are everywhere in an area that has much to offer lovers of culture and the countryside.

The Lot-et-Garrone, including what was once the Comté d'Agenais, lies between territories once held by the kings of France and the kings of England (also dukes of Aquitaine), and was the object of bitter dispute until it was finally won by France in 1472. In the 13th and 14th centuries, more than 40 *bastide* towns were built here on the orders of Raymond VII, Comte de Toulouse, of Alphonse de Poitiers, brother of Louis IX of France, and of Edward I of England. With their central arcaded squares and streets laid out to a grid pattern, such towns were built not only as a response to a rapidly growing population, but also to the conflict between France and England that raged over southwest France until well into the 15th century.

With its fertile, rolling hills and valleys, and pine forests that encroach across from the Landes, the Lot-et-Garonne is home to some of France's most stunning scenery. Over 200km (125 miles) of navigable waterways are provided by the Lot, the Garonne and the Baïse rivers, and the canal that runs alongside the Garonne. Once, these were the only means of transporting local produce between Guyenne and Languedoc.

Today, as a prime producer of fruit and vegetables, including its famous *prunes (see p153)*, the Lot-et-Garonne serves as the orchard of Europe. Its fine wines compare favourably with those of neighbouring Bordeaux and are an important element in the bounty of gastronomic specialities to be enjoyed in this corner of France.

A shaded lakeside, near Lauzun

◁ Half-timbered houses in a street in Pujols

Exploring the Lot-et-Garonne

The two great river valleys of the Garonne and its tributary, the Lot, cut right through this varied region. The Lot valley, in the centre, is by turns narrow and steep-sided, and wide and flat. Fruit, including the famous *prunes d'Agen* (a type of plum), and vegetables are grown on the fertile land along its banks. In the southeast are the Agenais and Pays de Serres areas, with their mix of broad plateaux and shallow valleys. In the southwest is the Albret, territory once controlled by the family of Henri IV. To the northwest is the Pays Marmandais, a land of vine-covered hillsides, fruit orchards and vegetable fields. The Pays du Drop, in the north, and the gentle hills of the Haut-Agenais are dotted with picturesque *bastide* towns. This area is also home to the mighty medieval Château de Bonaguil, in the east, and the grand Renaissance Château de Duras, to the west.

Flower-covered façade of a house in Pujols

The fortified church at Villeréal

GETTING AROUND

Agen, capital of the Lot-et-Garonne, has an airport and a railway station. By TGV (high-speed train), it is 4 hours from Paris and 1 hour from Toulouse and Bordeaux. The A62 runs from the north of Toulouse to Bordeaux, passing through the region from southeast to northwest. The N21 links Agen, Villeneuve-sur-Lot and the north. Following the banks of the Lot, then those of the Garonne, the D911 links Fumel and Marmande. The N113 follows the Garonne. Direct flights from Agen to Paris Orly West take just 1 hour 20 minutes.

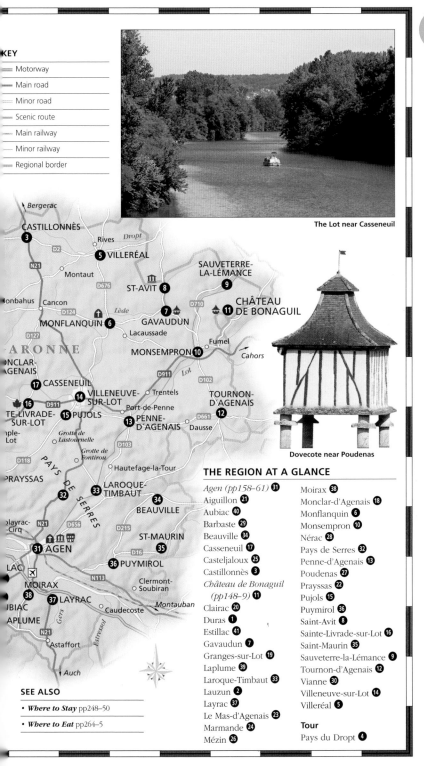

KEY

— Motorway
— Main road
— Minor road
— Scenic route
— Main railway
— Minor railway
— Regional border

The Lot near Casseneuil

Dovecote near Poudenas

THE REGION AT A GLANCE

SEE ALSO

• *Where to Stay* pp248–50

• *Where to Eat* pp264–5

Duras ❶

Road map D2. 22km (14 miles)
north of Marmande. 👥 *1,250.*
🚉 *Marmande.* ℹ️ *14 boulevard
Jean-Brisseau (05) 53 83 63 06.*
🍴 *Mon, in summer.*
🎭 *Fête de la Madeleine (Jul); Fête
des Vins (Aug); Les Médiévales (Aug).*

Built on the plan of a
bastide (see pp24–5),
this ancient fortified town
looks down from a high
promontory above the river
Dropt. The **Château de Duras**
was built in about 1137 and
later remodelled several
times. By the 14th century, it
was a fortress set with eight
towers; by the 17th century, it
had developed into a grand
residential château. During the
French Revolution, it was almost
reduced to a ruin. The state
acquired it in 1969.

Now largely restored, the
castle is open to visitors, who
can walk through almost 35 of
its great rooms. These include
the Salle des Maréchaux
(Marshals' Hall) and a barrel-
vaulted ballroom dating from
1740. The tower offers a
panoramic view of the
Pays de Duras. The
museum of local
history, in the
basement,
documents life in
Duras, focusing
on such aspects
of the area as
vinegrowing,
local crafts
and other folk
traditions.

**The 12th-century Château de Duras, once home to
the Ducs de Duras, now with several museums**

The **Musée Conservatoire du
Parchemin et de l'Enluminure**,
in the village itself, shows
how books were produced
in the Middle Ages. Rue
Jauffret, the main street, leads
to a small square with
picturesque old houses.

⚜ **Château de Duras**
***Tel** (05) 53 83 77 32.* 🕐 *Apr–Sep:
daily; Oct–Mar: on request.* 🎫 📷

🏛 **Musée Conservatoire
du Parchemin et
de l'Enluminure**
Rue des Eyzins. ***Tel** (05) 53 20 75
55.* 🕐 *Apr–Sep: pm daily (Jul–Aug:
also am daily).* 🎫 📷

Lauzun ❷

Road map D2. 26km (16 miles) east
of Duras. 👥 *791.* 🚉 *Marmande.* ℹ️
Rue Taillefer (05) 53 20 10 07. 🍴 *Sat.*
🎭 *Gasconnades (2nd Sun in Aug).*

The eventful life of the Duc
de Lauzun, marshal of France
and a courtier of Louis XIV, is
conjured up in the rooms of

Pays du Dropt ❹

Occupying the northwestern corner of
the Lot-et-Garonne, the Pays du Dropt
is bisected by the Dropt river. It is a region
of gentle valleys covered with vines and
plum trees, dotted with small, white, stone
Romanesque churches. The vineyards of
the Côtes de Duras occupy some 2,000ha
(4,940 acres), many of them part of small
family estates. The Côtes de Duras area
was granted its own *appellation* in 1937.

Sainte-Colombe-de-Duras ①
The choir of this small Romanesque church has
carved capitals. A fresco shows scenes from the
life of St Colomba.

Saint-Sernin-de-Duras ③
The church in this attractive village is
picturesquely covered in
Virginia creeper.
The building
was restored
in the 15th
and 19th
centuries.

TIPS FOR DRIVERS

ℹ️ *Allemans-du-Dropt (05) 53
20 25 59.*
Itinerary: About 57km (35 miles).
*Stopping-off places: The Étape
Gasconne at Allemans-de-Dropt
and the table d'hôte at Château
Monteton are recommended.
Sample M and Mme Dreux's prunes
at Esclottes and M and Mme
Ros's foie gras at Les Renards, in
Saint-Sernin-de-Duras.*

Esclottes ②
The village is named for
its *clottes* (boundary
stones) that marked the
borders of the dioceses
of Agen and Bazas. The
11th-century church here
has carved capitals
showing Christ in Majesty
and other scenes.

Monteton ⑧
Set above the Dropt valley, the charming
12th-century Romanesque church here has finely
carved capitals, featuring a host of fantasy beasts.

MONSÉGUR

MARMANDE

Duras

the **Château de Lauzun**, which was built in the 13th century and remodelled in the late 14th. The listed Renaissance wing has two monumental chimneypieces with carvings and marble capitals. The Gothic church in the village, opposite a house with caryatids, contains a 17th-century pulpit and altarpiece.

♠ Château de Lauzun
Tel (05) 53 94 18 89. ☐ Jul–Aug: 10am–noon & 2–6pm daily.

Castillonnès ❸

Road map D2. 12km (7 miles) east of Lauzun. 🏘 1,325. 🚉 Villeneuve-sur-Lot or Bergerac. ☐ 🛈 Place des Cornières (05) 53 36 87 44. ☐ Tue am.

Founded in about 1259, the *bastide* town of Castillonnès perches on a rocky spur. During the Hundred Years' War *(see p41)*, the town passed between the French and the English seven times, but was finally

A dovecote at Castillonnès, in a style typical of the Lot-et-Garonne.

taken by the French in 1451. Two gates are all that remain of the ramparts. On place des Cornières, the main square, is an unusual 20th-century covered market. On the other side of the square is the former Maison du Gouverneur, with a Renaissance courtyard. The building is now the town hall and tourist office.

The church, which was rebuilt after the 16th-century Wars of Religion, has a 17th-century Baroque altarpiece and stained glass by the master-craftsman Louis Franchéo.

Environs
About 13km (8 miles) to the west is **Miramont-de-Guyenne**, a *bastide* town dating from 1278, that was once owned by the Albret family. The central square has a reconstructed covered market and half-timbered houses line the narrow streets.

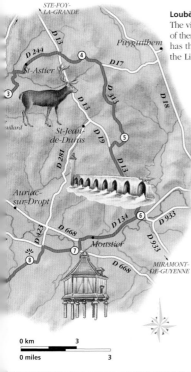

KEY
▬ Suggested route
═ Other roads
❊ Viewpoint

Loubès-Bernac ④
The village has four churches. One of them, the Église de Loubès, has the coat of arms of Richard the Lionheart on its doorway.

Soumensac ⑤
There are fine views from the remains of 12th-century ramparts at Soumensac.

La Sauvetat-du-Dropt ⑥
This village, in an ancient *sauve* (area of cleared land), has a large church with a 12th-century choir, and a Romanesque bridge.

Allemans-du-Dropt ⑦
The Église Saint-Eutrope is decorated with beautiful, listed 15th-century frescoes. They include depictions of the Last Supper, the Crucifixion, Hell, and the Last Judgment. The choir shows Moorish influence.

0 km 3
0 miles 3

The late 14th-century covered market at Villeréal

Villeréal ❺

Road map D2. 13km (8 miles) east of Castillonès. 🏛 *1,250*. 🚆 *Bergerac.* ℹ️ *Place de la Halle (05) 53 36 09 65.* 🛍 *Sat.* 🎪 *Bodega (Jul); Militaria (second Sun in Sep).*

Founded in 1265, the *bastide* town of Villeréal is laid out to a regular plan *(see pp24–5)*. The main square, at the centre of the town, is lined with arcades with corbelled houses above. The large, late 14th-century covered market has an upper storey, with half-timbered cob walls, which now houses the town hall. The fortified 13th-century church, which once served as a place of refuge, has two turrets that are connected by a wall-walk. Up to the 17th century access was still by drawbridge.

Environs
There is a cluster of interesting Romanesque churches in the villages around Villeréal. The 12th-century church at Bournel, 6km (4 miles) to the south is dedicated to Ste Madeleine, whose statue can be seen above the arched main doorway. The 12th-century church at **Rives**, 2km (1.5 miles) north, has an unusual triangular shaped bell tower, with two arches and a round apse. The 14th-century church at **Montaut**, 7km (4.5 miles) to the southwest, was extremely important, being the seat of the archpriest with around 91 parishes. It has a five-arched bell tower astride two towers, and has two bells.

Monflanquin ❻

Road map D3. 13km (8 miles) south of Villeréal. 🏛 *800*. 🚆 *Villeneuve-sur-Lot.* ℹ️ *Place des Arcades (05) 53 36 40 19.* 🛍 *Thu.* 🎪 *Foire aux Vins et Fromages (May); Festival Amateur de Théâtre (Jul); Journées Médiévales (Aug).*

This attractive *bastide* town, officially listed as one of France's prettiest villages, is laid out to an oval plan. It clings to the hillside rising sharply from the Lède valley. Built around 1240, with a grid pattern of streets, the *bastide* developed in 1252 under the leadership of Alphonse de Poitiers, but its defences were dismantled on the orders of Cardinal Richelieu. The streets intersect at place des Arcades, at the top end of the town.

Maison du Prince Noir

The main square is lined with arcaded houses *(see pp24–5)*, including the **Maison du Prince Noir** (House of the Black Prince; *see p41)*, with Gothic rib-vaulting and moulded panels. The church, the beautiful **Église Saint-André**, has a single-wall bell tower, whose façade dates from 1927, and a relief-decorated medieval doorway.

Rue de l'Union, rue des Arcades and rue Sainte-Marie are lined with fine stone houses with arcades on the ground floor and 16th-century half-timbered façades above.

Overlooking the town, on a rocky spur, stands the fortified Château de Roquefère (which is only open to the public on Journées Patrimoines).

The **Musée des Bastides** shows how *bastide* towns were constructed, from the 13th century onward, and how they served their purpose *(see pp24–5)*.

🛕 **Église Saint-André**
◯ *daily.*
🏛 **Musée des Bastides** Maison du Tourisme, place des Arcades.
Tel *(05) 53 36 40 19.*
◯ *daily.* 📷 💳

Environs
Cancon, 13km (8 miles) west of Monflanquin, is also a *bastide* town, perched on a hill overlooking Périgord and Quercy. Its old quarter has narrow streets lined by timbered 14th- and 15th-century houses.

BERNARD PALISSY'S "RUSTIC FIGULINES"

Bernard Palissy, the famous potter, was born in Lacapelle-Biron around 1510. He made large plates, dishes, ewers and other vessels encrusted with "rustic figulines" in high relief of reptiles, fish, shells and plants, modelled from life and realistically painted. He baked them in a kiln that he reputedly stoked with the furniture and floorboards of his own house. Patronized by the queen, Catherine de Medici and by the Connétable de Montmorency, he became "Inventor of rustic figulines to the King and My Lord the Duc de Montmorency", but was later imprisoned in the Bastille in 1589 for refusing to renounce his Protestant faith. He died in prison a few years later, in 1589 or 1590.

Bernard Palissy

Gavaudun ❼

Road map E3. 11km (7 miles) east of Monflanquin. 👥 327. 🚉 Monsempron.

Perched high up on a rocky hill, the village of Gavaudun stands proud of the wooded valleys all around it. The ruins of its 11th–13th-century fortress, particularly the huge **keep** with its limestone entrance, are very impressive. This stunning setting is regularly used for carnivals and musical events.

⚑ **Keep**
🕐 Jun & Sep: Sat–Sun; Jul–Aug: daily. **Tel** (05) 53 95 62 04. 🖼 🎥

Environs
2km (1 mile) north of Gavaudun is the small hamlet of **Saint-Sardos-de-Laurenque**, where there is a delightful Romanesque church with a carved doorway.

Saint-Avit ❽

Road map D2. 15km (9 miles) northeast of Monflanquin. 👥 430. 🚉 Monsempron. 🖼 Foire à la Poterie (second Sun in Aug).

This attractive hamlet on a hillside in the Lède valley has just one street. The 13th-century Romanesque church is decorated with frescoes. Saint-Avit is the birthplace of Bernard Palissy (see opposite). The **Musée Bernard-Palissy** here is devoted to his life and work, and also displays contemporary ceramics.

🏛 **Musée Bernard-Palissy**
Saint-Avit, Lacapelle-Biron. 🕐 May–Sep: Wed–Mon pm; out of season: Sun pm. **Tel** (05) 53 40 98 22. 🖼

Château des Rois-Ducs, at Sauveterre-la-Lémance

Sauveterre-la-Lémance ❾

Road map E2. 14km (8 miles) east of Saint-Avit. 👥 640. 🚉 Monsempron.

This village, dominated by the privately owned Château des Rois-Ducs, gave its name to the Sauveterrian, a major period of the Mesolithic age. The small **Musée de la Préhistoire**, displays objects found when excavations began in 1920 on a site known as Le Martinet.

A "rustic figuline" by Bernard Palissy

🏛 **Musée de la Préhistoire**
🕐 Apr–May & Oct: Tue–Fri & Sun pm; Jun–Sep: Tue–Sun. 🖼 🎥 **Tel** (05) 53 40 73 03.

Environs
At **Saint-Front- sur-Lémance**, 2km (1.5 miles) southwest, there is an interesting 11th–14th-century fortified church.

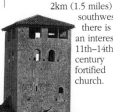

Monsempron ❿

Road map E3. 10km (6 miles) south of Bonaguil. 👥 2,200. 🚉 Monsempron. 🚌 🍴 Fumel: Place Georges-Escande. **Tel** (05) 53 71 13 70. 🕐 Thu am. 🖼 Annual fair & Fête du Printemps (Mar).

Here the imposing outline of the Benedictine priory of Saint-Géraud-de-Monsempron overlooks the confluence of Lot and the Lémance. This fortified village has a beautifully proportioned Romanesque church. Although it was remodelled in the 16th century, it retains some 12th-century elements, including a barrel-vaulted nave with carved capitals, a dome supported on stone columns above the central crossing and a severely plain doorway. The semicircular recesses of the apses overlap one another.

Environs
3km (2 miles) northeast, **Fumel** has a 12th–16th-century castle, surrounded by formal gardens.

The former Benedictine priory and its Romanesque church, above Monsempron

Château de Bonaguil ⑪

The colossal Château de Bonaguil stands majestically on a rocky spur at the foot of a wooded hill, its towers, ramparts and turrets fleetingly visible from behind lush greenery. Founded in the 13th century on an *aiguille creuse* (hollow peak), it became known as the castle *bona accus, or bonne aiguille*, in French, hence its current name. In 1483, it passed to Bérenger de Roquefeuil (1448–1530), who enlarged it. As the result of inheritance, ownership then changed several times, but in 1761 it was re-acquired by Marguerite de Fumel, who remodelled it. Abandoned during the French Revolution, it was eventually sold to Fumel's municipal authorities in 1860. It is an impressive example of the transition between medieval military architecture and an early Rennaisance noble residence.

The impregnable fortress of Bonaguil, perched on a rocky outcrop

Great hall

★ **Great Tower**
The key element of the castle's defences, the Great Tower is ringed by ramparts, which were once covered. It defended the inner courtyard.

Red Tower

Well
Located on the inner side of the main courtyard, the well was dug directly into the rock, its shaft reaching down to the water table below. Behind the well is an elegant Gothic doorway, which leads to the castle's outbuildings.

STAR FEATURES

★ Drawbridge

★ Great Tower

★ Keep

Barbican

This semicircular fortification acted as an area of defence between the inner and outer drawbridges. As one drawbridge was raised, the other was lowered.

VISITORS' CHECKLIST

Road map E3. 6.5km (4 miles) north of Fumel, near the village of Saint-Front-sur-Lémance. The castle can be reached either by road or on foot from the bottom of the village. **Tel** *(05) 53 71 90 33.* ☐ *mid-Feb–Oct: daily.* 🖼 🎭 *Festival de Théâtre (Aug).* **www**.bonaguil.org

★ Drawbridge

The inner ramparts and the barbican are connected by a drawbridge, which gave access to two gates, one for wheeled traffic and another for pedestrians. The drawbridge, which was converted into a standing bridge by Marguerite de Fumel, spans the castle's wide dry moats.

Outer courtyard

★ Keep

Because of the shape of the rock on which it was built, in the 13th century, the keep is strangely elongated. Eight hundred steps lead to the platform at the top of this lookout post, from which there are stunning views of the surrounding forests and valleys.

The *bastide* town of Tournon-d'Agenais, strategically set on a rocky plateau

Tournon-d'Agenais ⑫

Road map E3. 10km (6 miles) south of Fumel. 🏠 780. 🚌 *Penne-d'Agenais*. ⓘ *Place Centrale (05) 53 40 75 82.* 🛒 *summer: Fri evening; May: flower market.* 🎭 *Fête des Rosières (Aug); Foire à la Tourtière (Aug).*

Set on a rocky promontory in the Boudouyssou valley, this *bastide* town was built in about 1270, and soon after came under English control.

Houses built into the ramparts look down from the high clifftop. Constructed from a mix of uncut boulders and dressed stone, some, like those in rue du Bousquet, also have half-timbered walls. The 13th-century Maison de l'Abescat in rue de l'École housed the bishops of Agen during the Middle Ages. The bell tower in the square was built in 1637 and is crowned by a wooden steeple with a fine lunar clock that was added in 1843.

Above Place de la Mairie is a municipal garden, laid out on the site of a church that was destroyed in the 16th century during the Wars of Religion.

Penne-d'Agenais ⑬

Road map D3. 16km (10 miles) west of Tournon. 🏠 2,004. 🚌 ⓘ *Rue du 14-Juillet (05) 53 41 37 80.* 🎭 *Foire à la Tourtière (second Sun in Jul).*

By turns a mighty base for the warring Richard the Lionheart, a possession of the counts of Toulouse and of Simon de Montfort's Crusaders, this town was held alternately by the French and the English during the Hundred Years' War, then passed from the Protestants to the Catholics during the Wars of Religion. Filled with picturesque restored houses set on narrow paved streets that run down the hillside, it is crowned by the silvered dome of a great neo-Byzantine basilica, which was built from 1897 to 1947.

Remains of the medieval town include part of the 12th-century walls, as well as fine houses with Gothic doorways, and the square keep of the castle, which was dismantled in the reign of Henri IV (1589–1610).

Portrait in the Musée de Gajac

Some houses on the main square have windows with intricate Gothic tracery. A small, restored gateway, the Porte de Ricard, is framed by buttresses. The defence tower on rue des Fossés once formed part of the ramparts. Place du Mercadiel and place Paul-Froment are lined with old arcaded merchants' houses. Beneath the present town hall is the former "royal" prison.

Environs

Port-de-Penne, below the main town on the banks of the Lot, has a 12th-century Romanesque church. A section of its ancient ramparts also survive.

Villeneuve-sur-Lot ⑭

Road map D3. 10km (6 miles) west of Penne-d'Agenais. 🏠 24,600. 🚌 *Penne-d'Agenais.* 🚌 ⓘ *3 place de la Libération; (05) 53 36 17 30.* 🛒 *Tue & Sat; flower market (Apr).* 🎭 *Fête du Cheval (Sep).*

Straddling the Lot river, Villeneuve was founded by Alphonse de Poitiers in 1264. It is the largest *bastide* town of the Lot-et-Garonne.

The town's symbol is its ancient bridge, Pont Vieux, which was built across the Lot in 1287 and restored in the 17th century. It has five spans and was once set with three fortified towers. On the north bank of the river stands the Chapelle du Bout-du-Pont, built in the 17th century and dedicated to sailors and boatmen. Two majestic gates, Porte de Paris and Porte de Pujols, both 30m (98ft) high, once formed part

The silvered dome of the Basilique de Peyragude at Penne-d'Agenais

Porte de Ville, a fortified gate abutting the Église Saint-Nicolas in Pujols

of the town's 14th-century ramparts. Colourful markets are still held on place Lafayette, a square lined with arcades.

The Église Sainte-Catherine was built in the 19th century on the site of a demolished earlier building. In the Byzantine-Romanesque style, it has 15th- and 16th-century stained-glass windows and wooden statues. Église Saint-Étienne, on the opposite bank of the Lot, was built in the Gothic style and remodelled in the 16th century.

The **Musée de Gajac**, in a 16th-century disused mill, contains religious and 19th-century paintings.

The **Haras National** (National Stud), established in 1804, has many Arab and Anglo-Arab horses.

In the Quartier d'Eysses, a district in the north of Villeneuve, on the road to Monflanquin, is an archeological site with a 1st-century Gallo-Roman villa. Amphorae and various other objects discovered here are displayed at the site's small **Musée Archéologique**.

🏛 **Musée de Gajac**
2 rue des Jardins. *Tel* (05) 53 40 48 00. ⬜ daily. ⬤ Sat & Sun: am & public hols. 🈳 🈳

⚓ **Haras National**
Rue de Bordeaux. *Tel* (05) 53 70 56 84. ⬜ Mon–Fri: pm. 🈳 🈳

🏛 **Musée Archéologique**
Place Saint-Sernin-d'Eysses.
Tel (05) 53 70 65 19.
⬜ Jul–Aug: pm. 🈳

Pujols ⓯

Road map D3. South of Villeneuve-sur-Lot. 🏘 *3,844.* 🚉 *Penne-d'Agenais.* ℹ *Place Saint-Nicolas (05) 53 36 78 69).* ⬤ *Sun; pottery market (Aug).* 🈳 *Course du Mont-Pujols (Easter Mon).*

Officially listed as one of France's prettiest villages, this heavily fortified town was dismantled several times in the course of its history.

Porte de Ville, the fortified gate, is the only entrance to this walled town. The gate also serves as the bell tower of the 14th–15th-century Église Saint-Nicolas. The main street is lined with attractive 15th-century half-timbered and corbelled houses. The Église Sainte-Foy, decorated with 16th-century frescoes, hosts temporary exhibitions.

Environs
The nearby **Grotte de Lastournelle** and **Grotte de Fontirou** are caves with interesting natural rock formations.

Sainte-Livrade-sur-Lot ⓰

Road map D3. 9km (6 miles) west of Villeneuve-sur-Lot. 🏘 *6,200.* 🚉 *Penne-d'Agenais.* 🚌 ℹ *45 rue Nationale (05) 53 01 45 88.* ⬤ *Fri.* 🈳 *Championnat du Monde de Cracher de Pruneau (end Jul); Marché aux Saveurs (Aug).*

The church in this *bastide* town was built in the 12th to 14th centuries. It has an attractive stone-built Romanesque tiered apse and contains a white marble effigy of a 14th-century bishop. Another interesting feature of Sainte-Livrade is the Tour du Roy, a tower that formed part of a castle built here by Richard the Lionheart.

Roseraie Vicart, between Sainte-Livrade and Casseneuil, is a rose garden with 7,500 rose bushes representing 300 different varieties of rose.

🌺 **Roseraie Vicart**
Sainte-Livrade. *Tel* (05) 53 41 04 99. ⬜ May–Sep: daily. 🈳 🈳

Casseneuil ⓱

Road map D3. 🏘 *2,500.* 5km (3 miles) northeast of Sainte-Livrade. 🚉 *Penne-d'Agenais.* 🚌 ℹ *45 allée des Promenades (05) 53 41 13 33.* ⬤ *Wed & Sun; May: flower market.*

For centuries, this town, set on a peninsula, depended on river transport and river trade for its wealth. In 1214, it held out against the English under Simon de Montfort. Overhanging houses line the riverbank. The **Église Saint-Pierre** contains 13th and 15th century frescoes.

🔒 **Église Saint-Pierre**
Tel (05) 53 41 13 33 (tourist office).
⬜ daily. 🈳

Tour du Roy and its stairway, at Sainte-Livrade-sur-Lot

The imposing church at Monclar-d'Agenais, above the Tolzac valley

Monclar-d'Agenais ⓲

Road map D3. 10km (6 miles)
northwest of Sainte-Livrade. 🏛 862.
🚉 Tonneins. 🛈 Rue de Marmande
(05) 53 41 87 44.

Perched on a narrow spit of
land, the *bastide* town of
Monclar was founded by
Alphonse of Poitiers in 1256.
From its elevated situation the
town offers magnificent views
of the Tolzac valley. One side
of the town's main square is
lined with arcades. The
covered market abuts the
Église Saint-Clar, which has
a 16th-century porch.

Environs
Castelmoron-sur-Lot, 6km
(4 miles) to the southwest, has
a pleasant man-made lake,
beside which stands a Moorish
town hall. The church at
Fongrave, 8km (5 miles) south,
has a fine wooden altarpiece.
Temple-sur-Lot, 10km (6.5
miles) south, has a 15th-
century building that was once
the headquarters of the Knights
Templar. Here, visitors can
see over 200 types of water
lily in **Jardin des
Nénuphars
"Latour-
Marliac"**.

Granges-sur-Lot ⓳

Road map D3. 15km (9 miles) west
of Sainte-Livrade. 🏛 600.
🚉 Tonneins or Aiguillon.

Founded in 1291 on the banks
of the Lot, this *bastide* town
was largely destroyed during
the Hundred Years' War.
The **Musée du Pruneau
Gourmand** is devoted to the
history of the local prune
industry. It has displays of
19th–20th-century ovens,
drying cupboards, and other
equipment, as well as old
documents. The museum is
set in an orchard with over
3,000 plum trees.

🏛 **Musée du Pruneau
Gourmand**
Tel (05) 53 84 00 69. ☐ daily.
● Sun am & second 2 weeks in
Jan. 🎫 ✔

Environs
2km (1 mile) northwest is the
bastide town of **Laparade**.
At the Ferme du Chaudron
Magique at **Brugnac**, 11km
(7miles) north, visitors can buy
mohair from the angora goats
kept there.

The former headquarters of the Knights Templar at Temple-sur-Lot
For hotels and restaurants in this region see pp248–50 and pp264–5

Clairac ⓴

Road map D3. 29km (18 miles)
west of Villeneuve-sur-Lot. 🏛 2,660.
🛈 18 rue Gambetta (05) 53 88 71 59.
🕒 Thu. 🎪 Foire au Printemps (Mar);
Fête de la Fraise (May); Semaine
Musicale (Jul–Aug).

Once a Protestant town,
Clairac was besieged by
Louis XIII in 1621 and its fortifications were razed. However,
several 15th-century half-
timbered houses survive. The
town's **Benedictine abbey** was
founded in the 7th century and
by the 13th century it had
become the most influential
abbey in the Agenais. Now
restored, it houses a museum,
which re-creates the abbey's
history and daily life during
the Middle Ages. There is also
an exhibit on ancient trades
and crafts of the area.

Environs
The town of **Tonneins**, 8km
(5 miles) northwest, on the
banks of the Garonne, was
once the capital of ancient

An arcaded dovecote at Clairac

Gaul. A Garonna, a complex
in the former Manufacture
Royale des Tabacs (Royal
Tobacco Factory) here, built
in 1726, re-creates the world
of boating on the Garonne.
Just 8km (5 miles) southeast
of Clairac, in a wooded valley,
is the village of Lacepede. At
the edge of the village is Lac
Salabert, a reservoir and
nature reserve. The Maison de
la Nature here has information
on the local flora and fauna.

🏛 **A Garonna**
Tel (05) 53 79 22 79. ☐ Mar–Oct:
by prior arrangement. 🎫 ✔

🎿 **Lac Salabert**
Tel Maison de la Nature (05) 53 47 18
33. ☐ Mon–Fri: 9am–noon, 2–6pm.

Boats at the double lock at Buzet-sur-Baïse

Aiguillon ㉑

Road map D3. 11km (7 miles) south of Tonneins. 🏠 4,500. 🚉 🚌
🛈 Place du 14-Juillet (05) 53 79 62 58. 🔄 Tue & Fri. 🎭 Fête des Fleurs (May); Festival de Jazz (Aug).

Aiguillon, at the confluence of the Lot and the Garonne, has been inhabited since Gallo-Roman times, and was a focus of conflict during the Hundred Years' War. The Château des Ducs was built by the Duc d'Aiguillon between 1775 and 1781. This luxurious residence was pillaged during the French Revolution, and in 1966 it was converted into a school.

The **Musée Raoul-Dastrac** contains Roman mosaics and 19th-century pilgrims' staffs.

Château des Ducs in Aiguillon, now a school

🏛 **Musée Raoul-Dastrac**
Rue de la République. **Tel** (05) 53 84 41 44 or (05) 53 88 16 45. 🔄 Apr–Aug: Tue–Sun. 🎭 🎥

Environs
Pech-de-Berre, 4km (2.5 miles) north of Aiguillon, offers wide views of the Lot and Garonne valleys. **Damazan**, 7km (4 miles) to the west, is a *bastide* town with fine half-timbered houses and a covered market with the town hall on its upper floor.

5km (3 miles) southwest of Aiguillon, houseboats can be seen on the canal at **Buzet-sur-Baïse**, which is noted for its vineyards. 7km (4 miles) southwest at **Saint-Pierre-de-Buzet** is an attractive 12th-century fortified church.

Prayssas ㉒

Road map D3. 15km (9 miles) east of Aiguillon. 🏠 937. 🚉 Aiguillon.
🛈 Place de l'Hôtel-de-Ville (05) 53 66 36 57. 🎭 Fête du Fruit (Aug).

Surrounded by low hills covered with fruit trees and Chasselas vines, this attractive *bastide* town *(see pp24–5)* was built on an oval plan in the 13th century. Its church has a fine Romanesque apse.

Environs
The fortified village of **Clermont-Dessous**, 7km (4 miles) to the southwest, is dominated by its castle. There is also an 11th-century Romanesque church here.

PRUNES D'AGEN
No less than 65 per cent of all plums grown in France come from the Agenais. The trees take between seven and eight years to reach maturity. They are pruned in winter and their fruit is harvested between August and September. The plums are gathered by shaking the tree by hand, and by machine. After being sorted by size, most of the plums are laid out in drying tunnels, where they are exposed to a temperature of 75°C (167°F) for 24 hours. This removes 21 to 23 per cent of their moisture, turning them into prunes. About 3kg (6–7lb) plums produce about 1kg (2lb) prunes. Noted for their high quality, *prunes d'Agen* have been produced in the Agen area since the Middle Ages.

Poster for Agenais plums

Gilded woodcarving of the Christ's burial in the church at Marmande

Le Mas-d'Agenais ㉓

Road map D3. 11km (7 miles)
west of Tonneins. ⚑ 1,500. 🚉
Marmande or Tonneins. ℹ *Place de
la Halle (05) 53 89 50 58.* 🛒 *Thu.*

The village spreads out along
the canal that runs parallel to the
Garonne. Evidence of Roman
occupation has been
discovered here, including a
marble statue known as the
Vénus du Mas, now in
the Musée des Beaux-
Arts in Agen *(see p160).*
The Collégiale Saint-
Vincent, a fine
11th–12th-century
abbey church, has
17th-century choir
stalls and finely carved
capitals. It also
contains a painting of
Christ on the Cross
(1631) by Rembrandt.
The 17th-century corn
market in the square
has a fine wooden
roof. The wash house
nearby is also worth
a detour.

**Vénus du Mas,
from Mas-
d'Agenais**

Marmande ㉔

Road map D3. ⚑ 18,000. 🚉 🚌
ℹ *Boulevard Gambetta (05) 53 64
44 44).* 🛒 *Tue, Thu, Sat.* 🎉 *Fête des
Fleurs et de la Fraise (May); Fête de la
Tomate (Jul); Nuits Lyriques en
Marmandais (Aug); Festival du Cheval
de Trait (Aug).*

The Marmande area has been
a major producer of tomatoes
since the 19th century, and
now also grows strawberries.
Rival factions fought over the
town during the Hundred
Years' War, but in 1580 it was
finally won by France.
The **Église Notre-Dame**,
founded 1275, has a listed

organ built by Cavaillé-Coll in
1859. The church's Chapelle
Saint-Benoît contains a 17th-
century altarpiece with two
carved scenes at the centre.
Access to the 16th-century
cloister is through gardens.
Rue Labat is lined with
half-timbered houses and the
old ramparts are decorated
with a modern mosaic,
depicting major episodes in
the town's history.

> 🔒 **Église Notre-Dame**
> Rue de la République. ⬜ *daily.* 🎦

Environs
5km (3 miles) northwest is
the **Musée Archéologique
André-Larroderie** at the Gallo-
Roman site of **Sainte-Bazeille**.
It contains artefacts from the
Iron Age to the time of Louis
XIV, found at various digs in
the Marmande area.

> 🏛 **Musée Archéologique
> André-Larroderie**
> Place René-Sanson. *Tel* (05) 53 94
> 40 28. ⬜ *Jul–Aug: Mon &
> Wed–Sun pm; Sep–Jun: Sun pm.* 🖼

Casteljaloux ㉕

Road map C3. 23km (14 miles)
south of Marmande. ⚑ 4 900.
🚉 *Marmande.* ℹ *Maison du Roy
(05) 53 93 00 00.* 🛒 *Tue & Sat.*
🎉 *Fête des Vins, Pains et Fromages
(Jul); Festival de la Jeune Chanson
Française "Cadet d'Argent" (Jul).*

On the edge of the Landes
forests, this spa town is
closely associated with the
Albret dynasty. Some 40 half-
timbered corbelled houses,
built in the 15th and 16th
centuries, date from the
period when the town was
the capital of Gascony and a
base for Henri IV's hunting
expeditions *(see p43).*
The Maison du Roy (King's
House) is a fine 16th-century
residence associated with
Louis XIII and Louis XIV. Tour
Maquebœuf is one of the few
surviving vestiges of the
town's 14th-century
fortifications.

Environs
At **Clarens**, 2km (1 miles)
south of Casteljaloux, is a 17-
ha (42-acre) lake surrounded
by pine trees and fringed by
sandy beaches. Here people
of all ages can enjoy a range
of watersports. **Bouglon** has a
viewpoint that offers fine
views of the Landes forests.
The **Église Saint-Savin**, 1km
(0.5 mile) south of Villefranche-
du-Queyran, is a jewel of
Romanesque architecture.
Dating from the 11th–12th
centuries, it has a beautiful
12-arched choir and some 20
magnificently carved capitals.

The Renaissance cloister of the Église Notre-Dame in Marmande

The massive 13th-century church at Mézin, which towers over the village

Mézin ②

Road map D3. 12km (7 miles) southwest of Nérac. 🏃 *1,500*. 🚊 *Agen*. 🚌 🛈 *Place Armand-Fallières (05) 53 65 77 46*. 🔄 *Thu & Sun*.

The town of Mézin grew up around its medieval monastery, of which nothing now remains, and its church.

The main square is lined with picturesque arcades. In the narrow, winding streets all around there are half-timbered houses and a number of fine stone-built residences. The Gothic-arched Porte de Ville, a gateway also known as Porte Anglaise, is a vestige of the town's 13th-century ramparts.

On the square stands the restored 13th-century **Église Saint-Jean-Baptiste**. Despite the ugly, slightly leaning, six columns that flank the nave, the church has an elegant interior. The climb up the bell tower's 90 steps is no longer permitted because it is too dangerous. The wrought-iron cross to the left of the main doorway into the church dates from 1815. It bears the instruments of the Passion, which are surmounted by the cock that crowed when Peter denied Jesus.

There are several gardens in the town; it is particularly pleasant to walk around the ramparts, in the rue Neuve quarter and also along the rue des Jardins.

The **Musée du Liège et du Bouchon**, reorganized in 1999, is devoted to the cork-making industry, for which the town was famous in the 19th and early 20th centuries.

🏛 **Église Saint-Jean-Baptiste**
Place Armand-Fallières. ◯ *daily*. 📷

🏛 **Musée du Liège et du Bouchon**
Rue Saint-Côme. *Tel (05) 53 65 68 16.* ◯ *Tue–Sun: pm.* ● *Mon.* 📷 📷

Environs
Sports-lovers will enjoy the leisure centre 3km (2 miles) away at **Lislebonne**.

There are dozens of interesting Romanesque churches in the area. Those at **Villeneuve-de-Mézin**, 5km (3 miles) south, **Lannes**, 4km (2 miles) southeast, and **Saint-Simon-Saint-Pé**, 10km (6 miles) southwest, are especially fine.

The village of **Moncrabeau**, 10km (6 miles) to the east, is known as the liars' capital. It won this title in a competition that has been held on the first Sunday in August, every year since the 18th century.

A CENTURY OF CORK-MAKING

At the beginning of the 19th century, when the countryside around Mézin was France's major source of raw cork, cork-making was the Lot-et-Garonne's foremost manufacturing industry. Some 50 factories exported several million corks per day to all parts of the world. The industry's decline began in the second half of the 19th century, with the arrival of maritime pine and imports of raw cork from Spain, Portugal and Algeria. Today only 60 per cent of the raw cork grown around Mézin is used to make corks, and of the cork-oak forests that covered 5,600ha (14,000 acres) in 1851, only 5,000 trees remain.

Corkmaker in a traditional workshop

The mill at Poudenas, on the banks of the Gélise river

Poudenas ㉗

Road map D3. 4km (2 miles) west of Mézin. 🏠 253. 🎫 (05) 53 65 77 46. 🚌 Agen. 🎭 Foire d'Antan (Aug).

This medieval village was once a staging post, where Henri IV was a frequent visitor. The **château** above the village was built by the lords of Poudenas, who were vassals of King Edward I of England.

In the 16th century the castle, which is set in wooded parkland, was converted into a seigneurial residence. It is fronted by arcaded galleries.

🏰 **Château de Poudenas**
Tel (05) 53 65 70 53. 🕐 groups only, by prior arrangement. 🖼 🎥

Nérac ㉘

Road map D3. 27km (17 miles) southwest of Agen. 🏠 7,500. 🚌 Agen. 🚃 🎫 7 avenue Mondenard (05) 53 65 27 75. 🗓 Sat. 🎭 Fêtes du Grand Nérac (May); Festival de la Baïse au Mississipi (Oct); Festival Musique en Albret (Aug–Oct).

The Baïse, now a navigable river, runs through the centre of Nérac, with the castle and the new town on one bank, and the district of Petit Nérac on the other. In the 14th century, Nérac, capital of the Albret region, was a favourite base of the Albret family. They had settled in the region in the 12th century and married into the Navarrese and the French royal family. Nérac was a Protestant stronghold and, in 1621, its

fortifications were dismantled on the orders of Louis XIII.

The **castle**, built above the Baïse in the 14th to 16th centuries, reflects the importance of the Albret family at the height of their power. The castle once consisted of four wings set with circular towers. It was abandoned after the 16th century, and only the north wing now remains. It has an elegant corbelled gallery of twisted columns, built by Alain le Grand d'Albret between 1470 and 1522. Since 1934 the wing has housed the **Musée de Nérac**, with exhibits on the Albret family and life at court in Nérac. A section focuses on local Neolithic and Roman finds.

The 18th-century **Église Saint-Nicolas**, with a Neo-Classical façade, is known for its 19th-century stained-glass windows, which show

Église Saint-Nicolas, at Nérac

monumental figures of the prophets, and for its frescoes.

The Maison des Conférences, a 16th-century town house on rue des Conférences, has its original tiered galleries and a façade decorated with Renaissance motifs. It is named for the meetings *(conférences)* that Catherine de Medici and Henry of Navarre held here from 1578, to bring about a reconciliation between Catholics and Protestants.

Petit Nérac is full of half-timbered houses. It lies along the Baïse, near the lock (dating from 1835). The district's main feature is the 19th-century Église Notre-Dame. The Maison de Sully, at the other end of the Vieux-Pont, rebuilt in the 16th century, was home to the young Duc de Sully in 1580. He later became first minister to Henri IV.

The **Parc de la Garenne**, now a public park, stretches for 2km (1 mile) along the river bank. It has several fountains, including the Fontaine du Dauphin, built in 1601 to mark the birth of Louis XIII, and the Fontaine de Fleurette, named after a young girl who drowned herself, after being seduced and abandoned by the Prince of Navarre.

🏰 **Castle and Museum**
Impasse Henri IV. **Tel** (05) 53 65 21 11. 🕐 Mon. 🖼 🎥

🏛 **Église Saint-Nicolas**
Place Saint-Nicolas. 🕐 daily.

🌿 **Parc de la Garenne**
🕐 daily. 🎥 via the tourist office.

Half-timbered houses in the district of Petit Nérac, on the Baïse river

The ten-span Romanesque bridge at Barbaste

Barbaste 🄮

Road map D3. 6km (4 miles) northwest of Nérac via the D930. 🏃 *1,550.* 🚆 *Agen.* 🛈 *Place de la Mairie (05) 53 65 84 85.* 🎭 *Fête Nationale des Moulins (Jun).*

Built in the 13th century and set with four towers, the **fortified mill** here looks out over the Gélise river, onto a ten-span Romanesque bridge. In the mid-19th century, Antonin Bransoulié converted it into a flour mill. He also installed a walkway that linked the towers and mill to the west bank, and built warehouses. In the late 19th century, the building was converted into a cork factory *(see p155)*. It was damaged by fire in 1906 and again in 1937.

🏭 **Fortified Mill**
🕐 *by prior arrangement.*
***Tel** (05) 53 65 09 37.*

Environs
The *bastide* town of **Lavardac**, 2km (1 mile) to the northeast, was founded in 1256. The harbour, on the Baïse, was prosperous when river traffic was at its height; it is now a stopping-place for pleasure boats. The 13th-century tower is all that remains of a medieval castle.

Just 6km (3 miles) west of Barbaste, on the D665, lies the tiny village of **Durance**. This 13th-century *bastide* village is surrounded by pine forest. All that remains of the fortifications is the south gate, next to the ruins of Henri IV's château.

Vianne 🄯

Road map D3. 8km (5 miles) northwest of Nérac. 🏃 *1,260.* 🚆 *Agen.* 🛈 *Place des Marronniers (05) 53 65 29 54.* 📷 *Jun–Sep: until late eve Fri.* 🎭 *Journée des Nations (Jun).*

This *bastide* town, which still has its fortifications, was set up in 1284 on the banks of the Baïse. Its focal point is a fine 12th-century church. While the nave, choir and carved capitals are Romanesque, the doorway, the decoration of the apse and the bell tower's fortifications are all in the Gothic style.

A glassmaker's workshop set up here in 1928, keeps the local tradition alive *(see p270)*.

Environs
Xaintrailles, 5km (3 miles) south, has a 15th-century square keep. You can see how honey is made at the **Musée de l'Abeille** here. About 12km (8 miles) west of Vianne lie the remains of Henri IV's castle at **Durance**, and around 16km (10 miles) to the north is the 13th-century *bastide* town of **Francescas**.

🏛 **Musée de l'Abeille**
***Tel** (05) 53 65 90 26.* 🕐 *Jul–Aug: daily pm.* 📷

One of the fortified gateways in the ramparts at Vianne

WOMEN AT THE COURT OF NÉRAC

Jeanne d'Albret, mother of Henri IV

Women at the court of Nérac played an important role in its flowering during the 16th century. Marguerite d'Angoulême (1492–1549), wife of Henry of Navarre and sister of François I, came to Nérac in about 1530, followed by scholars, poets and humanist philosophers such as Lefebvre d'Etaples and Clément Marot. Her daughter, Jeanne d'Albret (1528–72), mother of Henri IV, became a Protestant and devoted herself to spreading Calvinism.

Street-by-Street: Agen ③

Hôtel Amblard

Manuscript from Agen

The French capital of rugby and of prunes – even though the famous *prunes d'Agen* do not in fact come from here – Agen (Aginnum) was originally a Gallo-Roman town. It grew rapidly during the late Roman Empire, but suffered as the result of invasions in the 5th and 6th centuries, and was later incorporated into the Grand State of Aquitaine, formed in 1032. Fought over by the king of England (who was also Duke of Aquitaine) and the king of France, control of the town passed from one to the other during the Hundred Years' War. In the 16th-century Wars of Religion, the town's Protestants were expelled. Agen later became a major manufacturing and trading base, exploiting its position on the river Garonne to export its produce. Today, it is an important administrative centre and university town.

Maison du Sénéchal (14th-century)

Théâtre Ducourneau
Renowned for its acoustics, this Neo-Classical theatre opened in 1906.

★ Rue Beauville
This well restored thoroughfare is one of the most picturesque in Agen. Both sides are lined with half-timbered houses with an overhanging upper storey.

RUE JEAN THORTE

RUE AUGUS

DES

RUE FLOIRAC

RUE DU PUITS DU SAUMON

RUE DE LA GRANDE HORLOGE

RUE DE GARONN

RUE MOLIÈRE

RUE MONCORNY

RUE BEAUVILLE

RUE RICHARD COEUR DE LION

STAR SIGHTS

- ★ Cathédrale Saint-Caprais
- ★ Musée des Beaux-Arts
- ★ Rue Beauville

| 0 metres | 100 |
| 0 yards | 100 |

KEY

- - - Suggested route

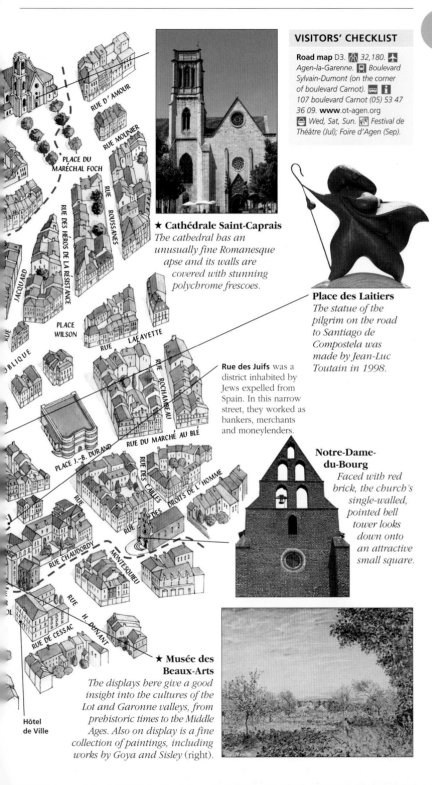

VISITORS' CHECKLIST

Road map D3. 🚗 32,180. 🚆
Agen-la-Garenne. 🚌 Boulevard
Sylvain-Dumont (on the corner
of boulevard Carnot). 📧 ℹ️
107 boulevard Carnot (05) 53 47
36 09. www.ot-agen.org
🛒 Wed, Sat, Sun. 🎭 Festival de
Théâtre (Jul); Foire d'Agen (Sep).

★ **Cathédrale Saint-Caprais**
*The cathedral has an
unusually fine Romanesque
apse and its walls are
covered with stunning
polychrome frescoes.*

Place des Laitiers
*The statue of the
pilgrim on the road
to Santiago de
Compostela was
made by Jean-Luc
Toutain in 1998.*

Rue des Juifs was a
district inhabited by
Jews expelled from
Spain. In this narrow
street, they worked as
bankers, merchants
and moneylenders.

**Notre-Dame-
du-Bourg**
*Faced with red
brick, the church's
single-walled,
pointed bell
tower looks
down onto
an attractive
small square.*

★ **Musée des
Beaux-Arts**
*The displays here give a good
insight into the cultures of the
Lot and Garonne valleys, from
prehistoric times to the Middle
Ages. Also on display is a fine
collection of paintings, including
works by Goya and Sisley (right).*

Hôtel
de Ville

Exploring Agen

The largest town in the Garonne valley between Toulouse and Bordeaux, Agen still has many fine buildings dating from it periods of prosperity as a manufacturing and trading centre. In the heart of the town, between boulevard Carnot and the Garonne, are narrow streets with restored half-timbered, medieval houses, grand 16th- and 17th-century town houses and arcaded squares. There are also some early 20th-century Neo-Classical buildings and a fine museum. Between esplanade du Gravier, on the Garonne, and the canal running parallel with the river, there are many pleasant areas of greenery.

Statue, Église des Jacobins

Renaud et Armide (16th century) by Domenico Tintoretto

Le Plongeur (1877) by Gustave Caillebotte

🏛 Musée des Beaux-Arts

ℹ Place du Docteur-Esquirol.
Tel (05) 53 69 47 23. 🕐 *Tue & public hols.* 📷 📹

Founded in 1876, this museum, whose collections cover almost every period from prehistory to the 20th century, is one of the finest in southwest France. The works are displayed in four beautiful 16th- and 17th-century town houses. On show here is the *Vénus du Mas*, a Roman statue from Le Mas-d'Agenais (*see p154*), as well as Flemish, Dutch, French and Italian paintings of the 16th and 17th centuries and an important collection of 18th- and 19th-century Spanish paintings, including five works by Goya. Paintings by Courbet, Corot and Sisley cover the 19th century, and canvases by Roger Bissière and sculptures by Claude and François-Xavier Lalanne represent the 20th century.

🏛 Vieille Ville

This part of town is crammed with many interesting features. These include buildings as diverse as the 13th-century **Chapelle Notre-Dame-du-Bourg**, in rue des Droits-de-l'Homme, which has a single-walled belfry, and one of France's earliest reinforced concrete buildings, the 1906 **Théâtre Ducourneau**, in place du Docteur-Esquirol.

Rue Beauville, a narrow street, is lined with beautiful 15th-century half-timbered houses. The **Église Notre-Dame-des-Jacobins**, once the chapel of a Dominican monastery built here in 1249, is now used for exhibitions. Arcaded galleries line the nearby **place des Laitiers. Ruelle des Juifs**, a narrow alleyway was, until the end of

The canal along the Garonne river, on its course through Agen

the 14th century, a street of bankers' and merchants.

Rue des Cornières, on the other side of boulevard de la République, was a major thoroughfare for trade in the 13th century. It is now lined with attractive restored houses, set above rows of arcades in a variety of styles.

Other houses worth seeing are the beautiful 14th-century **Maison du Sénéchal** in rue du Puits-du-Saumon, and the 18th-century **Hôtel Amblard**, at 1 rue Floirac.

🔒 Cathédrale Saint-Caprais
Place du Maréchal-Foch. ⬚ *daily.* ☑
Tel *(05) 53 66 37 27.*
Originally built in the 12th century, the cathedral has been remodelled several times. It has a magnificent Romanesque apse and its walls are covered with richly coloured frescoes.

🏛 Place Armand-Fallières
The bishop's palace here, now used as the offices of the local council, was built in 1775 and added to later.

A grand staircase, flanked by allegorical statues, fronts the Neo-Classical lawcourts.

🍀 Le Gravier
During the reign of Louis XIII, this small island near the river bank hosted regional fairs. The esplanade, laid out in the 18th and 19th centuries, is now a popular place for strolling. On avenue Gambetta is **Hôtel Hutot-de-la-Tour**, an 18th-century, pink brick building that was the tax-collector's house. To its right is the **Tour de la Poudre**, once part of the 14th-century ramparts.

🏛 Pont Canal
This 23-span stone bridge is 580m (1,903ft) long, one of the longest bridges in France.

Environs
Parc Walibi Aquitaine, 3.5 km (2 miles) west of Agen, has around 20 different rides and other attractions *(see p286)*.

At **Les Serres Exotiques Végétales Visions**, in Colayrac-Saint-Cirq, 6km (4 miles) to the west of Agen,

Half-timbered houses in rue Richard-Cœur-de-Lion

greenhouses full of rare exotic plants are on display.

🍀 Parc Walibi Aquitaine
Château de Caudouin, Roquefort.
Tel *(05) 53 96 78 32.*
⬚ *mid-Apr–Oct.*
www.sixflagseurope.com ♿

🍀 Les Serres Exotiques Végétales Visions
Tel *(05) 53 67 07 77.* ⬚ *Jul–Aug: daily; Sep–Jun: Tue–Sun.* ♿ ☑

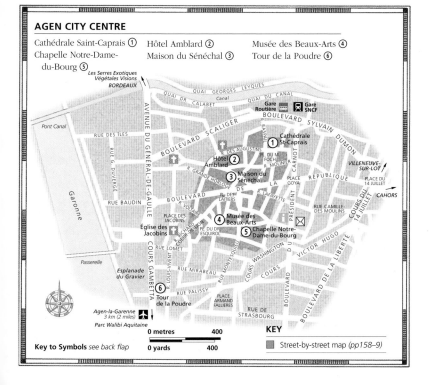

AGEN CITY CENTRE

Cathédrale Saint-Caprais ①   Hôtel Amblard ②   Musée des Beaux-Arts ④
Chapelle Notre-Dame-du-Bourg ⑤   Maison du Sénéchal ③   Tour de la Poudre ⑥

Les Serres Exotiques Végétales Visions
BORDEAUX

QUAI GEORGES LEYGUES
QUAI OR CALABET
Canal
QUAI DU CANAL

Gare Routière
Gare SNCF

BOULEVARD SYLVAIN DUMON

Pont Canal

RUE DES ÎLES

AVENUE DU GÉNÉRAL-DE-GAULLE

BOULEVARD SCALIGER

R. RASPAIL

Cathédrale St-Caprais ①

R. DES AUGUSTINS
PL. DU M FOCH
R. MOLINIER

CARNOT

RÉPUBLIQUE

VILLENEUVE-SUR-LOT

RUE G. DUVERGÉ

Hôtel ② Amblard
R. GRAND HORLOGE

Maison du ③ Sénéchal

PLACE GOYA

PLACE DU 14 JUILLET

CAHORS

Garonne

RUE BAUDIN

BOULEVARD DE

R. VOLTAIRE
PL. DES LAITIERS

LA LAFAYETTE

PRÉSIDENT

RUE CAMILLE-DES-MOULINS

COURS DU 14 JUILLET

PLACE DES JACOBINS
R. RICHARD-CŒUR-DE-LION

Musée des ④ Beaux-Arts

Église des Jacobins

PL. DE DR ESQUIROL

Chapelle Notre-Dame-du-Bourg ⑤

DU

VICTOR HUGO

Passerelle

RUE LOMET

RUE MIRABEAU

COURS WASHINGTON

BOULEVARD

BOULEVARD DE LA LIBERTÉ

Esplanade du Gravier

COURS GAMBETTA

R. LOUIS-VIVENT

RUE PALISSY

RUE MONTESQUIEU

COURS

Tour ⑥ de la Poudre

PLACE ARMAND FALLIÈRES

RUE DE STRASBOURG

Agen-la-Garenne
3 km (2 miles)
Parc Walibi Aquitaine

Key to Symbols *see back flap*

0 metres   400
0 yards   400

KEY

▨ Street-by-street map *(pp158–9)*

One of the many Romanesque churches in the Pays de Serres

Pays de Serres **32**

Road map D3.

The steep valleys and plateaux of the Pays de Serres form a geologically distinct area of land, bordered by the river Lot to the north and the Garonne to the south. Narrow bands of lime-stone, known as *serres* ("long crests") run right across this landscape, which is dotted with villages and old *bastide* towns that perch on the outcrops of rock. There are also many picturesque man-made structures, such as dovecotes, farmhouses and a number of Romanesque churches and chapels, Their typically white stone walls stand out in sharp contrast to the surrounding landscape.

Tuscan columns of the covered market in Laroque-Timbaut

Laroque-Timbaut **33**

Road map D3. 16km (10 miles) northeast of Agen. 🏘 *1,300.*
🚉 *Agen.* 🛈 *Rue du Commerce (05) 53 95 79 50.* 🕑 *Thu am.*
🎭 *Festival Médiéval (Aug).*

The village of Laroque-Timbaut was founded on a rocky outcrop. Its 13th-century covered market has a fine wooden roof, supported on Tuscan columns.

Walking down the pretty rue du Lô, visitors can see the foundations of a 13th-century castle and its old outbuildings. Just outside the village is a memorial to its famous sons, who include the cyclist Paul Dangla (1878–1904) and Louis Brocq (1856–1928), famous for his pioneering work in the treatment of skin disorders.

In the valley is a chapel dedicated to St German, where pilgrims gather on the last Sunday of May each year.

Environs
Hautefage-la-Tour, 7km (4 miles) north of Laroque-Timbaut, has an unusual, hexagonal, tower, built in the 15th century. The 16th-century church has a fine wooden roof.

About 6km (4 miles) to the northwest of Laroque-Timbaut is the fortified medieval village of **Frespech**. The **Musée du Foie Gras** in nearby **Souleilles** traces the 4,500-year-old history of foie gras, a local speciality.

🏛 **Musée du Foie Gras**
Tel (05) 53 41 23 24. ⬜ Mon–Sat.
⬤ Jan. 🎫 🎫

Beauville **34**

Road map D3. 11km (7 miles) east of Laroque-Timbaut. 🏘 *560.*
🚉 *Agen.* 🛈 *Place de la Mairie (05) 53 47 63 06.* 🛒 *mid-Jun–Aug: Sun.*

Sheltering behind a row of trees, the old *bastide* town of Beauville clings to the hillside, commanding an impressive view of the surrounding landscape. The attractive arcaded main square is lined with half-timbered houses. The castle, built in the 13th century with later alterations, is currently undergoing restoration. The 16th-century church has a bell tower at the entrance.

Beauville's main square, lined with arcaded houses

Saint-Maurin **35**

Road map D3. 28km (17 miles) northeast of Agen. 🏘 *450.* 🚉 *Agen.*

This peaceful village, set in a lush valley, developed around an 11th-century Benedictine abbey. The abbey was partly destroyed during the Crusades, then further damage was inflicted by the English in the 14th century. Now all that remains is part of the church and the abbot's house. Built on the plan of a Latin cross, this church has a semicircular choir with six exquisitely carved capitals, including a depiction of the martyrdom of St Maurin. The nave once covered what is now part of the village square. Other vestiges of the abbey lie between newer buildings. The abbot's house contains a **museum**. Designed by the village's inhabitants and with exhibits contributed by them, it documents daily life in the area in the early 20th century. There is also a model of the abbey as it was at the height of its splendour.

On the square in front of the abbot's house are an attractive covered market hall, restored in 1625, a well and several pretty half-timbered houses.

The Église Saint-Martin-d'Anglars, above the village, was founded in the 13th century and rebuilt in the 16th. The furnishings inside it include a 17th-century carved wooden altar and an 18th-century statue of St Joseph.

🏛 **Abbey museum**
Palais abbatial. ⭕ *Jul–Aug: pm.* 🌑 *Tue.* **Tel** *(05) 53 47 63 06 (Beauville).* 📷 📄

Puymirol ㊱

Road map D3. 17km (10 miles) east of Agen. 🏠 *880.* 🚉 *Agen.* 🛈 *83 rue Royale (summer only), (05) 53 95 32 30.*

Founded in 1246, Puymirol was the first *bastide* town to be built in the Agenais. From the heights of the rocky spur on which it perches, the town looks down into the Séoune valley.

Puymirol is surrounded by ramparts with a wall-walk, and entry is via a gate known as Porte Comtale. The main street is rue Royale, and the main square, which is lined with arcades, still has its ancient well. The church, rebuilt in the 17th century, has a 13th-century doorway with a wide carved archway. In the Middle Ages, Puymirol was well known for the fairs held there.

Environs
8km (5 miles) to the southeast is the hilltop village of **Clermont-Soubiran**, with stunning views of the rolling landscape and woodland all around. It has a 12th-century church with a

The Église Saint-Martin, Layrac, with a dome over the central crossing

single-walled belfry. The Château de la Bastide houses the Musée du Vin et de la Tonnellerie, a small museum with exhibits on local wines.

Layrac ㊲

Road map D3. 10km (6 miles) south of Agen. 🚉 *Agen.* 🛈 *Rue Docteur-Ollier (05) 53 66 51 53.*

Layrac commands stunning views over the Gers and Garonne valleys. The 12th-century Église Saint-Martin is crowned by an 18th-century dome, and it has a particularly fine apse. The capitals on the church's façade are carved with monsters and demons. The church contains a marble altarpiece and on the floor are traces of an 11th–12th-century

Half-timbered house in Caudecoste

mosaic, depicting Samson overcoming the lion. The bell tower is all that remains of the older church, which was destroyed in 1792. On place de Salens are a fountain and a washhouse, built against the remains of the ramparts.

Environs
Astaffort, a small town in the Brulhois area, about 11km (7 miles) south of Layrac, is the birthplace of the singer Francis Cabrel. It has some half-timbered houses and the remains of ramparts. The Romanesque Église Saint-Félix was remodelled in the 17th century.

Caudecoste, on a hilltop, 9km (6 miles) south of Layrac, was built in 1273. It is one of the few *bastide* towns to have been founded by a religious order. Half-timbered houses on wooden pillars cluster round its small arcaded square. The church, on the edge of the town, is also worth a visit.

The apse of the Romanesque Église Notre-Dame at Moirax

Moirax ❸

Road map D3. 7km (4 miles) south of Agen. 🏠 *1,023*. 🚉 *Agen*. 🛈 *Place du Prieuré (05) 53 87 03 69.*

The ancient village of Moirax, which clusters around its majestic Romanesque church, looks out onto the flatlands of the Agenais.

In the mid-11th century, the local baron, Guillaume de Moirax, donated land to the Cluniac order, and a monastery was built here. Suffering at the hands of various warring factions, the monastery experienced turbulent times during the Middle Ages. Towards the end of the 17th century, a major programme of rebuilding work was started, but this was brought to an abrupt halt by the outbreak of the French Revolution in 1789.

The **Église Notre-Dame**, which was once part of the monastery, is an exquisite example of Romanesque architecture, and has been superbly restored. An arcaded bell tower now rises above the projecting central section of the façade. This is crowned by a limpet-shaped roof. A double tier of arches lines the buttressed aisles. The arches of the porch are decorated with beading and carved foliated scrolls, and rest on four slender columns. The Gothic arch above frames a semicircular window. Over the choir is a dome decorated with shingles and crowned by a lantern. The arched windows of the apse and side apses are decorated with further beading. The church is laid out to the plan of a basilica, having a nave that is flanked by aisles, a feature which is quite rare in the southwest of France. The only lighting for the nave comes from the window in the west wall.

The strictly symmetrical transept is divided into three equal sections. Each arm of the transept, which is lit by a set of double windows, has steps that lead up to a raised platform or stand. The dome that sits above the central crossing point has been rebuilt in a star-shape.

The choir is lit by arched windows framed by slender columns. Four supporting arches rise up from its square base to the octagonal dome above. Five arched windows illuminate the vaulted apse.

More than 100 ornate capitals decorate the various columns found in this church. As well as abstract geometric and plant motifs, the lion motif features on many of them, while birds, rams and all manner of fantastic monsters also appear. Thirteen of the capitals are carved with Biblical scenes, that include depictions of Adam and Eve in the Garden of Eden, St Michael killing the dragon and Daniel in the lions' den. The aisles are decorated with 17th-century wood carvings, showing various scenes taken from the Old Testament.

🔒 **Église Notre-Dame**
🕐 *daily.* 📷 *by arrangement with the tourist office; (05) 53 87 03 69.*

The 18th-century five-sided wash-house outside Laplume

A picturesque stopping point on the canal at Sérignac-sur-Garonne

Laplume ➌

Road map D3. 14km (9 miles) southwest of Agen. 🏠 *1,250.* 🚉 *Agen.* 🚹 *64 Grande Rue; (05) 53 95 16 67.*

Once the capital of the small Brulhois area to the southwest of Agen, the village of Laplume looks out across the landscape from its vantage point, high on a rocky outcrop of limestone. Parts of the medieval village survive, including sections of the ramparts and two gates. The 16th-century Église Saint-Barthélemy was restored in the 17th and 18th centuries.

Just outside Laplume is the Lavoir de Labat, a curious five-sided wash-house that dates from the 17th or 18th century.

Aubiac ➍

Road map D3. 4km (3 miles) north of Laplume. 🏠 *870.* 🚉 *Agen.* 🚹 *(05) 53 95 16 67.*

Nestling in lush greenery, the beautiful fortified Romanesque Église Sainte-Marie towers over the village. The church was built between the 9th and the 12th centuries on the site of a Merovingian building. Appearing as a square, severely plain fortress from the outside, the church has a contrastingly ornate interior, with rounded arches in the apse and barrel vaulting above the doorway. The dome over the square

choir is decorated with 16th-century frescoes depicting the four Evangelists.

The 14th-century castle next to the church belonged to a branch of the Galard family. It was rebuilt in the 18th century.

An important archeological find from Aubiac is a Celtic bronze head of a horse, now in the Musée des Beaux-Arts in Agen *(see p160).*

Effigy of Blaise de Monluc, Estillac

Estillac ➍

Road map D3. 2km (1 mile) north of Aubiac. 🏠 *1,307.* 🚹 *(05) 53 67 80 36.*

A stronghold in the 13th century, Estillac was once owned by Blaise de Monluc, the writer and Maréchal de France, who led the Catholic armies in the 16th-century

Wars of Religion. His white marble effigy lies in the grounds of the **Château de Monluc**, where he lived. He also distinguished himself in the Franco-Italian wars, and is noted for his *Commentaires*, a treatise on soldiery. The styling of the 16th-century church is typical of architecture in this region.

⚜ Château de Monluc
Tel (05) 53 67 81 83. ◯ *daily.* 🍴🅿️

Environs

Sérignac-sur-Garonne, around 13km (8 miles) northwest of Estillac, was once a leading *bastide* town. Being on the canal, it is a popular spot for visitors on boating holidays. It has some fine half-timbered houses and an 11th-century church with a Romanesque porch and a spiral belfry, rebuilt in 1922, an exact replica of the 16th-century original.

The imposing fortified Romanesque church at Aubiac

LANDES

Thousands of visitors flock to the Landes region every year, drawn by the beauty of its forests and the long, sandy beaches along its Atlantic coastline, a paradise for surfers. But it is also well worth exploring the picturesque hinterland, with its wealth of fine architecture, colourful festivals and many gastronomic treats.

Lying at the heart of Aquitaine, the Landes cover an area of 9,800sq km (3,800sq miles). This largely unspoilt region of forests, lakes and rivers enjoys a gentle maritime climate. With its 106km (66 miles) of golden, sandy beaches and its many rivers (known locally as *courants*), lakes and vast wetlands, the Landes is the perfect setting for watersports. Inland the pine forests, interspersed with fields of maize, are sparsely dotted with traditional houses. Settlement of the Landes goes back to prehistoric times. The legacy of the Hundred Years' War can be seen in the many *bastide* towns, in strategic locations across the countryside. In this difficult, marshy terrain, life was hard. To keep watch over their sheep, local shepherds used to walk on stilts to make crossing the muddy ground easier. During the Second Empire (1852–1870), the landscape changed, as marshland was drained and extensive pine forests were planted for their resin and timber. Also at this time, the coming of the railways and better roads greatly improved communication between the towns and cities. The creation of the Parc Naturel Régional des Landes de Gascogne, in 1970, has helped to preserve the Landes' traditional way of life. Today, visitors come to the region for its fine Romanesque architecture, mostly sited along the former pilgrim routes to Compostela, as well as the superb surfing and hydrotherapy resorts. Bull-running festivals *(see p27)* are also a major attraction. And this beautiful region is a gourmet's paradise. *Foie gras de canard*, free-range chicken, Chalosse beef and sand-grown asparagus, as well as Armagnac and fine Tursan wines, are all on the Landes menu.

The Courant d'Huchet, plied by boatmen punting their craft along the river

◁ The choir of the Benedictine Abbaye de Saint-Sever

Exploring the Landes

The network of roads that covers this huge region make it easy to explore. From Biscarrosse, in the north, to Capbreton, in the south, the coastline has a succession of long beaches and high-class resorts. Inland, beyond the dunes, is a vast expanse of greenery and unspoiled countryside. A landscape that was once flatlands *(landes)* with a scattering of deciduous trees is now covered in pine forest. The Landes' two major towns are peaceful Mont-de-Marsan, the regional capital and administrative centre, and Dax, whose thermal springs attract those seeking health cures. The 290,000-ha (716,590-acre) Parc Naturel Régional des Landes de Gascogne is ideal for those who love the great outdoors. Further south lie the gently rolling hills of Armagnac, Chalosse and Tursan, at the foot of the Pyrenees.

Lac d'Aureilhan, near Mimizan, is very popular with amateur sailors

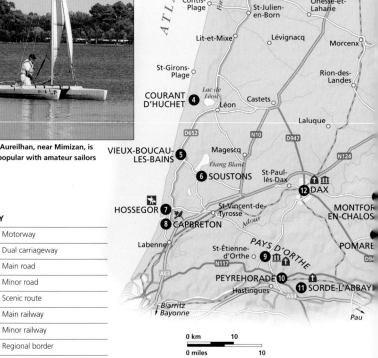

KEY

▬▬▬	Motorway
▬▬▬	Dual carriageway
▬▬▬	Main road
▭▭▭	Minor road
▬▬▬	Scenic route
▬▬▬	Main railway
▬▬▬	Minor railway
▬▬▬	Regional border

0 km   10

0 miles   10

For additional map symbols *see back flap*

Pine trees, now the
emblem of the Landes

THE REGION AT A GLANCE

A Landes house in an
airial (forest clearing)

GETTING AROUND

The nearest airports are at Bordeaux, to the north, Biarritz, to the south, and Pau, to the east. The region is also served by the TGV Atlantique (high-speed train) from Paris, which stops at Bordeaux, Mont-de-Marsan and Dax. The N124, which crosses the region from southwest to northeast, provides a road link between these three cities. The other main axis is the N10 between Bordeaux and Bayonne, in the Pays Basque, which also passes the Parc Naturel des Landes. The N134, D932 and D933, which run north to south, are the three other major roads through the region. Use of headlights, as a safety measure, is advisable when travelling along the minor roads, which tend to run in straight lines through the densely forested areas. Some local vehicles are fitted with an ultrasonic bleeper to frighten wild deer off the roads, as they approach. Bus services also run between towns and villages.

SEE ALSO

Parc Naturel Régional des Landes de Gascogne ❶

**Woman of
the Landes**

This paradise for nature-lovers lies
between the Atlantic seaboard to the
west, the vineyards of the Gironde to
the north and the foothills of the
Pyrenees to the south. It was created
in 1970 to preserve not only the
traditional architecture and culture
of the Landes, but also its wildlife,
protecting an environment on which
around 40,000 people depend for their
livelihood. A total of 41 villages, 20 of
which are in the Gironde and 21 in the

Boating on the river Leyre

Landes, have benefited. This extensive plateau,
which covers over 315,000ha (778,000 acres), is
covered with forests of deciduous trees and
evergreen pines, interspersed with large fields
of maize. The farmland is irrigated by the river
Leyre, which flows all the way through this
conservation area. Because the three routes to
Santiago de Compostela run through the park,
many pilgrims are among the visitors here.

Église Saint-Martin, Moustey
*Moustey has two churches, the Église Saint-
Martin, with fine carving on its doorway,
and the Église Notre-Dame, a stopping-off point on
the Santiago de Compostela pilgrimage route.*

Quartier de Marquèze
*At Marquèze, which forms part of the Écomusée
de la Grande Lande, there is a reconstruction of a
traditional village. Visitors can walk through a group
of typical late 19th-century Landes houses.*

Atelier des Produits Résineux de Luxey

The resin workshop at Luxey is a remnant of an industry that once played a leading role in the Landes' economy. Here also is the Musée de l'Estupr-huc (Firefighting Museum), with exhibits on dealing with forest fires.

VISITORS' CHECKLIST

40km (25 miles) south of Bordeaux via the N10. **Road map** B3/C3.
🚉 Sabres. 🛈 *Maison du Parc, 33 route de Bayonne, 33830 Belin-Beliet (05) 57 71 99 99.* **Fax** *05 56 88 12 72.* ◌ *Mon–Fri: 8:30am–12:30pm, 1:30–5:30pm.* ⬤ *public hols.* **www**.parc-landes-de-gascogne.fr

KEY

〓	Motorway
—	Railway line
▬	Major road
═	Minor road
🛈	Tourist information

HOSTENS

D 657

D 316   D 220E

elhade

SAINT-SYMPHORIEN

PARC DU HAOUT

PARC DE CALLEN

D 43

LAGUNE DES ARRIOUETS

BAZAS

Sore

D 143

D 104

D 49

Luxey

D 315

D 651

Landes pines, once important for their sap, or resin

LAGUNES DE LA BERMIOUSE

D 9

Labrit

D 353   D 626

MARAIS DE L'ANGUILLE

MARAIS DU BRAU DE PIAN

rein

Brocas

D 353   D 651

N 134

MONT-DE-MARSAN

PLANTS AND ANIMALS

The Leyre river, which winds its way across the flatlands of the Landes, is bordered by ferns and deciduous trees, such as Pyrenean oak and chestnut. The marshy land all around is home to the European pond turtle, otters and mink. In the delta, where fresh water meets salt water, storks, egrets and cranes live amongst bullrushes and glasswort. Forested areas, with pines, broom and heather, are punctuated by lagoons, which are inhabited by yellow-bellied toads, water rail and warblers.

Common crane in the Parc Régional

Exploring the Parc Naturel Régional des Landes de Gascogne

Located between the Gironde and the Landes, this vast conservation area lies in what was once known as the Grande Lande. Here sheep grazed under the watchful eyes of shepherds, who used stilts to cross the flat, muddy terrain. Most people lived in one of the many small villages, but houses were also built in open countryside, set in *airiaux* – unfenced grassy areas surrounded by deciduous trees. When Napoleon III decided to redevelop the area in the late 19th century, the marshes and pastures gradually disappeared under plantations of pines. Besides these forested areas, the park also contains a number of waterways and small lakes, including the unspoilt banks of the river Leyre, from which visitors can see picturesque villages, ancient farmhouses and splendid Romanesque churches.

Landes shepherds on stilts, once a common sight in the Landes

🎋 Vallées des Leyre
Road map B3. ℹ️ *Maison du Parc , 33 Route de Bayonne, 33830 Belin-Beliet (05) 57 71 99 99.*
Tel *(05) 56 88 12 72.* 🔲 *Mon–Fri.* 🌐 *public hols.* **www.**parc-landes-de-gascogne.fr
The river Leyre, formed by the Grande Leyre and Petite Leyre, flows into the Arcachon Basin. As it is the source of 80 per cent of the Basin's water, the river plays a key role in the ecological balance of that watery expanse. No roads run along its course, so the Leyre can only be explored by canoe or on foot. The forest, through which it flows for 100km (60 miles), is surrounded by valleys and marshland with a wealth of wildlife. Ancient churches and villages dot the landscape.

A genet in the Leyre forest

🏛 Solférino
Road map B3. In the southwest of the park.
The village of Solférino was founded by Napoleon III in 1863. He wanted to create an ideal model of rural life. To populate the region and promote agriculture, the Emperor purchased 7,000ha (17,000 acres) of flatland on which he built 10 farmhouses, 28 family houses, and 10 craftsmen's houses, as well as a church and a school.

🏛 Musée des Forges
Road map C3. Brocas.
Tel *(05) 58 51 40 68 or 58 51 62 63.* 🔲 *mid-Jun–mid-Sep: Tue–Sun.* 🏷 🏷
In the 19th century, Brocas was an important ironworking centre. The museum, in a disused flour mill, shows the tools and techniques that were used in this important industry, and also displays cast-iron objects such as firebacks. Next to the blast-furnace are workshops, a barn and ironworkers' houses.

🏛 Quartier de Marquèze
Road map B3. Marquèze, in the northeast of Sabres. ℹ️ *(05) 58 08 31 31.* 🔲 *Apr–Oct: daily.* 🏷
The Écomusée de la Grande Lande is an open-air museum with three separate locations: Luxey, which is devoted to resin-tapping; Moustey, which focuses on local religious traditions; and Marquèze, which illustrates daily life in past times, in one area of the Grande Lande. To help create the sense of going back in time, visitors may travel to the town by vintage steam train.
The Musée de Marquèze, which opened in 1969, explores traditional rural

Harvesting the traditional way, one of the park's many historical re-creations

and agricultural life in the Grande Lande, using the reconstruction of a small, local farming community from the late 19th-century. Each family would have lived in a house set in an *airial*, a clearing surrounded by deciduous trees; such areas were once the only patches of greenery in the bare flatlands all around. A wide range of different types of building is represented, including a manor house, several tied cottages and sheep barns. Specialist occupations as shepherding, flour-milling and resin-collecting *(see Luxey)*, as well as many other aspects of rural life, are demonstrated in a lively and informative way.

🐚 Luxey

Road map C3. In the northeast of Sabres. 🔲 *(05) 58 08 31 31 (Sabres).*

From the 1850s to the 1950s, the resin industry contributed greatly to the economic prosperity of the Landes. The resin-processing workshop run by Jacques and Louis Vidal at Luxey still has its old buildings, dating from 1859, along with the equipment that was used. Incisions were made in the trunks of the pine trees and, as the sap ran out, it was collected in vessels and transferred to barrels that were taken to the stills. Here the resin and turpentine were separated for use in the chemical industry.

One of the few clusters of deciduous trees in the Landes forests

The terrible fires that ravaged the forests of the Landes in 1947 and 1949 severely affected the resin industry. In Luxey, the **Musée de l'Estupe-huc** (meaning "put out the fire" in Gascon) documents the dangerous and difficult task of fighting forest fires in the Landes.

🏛 Musée d'Estupe-huc
Luxey. **Tel** *(05) 58 04 70 70.*
🔲 *reservation only.* 🖼

🐚 Moustey

Road map B3. 🔲 *(05) 58 08 31 31.* 🔲 *Apr–Oct: daily.* 🖼

Moustey has two churches, which stand opposite one another. The late 15th-century parish church of St Martin, to the north, is in the late Gothic style. The Église Notre-Dame, which was connected to a hostel, served pilgrims. It has an interesting 16th-century keystone.

Apse of the 11th-century church at Belhade

🔒 Romanesque churches

Built during the Roman epoque, the churches of this area were important meeting places for the St Jacques de Compostela pilgrims. Certain sanctuaries were built by the pilgrims themselves, who were almost the only people to cross the marshy flatlands of Les Landes at this period. At **Belhade**, the Eglise St-Vincent de Xaintes de Belhade has an apse, nave and belfry that date from the 11th–12th centuries. The Eglise St-Pierre de Mons, near **Belin-Beliet** was particularly important on the pilgrim route since legend says that followers of Charlemagne who died at Roncevaux were buried here. Inside there are beautiful wood carvings and sculptured capitals. Eglise St-Michel du Vieux Lugo at **Lugos** is a 12th-century church located in the heart of the forest. A unique apse and nave house painted 15th-century murals. The churches may be closed to the public out of season.

ARNAUDIN'S PRICELESS LEGACY

Berger et Bergerot au Pardéou by Arnaudin

Félix Arnaudin (1844–1921), who lived at Labouheyre (in the southwest of the park), travelled the length and breadth of the Landes, both by bicycle and on foot, with his cumbersome photographic equipment. He recorded a world that was slowly disappearing, photographing shepherds, storytellers and other scenes of country life, as well as the landscape and its architecture. This picture of the late 19th-century Grande Lande, where people lived by planting crops, raising animals and growing timber, on flat expanses that seemed to stretch to infinity, is part of a treasured historical record.

Biscarrosse, one of the most popular resorts on the Landes coast

Biscarrosse ❷

Road map B3. 🏘 *10,000*. 🚌
🛈 *55 place Georges-Dufau (05) 58
78 20 96*. 🛒 *Jul–Aug: daily am.*
🛩 *Rassemblement International
d'Hydravions (May, every two years);
Festival Rue des Étoiles (Jul); Fête de
la Plage (Aug).*

Biscarrosse, with a beach that
stretches for 15km (9 miles),
as far as the Adour river,
marks the beginning of the
Côte d'Argent (Silver Coast).
Sited between the ocean and
the forest, the town has two
lakes, which offer a range
of watersports.

   Visitors with an interest in
aviation will enjoy the **Musée
Historique de l'Hydraviation**,
which is devoted to sea-
planes. The museum stands
next to the Établissements
Latécoère, which produced
seaplanes from 1930 to the
end of the 1950s. The **Musée
des Traditions et de l'Histoire
de Biscarrosse** documents the
town's history and the lives of
resin collectors and shepherds
on the Landes.

🏛 **Musée Historique
de l'Hydraviation**
332 avenue Louis-Bréguet.
Tel *(05) 58 78 00 65.* ◯ *Jul–Aug:
daily; Sep–Jun: Wed–Mon pm.*
🖳 *www.latecoere.com*

🏛 **Musée des Traditions et
de l'Histoire de Biscarrosse**
216 avenue Louis-Bréguet. **Tel** *(05)
58 78 77 37.* ◯ *Jul–Aug: daily (not
Sun pm); Jun & Sep: Tue–Sat; mid-Feb–
May: Tue–Sat pm.* ◉ *Oct–Jan.* 🖼

Environs
4km (2.5 miles) north of
Biscarrosse is the Lac de
Sanguinet. Its 5,600ha (13,800
acres) of clear, fresh waters
are ideal for fishing and
watersports. Sanguinet itself,
on the site of a Gallo-Roman
village, has an interesting
archeological museum.

🏛 **Musée des Sites
Archéologiques Sublacustres**
Tel *(05) 58 82 13 32; out of season,
call (05) 58 78 54 20.* ◯ *Jul–Aug:
daily.* 🖼

Mimizan ❸

Road map B3. 🏘 *10,000 (with
surrounding villages).* 🚉 *Labouheyre
or Morcenx.* 🚌 🛈 *38 avenue
Maurice-Martin (05) 58 09 11 20.*
🛒 *Mimizan-Bourg: Fri am; Mimizan-
Plage: 15 Jun–15 Sep: Thu am.*
🛩 *Fêtes de la Mer (1 May).*

The 13th-century bell tower of
the abbey church at Mimizan

In summer, Mimizan attracts
large numbers of visitors,
who come to enjoy its 10km
(6 miles) of beaches, as well
as its forests, with their 40km
(25 miles) of cycle tracks. The
town has an abbey church
whose 13th-century bell tower
is listed by UNESCO.

   A small museum on the
abbey grounds illustrates
life here during the Middle
Ages. Destination Bois (Into
the Woods), organized by
the tourist office, introduces
visitors to forestry in the area,
with tours of local woodland
and forestry businesses.

🏛 **Clocher Porche du Prieuré
de Mimizan**
Rue de l'Abbaye. **Tel** *(05) 58 09 00
61.* ◯ *Jun–Aug: Mon–Sat; by
appointment rest of year.* 🖼

🏛 **Destination Bois**
*Information available from Mimizan's
tourist office (05) 58 09 11 20.*

Environs
At **Saint-Julien-en-Born**, 12km
(7.5 miles) south of Mimizan,
a river, the Courant de Contis,
flows down to the Plage de
Contis, a beach with a
lighthouse. At **Lit-et-Mixe**,
4km (2 miles) further south, is
the **Musée "Vieilles Landes"**,
which documents local crafts.
At **Lévignacq**, 23km (14 miles)
southeast of Mimiza, the 14th-
century church has a painted
oak ceiling above the nave.

🏛 **Musée "Vieilles Landes"**
Lit-et-Mixte. **Tel** *(05) 58 42 89 17.*
◯ *Jul–Aug: Mon–Sat.* 🖼

Courant d'Huchet ④

Road map B4. *Léon.* 🚶 *Bureau des Nateliers, rue des Berges-du-Lac (05) 58 48 75 39.*

The coast of the Landes is dotted with watercourses, known as *courants*, that flow into the ocean. The best-known is the Courant d'Huchet, a river with wonderful plants and wildlife. Since 1908, visitors have been able to travel on it in *galupes*, flat-bottomed boats that are propelled along using a *palot* (punt). Starting from the Étang de Léon, the lake from where the *courant* flows, *galupe* tours follow a maze of watercourses, which are inhabited by a variety of birds, including teal, common herons and woodcock. The banks are covered with cypresses, hibiscus, irises, gladioli and bracken, and in summer there are ducks, otters, wild boar, mink, crayfish and eels that come here to spawn from the Sargasso Sea. *Galupes* owned by the Bateliers de Léon *(see p299)* sail down the river for 10km (6 miles) to the sea.

Statue of Mitterrand

Vieux-Boucau-les-Bains ⑤

Road map B4. 🚶 *1,400.* 🚌 *Dax (30km/19 miles) or Bayonne (35km/ 22 miles).* 🚍 🚶 *11 promenade du Mail (05) 58 48 13 47.* 🗓 *Tue & Sat am.* 🎡 *Bullrunning (Jun–Sep).*

Near Vieux-Boucau is the resort of Port-d'Albret, clustered round a 60-ha (148-acre) salt lake. Very popular in summer, the resort can only be reached via the leafy Promenade du Mail. The town's arena hosts the popular Landes bull-running festivals.

Soustons ⑥

Road map B4. 🚶 *6,000.* 🚌 *Dax.* 🚍 🚶 *(05) 58 41 52 62 (Grange de Labouyrie).* 🗓 *Mon am; summer market: Thu am, Fri pm.* 🎡 *Fête de la Tulipe (Mar–Apr).*

The main village of the Marensin district, Soustons stretches out along the banks of a large freshwater lake, which is popular with watersports enthusiasts. In the centre of Soustons is a statue of François Mitterrand, the former president of France, who liked to spend time at his residence, Latché, situated 3km (2 miles) from here. The **Musée des Traditions et des Vieux Outils** at Château de la Pandelle brings to life local trades such as roofing, carpentry and resin-collecting.

🏛 **Musée des Traditions et des Vieux Outils**
Château de la Pandelle, avenue du Général-de-Gaulle. **Tel** *(05) 58 41 39 09.* 🖼
⏰ *15 Jun–Aug.* ⬤ *Mar.*

Environs
The Marensin, an area that lies south of Soustons, is cut by rivers and dotted with lakes. These include the **Étang Noir**, a nature reserve, and the Étang Blanc.

🦋 **Réserve Naturelle de l'Etang Noir**
Tel *(05) 58 72 85 76.*
⬤ *Sat–Sun.* 🎫 🖼

Hossegor ⑦

Road map A4. 🚶 *3,500.* 🚌 *Dax or Bayonne.* 🚍 🚶 *Place des Halles (05) 58 41 79 00.* 🗓 *20 Apr–8 Jun: Sun; 9–30 Jun: Wed, Fri & Sun; Jul–Aug: Mon, Wed & Sun.* 🎡 *Les Musicales (Jul–Aug).*

Visitors in a *galupe*, a traditional river craft on the Courant d'Huchet

In the early 20th century, a number of writers, including Paul Margueritte and Rosny Jeune, fell under the spell of this picturesque village, surrounded by pine trees. Ever since, Hossegor has drawn a steady stream of visitors. In the 1930s, it became a coastal resort, and the Sporting-Casino was built, along with a traditional *fronton* where the ball game *pelote basque* is still played. The elegant villas around the golf course and the sea lake evoke the resort's heyday in the 1920s and 1930s. Built in a Basque-Béarn style *(see pp22–23)*, they have Basque features, such as white roofs and façades, as well as typical Landes features, such as half-timbering.

Hossegor is now also an international, surfing mecca. The Rip Curl Pro and Quiksilver Pro festivals that take place in late August and October attract the best surfers in the world.

The Sporting-Casino at Hossegor, a 1930s building in the Basque style

Anglers on the pier at Capbreton

Capbreton ❽

Road map A4. 🏠 6,700. 🚌 ℹ️
Avenue du Président-Pompidou (05)
58 72 12 11. 🛒 *Tue, Thu & Sat am.*
🎭 *Fête de la Mer (Jun/Jul); Festival de*
Contes (Aug); Déferlantes Franco-
phones (Jul); Fête du Chipiron (Sep).

Separated from Hossegor by a
canal, Capbreton is a pleasant
yachting centre and a popular
coastal resort. The **Écomusée
de la Pêche-Aquarium**, re-
creates the seafaring life of this
coastal town from the 10th to
the 16th centuries, when its
fishermen would go whaling,
far out into the Atlantic. The
wooden pier was built in the
late 19th century. Interesting
buildings in the town centre
include 15th-century houses
and the Église Saint-Nicolas.

🏛 **Écomusée de la Pêche-
Aquarium**
Ave du Président Pompidou.
Tel (05) 58 72 40 50. ◻ Apr–Sep:
daily pm (all day Jul–Aug); Feb–Mar
& Sep–Dec: Wed, Sat, Sun & public
hols. ● Jan. 📷 📙

The Église de Saint-Étienne-d'Orthe

Environs
The **Marais d'Orx** is a nature
reserve covering 800ha (1,980
acres). Every year, thousands
of migratory birds of over
200 species, including the
common spoonbill, stop here
on their annual journey south.

🦅 **Marais d'Orx**
Accessible from Labenne, 8 km
(5 miles) south of Capbreton. ℹ️
Maison du Marais; (05) 59 45 42 46.
◻ *daily.* ● *Sat & Sun: am.* 📷 📙

Pays d'Orthe ❾

Road map B4. 🚌 *Peyrehorade.*
ℹ️ *147 avenue des Évadés,*
Peyrehorade (05 58 73 00 52).

South of the Landes lies the
Pays d'Orthe, a region that
has sat at the crossroads of
travellers' routes through
southwestern France since
prehistoric times. The seat of
the Orthe family from the
11th century until the French
Revolution, the area has a
wealth of magnificent châteaux
and religious buildings. The
bastide town of **Hastingues**,
on the pilgrim route to
Compostela, not far from
where the roads from
Le Puy and Vézelay
meet, was founded
by the English in
the 13th century.
Its fortified gate
once formed
part of
the town's
original
ramparts.

The **Centre d'Exposition Saint-
Jacques-de-Compostelle**, in a
layby on the A64 motorway,
documents the pilgrimage to
Santiago de Compostela. East
of Hastingues and south of
Peyrehorade is the **Abbaye
d'Arthous**, founded by
Premonstratensians in the
12th century and remodelled
in the 17th and 18th centuries.
The Romanesque church here,
built in about 1167, has Gothic
elements, including pointed
arches in its south aisle, and

**European pond turtle, a protected
species in the Landes' lagoons**

capitals with superb carvings.
A ceramics festival, with
potters from the locality as
well as from further afield,
takes place in the gardens
each summer. The **Musée
d'Histoire** and the regional
**Centre Éducatif du
Patrimoine** also have
interesting displays.
 Saint-Étienne-d'Orthe,
north of Hastingues, is the
gateway to the alluvial plains
of the river Adour, now a
12,810-ha (31,650-acre) nature
reserve. This stretch of land
is home to a number of
protected species, including
white storks, European pond
turtles and Landes ponies.

Château d'Orthe, also known as the Château de Montréal, Peyrehorade

🏛 **Centre d'Exposition de Saint-Jacques-de-Compostelle**
Layby on the A64; also accessible from Hastingues.
Tel (05) 59 41 56 00 (Autoroutes du Sud de la France).

🔒 **Abbaye d'Arthous**
About 2km (1 mile) east of Hastingues. *Tel* (05) 58 73 03 89.
Abbey and Musée d'Histoire
⬜ Jan–mid-Dec: Tue–Sun. 🎦 ✂
Centre Éducatif du Patrimoine
⬜ Mon–Fri.

Peyrehorade ⓾

Road map B4. 🏔 *3,500* 🚉 🚌
🛈 147 ave des Evadés (05) 58 73 00 52. 🍽 Wed & Sat am; Nov–Mar: Wed am: foie gras market. 🎨 Festival des Abbayes (mid-Jun); Festival Nuits d'Été en Pays d'Orthe (Aug).

Located in the far south of the Landes, between two rivers, the Gave d'Oloron and Gave de Pau, Peyrehorade is the largest village in the Pays d'Orthe. It is also the most newly established, as it grew up only in the 14th century as the result of trade between Bayonne and Toulouse. The village is dominated by the **Château d'Aspremont**, built in the 13th century by the Vicomtes d'Orthe on the site of an 11th-century fortress, of which only the ruins of the keep remain. The **Château d'Orthe** (also known as the Château de Montréal), which now houses the town hall, is another splendid building. Dating from the 16th century, it was remodelled by Jean de Montréal in the 18th century. It is not open to the public but, with its four towers which look down on the Gave de Pau, it is an impressive sight.

Sorde-l'Abbaye ⓫

Road map B4. 🏔 *535.* 🚌 🛈 Place de l'Église; (05) 58 73 04 83. 🎨 Festival des Abbayes (Jun); La Compostellane (late Jul, every two years); Festival Nuits d'Été en Pays d'Orthe (Aug).

The spot where Sorde-l'Abbaye now stands has been continuously inhabited since prehistoric times. The Falaise du Pastou, a cliff opposite the Gave d'Oloron, contains four rock shelters (not open to the public) dating from the Magdalenian period (around 12,000 BC). For thousands of years, a natural fault in the cliff here provided a passage between France and Spain. From the 10th century, it was regularly used by pilgrims on their way to Compostela, and the village became an important stopping-point. In the Bourg-Vieux, the town's historic centre, is the **Abbaye Saint-Jean**, now a World Heritage Site. Benedictine monks, who settled here from around 975, founded it in the 12th century. Destroyed in the 16th century, during the Wars of Religion, and rebuilt in the 17th century and again by a Maurist community in the 18th century, the abbey was abandoned during the French Revolution. A medicinal herb garden has been re-created in front of it, which looks down on to the river. Next to the monastery buildings, now in ruins, is a Romanesque church with elements dating from the late 11th century (such as the mosaic floor in the choir) and the 12th century (the apse, doorway and carved capitals). There is also an underground boathouse with a vaulted ceiling, which opens on to the river. This boathouse, the only one of its kind in France, was used for storing cereals.

East of the monastery stands the 16th-century abbot's house, built on the site of a Gallo-Roman villa. Now privately owned, the house is not open to visitors, but the remains of 4th-century baths and mosaic floors can be seen. Sorde-l'Abbaye is now the largest producer of kiwi fruit in France.

🔒 **Abbaye Saint-Jean**
Place de l'Église.
Tel (05) 58 73 09 62. ⬜ Nov–Mar: Mon–Fri; Apr–Oct: Tue–Sun. 🎦 ✂

Ruins of the monastery buildings at the Abbaye Saint-Jean at Sorde

The bullring at Dax, a major bull-running venue, built in 1913

Dax ⑫

Road map B4. 🏃 20,000. 🚗 🚌
ℹ️ 11 cours Foch (05) 58 56 86 86.
🛒 Sat & Sun (covered market,
Halles, place Saint-Pierre).
🎭 Festival de la Comédie (Jun);
Festival des Abbayes
(Jun); Paso Passion
(Aug); Festival Toros y
Salsa (Sep); Festival
d'Art Sacré (Oct).

Dax, once a
lake settlement,
stretches out along
the banks of the
Adour between
flatlands and the
Pyrenees. Under
Roman rule, the
town grew, as it prospered
from its thermal springs. In
the 19th century, the arrival
of the railways made Dax the
foremost spa town in France.
In the centre, with its narrow
medieval streets, the town's
famous therapeutic waters
gush out of the Fontaine
Chaude, also known as the
Fontaine de la Nèhe.

The **Musée Jean-Charles
de Borda** was transferred in
2006 to the **Chapelle des
Carmes**, in the west of the
town. The museum traces the
town's past from prehistory,
through the Middle Ages to
present-day Dax. There is
also an art exhibition devoted
to Landais landscapes, and
temporary exhibitions of
modern art. The **Musée
Georgette-Dupouy** displays
paintings by this 20th-century
artist. In the north, along Parc

*La Landaise au
Chapeau, Musée
Georgette-Dupouy*

Théodore-Denis, are the
remains of Gallo-Roman walls,
and the town's bullring,
which was built in 1913.

The **Parc du Sarrat** is laid
out with an unusual mixture
of formal, Japanese and
vegetable gardens.
Many of the plants
and trees in the
gardens are rare
and protected
species. Further
south is the **Musée
de l'Aviation Légère
de l'Armée de
Terre**, a museum of
light army aircraft
where the exhibits
include vintage
army helicopters.
There is also a gallery of
aviation photography.

🏛 **Musée de Borda**
La Chapelle des Carmes.
Tel (05) 58 74 12 91.
◯ Mar–Nov: Tue–Sat.
📷 🎫

🛕 **Chapelle des Carmes**
11 bis rue des Carmes.
Tel (05) 58 74 12 91.

🏛 **Musée Georgette-Dupouy**
25 rue Cazade. **Tel** (05)
58 56 04 34. ◯ daily. 📷

🌿 **Parc du Sarrat**
Rue du Sel-Gemme. **Tel** (05) 58 56
86 86. ◯ Mar–Nov: Tue, Thu & Sat.
📷 🎫

🏛 **Musée de l'Aviation
Légère de l'Armée
de Terre** 58 avenue de
l'Aérodrome.
Tel (05) 58 74 66 19.
◯ Mar–May & Sep–Nov:
Tue–Sat pm; Jun–Aug: Mon–
Sat pm. 📷 🎫

Environs

The village of **Saint-Paul-lès-
Dax**, which lies 2km (1.5
miles) west of Dax, has an
11th-century church with
carved reliefs. Also worth
visiting here are the Forges
d'Ardy, an old metalworks,
and the house of the writer
Pierre Benoit (1886–1962),
who was a member of the
Académie Française. It is now
a museum of his life and work.

🏛 **Musée Pierre-Benoit**
650 avenue Pierre-Benoit.
Tel (05) 58 91 29 16. 📷 🎫 May–
15 Oct: Thu. 🎫 call in advance.

Montfort-
en-Chalosse ⑬

Road map B4. 🏃 1,400. 🚌
ℹ️ 25 place. Foch (05) 58 98 58 50.
🛒 Wed am. 🎭 Fêtes Patronales
(Jul); Festival Music'Arts (Jul); Fête
des Vendanges à l'Ancienne (Oct).

This ancient *bastide* town lies
in the heart of the Chalosse, a
fertile area that produces
high-quality beef, as well as
ducks that are fed on maize
grown on the Landes'
flatlands to produce the area's
famous foie gras. The fact that
Montfort was an important
stopping place on the route to
Compostela can be seen from
its church, the Église Saint-
Pierre. It has a 12th-century
nave and its tower dates from
the 15th century. The **Musée
de la Chalosse** is housed in a
17th-century estate, the manor
house and its outbuildings
providing a perfect setting for
the re-creation of daily life in
19th-century Chalosse.

🏛 **Musée de la Chalosse**
Domaine de Carcher. **Tel** (05) 58
98 69 27. ◯ Apr–Oct: Tue–Sun;
Nov–Mar: Tue–Fri. ● 15 Dec–Jan.
📷 🎫

11th-century relief in Église de
Saint-Paul-lès-Dax

The 17th-century Château de Gaujacq, near Pomarez

Pomarez ⑭

Road map B4. 1,479. 🚉 🚌
ℹ️ district tourist office in Amou
(05) 58 89 02 25. 🔄 Mon am.
🎭 Fête du Printemps (Mar); Festival
Art et Courage (Apr).

Although Pomarez, on the
Adour, is an old-established
river port, few traces of its
history remain. Popularly
known as a mecca for bullrunning, the town is a major
centre for this sport, which
has an enthusiastic following
in the Landes.

The Café Laborde, in
the centre, has a museum
of bullfighting, with a wide
array of exhibits. The
museum also demonstrates
how the rules of Gascon
bullfighting were formally set
out in 1830s. Nearby is the
town's covered bullring. It is
in this arena that bull-runners
parade to music before
performing breathtaking feats
of agility, as they deftly avoid
the charging beasts, which are
raised in local *ganaderías*
(cattle farms). Working in
teams, or *cuadrillas* (*see
pp26–7*), and dressed in
white trousers and a bolero,
they leap, dodge and make
their passes, while wind
bands, known as *bandas*,
play. In order to prevent
the bulls from goring the
bull-runners, the tips of
their horns are sheathed.

Environs
1km (0.5 miles) west of
Pomarez lies the 17th-century
Château de Gaujacq. The
Marquis de Montespan retired
to the château to seek solace
following his wife's liaison
with the king, Louis XIV.

♣ **Château de Gaujacq**
Gaujacq. **Tel** (05) 58 89 01 01.
◯ Jul–Aug: daily; Thu–Tue am
during rest of the year. 🎟️ 🖼️

Brassempouy ⑮

Road map B4. 268. 🚉 Orthez
or Dax. ℹ️ regional tourist office at
Amou (05) 58 89 02 25.

Founded in the 13th century,
this ancient *bastide* town is
associated with the famous
Vénus of Brassempouy, a
Stone Age figurine of a
woman that was discovered
in the Grotte du Pape, a
prehistoric cave near the
town, in 1894. Carved in
mammoth ivory more than
20,000 years ago, this figure is
the earliest representation of a
human face that has so far
come to light. It is on display
at the Musée des Antiquités
Nationales de Saint-Germain-
en-Laye, near Paris. A copy of
the figure can be seen in the
**Maison de la Dame de
Brassempouy**, next to the
Château de Poudenx, along
with other replicas of
prehistoric figures from
France and elsewhere, dating
from 35,000–15 000 BC.

🏛️ **Maison de la Dame
de Brassempouy**
Tel (05) 58 89 21 73. ◯ mid-
Feb–Jun & Oct–mid-Nov: Tue–Sun
pm; Jul–Sep: daily pm. ⬛ mid-
Nov–mid-Feb. 🎟️ Jun–Sep. 🖼️

SPAS IN THE LANDES
The Landes is the site of France's foremost spas. The
curative powers of the region's thermal waters and warm-
mud treatments were already famous in Roman times. Dax
is the region's oldest-established spa town, and its warm waters
are renowned for their pain-relieving properties. The spring
waters and warm mud at Eugénie-les-Bains, Saubusse,
Prechacq-les-Bains and Tercis also attract people seeking
cures for rheumatism and those wanting to lose weight.

The thermal springs at Dax, enjoyed since Roman times

Tour of the Tursan ⑯

The Tursan is an area of lush green valleys, where maize, grown to fatten geese and ducks for *foie gras*, is the major crop. Tursan wine has been produced for centuries and, in the 11th century, Eleanor of Aquitaine had it exported to the English royal court. Light red, very dry white and rosé wines are made from grapes grown on 460ha (1,140 acres) of steep, terraced vineyards. The road over these hills follows a scenic route past wine estates, a spa town and some very picturesque buildings.

Tursan wine

Eugénie-les-Bains ④
This spa resort, opened in 1861, is named after Empress Eugénie. Michel Guérard, who has a restaurant here, offers gourmet dishes and special health menus *(see p266)*.

Larrivière ⑤
In this town is the Église Notre-Dame-du-Rugby, a church dedicated to rugby. The sport is very popular throughout southwest France.

MONT-DE-MARSAN
VILLENEUVE-DE-MARSAN
Grenade-sur-l'Adour
N 124
Adour
D 52
Montgaillard
D 11
AIRE-SUR-L'ADOUR
D 25
Babus
D 65

Samadet ①
Renowned for its clay and for timber, Samadet was the home of the Royal Faïence Factory, which closed in 1831.

Bas
D 65
Vielle-Tursan
D 68
Babus-Soubiran
D 11
Urgons
D 2
Babus

KEY

▬▬▬ Suggested itinerary

═══ Other roads

– – Route du Puy

❋ Viewpoint

0 km   3
0 miles   3

Gabas
D 944
D 211
D 11
Miramont-Sensacq

TIPS FOR DRIVERS

Tour length: about 90km (56 miles).
Stopping-off places: there are several good gîtes and farmhouse-inns in the region, as well as many opportunities for tasting and buying the Tursan's excellent homemade products. Information from the tourist office at Geaune (05) 58 44 50 01.

D 117
PAU

Pimbo ②
This ancient *bastide* town has one of the Landes' oldest abbey churches, a vestige of the Benedictine communities that settled here. Pimbo is also the departure point for walks through spectacular scenery.

Geaune ③
The capital of the Tursan, Geaune has cellars where visitors can sample locally produced wines. For information, contact the tourist office at Geaune on (05) 58 44 50 01.

4th-century marble relief on the sarcoophagus in Église Sainte-Quitterie

Aire-sur-l'Adour ⑰

Road map C4. 🎇 *6,868.* 🚊 *Mont-de-Marsan.* 🛈 *Place 19 mars 1962 (05) 58 71 64 70.* 🚌 *Tue & Sat: am.* 🎭 *Fêtes Patronales (3rd weekend in Jun); Festival de Théâtre (Oct); Festival de la Bande Dessinée (Dec).*

This picturesque town on the banks of the Adour also stands on the pilgrim route to Compostela, and is the gateway to the Tursan. The site was inhabited even before the Romans arrived in 50 BC. The former bishop's palace, built in the early 17th century, now houses the town hall. Next to it stands the 14th-Palais de l'Officialité, the old lawcourts. The Cathédrale Saint-Jean-Baptiste dates from the 12th century, with later alterations. The **Église Sainte-Quitterie-du-Mas**, on the Colline du Mas, is a World Heritage Site. The church's large 11th-century crypt contains the tomb of the patron saint of Gascony. Other notable features are the arches of the 12th-century choir, above which is a brick-built bell tower, and the Baroque pulpit, carved in 1770.

🏛 **Église Sainte-Quitterie-du-Mas**
At the top of rue Félix-Despagnet. *Tel (05) 58 71 64 70 or (06) 77 02 43 44.* 🕐 *mid-May–Sep: Mon–Sat; Oct–mid-May: Mon–Fri; by appointment out of season.* 🖼 🎟

Saint-Sever ⑱

Road map C4. 🎇 *4,666.* 🚊 *Mont-de-Marsan, then by bus.* 🚐 🛈 *Place du Tour-du-Sol (05) 58 76 34 64.* 🚌 *Sat am.* 🎭 *Nuits des Peñas (Jun); Fêtes du Quartier Péré (Aug); Semaine Taurine (Nov).*

Founded in 993, Saint-Sever is a strategically positioned town with a number of architectural jewels. Remains of the early settlement are clustered on the Plateau de Morlanne, which, with the town's former abbey and its surrounding streets, makes up one of Saint-Sever's two main districts.

The **Abbey de Saint-Sever**, a World Heritage Site, stands on a square lined with fine 18th-century town houses. First established in 988, the abbey was at its full glory in the 11th and 12th centuries. Damaged by fire, earthquakes and wars, the building was restored on several occasions but was abandoned in 1790. In the 19th century, this architecturally important structure underwent some questionable restoration. Built to a Benedictine plan, the church has 150 capitals. Their colourful painted decoration has been restored.

At the **Couvent des Jacobins**, founded in 1280 and later remodelled, the cloister, the church, the chapter room and the old refectory are open to visitors (although some may be closed from time to

The *Beatus* of Saint Sever, Bibliothèque Nationale

time). Among the exhibits in the museum of the history of the town is a copy of the *Beatus*, a commentary on the *Apocalypse of St John*, illuminated by Stephanus Garcia. The original is in the Bibliothèque Nationale, Paris.

🏛 **Abbaye de Saint-Sever**
Place du Tour-du-Sol.
Tel (05) 58 76 34 64. 🕐 *daily.* 🎟

🏛 **Couvent des Jacobins**
Place de la République.
Tel (05) 58 76 34 64. 🕐 *daily.* 🎟

Environs
The ancient bastide village of **Montaut**, which is situated 8km (5 miles) southwest of Saint-Sever on the D32, is well worth a visit.

Grenade-sur-l'Adour ⑲

Road map C4. 🎇 *2,305.* 🚊 *Mont-de-Marsan.* 🛈 *1 place des Déportés (05) 58 45 45 98.* 🚌 *Mon & Sat am.* 🎭 *Fêtes Patronales (Jun).*

A bastide town founded by the English in 1322, Grenade-sur-l'Adour has 14th- and 15th-century houses and an attractive church, with a Gothic apse, dating from the late 15th century. The **Petit Musée de l'Histoire Landaise** holds a collection of pieces relating to popular traditions and a display of costumes.

🏛 **Petit Musée de l'Histoire Landaise**
Rue de Verdun. *Tel (05) 58 76 05 25.* 🕐 *Wed–Fri pm.* 🖼 🎟

Environs
Bascons, 4km (2.5 miles) north of Grenade is a bullrunning centre *(see pp26–7)*. It has a chapel and a **museum** with exhibits on the history of this popular regional sport. Displays include 19th-century posters advertising bullrunning events, and a collection of early 20th-century postcards attesting to the exploits of leading bullrunners.

🏛 **Musée de la Course Landaise**
Bascons. 🕐 *May–Oct: Wed–Fri pm. Tel (05) 58 52 91 76.* 🖼 🎟

The 14th-century Donjon Lacataye, with the Musée Despiau-Wlérick

Mont-de-Marsan ㉕

Road map C4. 👥 *32,000.* 🚃 🚌
ℹ️ *6 place. du Général-Leclerc*
(05) 58 05 87 37. 🛒 *Tue & Sat am.*
🎭 *Festival d'Art Flamenco,*
Fête de la Madeleine (Jul).

Mont-de-Marsan, the Landes'
administrative centre since
1790, is set on the banks of
the Midou and Douze rivers,
which join to form the
Midouze. Nicknamed the
"Three-River Town", Mont-de-
Marsan is a lively centre
of trade. Top Spanish bullfighters also come to take
part in bullfights here.

🏛 Musée Despiau-Wlérick

Donjon de Lacataye, 6 place
Marguerite-de-Navarre. *Tel (05) 58
75 00 45.* 🕐 *Tue & public hols.* 🎫
free on Mon. 🅿️

The Musée Despiau-Wlérick,
in the Donjon Lacataye, a
14th-century fortress, is the
only museum in France that is
devoted to French figurative
sculpture of the first half of
the 20th century. On show
here is the work of artists
from Mont-de-Marsan,
including Charles Despiau
(1874–1946) and Robert
Wlérick (1882–1944). Other
exhibits include works by

Alfred Auguste Janniot
(1889–1969), a sculptor of
the Art Deco period.

🏠 Église de la Madeleine
Rue Victor-Hugo.
This Neo-Classical church,
built in the early 19th century,
contains a high altar created
by the Mazetti brothers in the
18th century.
   Walking up towards the
Douze river, visitors will see
two **Romanesque houses**
at 6 and 24 bis rue
Maubec, built of the
local shelly stone.

🌿 Parc Jean Rameau
Entrance on place
Francis-Planté.
This 6-ha (15-acre)
park is named after
Jean Rameau
(1858–1942), the
Landes novelist
and poet. It was
created in 1793 and
now contains
sculptures and
Japanese-style
gardens, which are planted
with 80 different species of
tree and 165 types of plant.

Apollon by
Charles Despiau

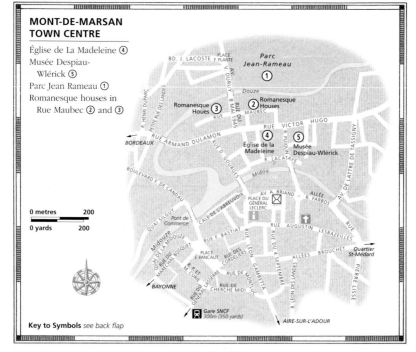

MONT-DE-MARSAN TOWN CENTRE

Église de La Madeleine ④
Musée Despiau-
   Wlérick ⑤
Parc Jean Rameau ①
Romanesque houses in
   Rue Maubec ② and ③

0 metres   200
0 yards   200

Key to Symbols *see back flap*

For hotels and restaurants in this region see pp250–52 and pp266–7

Half-timbered arcaded houses on Place Royale, Labastide-d'Armagnac

Quartier Saint-Médard
East of the centre is a 23-ha (57-acre) zoological garden, the **Parc de Nahuque**. At the end of avenue de Villeneuve. is the **Église Saint-Médard**.

🌼 **Parc de Nahuques**
Route de Villeneuve.
Tel (05) 58 75 94 38. ◐ Sat–Sun & public hols am.

Labastide-d'Armagnac ㉑

Road map C3. 🎋 700. 🚉 ℹ️ *Place Royale* (05) 58 44 67 56. 🛒 *Local produce market: Jul–Aug: Sun.* 🎉 *L'Armagnac en Fête (late Oct).*

Set in lush surroundings, this *bastide* town was founded by Bertrand VI, Comte d'Armagnac, in 1291, at a time when the area was held by Edward I of England.

The town has 13th-century houses, as well as a 15th-century wash-house. Around place Royale, the town's arcaded central square, are 14th–17th-century half-timbered houses. In the 15th-century Gothic church is a painted wooden *pietà*, which dates from the same period. The fortified bell tower is a sign of the town's turbulent history.

The **Écomusée de l'Armagnac** is an open-air museum that shows how Armagnac is made. It is said to be the oldest style of brandy in the world and has been exported from this area since at least the late 15th century or early 16th century. Also of interest here is **Notre-Dame-des-Cyclistes**, an 11th-

Painted *pietà*, Labastide

century Romanesque chapel dedicated to cycling and bicycle-touring. This unusual chapel has a museum, created by the Abbé Massie in 1959. It has numerous jerseys donated by former cycling champions, including Louis Bobet, Eddy Merckx and Lance Armstrong, as well as bicycles that were ridden in the Tour de France.

🏛 **Écomusée de l'Armagnac**
4 km (3 miles) southeast of Labastide. *Tel* (05) 58 44 88 38. ◐ Nov–Mar: Mon–Fri; Apr–Oct: daily (Sat–Sun pm only). 🎫 📷 for groups.

⛪ **Notre-Dame-des-Cyclistes**
Quartier Géou, on the road to Cazaubon. *Tel* (05) 58 44 86 46. ◐ May–Jun & Sep–mid-Oct: Tue–Sun; Jul–Aug: daily.

Environs
The **Domaine Départemental d'Ognoas**, 10km (6 miles) northeast of Labastide, is an estate with an experimental farm. Here 200 cows graze peacefully amid 25ha (62 acres) of Armagnac-producing grapes. Visitors can see how Armagnac is distilled using traditional methods.

Domaine Départemental d'Ognoas
Arthez-d'Armagnac. *Tel* (05) 58 45 22 11. ◐ May–Sep & public hols: daily (Sat–Sun & public hols pm only); Oct–Apr: Mon–Fri. 🎫 📷

ARMAGNAC

Bottles of Armagnac and a wide-bowled brandy glass

Exported since the late Middle Ages, Armagnac is a brandy that has probably been made since ancient Gaulish times. Particular varieties of grape (such as Baco 22A, Colombard, Folle Blanche or Ugni Blanc) are harvested in October. Their juice is extracted and distilled using a copper still. The brandy is aged for two years in oak barrels, from which it acquires its light brown colour and distinctive flavour. It is then bottled. Armagnac should be drunk from a wide-bowled glass.

PAYS BASQUE

*O*n the western side of the département of Pyrénées-Atlantiques
lies the Pays Basque (Basque Country), between the Adour river
and the Pyrenees. From Hendaye northwards to Anglet, it is
bordered by the Atlantic Ocean, with a coastline of clean, sandy beaches
to which tourists flock year after year. Inland, picturesque villages dot
the wide expanses of lush, unspoilt greenery, grazed by flocks of sheep.

Since the early 20th century, when the coastal resorts of the Pays Basque began to develop, most visitors have come to the region for its fine beaches. The attractive hinterland, however, has a rich historical heritage. There is evidence of settlement in this part of France going back to Neolithic times (5000–2000 BC). Later it was invaded by the Celts, then the Romans, who in turn were driven out by Germanic tribes from the east. In 778, the Franks, led by the Emperor Charlemagne, were repulsed, as was an invasion by Louis IX of France (1226–1270) in 824. After this the Pays Basque became part of the newly created kingdom of Pamplona.

In 1530, Charles V (1364–1380) made Basse-Navarre part of France, with Labourd and Soule, the other northern provinces of the region, being added in 1589. Spain retained Biscay, Guipuzcoa, Alava and Navarre. In 1659, the Peace of the Pyrenees brought about a reconciliation between France and Spain, which was consolidated by the marriage of the young Louis XIV of France to the Spanish infanta at Saint-Jean-de-Luz in 1660.

At the end of the 18th century, the Pays Basque entered a period of economic decline, which ended only with the birth of tourism. Today the region is not only a paradise for water-sports enthusiasts, but has also seen a renewal of interest in the ancient pilgrimage routes to Compostela that criss-cross it. These were designated as World Heritage Sites in 1993.

Down the centuries, despite the many changes of government, the Pays Basque has held on firmly to its national identity. Today, this is expressed as much as in the use of Euskara, the Basque language, as in the region's architecture, its religious and secular festivals, and its food specialities.

Partie de Cartes by Ramiro Arrue (1892–1971), showing four men playing *mus*, a Basque card game

◁ The Grande Plage at Biarritz

Exploring the Pays Basque

The part of the Pays Basque that lies in French territory comprises the three historical provinces of Basse-Navarre, Labourd and Soule. Basse-Navarre has several towns, most notably Saint-Palais and Saint-Jean-Pied-de-Port, that were once major stopping places on the ancient pilgrim routes to Santiago de Compostela. With the Gulf of Gascony to the west, Labourd consists of rolling hills and mountains, such as the Rhune, the Axuria and the Artzamendi, with many scenic villages, such as Ainhoa and Ascain. Soule, the wilder of the three areas, encroaches on the Pyrenean foothills that form part of Béarn. It has some truly stunning scenery, including the Forêt des Arbailles and Forêt d'Iraty, and three dramatic limestone canyons: the Gorges de Kakouetta, Gorges d'Holzarté and Gorges d'Olhadubi.

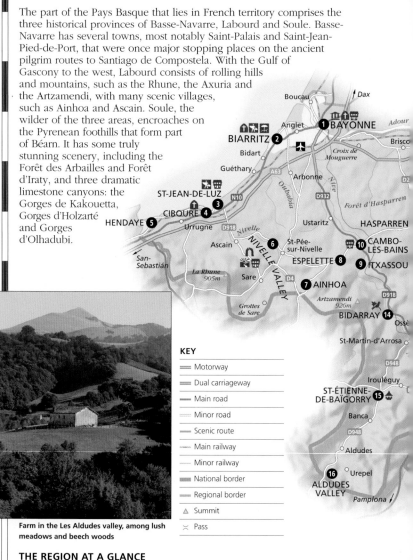

Farm in the Les Aldudes valley, among lush meadows and beech woods

KEY

▬▬	Motorway
▬▬	Dual carriageway
▬▬	Main road
····	Minor road
▬▬	Scenic route
▬▬	Main railway
—	Minor railway
▬▬	National border
▬▬	Regional border
△	Summit
╳	Pass

THE REGION AT A GLANCE

GETTING AROUND

Biarritz-Anglet-Bayonne is the regional airport. There is also a TGV (high-speed train) service between Paris and Bayonne. Bayonne is accessible via two motorways, the A64-E80 from Toulouse and Pau, and by the A63-E5-E70 from the Landes and Bordeaux. From Bayonne, the D932 leads to Cambo-les-Bains. In the west, the D918 links Espelette, Ainhoa, Saint-Pée-sur-Nivelle and Ascain, in Labourd, then continues southward to Saint-Jean-Pied-de-Port. The D918 leads into the mountains of Soule, where the villages of Larrau and Sainte-Engrâce, and the Gorges d'Holzarté and de Kakouetta are found.

Rocks shaped by the action of the waves on Plage Miramar in Biarritz

SEE ALSO

- *Where to Stay* pp252–3
- *Where to Eat* pp268–9

Orthez

13 BIDACHE

Notre-Dame-de-Belloc

Donjon

12 LA BASTIDE-CLAIRENCE

Masparraute

Orthez

Guinarthe-Parentier

Grotte d'Isturitz & Grotte d'Oxocelhaya

Garris

Laàs

Méharin

18 ST-PALAIS

Nabas

Iholdy

Sus

PYRÉNÉES - ATLANTIQUES

Gave d'Oloron

Irissarry

Ostabat

Gurs

Col d'Osquich

Espès-Undurein

L'HÔPITAL-ST-BLAISE **19**

Lacarre

Ordiarp

20 MAULÉON-LICHARRE

Oloron-Ste-Marie

7 ST-JEAN-PIED-DE-PORT

Gotein

Bastida

Aussurucq

Trois Villes

MASSIF DES ARBAILLES

22 TARDETS-SORHOLUS

Aramits

21

Laguinge-Restoue

Arette

Ahusquy

St Sauveur

FORÊT D'IRATY

23

26 D26

GORGES D'HOLZARTÉ & GORGES D'OLHADUBI **24** **25**

LARRAU

27 STÉ-ENGRÂCE

Pic d'Orhy 2017m

Col de Larrau

26 GORGES DE KAKOUETTA

Traditional Basque houses in Saint-Jean-Pied-de-Port

Train on the narrow-gauge railway up the Rhune mountainside

0 km   10
0 miles   10

Street-by-Street: Bayonne ❶

The cultural capital of the northern Pays Basque,
Bayonne grew and prospered from maritime
trade and its strategic position near the border
with Spain. It was long held by the English but
was finally taken by the French in 1451. In the
16th century Bayonne also opened its gates to
many Jewish refugees, who came here to escape
persecution during the Spanish and Portuguese
Inquisitions. At the confluence of
the great Adour, near its estuary,
and the smaller Nive, Bayonne
has a remarkable architectural
heritage. It is also well
known for its August
festivals and for holding
the longest-established
bullfighting fiestas in France.

★ Musée Basque
*This museum, in the late
16th-century Maison
Dagourette, documents every
aspect of Basque culture.*

Place de la Liberté
In this square the keys
of the city are thrown into
the crowd at the start of
the city's August festivals.

PLACE
DE LA
LIBERTÉ

Theatre
*Set on the Nive,
at the point
where it joins the
Adour, the theatre
was built in 1842.
It houses the town
hall, from whose
balcony Bayonne's
festivals are announced.*

Château-Vieux

| 0 metres | 200 |
| 0 yards | 200 |

**★ Cathédrale
Sainte-Marie**
*This Gothic
building stands in
the heart of Bayonne's
historic centre. Its twin spires
are among the city's best-known
symbols. The cathedral's 14th-century
cloister is particularly fine.*

Map labels: RUE LAFFITTE · RUE BOURGNEUF · RUE MARSAN · PONT MAYOU · QUAI DES CORSAIRES · NIVE · QUAI DUBOURDIEU · PONT MARE · RUE BERNÈDE · LORMOND · RUE · RUE VICTOR HUGO · RUE PORTS-DE-CASTETS · RUELLE · GARDIN · RUE DU PORT NEUF · RUE DE · ORBE · RUE · THIERS · PLACE PORTES · RUE DES GOUVERNEURS · PLACE DU CHATEAU VIEUX · PLACE VANSTEENBERGHER · RUE MON · RUE DES PRÉBENDES · RUE DOUER · RUE

Église Saint-André

Built in the 19th century, this church contains an important painting of the Assumption by Léon Bonnat, and an organ of 1863 presented by Napoleon III.

VISITORS' CHECKLIST

Road map A4. Baiona *in Basque.*
42,000. Biarritz-Anglet-Bayonne 8km (5 miles) south of Bayonne. Place des Basques; (05) 59 46 01 46.
daily. Foire au Jambon (mid-Apr), Fêtes de Bayonne (early Aug), bullfights (Jul–Sep).

★ Musée Bonnat
The collection of paintings in this gallery includes works by Rubens, El Greco, Degas, Titian, Raphael, Watteau, Delacroix and Goya.

Nive Embankment
A popular place for a stroll in summer, the embankment along the Nive is filled with music and dancing in the festival season. It is now lined with restaurant terraces, but in the past it was where catches of fish and goods arriving from the Americas were unloaded.

RUE DES LISSES
MARENGO
TRINQUET
RUE PONTRIQUE
RUE
TONNELIERS
RUE DE COURSIC
RUE DES
GALUPERIE
MANDANT ROQUEBERT
PONT PANNECAU
POISSONNERIE
DE LA
ESPAGNE

STAR SIGHTS

★ Cathédrale Sainte-Marie

★ Musée Basque

★ Musée Bonnat

KEY

– – – Suggested route

Citizens of Bayonne in festival costume in the old city centre

Exploring Bayonne
The best way to explore the city is to start with the south bank of the Adour, then walk along the Nive. Half-timbered Basque houses line the embankment, their dark red or green shutters giving the place its unique character.

Historic city centre
Until the 17th century, the old city, which clusters round the cathedral, was criss-crossed by canals. Some streets, like rue du Port-Neuf, were created when the canals were filled in. Rue Argenterie is named after the goldsmiths who had their workshops here, while rue de la Salie is in the cloth and spice merchants' quarter.

Nive Embankment
Starting at place de la Liberté, the Nive embankment runs past the covered market and open-air marketplace. Quai Jauréguiberry, with its typical Bayonne houses, and rue de Poissonnerie, a little further on, were hives of activity when Bayonne formed a major port for goods from the New World.

Château-Vieux
Rue des Gouverneurs.
Built in the 12th century and extended in the 17th, the castle incorporates elements of a Roman fort. It was once home to Bayonne's English governor, and two French kings, François I and Louis XIV, stayed here. It is not open to public, but visitors can walk into the courtyard.

🏛 Musée Basque

Maison Dagourette, 37 quai des Corsaires. *Tel (05) 59 46 61 90.* 🕐 *Mon & public hols (except Jul & Aug).* 🎫 🆓 *free for those under 18; combined entry to Musée Bonnat.* **www**.musee-basque.com

The museum is in the Maison Dagourette, a superbly restored 16th-century house that is listed as a historic monument. The collections, which have grown since the museum's foundation in 1922, concentrate on Basque culture. Laid out in 20 rooms, they give an insight into the folk art and customs of the Pays Basque. Displays cover a number of different themes, including local farm life and sea and river trade, as well as theatre, music, dance, games and sports, with a room devoted to pelota *(see p50)*. There are also sections on everyday clothing and traditional costume, architecture, religious and secular festivals and burial customs. Among the paintings are depictions of typical local scenes and activity.

🏢 Place Paul-Bert

In August, during Bayonne's festival season, this square in Petit Bayonne is where young cows are let loose as part of the traditional bull-running events. Nearby is the 19th-century **Église Saint-André**, where mass is celebrated in Basque. Directly opposite the church is **Château-Neuf**, built in the 15th century during the reign of Charles VII. It forms part of the defences that were later built around the city. In summer, the castle is the venue for large-scale temporary exhibitions mounted by the Musée Basque.

Game of Pelota by the Ramparts of Fontarabia, in the Musée Basque by Gustave Colin

🏢 Quartier Saint-Esprit

This district on the north bank of the Adour, east of **Pont Saint-Esprit**, is still largely working-class, with quite a cosmopolitan feel. It is where immigrants settled, especially Jews driven out of Spain and Portugal from the mid-16th century onward, helping build up sea trade. A synagogue and a Jewish cemetery are two vestiges of this period.

Environs

The **Croix de Mouguerre**, 8.5km (5 miles) from Bayonne, commemorates the fallen in a battle fought in 1813, during the Napoleonic Wars, between the English, led by Wellington, and the French, led by Maréchal Soult. From here the views of the Pyrenees, Bayonne, the Adour and the Atlantic Ocean are stunning.

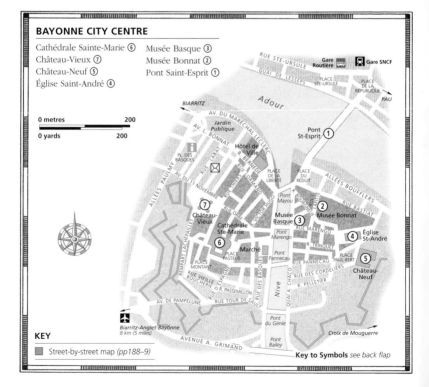

BAYONNE CITY CENTRE

Cathédrale Sainte-Marie ⑥
Château-Vieux ⑦
Château-Neuf ⑤
Église Saint-André ④
Musée Basque ③
Musée Bonnat ②
Pont Saint-Esprit ①

0 metres   200
0 yards   200

KEY

◼ Street-by-street map (pp188–9)

Key to Symbols *see back flap*

Musée Bonnat

Occupying a 19th-century building, the Musée Bonnat contains over 5,000 works of art. These date from antiquity right up to the early decades of the 20th century. The galleries are arranged round an inner courtyard and contain paintings, sculpture and ceramics, including works by Goya,

Ceramic platter (16th-century)

Rubens, Ingres, Degas, Van Dyck, Géricault and other major artists. Most of the pieces on display were collected by Léon Bonnat (1822–1922), a native of Bayonne, who was a very fashionable portrait painter.

The Bather (1807) by Ingres, one of the Musée Bonnat's finest works

ANTIQUITIES

The basement contains the museum's collection of Egyptian, Greek and Roman antiquities, among which are some very rare pieces.

PAINTINGS

This eclectic collection of 19th-century pictures contains studies by Géricault, Delacroix, Corot and Degas, as well as Impressionist works. It also includes a dozen paintings and 95 drawings by Jean Auguste Dominique Ingres, amongst which is the museum's most famous painting, *The Bather* (1807).

PORTRAITS BY LÉON BONNAT

A native of Bayonne, Léon Bonnat painted striking portraits of important people in Parisian high society in the

late 19th and early 20th centuries. These included the writer Victor Hugo, society ladies and men from the world of politics. Bonnat's early works are also shown, and in the courtyard there is a large-scale painting by Henri-Achile Zo of Bonnat with his Basque and Béarnese pupils on the hills above Bayonne.

RESERVE COLLECTIONS

In order to show as many works as possible, the museum has six rooms in which an assorted mix of allegorical, animal and figure studies and other genres are hung together. Only a tenth of the museum's holdings can be seen on its three other floors.

SPANISH PAINTING

Léon Bonnat studied art at the Prado in Madrid and, as a collector, he showed a strong preference for the

Spanish Old Masters. This is reflected in the museum's collection of works by Goya – such as *Don Francisco de Borja*, a self-portrait and *San José de Calasanz's Last Communion* – and by El Greco, such as *The Duke of Benavente* and *Cardinal Don Gaspar de Quiroga*, as well as several paintings by Murillo and Ribera.

GALLERY OF RUBENS' SKETCHES

This unique collection consists of preparatory sketches made by Peter Paul Rubens (1577–1640) as designs for tapestries. They depict allegorical themes, created for the king of Spain, and scenes from the life of Henry IV of France. Delicate terracotta sculptures from the Cailleux Collection are also on display here.

LE CARRÉ

In a neighbouring building, Le Carré serves as an extension of the museum. It is used for temporary exhibitions of contemporary art.

🏛 **Musée Bonnat**
5 rue Jacques-Laffitte.
Tel (05) 59 59 08 52. ☐ Jul–Aug: daily. ● Sep–Jun: Tue & public hols.
🎫 🎫 free on first Sun in the month; joint entry to Musée Basque.
♿ www.musee-bonnat.com

🏛 **Le Carré**
9 rue Frédéric-Bastiat.
Tel (05) 59 59 08 52.
☐ pm, during temporary exhibitions.

The Raising of Lazarus (1853), an early painting by Léon Bonnat

Bayonne Cathedral

Built in the 12th and 13th centuries on the site of a Romanesque cathedral, the Cathédrale Sainte-Marie, also known as Notre-Dame-de-Bayonne, is one of Bayonne's most visible emblems. This imposing structure, in the northern Gothic style, with its tall twin spires, can be seen from afar. Located in the heart of the old city, it was an important stopping-place for pilgrims travelling to Santiago de Compostela in Spain. In the 19th century, it underwent extensive restoration after suffering damage during the French Revolution, making what stands today the result of around 800 years of continuous building work and renovation.

Detail of *Woman of Canaan* window

The Flight into Egypt
This biblical scene by Nicolas-Guy Brenet (1728–92) hangs in the Chapelle Saint-Léon. A pupil of François Boucher, Brenet revived the grand manner of painting historical and allegorical scenes in the second half of the 18th century. He executed large-scale religious works for a number of churches in France.

West door

★ **Cloister**
In the Flamboyant Gothic style, the cloister is on the south side of the cathedral. Three of its arcaded galleries survive. The cloister also served as a burial site and many tombs can still be seen here.

STAR FEATURES

★ Cloister

★ Vestry

★ The Woman of Canaan Window

Elegant arches, enclosing four smaller arches with trefoil windows above, line the cloister.

VISITORS' CHECKLIST

Tel (05) 59 59 17 82.
Cathedral ☐ Mon–Sat:
10–11:45am, 3–5:45pm; Sun:
3:30–5:45pm. 🗹 **Cloister** ☐
Jun–Sep: 9am–6pm; Oct–May:
9:30am–12:30pm, 2–5pm.
♿ through west door. 🗹

Great Organ
The cathedral's original organ was made in 1488, and the present organ case was installed in the early 18th century.

Nave

North door

★ The Woman of Canaan Window
(detail) This stained-glass window, made in 1531, is in the Chapelle Saint-Jérôme.

Entrance to the cloister

Choir
This is the oldest part of the cathedral. The ciborium (canopy) in the centre dates from the mid-19th century.

★ Vestry
The vestry has a Gothic doorway with intricate 13th-century carvings.

Biarritz ❷

Road map A4. *Miarritze* in Basque.
🏠 30,000. 🚉 🚌 🛈 1 square
d'Ixelles (05) 59 22 37 10.
🎭 Jul–Aug. 🛒 daily. 🎪 Fête des
Casetas (late Jun), Biarritz Surf Festival
(mid-Jul). **www**.ville-biarritz.fr

Until the late 19th century,
when sea-bathing came into
vogue, Biarritz was just a
small whaling port. This new
trend, fuelled by expansion of
the railways and the town's
popularity with Napoleon III
and Empress Eugénie, led to
its discovery by the wider
world. Since then, Biarritz,
with its elegant villas, has
attracted a cosmopolitan
crowd, who come to surf and
enjoy a little luxury.

Exploring Biarritz
The resort's famous **Grande
Plage** (Great Beach) stretches
out in front of the **casino**, an
Art Deco building dating from
1924. On the right stands the
impressive **Hôtel du Palais**,
built in the early 20th century
on the site of Villa Eugénie,
the former imperial residence.
In the distance is the **Phare de
la Pointe Saint-Martin**. The
248 steps in this lighthouse
lead up to the lantern, from
where there is a panoramic
view, stretching all the way
from Anglet to the Landes.
Plage Miramar, an extension

of Grande Plage, is backed by
luxurious Belle Époque villas,
the finest of which are Villa San
Martino and Villa Casablanca.
The **Russian Orthodox church**
in avenue de l'Impératrice was
built in the late 19th century.
Further along is an exhibition
space known as **Le Bellevue**,
in the Empire style, which has
an Art Deco rotunda. The
fishing harbour, created in
1870, sits in a sheltered inlet
above which stands the Église
Sainte-Eugénie.
The city's emblem is the
Rocher de la Vierge, which is
connected to the promenade
by an iron walkway built by
Alexandre Eiffel. The rock is
crowned by a statue of the
Madonna. The **Villa Belza**,
built 1895, looks out to sea.
It is an unusual house with a
turret and a peaked roof. The
Plage du Port-Vieux, south of
the rocks, leads on to the
Côte des Basques.

🏛 Chapelle Impériale
Rue Pellot. **Tel** (05) 59 22 37 10. 🕑
Jul–Aug: Tue, Thu, Sat pm; during rest
of year, call for opening times. 🎫 🎟
This chapel on place Sainte-
Eugénie is dedicated to Our
Lady of Guadalupe, Mexico's
Black Madonna. It was com-
missioned by Empress Eugénie
in 1864. The exterior is in a
combination of Byzantine
Romanesque and Moorish
styles, which were in vogue

during the Second Empire. The
interior has a painted ceiling,
exposed beams and *azulejos*
(Moorish-style tiles) made at
the Sèvres factory.

🏛 Musée de la Mer
Plateau de l'Atalaye. **Tel** (05) 59 22
33 44. 🕑 Apr–Oct: daily; Nov–Mar:
Tue–Sun. 🌑 two weeks in Jan. 🎫
In a 1935 Art Deco building,
this museum describes the
Gulf of Gascony's marine life.
It has several aquariums and
displays on fishing. Visitors can
watch seals swim underwater.

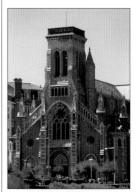

The 19th-century Chapelle Impériale
in Biarritz

🏛 Musée Historique
Rue Broquedis. **Tel** (05) 59 24 86 28.
🕑 Tue–Sat. 🎫 🎟
The history of Biarritz, from
small fishing village to high-
class resort, is covered by this
museum, in a former church.

🔦 Phare de la Pointe
Saint-Martin
Tel (05) 59 22 37 10. 🕑 Jul–Aug. 🎫
Built in 1834, the lighthouse
is 73m (240ft) high. Climbing
the 248 steps to the top is
worthwhile for the view of
the rocky Basque coastline.

Environs
Anglet, 4km (2.5 miles) east
of Biarritz, has a long beach,
as well as a pine forest, the
Chiberta golf course and the
legendary Grotte de la
Chambre-d'Amour. There are
fine views from the Chapelle
Sainte-Madeleine at **Bidart,**
5km (3 miles) south of
Biarritz, and at **Guéthary**, 2km
(1 mile) further south, the
Musée Municipal Saraleguinea
displays contemporary art.

The Grande Plage and lighthouse at Biarritz, from the marina

High Society in Biarritz

In the late 19th century, when Napoleon III and Empress Eugénie were putting Biarritz on the map as a coastal resort, the Second Empire gave way to the Belle Époque. It was then that Biarritz became an upper-class resort with a lively nightlife. Full of newly built Art Nouveau and Art Deco buildings, it held great allure for many prominent people, from both France and abroad. President Sadi Carnot and prime minister Georges

Caricature of bathers at Biarritz

Clemenceau and the writers Émile Zola and Edmond Rostand spent summer holidays here, and Sissi, or Elizabeth of Austria, came in search of a cure for her world-weariness. In the early 20th century, the town's casinos drew such celebrities as Sarah Bernhardt and the couturier Jean Patou. After World War II, the Marquess of Cueva threw extravagant parties, entertaining royalty and film stars such as Rita Hayworth, Gary Cooper, Bing Crosby and Frank Sinatra.

Edward VII, *the king of England, spent many summer holidays in Biarritz in the early 20th century.*

Bathing at Biarritz
was at its most fashionable in the first half of the 20th century.

BATHING

The fashion for sea bathing was born in Biarritz thanks to Napoleon III and Empress Eugénie, who reigned as "Beach Queen" until World War I and again in the interwar period. The heyday of that epoch's seaside holidays was brought to an abrupt end by the Wall Street crash of 1929 and the economic hardship of the 1930s that followed.

Charlie Chaplin *was one of a host of internationally famous people who regularly frequented Biarritz's many luxurious hotels, such as the Hôtel Miramar, in 1930s and 1940s.*

The British Royal Family, *following the lead set by King Edward VII, became regular visitors to Biarritz's sunny shores. This photograph of Edward, Prince of Wales, later the Duke of Windsor, and his younger brother George, Duke of Kent, was taken in 1925, while they were guests at the Villa Hélianthe.*

Saint-Jean-de-Luz ❸

Road map A4. *Donibane Lohizune* in Basque. 🏛 *13,600.* 🚪 🚌 ℹ *Place du Maréchal-Foch (05) 59 26 03 16.* 🛒 *Tue & Fri am.* 🎵 *Musique en Côte Basque & Académie Maurice Ravel (Apr & Sep).* **www**.saint-jean-de-luz.com

Once a pirates' stronghold, Saint-Jean-de-Luz lies in a bay with the Fort de Socoa on one side and Pointe de Sainte-Barbe on the other. For centuries the town grew rich from the fortunes amassed by its traders and pirates – who were at their most active from the 16th to the 19th centuries – and from whaling and cod, sardine and tuna fishing. The harbour is still a lively place today, and Saint-Jean-de-Luz has become a pleasant resort that is popular with surfers.

The coastline northeast of the town has many beaches: Erromardi, Lafitenia, Mayarco and Senix, shared with the neighbouring resort of Guéthary.

Place Louis-XIV, opposite the harbour and behind the tourist office, is lined with elegant residences. It is now filled with café terraces, laid out in the shade of plane trees. Rue Mazarin also has beautiful town houses, such as Maison de l'Infante, the Maison des Trois-Canons at no. 10, and Maison de Théophile de la Tour-d'Auvergne at no 18.

🛉 Église Saint-Jean-Baptiste

Rue Gambetta. **Tel** *(05) 59 26 08 81.* ⭕ *daily.* 🎟 *summer.*
Having been destroyed by fire in 1419 and then rebuilt in several stages, this sturdy looking church appears plain from the outside, but has a splendid 17th-century interior with a fine altarpiece. It was here that the marriage of Louis XIV and Marie-Thérèse of Austria took place on 9 June 1660 *(see p36).*

🏛 Maison Louis-XIV

Place Louis-XIV. **Tel** *(05) 59 26 01 56.* ⭕ *Jun–Sep: daily.* 🎟 🗲

Busy pedestrianized streets in the old quarter of Saint-Jean-de-Luz

This house was built in 1643 by Johannis de Lohobiague, a shipowner. Cardinal Mazarin (1602–1661), effectively ruler of France during the minority of Louis XIV, stayed here in 1660, as did Anne of Austria and Louis XIV himself, when he came to marry the infanta

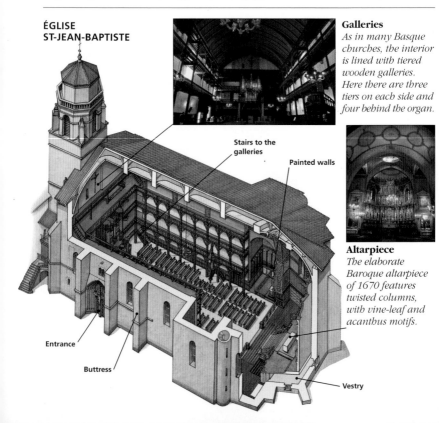

ÉGLISE ST-JEAN-BAPTISTE

Galleries
As in many Basque churches, the interior is lined with tiered wooden galleries. Here there are three tiers on each side and four behind the organ.

Stairs to the galleries

Painted walls

Altarpiece
The elaborate Baroque altarpiece of 1670 features twisted columns, with vine-leaf and acanthus motifs.

Entrance

Buttress

Vestry

Maison de l'Infante, on the harbour in Saint-Jean-de-Luz

Marie-Thérèse of Austria, to fulfil the terms of the Peace of the Pyrenees. Next door are **Maison Saubat-Claret**, with carved balconies, and the **Hôtel de Ville** (1654), which contains an equestrian statue of Louis by Bouchardon.

🏛 Maison de l'Infante
Quai de l'Infante. **Tel** (05) 59 26 36 82. ⬜ Jun–Sep: daily. 🎫 🖼
This house, also known as Maison Joanoenea and built in about 1640, belonged to the Haraneders, a shipowning family. The future queen of France stayed here in 1660.

🏛 Rue de la République
This street leads down to the sea front and **Grande Plage**. Having survived the fire of 1558, Maison Esquerrenea, at no. 17, is the town's oldest house. Like Maison Duplan at no. 10, it has a tower for observing ships entering the harbour. Off place Louis XIV is a pedestrianized street, **rue Gambetta**, with beautiful houses at nos. 18 and 20.

Environs
The town of **Urrugne**, 5km (3 miles) from Saint-Jean-de-Luz, has an interesting church, the 16th-century **Église Saint-Vincent**. It has a Renaissance doorway, a 45-m (148-ft) bell tower, an organ gallery and 22-m (72-ft) high wooden galleries. The **Château d'Urtubie**, which dates from 1341, was largely rebuilt in the 16th and 18th centuries. Louis XI stayed here in 1463.

⛪ Château d'Urtubie
RN 10. **Tel** (05) 59 54 31 15. ⬜ Mar–Oct: daily. 🎫 🖼

Ciboure ❹

Road map A4. *Ziburu* in Basque. 🏘 6,000. 🚉 ➡ *Saint-Jean-de-Luz.* 🛈 27 quai Maurice-Ravel (05) 59 47 64 56. ➡ Sun am. 🎉 Fête du Thon (second Sat in Jul). **www**.ciboure.fr

Just south of Saint-Jean-de-Luz, on the other side of the Nivelle River, is Ciboure. The town has many fine examples of traditional Basque architecture, with its whitewashed houses, red woodwork and balconies. The **Couvent des Récollets** was built in 1610 and, with the cloisters, it was used as a prison and tribunal during the French Revolution. On the quayside is a 17th-century house with a Dutch-style gabled façade: this is where the composer Maurice Ravel was born, and where the town's tourist office is now located.

The 16th-century **Église Saint-Vincent**, in rue Pocalette, has a fortified octagonal bell tower. The church's interior has wooden galleries arranged in three tiers, an impressive altarpiece and pictures from the Chapelle des Récollets.

The lighthouse here was built in 1936 to a design by the architect André Pavlovsky. The Fort de Socoa, built in the 17th century to defend the whaling port, stands at the tip of the harbour wall.

⛪ Couvent des Récollets
Quai Pascal-Elissalt. **Cloister**
Tel (05) 59 47 64 56. ⬜ daily. 🖼

Hendaye ❺

Road map A4. *Hendaia* in Basque. 🏘 12,000. 🚉 🚌 🛈 12 rue des Aubépines (05) 59 20 00 34. ➡ Wed & Sat am. 🎉 Fête Basque (2nd weekend in Aug). **www**.hendaye.com

The family resort of Hendaye, at the mouth of the Bidassoa river, has two distinct areas, Hendaye-Plage and Hendaye-Ville. The Église Saint-Vincent is notable for its 13th-century crucifix and a 17th-century altarpiece. The two distinctive rocks of Pointe Sainte-Anne mark the entrance to the Baie de Fontarrabie.

Environs
1.5km (1 mile) from Hendaye lies **Château d'Abbadia**, built by explorer Antoine d'Abbadia (1810–1897). Here odd oriental touches mix with the Gothic design.

⛪ Château d'Abbadia
Route de la Corniche. **Tel** (05) 59 20 04 51. ⬜ call ahead. 🎫 🖼

The sturdily built Neo-Gothic Château d'Abbadia at Hendaye

For hotels and restaurants in this region see pp252–253 and pp268–269

Train on the rack railway up the Rhune at Col de Saint-Ignace

Nivelle Valley ⑥

Road map A4.

Set against the backdrop of three soaring peaks – the Rhune, Mondarrain and Axuria – the landscape of this valley is a mix of rolling hills, open meadows and farmland, enclosed by neat hedges.

Ascain, 6km (4 miles) from the coast, nestles in the foothills of the Rhune. The village was immortalized by Pierre Loti (1850–1923) in his novel *Ramuntcho*. The old Labourd-style houses on the main square, together with the church, make a picturesque sight. Consecrated in 1626, in the presence of Louis XIII, the

Grottes de Sare, prehistoric caves in the Nivelle valley

church has an imposing west tower. Nearby is **Saint-Pée-sur-Nivelle**, which has 18th-century houses and a church, the Église Saint-Pierre, with tombstones – including one from the 16th century – set in the floor. Behind the church is the **Moulin Plazako Errota**, a 15th-century mill. It is no longer in use, but contains old grain-measures that were used by Basque millers. The state-owned forest has footpaths and bicycle tracks, as well as strangely shaped pollarded oaks. The **Lac de Saint-Pée**, 2km (1 mile) further on, via the D918, offers watersports activities.

The summit of the lofty **Rhune** (905m/2970ft) can be reached on foot or by a little train. The mountainsides here are dotted with megalithic monuments dating from the Neolithic period. Visitors will also see shepherds with their sheep, as well as *pottoks* and griffon vultures *(see p19)*.

The old smugglers' village of **Sare** has some fine 17th- and 18th-century Labourd-style houses *(see p22)*. Strolling through its various districts, visitors will come

across 14 oratories dedicated to the Madonna and various saints, built in thanksgiving by fishermen from the 17th century onwards.

Maison Ortillopitz, just outside Sare, is a stately 17th-century farmhouse. With half-timbered walls, a fine oak-beamed roof and thick stone walls, it is a typical *etxe*, or traditional Basque house *(see p22)*.

The **Grottes de Sare** lie 7km (4 miles) south of the village. Bones and flint tools that were discovered here show that these caves were inhabited in prehistoric times.

☷ Moulin Plazako Errota
Tel (05) 59 54 19 49.
◯ Jun–Sep: daily. ▨

✳ Lac de Saint-Pée
Tel (05) 59 54 11 69.
◯ Jul–Aug: daily. ▨

☸ Petit Train de la Rhune
Col de Saint-Ignace. *Tel* (05) 59 54 20 26. ◯ mid-Mar–mid-Nov. ▨

⋒ Grottes de Sare
Tel (05) 59 54 21 88. ◯ daily.
◯ Jan. ▨ ☑
www.grottesdesare.com

☷ Maison Ortillopitz
Tel (05) 59 85 91 92. ◯ Apr–Oct: daily. ☑ ▨ www.ortillopitz.com

---

POTTOKS

Since prehistoric times, the hills of the Pays Basque have been inhabited by a type of pony known as a *pottok* (pronounced "potiok"), meaning "little horse". *Pottoks* are hardy, having evolved in a harsh environment where food was scarce. They are typically bay or black and pot-bellied, with long manes, dainty legs and small hooves. These tiny horses are endangered but, in the 1970s, certain breeders began to take an interest in them. Once used for farm work or slaughtered for food, they are now protected and treated as the emblem of the Pays Basque.

Pottoks in their natural habitat, the hills of the Pays Basque

Ainhoa ⓓ

Road map A4. 🏘 611. 🚉
🚌 Bayonne, Saint-Jean-de-Luz.
ℹ️ Mairie (05) 59 29 92 60.

Said to be one of France's
prettiest villages, Ainhoa
has rows of splendidly
picturesque old houses with
red or green woodwork. Some
in the main street have carved
lintels. The 14th-century
church, in the main square, is
lined with galleries and
contains a gilt altarpiece. It
also has a five-tiered bell
tower and circular-topped
funerary stones in the
graveyard (see p29). A further
26 of these traditional Basque
gravestones can be found at
Notre-Dame-de l'Aubépine,
another church, higher up at
450m (1,477ft). Views from
here take in the Rhune peak,
the Atlantic and the frontier
district of Dancharia, in Navarre.

Espelette ⓔ

Road map A4. Ezpeleta in Basque.
🏘 1,900. 🚉 🚌 Cambo-les-Bains.
ℹ️ Château (05) 59 93 95 02. 🏪
Wed am & Sat (Jul–Aug). 🎪 Fête du
Piment (last weekend in Oct), pottok
market (last Tue–Wed in Jan).

Famous for its sweet red
peppers, this large village is
also noted as the birthplace
of Father Armand David
(1826–1900), who discovered
the great panda in China, as
well as a species of deer,
Elaphurus davdianus, which
is named after him. A plaque
marks Maison Bergara, where
he lived. Also worth a visit is

PIMENT D'ESPELETTE

**Strings of dried
piment**

Introduced into the Pays Basque from
Mexico in 1650, these sweet red peppers
first served as a medicine and only later as
a condiment and preservative. They are
used whole, either fresh or dried, or in
powdered form in many local dishes, and
even as a flavouring in chocolate. The
Gorria variety, known as *piment d'Espelette*,
is grown in ten villages around Espelette.
The peppers are picked in late summer,
threaded onto string and hung to dry,
often across the front of houses. The
symbol of Espelette, these peppers have an AOC, and a
festival in their honour is held on the last Sunday of October.

the 11th-century **Château des
Barons d'Ezpeleta**, which
now houses the village hall
and tourist office.
  The church, just outside,
has a painted ceiling, wooden
galleries, a 17th-century
altarpiece and a large bell
tower. In the cemetery are
ancient circular-topped
funerary stones and the Art
Deco tomb of the first woman
to become Miss France.

⚜ Château des Barons
d'Ezpeleta
145 rte Karrika-Nagusia. **Tel** (05) 59 93
95 02. ◯ Mon–Sat. 🔲 Sat pm, Sun.

Itxassou ⓕ

Road map A4/B4. Itsasu in Basque. 🏘
2,000. 🚉 Cambo. ℹ️ Mairie (05) 59
29 75 36. 🎪 Fête de la Cerise (first
Sun in Jun); Fête-Dieu (late Jun).

Itxassou is set in the heart of
a picturesque valley. In the
Urzumu quarter of the village
stands the 17th-century white-
walled Église Saint-Fructueux,

The village of Itxassou, capital of
black-cherry cultivation

which is lined with galleries
of turned and carved wood.
The cemetery contains over
200 circular-topped funerary
stones. Black cherries are a
speciality of the area and are
celebrated at a festival in
early June. Either fresh or
made into jam, these cherries
are delicious with a slice of
ewe's milk cheese (see p209).

Environs
1.5km (1 mile) from Itxassou,
a winding road runs alongside
the Nive river and the Gorges
d'Ateka-Gaitz as far as **Pas-de-
Roland**. According to legend,
Roland (see p204) pierced this
great rock with his sword,
Durandal. Here **Artzamendi**
(Basque for "Bear Mountain")
soars up to 926m (3,040ft)
and is within easy reach, by
car or on foot. Another gentle
walk along a marked path
leads up to the summit of
Mondarrain, at 750m (2461ft),
where there are ruins of a
Roman fortress that was
rebuilt in the Middle Ages.

White houses and the imposing bell tower at Espelette

Villa Arnaga, Edmond Rostand's house in Cambo-les-Bains

Cambo-les-Bains ⓾

Road map A4. *Kanbo* in Basque.
🏠 *4,500.* 🚆 *Cambo.* ⓘ *Avenue de la Mairie (05) 59 29 70 25.*
🚌 *Wed & Fri.* 🎭 *Festival de Théâtre (mid-Aug); Fête du Gâteau Basque (last Sun in Sep).*

Well known as a spa resort, Cambo-les-Bains is set above the Nive river. Many people, including artists, writers and other famous figures in the 19th and early 20th centuries, have come here to sample the sulphur- and iron-rich waters of its two springs. Amongst them were Napoleon III and the Empress Eugénie, who acquired a holiday home in Biarritz in 1856, the Spanish composer Isaac Albéniz, in 1909, and the painter Pablo Tillac, in 1921.

In clear weather, there are panoramic views of the river valley and the Pyrenees from rue du Trinquet and rue des Terrasses. The Église Saint-Laurent has a late 17th-century, Baroque altarpiece in gilded wood, with a central panel that depicts the martyrdom of St Laurence. In the graveyard are several examples of the circular-topped, Basque-style grave-stones *(see p29)*.

Avenue Edmond-Rostand leads to the hillside where Rostand built his home, **Villa Arnaga**, which is set in extensive gardens. Every room is decorated in a different style, including classical elements in the study. Displays relating to the writer's life and work fill the first-floor rooms.

🏛 **Villa Arnaga**
Route de Bayonne. **Tel** *(05) 59 29 83 92.* ☐ *Mar: Sat & Sun pm; Apr–Oct: daily.* 📷 📷

Hasparren ⓫

Road map B4. *Hazparne* in Basque.
🏠 *5,900.* 🚆 *Cambo-les-Bains, Bayonne.* ⓘ *2 place Saint-Jean (05) 59 29 62 02.* 🚌 *alternate Tue.*
🎪 *bull-running (Jul–Aug); Championnat de l'Irrintzina (Aug).*

Hasparren is surrounded by rolling hills and meadows grazed by flocks of sheep, and the landscape is dotted with villages and traditional half-timbered Basque farmhouses with white walls and red shutters. Once a centre for shoe-making and leather goods, Hasparren is now an industrial yet pleasant town.

The **Chapelle du Sacré-Cœur**, also known as the Chapelle des Missionnaires, was built in 1933. The walls of the nave are covered in huge frescoes depicting 48 saints, some of whom are shown with the instruments of their martyrdom. A Byzantine-style mosaic, *Christ in Majesty*, adorns the choir.

Maison Eyhartzea, in rue Francis-Jammes, at the entrance to the village, now houses a cultural centre, but from 1921 until his death in 1938 it was the home of the poet Francis Jammes.

Fresco in Chapelle du Sacré-Cœur

Environs
Between Cambo and Hasparren, the D22, known as the **Route Impériale des Cimes** (Mountaintop Road), offers panoramic views of the Nive valley, and of the Rhune, Artzamendi and Mondarrain mountain peaks. Turn off at a junction in the Pachkoenia district to return to Hasparren via Cambo-les-Bains and Bayonne-Saint-Pierre-d'Irube.

About 4 km (2 miles) from Hasparren, at **Ayherre**, there is a panoramic view of the Basque countryside. The Basque name for this village is *Eihera* which means "mill". There were 14 mills, but now only one is in working order. On the edge of the village stand the ruins of the former Château de Belzance, where the Treaty of Basse-Navarre was signed.

EDMOND ROSTAND

Cambo-les-Bains is closely associated with the writer Edmond Rostand (1868–1918). A member of the Académie Française and the author of the famous verse-drama *Cyrano de Bergerac* (1897), as well as *L'Aiglon* (1900) and *Chantecler* (1910), Rostand was a noted playwright and poet. Suffering from pleurisy, he came to Cambo in 1900 for its curative waters. He soon fell under its spell, and the following year had an elegant residence, the Villa Arnaga, built for himself and his family. Rostand lived here with his wife and two children for almost 15 years.

The Château de Gramont, at Bidache, above the Bidouze valley

About 13km (8 miles) from Hasparren are the **Grotte d'Isturitz** and **Grotte d'Oxocelhaya**, caves formed by an underground stretch of the Arbéroue river. Paintings and engravings of deer and horses, as well as bones, tools and a musical instrument made out of bone, were found here.

⋔ Grotte d'Isturitz and Grotte d'Oxocelhaya
Saint-Martin-d'Arbéroue. *Tel* (05) 59 29 64 72. ⬜ *Mar–mid-Nov.* 🖼
🖼 www.grottes-isturitz.com

La Bastide-Clairence ⓬

Road map B4. *Bastida* in Basque.
🏚 *900.* 🚉 *Bayonne.* 🚌 ▮ *Maison Darrieux (05) 59 29 65 05.* 🎨 *pottery market (second weekend in Sep).*

This beautiful *bastide* town, on the border with Gascony, was founded in 1312 by the king of Navarre. Its location very near Béarn allowed it to control traffic on the Adour river. In the Middle Ages, the village grew as a result of its weaving and leatherworking industries, as well as trade. The town still has its original medieval grid layout, with two main thoroughfares at right angles to six smaller streets, and half-timbered houses and arcades. The 14th-century Église Notre-Dame, in the upper part of the town,

stands in a courtyard with gravestones set into it. Further up the hill is a graveyard with about 60 headstones. This was the cemetery of a community of Sephardic Jews who came to the area from Portugal during the 17th century.

Environs
Located 3km (2 miles) from La Bastide-Clairence is the Benedictine abbey of **Notre-Dame-de-Belloc**. It was founded in 1875 and is inhabited by a community of monks who work the land and who publish books in Basque. The graveyard has a few circular-topped gravestones.

Bidache ⓭

Road map B4. *Bidaxune* in Basque.
🏚 *1,100.* 🚉 *Puyoô.* 🚌 *Bayonne.*
▮ *Rue des Jardins (05) 59 56 03 49.*

That Bidache was once the seat of a dukedom gives some idea of the town's historical importance. This is also evident from the ruins of the Château de Gramont, built by the duke here in the 13th century. It was remodelled several times up until the 18th century and has both medieval and Renaissance elements. The **Jewish cemetery** in the village is one of the oldest in France.

The Benedictine abbey of Notre-Dame-de-Belloc, near La Bastide-Clairence

Bidarray ⑭

Road map B4/B5. *Bidarrai* in Basque.
🏠 *700.* 🚉 *Pont Noblia-Bidarray.*
🚌 *Cambo-les-Bains.*
ℹ️ *Barbastaenea (05) 59 37 74 60.*

Pont-Noblia across the Nive river at Bidarray

This village is divided into
12 districts, each with typical
Basse-Navarre-style houses
(see p22). On the square at
the top of the hill stands a
small 12th-century church
with pink sandstone walls. Its
graveyard contains circular-
topped stones *(see p29)*.

The river Nive here is
suitable for watersports, and
several local centres organise
activities on the river. Being
located on the GR10, a long-
distance footpath, between
Ainhoa and Baïgorry, also
makes Bidarray a good starting
point for scenic walks up the
Iparla and Baygoura mountains
and Mont Artzamendi.

Environs

Ossès, 6km (4 miles) from
Bidarray, has fine half-
timbered houses, such as

Maison Harizmendi and
Maison Ibarrondo, and
houses with decorated lintels,
such as Maisons Arrosa and
Maison Arrosagaray. On the
square stands the Église Saint-
Julien, a 16th-century
Renaissance-style church with
a seven-sided bell tower and
a 17th-century Baroque
doorway. The interior has
carved wooden galleries, a
spiral staircase, and a
magnificent 17th-century
Baroque altarpiece.

Saint-Martin-d'Arrosa, 4km
(3 miles) away on the
opposite bank of the Nive,
has traditional houses with
carved lintels. The church, on
the promontory here, has a
gilded wooden altar and a
moulded ceiling. **Irrissary**, a
village at the centre of the
Pays Basque Nord, has a
remarkable 12th-century
priory hospital, which was
once the seat of a commander
of the Knights Templar St-Jean
de Jérusalem.

Aldudes Valley ⑯

At the head of the Aldudes
valley lies a region known as the
Pays Quint, or Kintoa. Although it
belongs to Spain, it is leased in
perpetuity to its inhabitants.
Like the Baztán, Erro and
Valcarlos valleys, over the
border in Spain, it is a land
of *estives* (summer pastures),
beech woods and isolated
farmsteads. Flocks of
black-faced sheep, known
as *manechs*, thrive here.

**Church at the
foot of the
valley**

**The church
at Les
Aldudes**

Venta Baztan ③
On the Spanish side of
the border, Basque
markets are known as
ventas. Found at
mountain passes,
ventas are good places
for buying souvenirs or
having a quick snack.

| 0 km | 0.5 |
| 0 miles | 0.5 |

Kuartela ④
At a spot near a disused
barracks, known as Kuartela,
drivers can turn off the N138
to go down to Urepel. This
narrow, twisting but scenic
route leads through beech woods
and lush green meadows.

N 138

N 138

*PAYS QUINT
OU KINTOA*

PAMPELUNE

Saint-Étienne-de-Baïgorry ⓯

Road map B5. *Baïgorri in Basque.*
🏠 *1,500.* 🚉 *Ossès.* 🚌 *Ossès.*
ℹ️ *Place de l'Église (05) 59 37 47 28.*
📷 *Journée de la Navarre (last week-end in Apr); Euskal Trial (Sep).*

From the central square where the *fronton* (pelota court) is located, there are fine views of Mont Buztanzelai and Mont Oilandoi, and over to Col d'Ispéguy. To the right of the main entrance to the 11th-century Romanesque **church** is the Porte des Cagots, a doorway for Baïgorry's *cagots*, villagers who were set apart for some unexplained reason. Their ghetto was in the Mitchelenea quarter, where there is a single-span bridge. Built in 1661, it is known locally as the **Roman bridge**.

With two medieval towers on its north side and two Renaissance parapets on the south, the **Château d'Etxauz** dominates Baïgorry. Its lord ruled here for 500 years. The castle has a small collection of items associated with Charlie Chaplin, who stayed here.

⛪ **Château d'Etxauz**
On the D949. *Tel (05) 59 37 48 58.*
◯ *phone for opening times.* 📷 🅿️

Environs

The vineyards of **Irouléguy**, 5km (3 miles) from Saint-Étienne, are the only ones in the northern Pays Basque to have their own **cave co-operative** (wine co-operative).

Just outside **Banca**, 8km (5 miles) away, are the remains of an 18th-century blast furnace, a vestige of the mines that were once active.

Les Aldudes has Navarre-style houses featuring red sandstone. At Salaisons des Aldudes, a meat-curing factory, visitors can learn about the Basque pork industry and sample its produce. Pierre Oteïza, the owner, has almost single-handedly revived the art of making traditional hams from *pie noir*, a local breed of black-spotted pig.

Large prehistoric stone circles stand on **Argibel**, a mountain west of the village.

🏛️ **Cave Coopérative d'Irouléguy**
On the D15. *Tel (05) 59 37 41 33.*
◯ *Mon–Fri (cave); Mon–Sat (shop).*
📷 🅿️

Château d'Etxauz in Saint-Étienne-de-Baïgorry

LES ALDUDES

Urepel ①
Gateway to the Pays Quint, Urepel is the birthplace of Fernando Aire, known as Xalbador (1920–76). He was a famous *bertxulari*, who would improvize in verse on any given theme. There is a memorial stone to him here.

TIPS FOR DRIVERS

Road map B5.
Tour length: *15km (9 miles), leaving Saint-Étienne-de-Baïgorry on the D948.*
Stopping-off places: *There is an auberge and small frontier super-market at Venta Baztán. The route passes meadows, beech woods and farmsteads, with many convenient stopping-places along the way.*

KEY

▬ Suggested route

═ Other roads

-·- Border with Spain

❋ Viewpoint

Larrategia ②
This area is typical of the Basque valleys, where most of the land is only suited to grazing livestock. Here visitors will find isolated farms and shepherds with their flocks.

The Nive river at Saint-Jean-Pied-de-Port, an important stopping-place for pilgrims to Compostela

Saint-Jean-Pied-de-Port ⑰

Road map B5. *Donibane Garazi in Basque.* 🏠 *1,400.* 🚗 🚌
ℹ️ *14 place Charles-de-Gaulle (05) 59 37 03 57 and (08) 10 75 36 71.*
🏢 *Mon.* 🎾 *game of bare-handed pelota main played in the trinquet (Mon); gastronomic fair (second week in Jul & third week in Aug); Basque strong-man contests (Jul–Aug).*

As the final stopping-place before the dangerous climb over the passes to Roncevaux, Saint-Jean-Pied-de-Port has been an important commercial town on the pilgrim routes to Santiago de Compostela since the 14th century. Known as the Garden of Navarre, this town, switched between sovereigns many times until 1589, when, under Henri IV, it became part of France.

Entry into the old town is from place Charles-de-Gaulle, through Porte de Navarre, a fortified gate with arrow-slits and battlements. Steps lead up to the wall-walk near the Citadelle, built in the 17th century. The attractive 14th-century Église Notre-Dame-du-Bout-du-Pont has pink sandstone columns and pillars. Maison Mansart, also built in pink sandstone, houses the town hall.

Rue de la Citadelle is lined with beautiful stone houses, with carved lintels and eaves over richly decorated beams.

One of the finest of these houses is Maison Arcanzola, built in 1510, with brick and half-timbered walls in its upper storey. Further up is the Prison des Évêques. In the 19th century it was used as a short-term prison, but the building dates from the times that the town was the seat of a bishopric – three times between 1383 and 1417. **Porte Saint-Jacques**, the gateway at the end of rue de la Citadelle, is a World Heritage Site, and pilgrims still pass through it.

Crossing the Nive by the picturesque Pont Notre-Dame to the rue d'Espagne quarter on the opposite bank, you will come to the ramparts. There is a covered market here, and a craft market is also held on Mondays.

Environs
10km (6 miles) away, just beyond Arnéguy and Valcarlos, in Spain, is **Roncevaux** (Roncesvalles in Spanish). The town lies below Col de Roncevaux (or Puerto d'Ibañeta), a pass at an altitude of 1,507m (4946ft). It has an 18th-century hostel, the 12th-century Chapelle de Sancti Spiritus and the 14th-century Église de Santiago. The town is 800km (500 miles) from Compostela and, for the pilgrims arriving there, the most arduous part of their journey was over.

BATTLE OF RONCEVAUX

15th-century illumination showing Charlemagne before the dead Roland

In 778, having attempted to lay siege to the then Moorish town of Zaragoza, the Christian army of the Holy Roman Emperor, Charlemagne, retreated to the Pyrenean passes. The exhausted rear guard, who were led by Charlemagne's nephew, Roland, were attacked by Vascons, who at the time supported the Moors, in the Roncevaux pass and suffered heavy losses. Roland himself was killed. A stone erected at Col d'Ibañeta stands in memory of these fallen heroes, whose deeds were immortalized in the *Chanson de Roland*, written over 300 hundred years later.

BASQUE LINEN

Basque linen is traditionally woven with stripes, which served to identify different families' linen at the village wash-house. Originally woven from flax on wooden handlooms, Basque linen is now made of both flax and cotton, using factory methods. Traditional patterns include variations on the Basque cross, and the ground may be a solid colour, rather than just the traditional white. Linen cloth had a wide range of uses, from tablecloths and napkins to curtains. The largest pieces were used to decorate the interior of Basque houses. Today only a few workshops – Jean Vier in Saint-Jean-de-Luz, Ona Tiss in Saint-Palais and Lartigue in Oloron-Sainte-Marie, in Béarn – keep this ancient skill alive.

Traditionally woven Basque linen in a shop in Saint-Jean-de-Luz

Saint-Palais ⑱

Road map B4. *Donapaleu* in Basque.
🏠 *2,000.* 🚆 *Puyoô.* 🚌 🛈 *14 place Charles de Gaulle (05) 59 65 71 78.* 🅿️ *Fri.* 🎭 *Festival de Force Basque (first Sun after 15 Aug); horse fair (26 Dec).*

Founded in the 13th century, the bastide town of Saint-Palais later became the capital of the kingdom of Navarre. As it stands at the crossroads of several pilgrimage routes, many markets were held here. It is also where the region's first Estates General, or governing assembly, met in the 16th century.

The town has some attractive old houses, particularly Maison des Têtes, which is decorated with carvings of heads, set within medallions. The **Musée de Basse-Navarre et des Chemins de Saint-Jacques**, in the courtyard of the town hall, documents local history and the history of pilgrimages to Compostela. The town also has **Ona Tiss**, one of the few remaining traditional Basque linen-weaving workshops.

🏛 **Musée de Basse-Navarre et des Chemins de Saint-Jacques**
Tel (05) 59 65 71 78. ☐ *daily.* 🎫 🛈

🧵 **Ona Tiss**
23 rue de la Bidouze. *Tel (05) 59 65 71 84.* ☐ *Sep–Jun: Mon–Thu; Jul–Aug: Mon–Sat.* 🛈

Environs
The 16th-century **Château de Camou**, 5km (3 miles) north of Saint-Palais, has an exhibition on tenant farming and models of Renaissance inventions. At **Garris**, 3km (2 miles) further northwest, a *pottok* fair takes place on 31 July and 1 August each year. **Ostabat**, 12km (7 miles) south of Saint-Palais, stands at the junction of the pilgrim routes from Tours, Vézelay and Le Puy. As such it was an important stopping-place for pilgrims.

The 12th-century church at Hôpital-Saint-Blaise

⛪ **Château de Camou**
Tel (05) 59 65 84 03. ☐ *Jul–Aug: daily pm.* 🎫 🛈

L'Hôpital-Saint-Blaise ⑲

Road map B5. *Ospitale-Pia* in Basque.
🏠 *75.* 🚆 🚌 *Oloron-Sainte-Marie.* 🛈 *Mairie (05) 59 66 11 12.*
🎭 *pilgrimage in honour of Saint-Blaise (early Feb).*

This tiny village, 13km (8 miles) northeast of Mauléon-Licharre, lies very close to the border with Béarn *(see p213)*. It was once the seat of a commander of the Knights Templar, and had a hostel where pilgrims would stay and rest, before continuing on their journey up to Col du Somport, via Oloron-Sainte-Marie or Saint-Jean-Pied-de-Port.

The striking 12th-century **Église de L'Hôpital-Saint-Blaise** is in the Romanesque style with Moorish elements. These are particularly noticeable in the stone latticework of the windows and in the capitals of the doorway. Moorish influence is also apparent inside the church: the stone-built dome has groin vaults that intersect to form an eight-pointed star. The interior also has a Baroque altarpiece and traditional Basque-style galleries *(see p196)*. Both these features date from a later period than the church itself.

🛈 **Église de L'Hôpital-Saint-Blaise**
Tel (05) 59 66 11 12.
☐ *daily.* 🎫 🛈

Weaver at Ona Tiss, the Basque linen workshop in Saint-Palais

Pilgrim Routes of Southwest France

The four main pilgrim routes – from Tours, Vézelay, Le Puy-en-Velay and Arles – to Santiago de Compostela run through southwest France. Since the discovery of the supposed tomb of the apostle St James at Compostela in 813, many have embarked on the perilous journey to visit it. James is believed to have preached in Spain, and it is thought that his body was taken there after his martyrdom in Jerusalem in the 1st century AD. Having crossed the Pyrenees via the Col de Somport or Col de Roncevaux, pilgrims still had 800km (500 miles) to travel before reaching the Cathedral of Santiago. The routes they used were added to Unesco's World Heritage List in 1993.

Street sign in Bordeaux
Pilgrims arriving from the Médoc and Tours, or by boat along the Garonne, stopped in the city. The shell of St James, emblem of the pilgrimage, is featured.

Backpacks hold the present-day pilgrim's luggage.

Book of Hours
Accounts of pilgrimages and guides to the routes were written from the 12th century onwards. Among them was the late 15th-century Codex Calixtinus, written by Aymery Picaud, a monk.

Pilgrims cross the Aspe at Oloron-Sainte-Marie, in Béarn.

The **sportelle**
This was a badge that pilgrims would sew onto their clothes. In some areas, it served as a kind of pass. Today's pilgrims carry a credencial, a passport that is stamped to record their progress and the places where they have stopped.

Map of the pilgrim routes to Compostela
Based on a 17th-century map, this shows the various pilgrim routes and the points at which they converge. Stopping-places are concentrated in the southwest.

Porte Saint-Jacques
Among the many monuments on the route to Compostela that are now listed as World Heritage Sites is this gateway at Saint-Jean-Pied-de-Port (see p204). The town sits at the foot of the Pyrenees, just below Roncevaux.

Religious buildings
Many churches, such as that at L'Hôpital Saint-Blaise, shown here, are World Heritage Sites. They testify to the strength of Christian faith in southwest France, as in the rest of Europe, during the Middle Ages.

Gîtes and refuges
Along the way there are many gîtes and refuges where pilgrims can spend the night, so long as they can show their credential, *which is given to them by their diocese.*

A cross is still carried by some pilgrims as a mark of their Christian faith.

Stèle de Gibraltar
At Ostabat, near Saint-Palais, is a column, that symbolically marks the convergence point of the pilgrim routes from Tours, Le Puy-en-Velay and Vézelay.

JACQUETS AND JACQUAIRES

In France, pilgrims travelling to Compostela are known as *jacquets* or *jacquaires*. Although their paths vary according to their point of departure, all pilgrim routes converge in the Pays Basque. Because of the spectacular scenery and the towns and the villages that they pass through, these routes are becoming very popular.

Pilgrim sculpture
Sited on the Spanish side of Col du Somport, this marks the route from Arles in France that later converges with four other pilgrim routes at Puente la Reina. From there, a single route, known as the Camino Francés *(French Road), continues straight to Compostela.*

Bell tower with three steeples on the 16th-century church at Gotein, near Mauléon

Mauléon-Licharre ⑳

Road map B5. *Maule-Lextarre in Basque.* 3,500. Oloron-Sainte-Marie. Place des Allées (05) 59 28 02 37. Tue & Sat am. Fête de l'Espadrille (15 Aug). www.valleedesoule.com

Capital of the Soule, the smallest and the most sparsely populated of all the provinces of the Pays Basque, Mauléon-Licharre, also known as Mauléon-Soule, stretches out along the banks of the Saison river. In Mauléon, the upper part of the town, stands the 12th-century **Château Fort**. This small fortress, perched on an outcrop of rock that towers over the valley, contains dungeons and old cannons. The old *bastide* town of Mauléon was built in the 13th century, when Edward I of England ruled Aquitaine. Licharre, the lower town to the west, was the province's administrative centre. At the far end of the allées de la Soule, a long esplanade fronts the Hôtel de Montréal, a 17th-century building that now houses the town hall, a bandstand and a *fronton* (pelota court). **Château d'Andurain**, built in the 16th and 17th centuries, has a shingle and slate, keel roof. Still inhabited by the descendants of Arnaud de Maytie, this residence has Renaissance-style decoration, including listed carved mantelpieces, as well as antique furniture and rare books.

♣ Château Fort de Mauléon
Tel (05) 59 28 02 37.
15 Jun–15 Sep: daily.

♣ Château d'Andurain de Maytie
1 rue du Jeu-de-Paume. *Tel* (05) 59 28 04 18.
Jul–20 Sep.
Thu, Sun am.

Environs
Gotein, 4.5km (3 miles) from Mauléon-Licharre, has a 16th-century church, which contains an 18th-century altarpiece. Its bell tower, with three steeples, each topped by a small cross, is typical of the Soule region.
Ordiarp, 6km (4 miles) further on, towards Col d'Osquich, was a stopping-place on the route to Compostela. It has several medieval houses, a 12th-century church where mass is said in Basque, and several circular-topped gravestones *(see p29)*. Next to the town hall stands the **Centre d'Évocation de Saint-Jacques de Compostelle**. It documents the Romanesque art and architecture that relates to the history of pilgrimages to Compostela.
At Trois-Villes, 10km (6 miles) away, is the **Château d'Élizabea**. Built in 1660 and surrounded by gardens, it belonged to the Comte de Tréville, captain of Louis XIII's musketeers. It figures in *The Three Musketeers* (1844), the famous novel by Alexandre Dumas. The route leading to Les Arbailles passes a Soule-style church at **Aussurucq**.

♣ Château d'Élizabea
Tel (05) 59 28 54 01. call ahead. 10–30 Jun; Aug.

🏛 Centre d'Évocation de Saint-Jacques-de-Compostelle
Adjoining the town hall.
Tel (05) 59 28 07 63.
mid-Jun–Sep: Mon–Fri.

Massif des Arbailles ㉑

Road map B5. Oloron-Sainte-Marie. Place Centrale, Tardets (05) 59 2851 28. Transhumance (May, around Ascension); Fête des Bergers, Col d'Ahusquy (first Sun after 15 Aug).

The dense and magical Forêt des Arbailles, which has inspired many Basque legends, covers a mountainous area of limestone rocks. Heavy rainfall there has led to the formation of around 600 rock cavities. Pitted with sinkholes, crevasses and chasms, parts of the area resemble a giant Gruyère cheese. Because the terrain is often so uneven, walkers are advised not to stray off footpaths. From earliest times, the people of Les Arbailles have derived their livelihood from grazing sheep. Shepherds live in huts known as *cayolars* and, from May to October, ewes are milked and cheeses, including Ossau-Iraty, are made.
The D117 leads to **Ahusquy**, where there is a spring whose pure, almost mineral-free waters are thought to have curative and diuretic properties. Ahusquy is a gateway to the Forêt des Arbailles, which is dotted with megalithic monuments, such as the **Cercle de Pierre de Potto** and the Dolmen d'Ithé.
Besides livestock, this fragile, unspoilt environment is inhabited by deer and feral goats, and its cliffs are home to peregrine falcons, eagle owls, bearded vultures and great spotted woodpeckers.

A great spotted woodpecker in the Forêt des Arbailles

OSSAU-IRATY

Ossau-Iraty, made by traditional methods

In an area between the Forêt d'Iraty and the Pic du Midi d'Ossau, with the mountains of the Pays Basque on one side and those of Béarn on the other, Ossau-Iraty is made. This unpasteurized ewes' milk cheese has its own AOC. In May, around 2,000 flocks of sheep, with a total of 300,000 ewes, make their way up to high-altitude pastures known as *estives*. Here they graze on the nourishing and diverse greenery that gives the cheese its flavour. After the ewes have been milked, the milk is curdled, and the cheese cut, fermented and pressed into moulds. It is then matured for two to three months. It can be eaten as an appetizer, in salads, or is delicious as a dessert with black cherry jam.

Tardets-Sorholus ❷

Road map B5. *Atharratze-Sohorolüze* in Basque. 🏠 *700.* 🚌 *Oloron-Sainte-Marie.* 🚏 ℹ️ *Place Centrale (05) 59 28 51 28.* 🗓️ *Sep–Jun: alternate Mon; Jul–Aug: Mon.* 🎪 *Foire aux Fromages; Fêtes de Tardets (third week in Aug).*

The origins of Tardets-Sorholus go back to 1289, when it was founded as a *bastide* town. The central square, its focal point, is lined with 17th-century arcaded houses. In the town hall district is a *fronton* where games of pelota are played. Some of the houses along the banks of the Saison river have wooden galleries. The Soule-style farmhouses in the surrounding foothills are similar to the slate-roofed buildings of Béarn.

Environs
5km (3 miles) from Tardets-Sorholus, in the direction of Barcus, is the 16th-century **Chapelle de la Madeleine**.

From here visitors can enjoy stunning views of the Soule and the Pyrenean mountain chain. A Latin inscription inside the church mentions an ancient Basque deity.

Forêt d'Iraty ❸

Road map B5. ℹ️ *(05) 59 28 51 29.*

Straddling the border between France and Spain, the Forêt d'Iraty covers more than 17,000ha (42,000 acres). On the French side, altitudes range from 900 to 1,500m (2,950 to 4,900ft). The heavy annual rainfall results in luxuriant growth. Both pines and beech trees thrive here – this is Europe's largest beech forest. Like the Massif des Arbailles, the terrain is dotted with the remains of ancient megalithic monuments.

The area also has many peat bogs. Because ancient plant matter is preserved by the airless conditions in the bogs, they act as a record of evolutionary change over thousands of years. The bogs are also home to most of the forest's wildlife, including wild boar, deer, foxes and squirrels.

At Col de Bagarguiac, beyond Col d'Organbidexka, close to a chalet housing a visitor centre, are several marked paths for circular walks of 1¹/₂ to 4 hours, or for cross-country skiing in winter. The GR10, a long-distance footpath, crosses the northern part of the area. You can also drive through Iraty on the D18 from Larrau to Saint-Jean-Pied-de-Port.

The village of Larrau, beneath the Pic d'Orhy

Larrau ❹

Road map B5. *Larraine in Basque.* 🏠 *250.* 🚏 ℹ️ *Place Centrale (05) 59 28 51 28.* 🗓️ *Mon, in Tardets.*

Larrau, a village of slate-roofed houses, clings to the sides of the Pic d'Orhy, a mountain that figures in local legends. On the edge of the Forêt d'Iraty, the village is the main centre of wood pigeon-hunting, a traditional sport with a lively local following.

Environs
About 12km (7 miles) from Larrau is **Col de Larrau**, a pass at 1,573 m (5,163ft). This is a good place to stop on the way up to **Pic d'Orhy**, at 2,017m (6,619ft), which is 1¹/₂ hours' walk away. 12.5km (8 miles) further on is **Col d'Organbidexka**, at 1,284m (4,214ft). In the autumn, birdwatchers come here to see migrating birds.

🦅 **Col d'Organbidexka**
Tel (05) 59 65 97 13.

Houses in Tardets-Sorholus, a 13th-century *bastide* town

Tour of the Gorges d'Holzarté and Gorges d'Olhadubi ㉕

The Gorges d'Holzarté and Gorges d'Olhadubi, near Larrau, are two great canyons cut into the limestone by the action of water. There are dramatic views across the river valleys of both from the Passerelle d'Holzarté, a footbridge over the Gorges d'Olhadubi. Those who suffer from vertigo may find this bridge unnerving, but it is perfectly safe, and there are even picnic places where visitors can stop for lunch.

Latsagaborda ③
These newly restored shelters are now used by hunters of wood pigeons. Dotting the Basque mountains, they were built originally for shepherds.

Gîte d'Étape de Logibaria ①
Logibaria lies at the bottom of a valley, amid a verdant mountain landscape. On the GR10 long-distance footpath, this gîte is a good stopping-place for a meal or an overnight stay.

Pont de la Mouline ②
This bridge spans the Gave de Larrau. A monument here commemorates a battle between members of the French Résistance and a phalanx of retreating German soldiers during World War II.

Passerelle d'Holzarté ⑥
This footbridge has been strengthened since it was built in 1920. Timber from the Forêt d'Iraty was once carried over it.

| 0 | 500 m |
| 0 | 0,5 miles |

KEY

- ▬▪ Suggested route
- ═ Other roads
- ☼ Viewpoint

Gorges d'Holzarté ⑦
Near the end of their journey, visitors can admire the Gorges Holzarté, a breathtaking chasm carved into the limestone by the swift-flowing water of the river.

Col d'Ardakhotxia ④
This pass commands stunning views of the Larrau valley below. The valley's undulating terrain is typical of the region.

Pont d'Olhadubi ⑤
magnificently wild surroundings with small waterfalls, this bridge rs spectacular views. Visitors can e in the pools by the bridge and, a little further on, experienced anoeists may wish to attempt an hilarating descent of the canyon.

The Gorges de Kakouetta, with walkways for visitors

Gorges de Kakouetta ㉖

Road map B5. Sainte-Engrâce. ◻
15 Mar–15 Nov: daily. **Tel** (05) 59 28
60 83 & 59 28 73 44. ▨ Sturdy
walking boots are recommended.

First explored by Édouard-Alfred Martel in 1906, these narrow gorges near Sainte-Engrâce were carved out of the rock by the action of water over thousands of years. You can walk all the way round the canyon in a 6½ hour trek. You can also walk for 2km (1 mile) right up into the gorge along metal walkways.

The drop from the clifftops on either side to the bottom of the canyon is about 300m (985ft). Some of the narrow passages, including the Grand Étroit, which is one of the most magnificent in France, are no more than a few metres wide, but walking them is a thrilling experience. The moist conditions in these deep gorges allow lush vegetation to thrive.

After walking for about an hour, you will come to a 20-m (65-ft) waterfall, whose source has still not been discovered. About 200m (220yds) further on, the walk comes to an end when you reach the Grotte du Lac, a cave with spectacular stalactites and stalagmites.

Carved capital, Sainte-Engrâce

Sainte-Engrâce ㉗

Road map B5. *Santa Graxi in Basque.*
👥 250. 🚉 Oloron-Ste-Marie. 🚌
Mauléon. 🏛 Mairie (05) 59 28 60 83.
⛪ Patronal festivals (Whitsun).

In the heart of the upper Soule, at 630m (2,068ft), the shepherds' hamlet of Sainte-Engrâce lies almost on the border with Béarn and very near Navarre, a province of the Spanish Basque country. It consists of about 100 farmsteads, and "districts" spread out over a wide area of unspoilt countryside. At the confluence of the Gorges de Kakouetta and Gorges d'Ehujarre, it seems to stand guard over the great amphitheatre of hills all around. The 12th-century Romanesque abbey church is dedicated to Santa Gracia, after whom the village is named. She was a young Portuguese woman who was put to death around 300, when Christians were being persecuted in Moorish Zaragoza. The original chapel on the site was built to house a relic of the saint – her arm, which was miraculously recovered. The chapel was later attached to the monastery at Leyre, in Navarre. It has a wooden pulpit and 21 capitals carved with a wealth of biblical scenes. The wrought-iron rood screen and Baroque altarpieces are also noteworthy. The graveyard has several circular-topped Basque gravestones.

BÉARN

With the Pays Basque, Béarn forms part of the département of the Pyrénées-Atlantiques. Bordered by Aragón, in Spain, to the south and the Hautes-Pyrénées to the east, Béarn enjoys a gentle climate. The mountains, forests and lush green hills of Haut Béarn contrast with the flatlands of the Gave de Pau and Gave d'Oloron.

With the rugged Pic du Midi d'Ossau in the east and the low-lying plains that merge into the Landes and Gascony to the west, the Béarn has a very varied landscape. Its cultural identity is clearly expressed by the use of its own language, Gascon, and by gastronomic specialities such as *garbure (see p257)*, *confit* of duck, ewes' milk cheese, and wines from Jurançon and Madiran.

Béarn also has a turbulent history. There is evidence of Roman settlement and it was later incorporated into the Spanish kingdom of Aragón. But, by the 9th century, Béarn was under Gascon rule and, by 1290, had passed to the counts of Foix, who ruled it as an independent territory, despite treaties claiming it as part of France. Inheritance led to its inclusion in the kingdom of Navarre and, in 1560, the ruler, Jeanne d'Albret *(see p43)*, declared it a Protestant state, contributing to its bloody role in the Wars of Religion. Her son, Henri IV, was crowned king of France in 1589, but Béarn-Navarre was to remain a separate state until 1620, when Louis XIII brought it under the French crown. After the French Revolution, Béarn was linked with the Pays Basque to create the new *département* of the Basses-Pyrénées, which was renamed the Pyrénées-Atlantiques in 1970.

The modern world seemed barely to touch Béarn in the early 20th century. But it has changed enormously since 1950, thanks to the discovery of gas at Lacq, the intensive cultivation of maize and the expansion of the capital, Pau. Improvements to the road network have also helped to open up this breathtakingly beautiful, unspoilt region, with its unique wildlife.

A herd of *pottoks* in the Soussouéou valley

◁ Detail from the doorway of Cathédrale Sainte-Marie in Oloron-Sainte-Marie

Exploring Béarn

This diverse region, with its rich history and architectural heritage, as well as stunning landscapes, lies within easy reach both of the Atlantic, one hour's drive from Pau, and of the high Pyrenees, just 30 minutes from Pau. In summer, the Aspe, Ossau and Barétous valleys are ideal for hiking, and in winter, skiers come to the resorts of Gourette, Artouste and Pierre-Saint-Martin. Pau, the capital of Béarn and administrative centre of the Pyrénées-Atlantiques, is an elegant city with many green spaces and the château where Henri IV of France, heir of the rulers of Béarn and Navarre, was born.

THE REGION AT A GLANCE

0 km   10
0 miles   10

SEE ALSO

• *Where to Stay* p253

• *Where to Eat* p269

Rafting on the Gave de Pau, near Bétharram

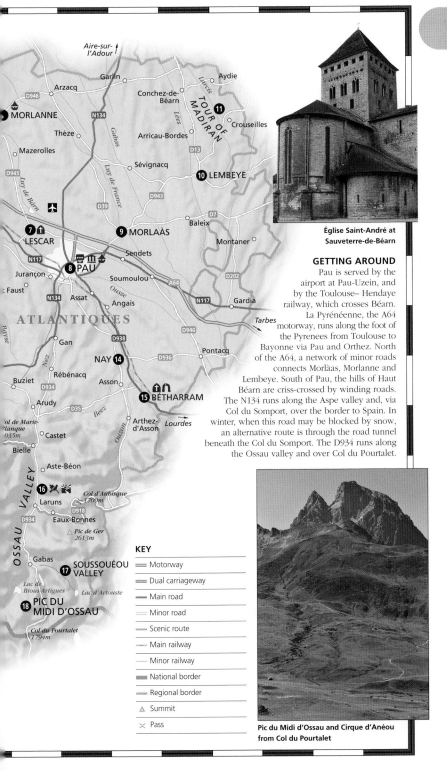

**Église Saint-André at
Sauveterre-de-Béarn**

GETTING AROUND

Pau is served by the
airport at Pau-Uzein, and
by the Toulouse– Hendaye
railway, which crosses Béarn.
La Pyrénéenne, the A64
motorway, runs along the foot of
the Pyrenees from Toulouse to
Bayonne via Pau and Orthez. North
of the A64, a network of minor roads
connects Morlàas, Morlanne and
Lembeye. South of Pau, the hills of Haut
Béarn are criss-crossed by winding roads.
The N134 runs along the Aspe valley and, via
Col du Somport, over the border to Spain. In
winter, when this road may be blocked by snow,
an alternative route is through the road tunnel
beneath the Col du Somport. The D934 runs along
the Ossau valley and over Col du Pourtalet.

KEY

━━━ Motorway

━━━ Dual carriageway

─── Main road

···· Minor road

━━━ Scenic route

┄┄┄ Main railway

─── Minor railway

▬▬▬ National border

━━━ Regional border

△ Summit

╳ Pass

**Pic du Midi d'Ossau and Cirque d'Anéou
from Col du Pourtalet**

The 13th-century Église Saint-Laurent in Morlanne

Morlanne **❶**

Road map C4. 🏚 *430.* 🚌 *Orthez.*
🚍 *Arzacq.* 🛈 *La Grange, Carrère-
du-Château (05) 59 81 42 66.* 📷
Fête de Saint-Laurent (early Aug).

This characterful village has
17th- and 18th-century houses
in a style typical of northern
Béarn. The **Église Saint-
Laurent**, built in the 13th
century and fortified in the
14th, is lit by Gothic windows
in its west wall and apse. The
village's main street runs from
Maison Domecq, a 15th-
century abbey, to **Château de
Morlanne**. Built in 1373 by
the half-brother of Gaston
Fébus *(see p222)*, this fortress
has a 25-m (82-ft) high, brick-
built keep. A drawbridge once
spanned the moat, which is
6m (20ft) deep. The building's
original features were restored
in the 1960s. On the guided
tour of the castle, visitors
will see medieval furniture
and other pieces, pictures by
Fragonard, Nattier, Canaletto
and Van de Velde, as well as
some fine 16th–18th-century
furniture. The grounds feature
a formal garden.

♣ **Château de Morlanne**
Tel *(05) 59 81 60 27.* ⏰ *Jul–Aug:
daily; Apr–Oct: Sat & Sun pm.* 📷 📷

Environs
Arzacq, 12km (7 miles)
from Morlanne, is a *bastide*
town built by the English. Its
focal point is the arcaded
place de la République. A local
administrative centre, the
town is on the pilgrim route to
Compostela. The parish church
has a stained-glass window
with a depiction of St James
and a 16th-century painted
wood statue of the Madonna
and Child. Also in the town is
the **Maison du Jambon de
Bayonne**, a museum devoted
to the history and production
and Bayonne ham *(see p256)*.
   Château de Momas, 13km
(8 miles) away, dates from the
the 14th to the 16th centuries
and was the residence of the
lords of Momas. The present
owner takes visitors on a tour
of the garden here, which is
planted with rare flowers,
shrubs and vegetables.

🏛 **Maison du Jambon
de Bayonne**
Route de Samadet. **Tel** *(05) 59 04
49 35.* ⏰ *Jul–Aug: daily; Sep–Jun:
Tue–Sat.* 📷
www.jambon-de-bayonne.com

♣ **Château de Momas**
Tel *(05) 59 77 14 71.* 📷 *Apr–Oct:
Sat–Sun and by arrangement.*
📷 📷

Salies-de-Béarn **❷**

Road map B4. 🏚 *5,000.* 🚌
Puyoô. 🚍 🛈 *Rue des Bains (05) 59
38 00 33.* 🍴 *Thu & Sat; farmers'
market: Jul–Aug: Tue.* 📷 *Fête du Sel
(second weekend in Sep).*

The town's historic district
centres around Place du
Bayaà, where, opposite the
town hall, stands the Fontaine
du Sanglier, named after the
legend of the wounded boar
that led to the discovery of
Salies' famous salt spring *(see
p217)*. Flowers hang down
the buildings lining the town's
ancient narrow streets. The
Musée du Sel, a salt museum
that features a salt-panner's
workshop, stands among
17th- and 18th-century
houses. In front of it is a
coulédé, a stone trough where
water drawn from the salt-
water fountain was kept
before being transferred to
reservoirs. Historical artifacts
and furniture by Salies'
cabinetmakers illustrate aspects
of local history.
   The **Musée des Arts et
Traditions Béarnaises** is
housed in a 17th-century
residence opposite the town
hall. Beyond Pont de la Lune
are half-timbered houses on
pillars and, opposite, Maison
de la Corporation des Part-
prenants (who won the legal
right to use the salt-water

Houses on pillars in the centre of Salies-de-Béarn

Pont de la Légende over the Gave d'Oloron at Sauveterre-de-Béarn, on an ancient route to Navarre

fountain in 1587). The old town ends at the spa quarter. The grand hotels here, such as the Hôtel du Parc (1893), were built during the spa's heyday at the end of the 19th century. Nearby are baths, built originally in 1857 and rebuilt in the Moorish style after a fire in 1888.

🏛 **Musée du Sel**
Rue des Puits-Salants.
Tel (05) 59 3800 33. ◯ May–Oct:
Tue–Sat. 🖼 🖊

🏛 **Musée des Arts et Traditions Béarnaises**
Place du Bayaà. ◯ As for Musée du Sel. 🖼 🖊

Sauveterre-de-Béarn ❸

Road map B4. 🏘 *1,370.* 🚉 *Puyoô and Orthez.* 🚌 🛈 *Place Royale (05) 59 38 58 65.* 🏛 *Sat.*

Until the end of the Middle Ages, this fortified town helped to defend and preserve Béarn's independence. The 13th-century, 33-m (108-ft) high Tour Monréal was the keep of the viscount's castle and served as Gaston Fébus's hunting lodge. Below the steps to the tower, a path heading down to the river leads to Pont de la Légende, the town's 12th–14th-century fortified bridge. It led to the Île de la Glère, an island covered in lush vegetation. According to legend it was here that a harsh judgment was meted out to Queen Sancie. Accused of murdering her newborn son, she was cast into the river, and was washed up on the island. Entering the old town by Porte de Lester, visitors will come to the town's former arsenal, now restored, and the fortified Porte de Datter. The Église Saint-André is in a transitional Romanesque-Gothic style. The Porte des Cagots, on the south side of the church, was a doorway for people who, for reasons that are still unclear, were forbidden from mixing with the townspeople. They may have been converted Muslims, gypsies, Jews or lepers.

Environs

About 2km (1 mile) from Sauveterre, on the road to Laàs, is the little **Chapelle de Sunarthe**, a stopping-place on the pilgrim route to Compostela. Inside is a model of medieval Sauveterre, brought to life by a son et lumière show.

🛈 **Chapelle de Sunarthe**
Tel (05) 59 38 58 65. ◯ Jul–Aug: Tue–Sat. 🖼 🖊

SALIES-DE-BÉARN'S SALT LEGEND

Salt has been panned at Salies-de-Béarn since the Bronze Age. However, according to a medieval legend, the salt-rich waters of the area were only discovered when a boar that hunters had wounded was found in a marsh, covered in salt crystals. In 1587, a law was passed to ensure fair access to this source of salt. The *jurats du sel*, officials who oversaw the drawing of this water, in-scribed nine articles of good conduct in the *Livre Noir*. The annual Fête du Sel (*see p34*) features a barrel race in which brine barrels are rolled along. The local salt marshes, which produce 800 tonnes of salt a year, are still in use today.

Fontaine du Sanglier on Place du Bayaà in Salies-de-Béarn

Pont Vieux, with its keep, over the Gave de Pau at Orthez

Orthez ❹

Road map B4. 🏠 11 000. 🚉 Pau. 🚌 🚏 ❓ Maison Jeanne-d'Albret, rue Bourvieu (05) 59 38 32 84. 🐟 Tue; foie gras market: Nov–Mar: Sat. 🎭 Feria (Jul).

The emblem of Orthez, Béarn's "second capital", is the **Pont Vieux**, built there across the Gave de Pau in the 13th century, under the rule of Gaston VII de Moncade. The tower was added by Gaston Fébus, who inscribed it with a Gascon saying: *Toquey si gaouses* ("Touch it if you dare"). The **Château de Moncade** (or Tour de Moncade) towers above the town. Built in the 13th and 14th centuries, it witnessed the flowering of Fébus's court *(see p222)*, but was torched in 1569 during the Wars of Religion. What remained was sold during the French Revolution. It was finally restored in the 19th century.

The 16th-century house where Jeanne d'Albret *(see p43)* lived has a stair-tower, mullioned windows and a formal garden. It houses the **Musée Jeanne-d'Albret**, which documents the history of Protestantism in Béarn. The **Église Saint-Pierre**, built in the 13th and 14th centuries as part of the town's fortifications, has a nave in the Languedoc Gothic style. **Maison Chrestia**, home of the Béarnese poet Francis Jammes from 1897 to 1907, illustrates his life and work.

🏛 **Château de Moncade**
Rue Moncade. **Tel** (05) 59 69 36 24 (tourist office). ⬜ Jun–Sep: daily. 📷 🎟

🏛 **Musée Jeanne-d'Albret**
Rue Bourvieu. **Tel** (05) 59 69 14 03. ⬜ Apr–Sep: Mon–Sat; Oct–Mar: Tue–Sat. ⬤ Jan. 📷 🎟

🏛 **Maison Chrestia**
7 avenue Francis-Jammes. **Tel** (05) 59 69 11 24. ⬜ Mon–Fri. ⬤ Oct–May: pm

Painted keystone, Saint-Pierre d'Orthez

Environs
The **Monument du Général Foy**, 3.5km (2 miles) north on the D947, honours the Battle of Orthez and Wellington's victory over the Soult army. The area is dotted with Béarn farmhouses with their steep roofs.

Navarrenx ❺

Road map B4. 🏠 1,200. 🚉 Orthez. 🚌 ❓ Rue St Germain (05) 59 38 32 85. ⬤ Wed. 🎭 La Saumonade (mid-Jul).

Overlooking the Gave d'Oloron, this fortified town was built in the 16th century by Henri d'Albret. It came under attack during the Wars of Religion and was besieged in 1569. The **Arsenal**, built in 1680, was originally the residence of the kings of Navarre. As its name implies, it later served as an arsenal and also as a provisions store for the viscounts of Béarn. The building is now a cultural centre and tourist office. In rue Saint-Antoine is a 16th-century house known as Maison de Jeanne-d'Albret, ruler of Béarn in 1555. The 16th-century Église Saint-Germain has arches decorated with carved and painted heads.

FRANCIS JAMMES

Born in Tournay in 1838, this poet and novelist took literary Paris by storm. However, he never left his native Béarn, choosing to live a quiet life in Orthez. At the age of 40 he became a devout Catholic. His major works include *De l'Angélus de l'Aube à l'Angélus du Soir* (From the Dawn Angelus to the Dusk Angelus; 1898), *Le Deuil des Primevères* (Primroses in Mourning; 1901), and two novels *Clara d'Ellébeuse* (1899) and *Almaïde d'Étremont* (1901).

Francis Jammes by Jacques-Émile Blanche

🏛 Arsenal
Navarrenx through the Centuries (exhibition). ◯ Jun–Sep: daily. 🎫 📷

Environs
4km (3 miles) from Navarrenx, on the D936 to Oloron, is **Camp de Gurs**. Here Spanish republicans were interned after the Civil War and Jews held before deportation. About 12km (7 miles) away, at the 17th-century **Château de Laàs**, is a decorative arts museum.

🏛 Camp de Gurs
Tel (05) 59 39 34 68.

♣ Château de Laàs
Tel (05) 59 38 91 53. ◯ call ahead.

Monein ❻

Road map C4/C5. 🏠 4,300.
🚉 Artix. 🚌 🏠 Mon. 🛈 58 rue du Commerce (05) 59 21 29 28.

The town is set in the rolling hills of the Jurançon, a region that produces a renowned wine. A 19th century building with pillars and stone arches, on place Lacabanne, houses the town hall and covered market.

Église Saint-Girons, built in 1530, is the largest Gothic church in Béarn. A thousand oak trees were needed to build its magnificent hull-shaped roof. The roof beams were originally dowled rather

Altarpiece of the Église Saint-Girons in Monein, the largest Gothic church in Béarn

Mosaic in Cathédrale Notre-Dame at Lescar

than nailed. A son et lumière show explains the roof's unusual construction.

⛪ Église Saint-Girons
Tel (05) 59 21 29 28. ◯ Sat.
📷 📷

Environs
10km (6 miles) southeast of Monein, at Saint-Faust, is **Cité des Abeilles** (Honeybee City), which is devoted to beekeeping.

🏛 Cité des Abeilles
Saint-Faust. *Tel* (05) 59 83 10 31. ◯ Apr–Jun & Sep–mid-Oct: Tue–Sun; Jul–Aug: daily; mid-Oct–Mar: Sat–Sun. ◯ 15 Dec–15 Jan. 📷 📷 ♿ www.citedesabeilles.com

Lescar ❼

Road map C4/C5. 🏠 9,000. 🚉 Pau. 🚌 🛈 Place Royale (05) 59 81 15 98. 🏠 First & third Wed in the month.

Not far from Pau, Lescar, historically the capital of Béarn, perches on a walled promontory that looks towards the Pyrenees. In the 12th century, the town became a fortified bishopric, with work on the **Cathédrale Notre-Dame** commencing in 1120. A plaque set into the cathedral floor lists the tombs of some of the kings of Navarre that are buried here. The floor near the altar is covered with mosaics depicting hunting scenes. The building also has some

fine 17th-century sculptures of Christ, the apostles and local saints. Around the cathedral stand the 14th-century Tour de l'Esquirette and two 16th-century towers, the Tour de l'Évêché and Tour du Presbytère.

From the community centre *(salle des fêtes)*, a short walk leads along the ramparts to the upper town. The **Musée Art et Culture** here displays the work of contemporary painters and also has pieces of Iron Age pottery that were unearthed in excavations at Neandertal, as well as artifacts from a Gallo-Roman villa that was discovered just outside the town.

⛪ Cathédrale Notre-Dame
Place Royale. ◯ daily. 🎫 fee.

🏛 Musée Art et Culture
Rue de la Cité. *Tel* (05) 59 81 06 18. ◯ Apr–Nov: daily. 🎫 fee.

Environs
About 10km (6 miles) from Lescar are the **Cave des Producteurs de Jurançon**, at Gan, and the **Maison des Vins de Jurançon** at Lacommande. At both, visitors can taste and buy local wines. The area's white wine was said to be a favourite of Henri IV, who first tasted it at his Christening.

🍷 Cave des Producteurs de Jurançon
Gan. *Tel* (05) 59 21 57 03. ◯ Mon–Sat. 🎫 tour of the wine cellars, with wine-tasting.

🍷 Maison des Vins de Jurançon
Lacommande. *Tel* (05) 59 82 70 30. 🎫 second Sun in Dec: open house and wine-tasting in the cellars.

Pau ⑧

Window in the château

The capital of Béarn and seat of the royal court of Navarre, Pau is the birthplace of Henri IV of France and of the Bourbon dynasty. In the first half of the 19th century, the city's gentle climate attracted many visitors, including a number of wealthy English people, who came to spend their winters here. The elegant villas, sumptuous parks and gardens, luxurious hotels and sophisticated town planning from that time help to make Pau a charming and discreetly elegant place.

Discovering Pau

At the beginning of the 19th century, Pau was discovered by foreign aristocrats, in particular the English gentry, after Alexander Taylor, a Scottish doctor, published an account of the curative properties of the air there. Soon luxurious villas were being built and splendid municipal gardens were laid out. In 1856, the first golf course to be built on the continent of Europe opened in Pau, which also has an Anglican church, the Église Saint-Andrew, on the corner of rue O'Quin and rue Pasteur. Another English-inspired institution is the Pau Hunt, which keeps the British tradition of fox hunting alive in this corner of France.

🏛 Villa Saint-Basil's

61 avenue Trespoey. 🔲 *Mairie (05) 59 27 85 80.*

The **Quartier Trespoey** has several grand houses, almost all of them privately owned. However, **Villa Saint-Basil's**, built between 1885 and 1888

and set in parkland, is open to visitors. There are other privately owned villas north of the castle, beyond rue Gaston-Fébus.

🏛 Quartier du Château and Quartier du Hédas

The medieval and Renaissance town clusters around the castle. Remodelled in the 18th century, it has paved streets and several town houses, including **Maison Peyré**, also known as Maison Sully, at 2 rue du Château. Its door knocker, in the shape of a basset hound, is said to be lucky.

Quartier du Hédas, the city's oldest district, has fine 16th-century town houses in rue René-Fournets and at place Reine-Marguerite on rue Maréchal-Joffre.

🏛 Boulevard des Pyrénées

This pedestrian promenade was laid out in the late 19th century by Adolphe Alphand, a pupil of the great town planner Baron Haussmann.

The 1908 funicular on Boulevard des Pyrénées

Key to Symbols *see back flap*

PAU CITY CENTRE

Château de Pau, first a medieval fortress, then the Renaissance château of the viscounts of Béarn, and remodelled in the 19th century

For hotels and restaurants in this region see p253 and p269

About 1,800m (1 mile) long, it lies on a natural terrace between Parc Beaumont and Parc du Château, and in clear weather offers both glorious views of the Château gardens below and of the highest peaks of the Pyrenees, which are often snow-capped all year round. Opposite 20 boulevard des Pyrénées there is even an orientation table which names and gives heights of the visible peaks.

The boulevard is lined with the terraces of cafés, restaurants and bars which become lively on summer evenings, spilling out on the pavement. The funicular, installed in 1908, carries

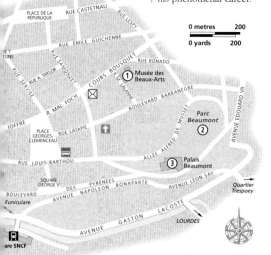

Pyrénées, this museum displays some fine examples of painting from the Dutch, Flemish, Spanish, Italian, French and English schools of the 15th to the 20th centuries. Among the museum's most famous works are *Portraits dans un Bureau de La Nouvelle-Orléans* (1873) by Degas, and works by Rubens, Greco, Rodin and Morisot. Major temporary exhibitions are also regularly held at the the museum.

⛩ Musée Bernadotte
8 rue Tran. *Tel* (05) 59 27 48 42. ⬤ *Mon.* 📷 🎦
The birthplace of Jean-Baptiste-Jules Bernadotte, one of Pau's greatest sons, is now a museum, documenting his phenomenal career.

Having joined the French army as a private in 1780, Bernadotte rose through the ranks to become a Maréchal d'Empire in 1804. With the help of Napoleon, he was created a royal prince of Sweden in 1810, succeeding to that country's throne in 1818, as Charles XIV.

⛩ Palais Beaumont
Tel (05) 59 27 27 08.
This winter palace, with a Neo-Classical south façade and decorative plasterwork, was built in 1900 to cater for foreign visitors and has since been restored. Set in stunning parkland, it also has a casino and a conference centre.

❧ Parc Beaumont
The variant species of flora growing in the delightful Parc Beaumont, from Californian redwoods to Himalayan cedars, is ample testament to the gentle climate of Pau – just about anything grows here. There is also a lovely rose garden, Pyrenean flowers, a lake and a waterfall.

passengers from place Royale to the railway station. Nearby is the **Église Saint-Martin**, next to a tree-lined square.

⛩ Former Hôtel Gassion
This palace, just beyond boulevard des Pyrénées, was completed in 1872. It stands as a symbol of Pau's heyday in the late 19th century.

⛩ Musée des Beaux-Arts
Rue Mathieu-Lalanne. *Tel* (05) 59 27 33 02. ⬤ *Tue.* 🎦 📷
In a 1930s building, a stone's throw from the Palais Beaumont and boulevard des

Portraits dans un bureau de La Nouvelle-Orléans (1873) by Edgar Degas

Château de Pau

Porcelain in the château

As it lay between his territory in Ariège and his court at Orthez, Gaston Fébus, Comte de Foix-Béarn, chose Pau as a strategically located base. The original castle, built in 1370, was a fortress with a triple line of defences. During the Renaissance, it became the residence of the viscounts of Béarn, allies of the Albrets, rulers of Navarre. The birthplace of Henri IV, future king and France's first Bourbon monarch, it served as the centre of a Protestant state created by Henri's mother, Jeanne d'Albret. Later, the castle became a shrine to Henri, and in the 19th century Louis-Philippe, himself a Bourbon, ordered a major programme of restoration, which was continued by Napoleon III. The château contains many works of art, including some of the finest Flemish and Gobelins tapestries in France.

Henri IV on horseback, by Guillaume Heaulme (1611)

The main courtyard is entered via a three-arched portico. The buildings on either side of it have windows with Renaissance-style carving and 19th-century decoration.

Jeanne d'Albret's Bedchamber
The room is hung with 18th-century tapestries. Cybèle Imploring Spring to Return *features allegories of Wind and Rain.*

Tapestries
The king's bedchamber has some of the richest furnishings of any royal residence in France. This detail is from Les Mois Arabesques, designed by Giulio Romano

★ Chambre du Roi de Navarre
The turtle shell here is supposed to have served as Henri IV's cradle. The embroideries, flags and the plumed helmet were placed in the room in the early 19th century.

Salon de famille

Statue of Gaston Fébus

Statue of Henri IV
With a wreath of laurels, this statue of the king was carved by Barthélemy Tremblay and Germain Gissey in the 17th century, and contributed to the cult of "Good King Henry".

Main staircase
Paintings, including this view of the castle by Pierre-Justin Ouvrié, decorate the stairwell.

Chapel

Cupid and Psyche
This 17th-century tapestry with mythological scenes was woven to a design by Raphael.

STAR FEATURES

★ Chambre du Roi de Navarre

★ Salle aux Cent Couverts

★ Salle aux Cent Couverts
This large room was once the castle's guardroom. It takes its name from the table round which 100 diners can be seated.

The Last Judgment fresco in the Église Saint-Michel, Montaner

Morlaàs

Road map C4. 🏠 *4,000.*
🛈 *Place Sainte-Foy (05) 59 33 62 25.* 🗓 *Fri am (twice a month).*

Capital of Béarn from 1080 to 1260, and a stopping-place on the pilgrim routes to Compostela, Morlaàs was once an important stronghold of Gaston Fébus (*see p222*) and had its own mint. Most of the town was destroyed during the Wars of Religion in the 16th century, and very little remains of its prestigious past other than the Église Sainte-

Foy. This church, built in 1080, has a Romanesque doorway, carved with a depiction of St John's vision of the Apocalypse. Inside, the capitals in the apse are carved with scenes from the life and martyrdom of St Foy. The church is in a similar style to other buildings on the pilgrim route, particularly those in Jaca in the Spanish province of Aragon, on the other side of the Pyrenees.

Like Orthez, Salies-de-Béarn and other towns in the area, Morlaàs is also noted for traditional furniture-making.

Lembeye ❿

Road map C4. 🏠 *690.*
🚋 *Pau, 35 km (22 miles).* 🛈 *38 place Marcadieu (05) 59 68 28 78.* 🗓 *Thu am.* 🎭 *Les Médiévales (Montaner, Jul).*

Set on a steep hillside, Lembeye was founded by Gaston VII of Béarn in 1286, and became the capital of Vic-Bilh ("Old Villages"), an area adjoining Bigorre and Gascony. Not far from place Marcadieu, near some old arcaded houses, is a fortified gate, known as Tour de l'Horloge ("Clock Tower"). Lembeye's large Gothic church has an interesting carved doorway.

Environs
About 17km (11 miles) from Lembeye is the **Château de Mascaraas**, with 17th- and 18th-century decoration. 21km (13 miles) away, at **Montaner**, is the 14th-century **Château**, built on the order of Gaston Fébus, and the **Église Saint-Michel**, a church with a remarkable set of frescoes, dating from the 15th and 16th centuries.

🏰 **Château de Mascaraas**
Tel (05) 59 04 92 60. 🎦 📷

🏰 **Château de Montaner**
Tel (05) 59 81 98 29. 🎦 📷

🛈 **Église Saint-Michel**
Tel (05) 59 81 98 29. 🎦 📷
Jul–Aug.

Detail of the Romanesque doorway of the Église Sainte-Foy in Morlaàs

Tour of Madiran ⓫

The vineyards of Madiran and Pacherenc du Vic-Bilh lie at the intersection of Béarn, the Gers and the Hautes-Pyrénées. Madiran's robust, dark red wine acquired an AOC in 1948. Long used as a communion wine, it became known to the wider world thanks to pilgrims who passed through the area on their way to Compostela. Since then, as the quality of Madiran wine has improved, it has become even better known. The lesser-known Pacherenc vineyards produce both a dry and a sweet white wine.

Bottle of Madiran wine

TIPS FOR DRIVERS

Road map C4.
Tour length : 38.5km (24 miles).
Stopping-off places: Two pleasant places to stop are the Château d'Aydie on the Domaine Laplace (05) 59 04 08 00, and the priory in the village of Madiran, where there is a Maison des Vins (05) 62 31 90 67.

Aydie ④
Between Béarn, Bigorre and the Landes, Aydie is a major centre for the production of Madiran wine, as well as the wines of five other estates. The village is also associated with the writer Joseph Peyré, who lived in a villa here.

Conchez-de-Béarn ③
From the 16th century, Conchez was the home town of Béarn's aristocracy. It also has some more bourgeois 16th- and 17th-century houses.

Madiran ⑤
A characterful Gers village, it has given its name to a local wine *appellation*. A former priory here houses the Maison des Vins et du Pacherenc.

Crouseilles ⑥
The Crouseilles-Madiran wine co-operative was founded here in 1950. It has 162 members, 28 of whom are in the Pyrénées-Atlantiques. The others are in the Gers and Hautes-Pyrénées The co-operative is open to visitors.

Arricau-Bordes ②
Although the magnificent château here is closed to the public, visitors are welcome to explore the wine cellars, in the former stables. They can also participate in tutored wine tastings. The 25ha (62 acres) of Arricau-Bordes vineyards produce a very fine wine.

Lembeye ①
In the 17th century, this *bastide* town, 35km (22 miles) from Pau, was the sixth largest in Béarn.

Map labels: AIRE-SUR-L'ADOUR, D 22, D 348, D 317, D 48, D 548, D 65, D 58, D 292, D 66, D 219, D 136, D 648, Cadillon, D 219, D 205, D 298, Larcis, D 139, D 139, D 143, D 228, Castillon, D 13, D 139, D 205, D 142, MONTANER, Lasserre, D 142, D 221, D 943, MORLAAS, D 943, D 47, MAUBOURGUET

KEY

▬ Suggested route

═ Other roads

0 km   2

0 miles   2

Oloron-Sainte-Marie ⑫

Situated at the confluence of the Gave d'Aspe and Gave
d'Ossau, Oloron-Sainte-Marie is the capital of Haut Béarn
and the gateway to the Aspe valley. In the 11th century,
Oloron and the neighbouring bishopric of Sainte-Marie
began to expand and merge, becoming a strategic point of
trade with the Spanish kingdom of Aragon, as well as a
major textile-weaving centre. The two were officially united
to create one city in 1858. The most notable
feature here is the magnificent 12th-century
Romanesque carved doorway of Cathédrale
Sainte-Marie. Covered by a porch, it is
certainly the finest and best-preserved such
doorway in Béarn and features on Unesco's
World Heritage List.

**Detail of the doorway of
Cathédrale Sainte-Marie**

Carving detail
*One of the 24
Elders of the
Apocalypse is
shown holding a
mandolin.*

Christ in Majesty
*Crowned by a halo, symbol of divine
power, Christ is shown appeasing two
lions, which sit on either side of Him.*

Salmon panel
*A series of scenes
show salmon-
fishing in the
Gave d'Oloron,
with the fish being
cut up and
smoked.*

Doorway capital
*Bowed down by an
invisible burden
and grimacing
with pain,
these figures
symbolize
human
suffering.*

**The 12th-century Romanesque doorway of
Cathédrale Sainte-Marie**

Back-to-Back Atlantes
*This carving is also
known as "The Chained
Saracens".*

**Monster Swallowing
the Damned**
*The hideous monster shown
swallowing two heads is next
to a bearded grape-picker.*

🏛 Quartier Sainte-Croix
The Quartier Sainte-Croix is
set above the lower part of
Oloron-Sainte-Marie. It stands
on the site of a former Roman
settlement, known as Iluro.
The Église Sainte-Croix, built
in the 11th century, has an
unusual tower-like belfry.
With its Moorish design, the
interior of the dome is unique
in France. Opposite the
church is an attractive group
of medieval buildings. The
17th-century Maison Marque
houses the **Maison du
Patrimoine**. As well as artifacts

from ancient Iluro, the
museum has an exhibition on
the French concentration
camp that was set up at Gurs
during World War II.

🏛 Quartier Notre-Dame
Of interest here are the 19th-
century Église Notre-Dame, a
former **Capuchin monastery**
and **Marcadet** on place
Gambetta, which comes to
life when the Friday morning
market takes place. It is also
pleasant to stroll along the
mills in the fountains district,
next to the village of Estos.

🏛 Contemporary
Sculptures
Oloron's streets and parks are
graced with eight contemporary
sculptures. These refer to
the artistic activity that was
associated with the traditional
pilgrim routes to Compostela.
Oloron is a stopping-place on
the pilgrim route to Santiago
via Col du Somport. The city's

tourist office is especially
geared to catering to the
needs of pilgrims.

🏛 Tissages Lartigue
Avenue Georges-Messier.
Tel *(05) 59 39 50 11.* ⬜ *Mon–Fri.*
🗓 *Jul–Aug: Mon–Sat or by request.*
Along with Nay, Oloron is the
major manufacturing centre of
the traditional Basque béret.
Textiles are still important to
the town, although Tissages
Lartigue, in Quartier Sainte-
Marie, is the only surviving
weaving workshop that still
uses traditional methods.

VISITORS' CHECKLIST

Road map B4/B5.
👥 *11,800.* 🚃 🚌
ℹ️ *Allée du Comte-de-Tréville;
(05) 59 39 98 00.*
🎪 *Fri am; traditional fair on 1
May.* 🎭 *International folklore
festival (even years: early Aug),
Garburade (first Sat in Sep).*

Oloron-Sainte-Marie, on the Gave d'Aspe

The mountain pastures of Col de la Pierre-Saint-Martin, dotted with outcrops of white limestone

Barétous Valley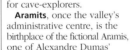

Road map B5. 🚉 🚌 *Oloron-Sainte-Marie*. 🛈 *Arette (05) 59 88 95 38, or La Pierre-Saint-Martin (05) 59 66 20 09*. 🚍 *Sun in Aramits.* 📅 *Junte du Roncal (13 Jul); Fête des Bergers d'Aramits (third weekend in Sep).*

Near the border between the Pays Basque, in France, and Navarre, in Spain, the Barétous valley is a region of sharp contrasts. Woodland, green hillsides and *estives* (summer pastures), grazed by sheep, mix with steep gorges, the lofty, 2,504-m (8218-ft) high Pic d'Anie and the Col de la Pierre-Saint-Martin, a long, arid limestone chasm, thought to be the deepest in the world, that is a paradise for cave-explorers.

Aramits, once the valley's administrative centre, is the birthplace of the fictional Aramis, one of Alexandre Dumas' famous three musketeers. In 1221, the *jurats* (municipal officers) for the Barétous area, met at the Maison de la Vallée here.

Lanne-en-Barétous, birthplace of Porthos, another of Dumas' fictional musketeers, stands near the border with the Pays Basque. Here, a footpath leads to a set of suspended nets that are used to trap passing wood pigeons, on their migratory route over the Pyrenees.

Musée du Béret, Nay

Arette, with 1,125 inhabitants, is the valley's largest town. On 13 August 1967, it was hit by an earthquake. The Centre Sismologique here (tours can be arranged through the tourist office), registers earth tremors in the region. The **Maison de Barétous**, at the tourist office, has an exhibition on life in the valley, and a feature on the Junte du Roncal.

At **Pierre-Saint-Martin**, on Col du Roncal, is an enormous limestone chasm where water rushes through underground caverns and galleries.

Nay 🟥

Road map C5. 🏠 *3,800.* 🛈 *Office de Tourisme Communautaire de la Vath Vielha (05) 59 13 94 99.* 🚉 *Coarraze-Nay.* 🚍 *Tue & Sat.* 📅 *Festival du Conte (Jul); Fêtes de Nay (last weekend in Aug).*

At the beginning of the 12th century, monks from Sainte-Christine in Gabas founded Nay (pronounced "Nye") to provide food and shelter for pilgrims travelling to Compostela. This small town, on the edge of the Hautes-Pyrénées, stands on the Gave de Pau, which becomes swollen with meltwater in spring. In 1302, Marguerite de Moncade made Nay a fortified *bastide* town. It began to prosper during the Middle Ages, thanks to the growth of

---

JUNTE DU RONCAL

On 13 July each year, at the Col de la Pierre-Saint-Martin, the Junte du Roncal, also known as the *Tribut des Trois Génisses* (Gift of Three Heffers), commemorates a peace treaty, that has been in force since 1375, between the inhabitants of the Barétous valley and those of the Roncal valley, in the Spanish province of Navarre. The mayors of each valley take an oath and, to mark it, the Béarnese present the Navarrese with three heffers. In exchange, they can graze their sheep on the *estives* (summer pastures) of their neighbours in the Roncal.

Mayors' oath of agreement

The Four Évangelists on the façade the Chapelle Notre-Dame, Bétharram

the weaving industry, reaching the height of its prosperity in the 18th century with the manufacture of Basque berets and textiles. In 1543, Nay was severely damaged by fire. The Église Saint-Vincent, a single-nave church in the Languedoc Gothic style, originally from the 15th–16th-century, was remodelled when the rest of the town was rebuilt.

The 16th-century **Maison Carrée**, built by Pedro Sacaze, a rich merchant from Aragon, is a Renaissance-style town house with Italian loggias and a beautiful inner courtyard. It fell into ruin in the 18th century and was finally restored between 1994 and 1999. The upper floors house the **Musée Béarnais**, which features a display on industry in Nay through the ages, with sections on local metalwork, weaving and quarrying.

The **Musée du Béret**, in a former industrial building, traces the history of the beret and shows the stages in its manufacture. Despite being associated with the Pays Basque, this famous type of headgear in fact originates in the Ossau valley. From the industrial revolution onwards, its manufacture was a major source of income in Nay and Oloron-Sainte-Marie. However, beret-making is now in decline.

🎌 **Maison Carrée and Musée Béarnais**
Place de la République. **Tel** (05) 59 13 99 65. ⬜ May–Jun & Sep–Oct: Tue–Sat; Jul–Aug: Tue–Sun; Nov–Apr: Sat. 🈂️ 🎫

🏛 **Musée du Béret**
Place Saint-Roch. **Tel** (05) 59 61 91 70. ⬜ Apr–Jun & Sep–mid-Nov: Tue–Sat; Jul–Aug: daily; Jan: Tue & Sat pm 🈂️ 🎫

Bétharram ⓯

Road map C5. 🏘 1,035.
🚉 Coarraze-Nay. 🎪 Fête de la Saint-Jean (usually 24 June).

The town's main attraction is a series of caves, the **Grottes de Bétharram**, on five levels, that visitors can explore on foot, by boat or on a small train. An amazing array of draped, fringed and lace-like rock formations hang from the walls and ceilings of these great caverns, which have names such as Le Chaos and La Salle des Lustres (Hall of the Chandeliers).

Bétharram also has a Baroque chapel, the **Chapelle Notre-Dame**, built in the 17th century on the orders of Louis XIII and the counts of Béarn. According to legend, the original chapel here was built in the 14th century, after the Madonna had appeared on the banks of the Gave de Pau. A second chapel was destroyed by fire in 1569. The west front of the present chapel is of grey marble, with statues of the Four Evangelists and the Madonna and Child. The interior is unusually opulent: it has black marble pillars, a 17th-century altarpiece, paintings and gilded wooden sculptures.

The chapel is associated with Michel Garicoïts (1797–1863), a priest who is buried here. The founder of the Society of the Priests of the Sacred Heart of Bétharram, he was canonized in 1947.

🕳 **Grottes de Bétharram**
Saint-Pée-de-Bigorre. **Tel** (05) 62 41 80 04. ⬜ Feb–Mar: Mon–Fri ; Apr–Oct: daily. ⬛ Nov–Jan. 🈂️ 🎫 **www**.grottes-de-betharram.com

⛪ **Chapelle Notre-Dame de Bétharram**
Lestelle-Bétharram. **Tel** (05) 59 71 98 40. ⬜ Apr–Oct: daily. 🈂️ 🎫

Vintage poster advertising the Grottes de Bétharram

Ossau Valley ⑯

After the Aspe and Barétous valleys, the Ossau valley is the third-largest in Béarn. Beginning south of Pau, it lies at right angles to the Pyrenees and runs right up to Col du Pourtalet, at 1,794m (5,888ft), on the border with Spain. Glaciers covered this whole area during the last Ice Age. The lower part of the valley stretches between the towns of Arudy and Laruns. In the upper valley, villages such as Eaux-Chaudes, Gabas and Bious are sited in basins, amid deep gorges and broad plateaux, such as those at Cezy, Soussouéou and Aule, encircled by the rocky outcrops, like the Cirque d'Anéou, below Le Pourtalet. The highest peak in this majestic landscape is the 2,884-m (9,465-ft) high Pic du Midi d'Ossau. The collapsed cone of an extinct volcano, it serves as the emblem of the Haut Béarn.

★ **Falaise aux Vautours**
This centre at Aste-Béon (see p233) is dedicated to the observation of the griffon vulture. Hides set into the cliffside allow visitors to watch these carrion birds in flight, as well as when attending to their nesting chicks.

Eaux-Chaudes
The village takes its name from the hot springs that made it famous, and that were very popular in the 19th and early 20th centuries. Various health treatments are still available here.

KEY

▬	Main road
═	Minor road
─	Border with Spain
++	Railway line
🚂	Tourist train
🐴	Horseback riding
🛶	Canoeing
🎿	Skiing
♨	Spa
🏠	Refuge
🦋	Nature reserve
☀	Viewpoint

Haut Ossau
Throughout the summer, flocks of sheep graze on the high-altitude pastures here, watched over by shepherds.

Map labels:
PAU
Rébénac
OLORON-SAINTE-MARIE
D 918
D 920
D 232
Sévignacq-Meyracq
Arudy
Iseste
Col
COL DE MARIE BLANQUE
1,035 m (3,397 ft)
ESCOT
Bénou
D 294
Bilhères
Bielle
Louvie-Juzon
Castet
PORT D CASTE
Aste-Béon
Louvi
Soub
Laruns
Béc
Eaux-Bonnes
Eaux-Chaudes
Gave d'Ossau
D 934
Gabas
Artouste-Fabrèges
D 231
LAC DE BIOUS-ARTIGUES
LACS D'AYOUS
PIC DU MIDI D'OSSAU
2,884 m (9,465 f
PARC NATIONAL DES PYRÉNÉES
CIRQUE D'ANÉOU
COL DU POURTA
1,794 m
ZARAGOZA

VISITORS' CHECKLIST

Road map C5. From Pau, take the N134 to Jurançon and Gan, then the D934 to Laruns. At Col du Pourtalet, the road crosses the border into Spain, then leads down the Tena valley, in Aragón. 🚉 *Oloron-Sainte-Marie.* 🚌 ℹ️ *Place de Laruns, Laruns (05) 59 05 31 41, or Maison du Parc National des Pyrénées, Avenue de la Gare, Laruns (05) 59 05 41 59.*

★ Col d'Aubisque

The road over this pass, which is open from June to September, offers stunning views of the Cirque de Gourette and Cirque du Litor.

Train to Lac d'Artouste

Running along a narrow-gauge track laid out in 1924, when the dam at Artouste was being built, a little train takes visitors to Lac d'Artouste. This scenic journey, at an altitude of 2,000m (6,564ft), takes 50 minutes.

★ Lac d'Artouste

The departure point for several good walking routes, the lake can also be reached in about 3 hours, along a footpath that starts near the hut at Soques, at the bottom of the valley.

STAR SIGHTS

★ Col d'Aubisque

★ Falaise aux Vautours

★ Lac d'Artouste

0 km   4

0 miles   4

Exploring the Ossau Valley

Gentian

The Ossau Valley, which is divided into the Bas Ossau (lower valley), and the Haut Ossau (upper valley) has a strong cultural identity. This is expressed through traditional songs and dances and the continuing use of the Gascon dialect. Life here is centred around the raising of livestock, the main source of income in the area. Until the French Revolution, every village elected *jurats*, municipal officers who took care of the community's welfare and defended its rights and customs. Being governed by such democratic principles gave the valley a certain degree of independence from the central government of France.

Gothic doorway of Église Saint-Vivien in Bielle

Arudy

ℹ Place de l'Hôtel-de-Ville (05) 59 05 77 11. 🚌 Wed & Sat. 🎻 Estives Musicales (Jul–Aug).

Arudy is famous for its fine marble. This ranges from a blueish-grey variety, the most common, to the rarest, which is veined with red or a mix of several colours.The Église Saint-Germain, dating from the 16th and 17th centuries, has a pointed dome and capitals carved with bears and cows, the emblems of Ossau.

The 17th-century abbey now houses the **Maison d'Ossau**. This is a visitor centre with displays on the plants and wildlife of the Parc National des Pyrénées and a museum of prehistory. A prehistoric site was discovered here that gave its name to the Arudyan period of the Magdalenian

era (14,000–7,500 BC). The village also has some 50 engraved lintels, dating from 1674 to 1893.

🏛 Maison d'Ossau
Rue de l'Église. **Tel** (05) 59 05 61 71. 🖼

Sainte-Colome

2km (1 mile) east of Arudy.
ℹ (05) 59 05 62 65 (Mairie).

This was a stopping-place on the stretch of the pilgrim route to Compostela that passed through the foothills of the Pyrenees. The town has a 12th–13th-century fortified house, some sturdily built, Ossau-style decorated houses and the Église Saint-Sylvestre, a 15th-century church.

Louvie-Juzon

2.5km (2 miles) southeast of Arudy.
ℹ Place de la Mairie (05) 59 05 61 70.
🎭 Festivals in hamlets of Pedehourat and Pedestarres (third weekend in Jul).

The 16th-century **Église Saint-Martin** here is in a very late Gothic style. Its capitals are beautifully carved with depictions of the four ages of man, and with angels, devils and a bestiary. The church also has some interesting furnishings and an 18th-century organ.

Castet

4.5km (3 miles) southeast of Arudy.
ℹ (05) 59 05 79 51 (Mairie).

This attractive village takes its name from the castle here, the valley's only fortification. Built on a rocky outcrop in the 13th century, it was dismantled by the valley's inhabitants in 1450, and all that remain are two towers. There is also a Romanesque church, the Église Saint-Polycarpe. A road leads down to the harbour, beside a lake on the Gave d'Ossau. Here there are marked pathways and an "espace naturel" devoted to the wildlife living in and around these waters.

Bielle

6km (4 miles) south of Arudy.
ℹ (05) 59 82 60 36 (Mairie).

As the town where the *jurats* sat, Bielle was the valley's political capital. It remained autonomous until the French Revolution in 1789. The records of the community's legal business were stored in a triple-lock chest, now displayed in the **Église Saint-Vivien**. The tympanum of this 16th-century church is carved with a bear and a cow, emblems of Ossau. Among the town's richly decorated 15th–18th-century houses are Maison Trille and the former convent, which has a square pavilion and a circular tower, with an arched doorway.

Workshop in Nay, making the bells worn by sheep in the Ossau valley

Bilhères

6km (4 miles) southwest of Arudy.
(05) 59 82 60 92 (Mairie).

Bilhères lies on the D294, which
connects the Ossau and Aspe
valleys via **Col de Marie-
Blanque** at 1,035m (3,397ft).
The doorways of some of the
16th- and 17th-century houses
here are carved with keys. The
Église Saint-Jean-Baptiste has
a painted wooden canopy.

✗ Falaise aux Vautours d'Aste-Béon

Tel 05 59 82 65 49. 🖼 📷
🔲 *Apr–Sep: daily; school hols.*

The cliffs at the villages of Aste
and Béon are a protected
nature reserve. The visitor
centre at the foot of the cliffs
displays information about the
griffon vulture. Hides in the
cliffs allow these birds to be
observed at close quarters.

Laruns

🔲 *Place de Laruns (05) 59 05 31 41.*
🔲 *Maison du Parc National des
Pyrénées, Avenue de la Gare*
Tel (05) 59 05 41 59. 📷 *"Nouste
Dame" fete (15 Aug); Cheese fair (first
weekend in Oct).*

Laruns is home to the Ossau's
tourist office and the **Maison
du Parc National**. Here the
valley's traditional culture is
kept alive at the festival of
music and dancing that takes
place on 15 August each year.
The Pon quarter, in the south
of the town, has 16th- and
17th-century houses.

Laruns's municipal district
includes the spa town of
Eaux-Chaudes, about 5km
(3 miles) to the sourth, which
was at its peak during the
19th century. There are seven
hot springs near the baths.

Dancing in traditional dress at the Laruns festival on 15 August

🎿 Route de l'Aubisque

This pass, which leads
through stunning mountain
scenery, lies beyond Laruns
on the D918 to Gourette.
Empress Eugénie instigated
the construction of this "spa
route", and encouraged the
development of the health
spa of **Eaux-Bonnes** along it.

Béost

2km (1 mile) northeast of Laruns.
🔲 *(05) 59 05 31 93 (Mairie).*

A narrow street in this high-
set hamlet leads to a 12th-
century castle and a church
with a fine 14th-century
doorway. Some of the 16th-
century houses here have their
original bread-ovens

Louvie-Soubiron

4km (3 miles) northeast of Laruns.
🔲 *(05) 59 05 37 09 (Mairie).*

White marble from here was
used at La Madeleine in Paris
and for statuary on Place de la
Concorde, and also at the
Palais de Versailles. The
Romanesque church has a
12th-century font and baptistry.

Soussouéou Valley ⑰

Road map C5. Beyond Laruns,
towards Gabas.

The breathtakingly beautiful,
high Soussouéou valley is
about 10km (6 miles) long.
Information on hiking here is
available from the tourist office
at Laruns. If you intend to
walk in the valley, drive out of
Laruns on the Gabas road,
follow it to the Miégebat power
station and, 2km (1 mile) from
there, take a left turn to Pont
de Goua, a bridge by which
you can park your car. From
here a footpath leads through
the undergrowth. A 30-minute
walk brings you to the GR10,
a long-distance path. From
here, a day's walk along this
irregularly signposted but
well-used track will take
you to Lac d'Artouste.

An alternative route up the
valley is to drive through
Gabas and park at the **Lac de
Fabrèges cable-car** car park,
4km (3 miles) further on.
From here, a 12-minute ride
will take you up to **Col de la
Sagette**, where you can catch
the **Artouste train**, which
follows a track up the side
of the valley. The journey,
in open carriages, takes 55
minutes and offers splendid
views of the Pic d'Ossau.
From the terminus, it takes
about 15 minutes to reach
Lac d'Artouste on foot.

You can also walk down
from Col de la Sagette to
the Soussouéou plateau and,
in summer, you can ride up
again on a chair lift, the
Télésiège de l'Ours.

Brown bears in the mountains between the Ossau and Aspe valleys

Pic du Midi d'Ossau ⑱

Edelweiss, a Pyrenean flower

Standing out like a giant shark's tooth, the Pic du Midi d'Ossau soars up to a height of 2,884m (9,465ft). Climbing to the top is safe only for experienced mountaineers, but its lower slopes are more easily accessible, and offer pleasant walks as well as a number of family attractions. From the lakes and passes around the peak there are spectacular views of Béarn's mountains. Hikers, however, should never set out without a good map and suitable equipment.

One of the many varied landscapes in the Pic du Midi d'Ossau

Lac de Bious-Artigues (1,422m/4,667ft) ①
This artificial lake in Haut Béarn is a gateway to the Parc National des Pyrénées. The peaceful, shaded lakeside is a perfect place to relax and, from here, the distinctive shark's-tooth outline of the Pic du Midi d'Ossau is in full view.

Pont de Bious (1,500m/4,923ft) ②
This bridge over the Gave de Bious is an intersection and landmark on the GR10 footpath.

GR 10

Lac du Miey ③

Lac Gentau

Lac Roumassot

Gave de Bious

Pic de Larry ▲ 2,337 m (7,670 ft)

Lacs d'Ayous (1,947m/6,390ft) ③
This lake is one of the most beautiful and best-known sights in the Haut Ossau. From the staffed refuge, where you may spend the night, you can see the rays of the setting sun reflected on the water and the mountainside.

Pic Hourquette 2,384 m (7,824 ft) ▲ ④

⑤

Lac Bersau (2,083m/6,836ft) ④
This lake was formed when glaciers melted at the end of the last Ice Age. It is one of the largest glacial lakes in the Pyrenees.

Lac Castérau ⑤
A little way beyond Lac Bersau, the footpath branches off to the left, leading due east down to the hut at Cap de Pount. Lac Castérau, which is well known to mountaineers, is frozen in winter but in summer its cool water is perfect for a paddle, to help reinvigorate tired feet.

KEY

- ▪ Suggested route
- ═ Other roads
- ☼ Viewpoint

0 km   1
0 miles   1

Col Long de Magnabaigt (1,698m/5,573ft) ⑧

The 11 cromlechs and two tumuli at Magnabaigt show that the area was inhabited in Neolithic times. From the pass there is a gentle walk down to Lac de Bious-Artigues. The footpath leads through more thickly wooded landscape, with dense beech forests.

Lac de Pombie and its staffed refuge, where hikers can have a meal and spend the night

Col de Suzon (2,127m/6980ft) ⑦

This ascent is relatively gentle, and on this stretch, via the Pic Saoubiste, you will see another aspect of the Pic du Midi. You can either spend an extra night at the refuge at Pombie or walk back down to Bious-Artigues, just a few hours away.

TIPS FOR WALKERS

Road map C5.
Tour length: In good weather the whole tour takes 2 days. The refuges at Lac d'Ayous (05) 59 05 37 00 and Lac de Pombie (05) 59 05 31 78 are open Jun–Sep. The walk round Lac de Bious-Artigues takes 1 hour, and round both Lac d'Ayous and Lac Bious-Artigues it takes 5 hours.
Access: To reach the Pic du Midi d'Ossau, take the D934 out of Laruns, then follow the D231. The road from Gabas to Bious-Artigues is open May–Nov, depending on weather conditions.

Col de Peyreget (2,208m/7,247ft) ⑥

From Col de Peyreget there is a clear view of the four peaks of the Pic du Midi d'Ossau. They each have a name: Petit Pic, Grand Pic, Pointe Jean Santé and Pointe d'Aragon, which is the nearest to Spain.

Map labels:
LARUNS
P
D 231
GR 10
Barrage
①
P
⑧
TOUR OF PIC DU MIDI D'OSSAU
②
Pic Saoubiste ▲ 2,261 m (7,421 ft)
⑦
Pic du Midi d'Ossau 2,884 m (9,465 ft) ▲
Petit Pic du Midi d'Ossau 2,802 m (9,196 ft)
TOUR DU PIC DU MIDI D'OSSAU
Lac de Peyreget
⑥
Lac de Pombie
▲ Pic de Peyreget 2,338 m (7,673 ft)

The Romanesque chapel at Jouers, in the Bedous valley

Aspe Valley ⑲

Road map C4/C5. 🚹 2,800.
ℹ Place Sarraillé, Bedous (05) 59 34
71 48. 🚉 Oloron-Sainte-Marie.
🚌 Oloron–Canfranc route. 🛒 Thu
in Bedous; Sun in Etsaut (Jul–Aug).
🧀 cheese fair at Etsaut (late Jul).

The Aspe Valley, south of
Oloron-Sainte-Marie, is
washed by the Gave d'Aspe.
The railway viaduct here was
built in 1910 to carry the now-
defunct Pau–Canfranc line.
Notre-Dame-de-la-Pierre, at
Sarrance, is the first of four
stops along a trail that makes
up the **Écomusée de la Vallée
d'Aspe**, the valley's open-air
museum. This stop focuses on
the legend of Sarrance and its
pilgrims. Visitors can then see

the 17th-century church and
cloister. At **Lourdios Ichère**,
the open-air museum's next
stop, an audiovisual presentation
explains the daily life of the
inhabitants of this mountain
village. **Bedous** is the valley's
commercial centre. The GR65,
a long-distance path known
as the Chemin de Saint-Jacques,
runs from Bedous to **Accous**.
Here visitors can taste cheeses
made by local farmers. The
imposing Église Saint-Martin
d'Accous suffered severe
damage twice in its history,
first in 1569, then again 1793.
The **Cirque de Lescun**, at the
head of the valley, is a huge
green plateau dotted with
barns and surrounded by peaks,
the Pic Billare, Pic d'Anie and
Aiguilles d'Ansabère. **Cette-**

Eygun has a fine 12th-century
church, the Église Saint-Pierre.
The **Maison du Parc
National des Pyrénées at
Etsaut** has an exhibition
about the Pyrenean brown
bear. About 2km (1 mile)
beyond Etsaut, a track joins
the **Chemin de la Mâture**.
This stretch of the GR10 is
dug into the rockface above
a sheer drop. In the mid-18th
century, pine trunks to be
used as masts (mâture) for
French navy ships were
dragged through here. The
Chapelle Saint-Jacques, known
as L'Hospitalet, at **Borce** once
took in pilgrims. It now
contains a museum about the
Chemin de Saint-Jacques. The
main street has picturesque
15th- and 16th-century houses
with mullioned windows, Gothic
doorways, carved lintels and
bread-ovens. The striking
Fort du Portalet (1860), above
the Gorge d'Enfer and its
river, was used as a state
prison during World War II.

🏛 **Écomusée
de la Vallée d'Aspe**
Tel (05) 59 34 76 06. ⬜ daily at
Accous & Borce; Jul–Sep: daily &
Oct–Jun: Sat–Sun at Sarrance &
Lourdios. ⬛ Accous & Borce: Sun
mid-Sep–Jun; Sarrance & Lourdios:
Jan. 🅿 🖾 free at Accous & Borce.

🏛 **Maison du Parc National
des Pyrénées**
Etsaut. **Tel** (05) 59 34 88 30.
⬜ May–Oct: daily.

Pic de Billare (2,309m/7578ft) and Pic d'Anie (2,504m/8,218ft) from the Labérouat refuge, above Lescun

Livestock in Béarn

The shepherds and stock breeders of the mountains of the Haut Béarn earn their living largely from the production of fine cheeses, mostly made from unpasteurized ewe's milk. The shepherds who take their flocks up to the *estives* (high-altitude summer pastures) of the Aspe, Ossau and Barétous valleys not only

A shepherd and his bells

help to preserve this beautiful landscape, but also keep alive a traditional way of life that survives nowhere else in the Pyrenees, except in the Pays Basque. Some of Béarn's highest *estives* are difficult and often dangerous to reach. In the more remote pastures, flocks may be attacked by bears, who sometimes take ewes for food.

THE YEARLY ROUND
When the snow begins to melt, herds of cows and flocks of sheep return to the high-altitude pastures, or *estives*. Over the summer shepherds live in huts, close to their flocks, although with such modern equipment as radios and solar power, their lives are now much easier.
Cheeses made in the mountains are carried down to the villages by donkey.

A small reconstructed farmstead, high up in the mountains

Ossau customs *are vigorously kept alive, particularly through traditional music and local dancing.*

Ewe's milk cheese *is made in the summer. For this, the ewes are milked twice a day.*

Traditional instruments *are still used today. The most common are a three-hole flute and a stringed tambourine known as a* ttun-ttun.

Sheep shearing *is always done in spring, before the flocks are driven up to the* estives. *However, these fleeces now fetch relatively low prices.*

Sheep-rearing *in Béarn survives thanks to demand for the cheeses that are made on the* estives, *and to subsidies that allow breeders to live in the mountains. Although a younger generation continues to take up this traditional way of life, it is still in danger of dying out.*

TRAVELLERS' NEEDS

WHERE TO STAY

CHAMBRES
B&B
Bed & Breakfast sign

From Château De Cordeillan-Bages, in Pauillac, to Château d'Urtubie, in Saint-Jean-de-Luz, the region is dotted with attractive hotels, many of them rich in history. Among the most luxurious are the Relais Margaux, Les Sources de Caudalie and Les Prés d'Eugénie. Numerous grand 18th- and 19th-century townhouses and country residences have been converted into comfortable guest houses. These are ideal for both one-night stops and for longer stays.

RESERVATIONS

In summer, it can be difficult to find a hotel room without booking several months in advance, particularly from mid-July to mid-August, the peak holiday season. Outside this period, hotels are also likely to be fully booked for the duration of major regional events such as Vinexpo, Bordeaux's biennial wine fair, and the world surfing championships at Lacanau in early August. Even hotels and guest houses at a considerable distance from such events often have no vacant rooms.

Generally, however, the further away from the coast you go, the greater your chances of finding a room, especially in large towns and cities, which are quieter in summer. When you book, always ask about special offers. According to the time of year, you may also be able to negotiate a lower price if you are booking in advance. Town hotels often offer special weekend deals *("Bon week-end en ville")*, details of which are generally available from local tourist offices.

Swimming pool at Les Loges de l'Aubergade, Puymirol *(see p249)*

◁ The shady terrace of an auberge

Les Hortensias du Lac, a hotel at Hossegor *(see p251)*

Many hotels close in winter, usually between November and February. Wherever you wish to stay in the southwest, and whatever your budget, information and advice are available from Maison Aquitaine in Paris *(see p286)*.

CATEGORIES

All accomodation, from simple rooms in guest houses to luxurious hotel suites, is graded by the French Ministry of Tourism. Various levels of comfort are indicated by stars, daggers, keys and other symbols. Be aware, however, that the classification may not take into account considerations such as the general appeal of a place or an attractive setting. By contrast, the more upmarket hotel associations such as **Relais et Châteaux, Relais du Silence** and **Châteaux et Hôtels de France** do take such factors into account. Each of these produces an annually updated listing and operates a central booking system.

PRICES

By law hotels must clearly display their charges, and these should include service and taxes. You may, however, be able to negotiate a lower price outside the peak summer season. For a stay of several days, some hotels offer rates for half-board or for full-board. Sometimes these can be excellent value, especially if the hotel has a good restaurant, with local produce on the menu. Many guest houses include breakfast in the price of the room.

CHAIN HOTELS

Although they provide a guaranteed standard of comfort, chain hotels are often rather impersonal and lacking in atmosphere. Exceptions to this rule are some of the larger hotels, including those in the **Sofitel** or Holiday Inn chains. **Mercure** hotels, such as the Splendid in Dax *(see p250)*, stand out for their tasteful and individual interior decoration.

TRADITIONAL FAMILY-RUN HOTELS

These establishments usually offer comfortable rooms at very reasonable prices. Good examples are Hôtel du Centenaire at Les Eyzies-de-Tayac *(see p247)*, and certain of the hotels listed by **Pierre et Vacances**; some of these have stunningly beautiful settings, on a golf course, in a pine forest or near the coast.

Others, like La Maision de Navarre in Sauveterre de Béarn *(see p253)* and L'Oyat in Lacanau-Océan *(see p245)*, welcome families all year round. Establishments marked "Station Kid" are particularly suitable for families with very young children. Alternatively, there is **Logis de France**, whose members offer accommodation with charm and character, as well as a warm welcome. The **Fédération Nationale des Tables et Auberges de France** provides information about a host of other places to stay.

LUXURY HOTELS

All large towns and cities in Aquitaine have top-class hotels. Bordeaux's Hauterives & Restaurant St James *(see p245)*, set in four pavilions around a 17th-century vinegrower's house, is just one example. Some of the most luxurious are located in the heart of the countryside. In the Médoc, there is the Château de Cordeillan-Bages *(see p245)*, and at Château d'Urtubie, in Saint-Jean-de-Luz, *(see p253)* guests are welcomed by the count himself. Château de Brindos, near Biarritz *(see p252)*, has a stunning lakeside location. The annually updated guides of Châteaux et Hôtels de France and Relais et Châteaux list many such establishments.

GUEST HOUSES

By renting a room in a guest house *(chambre d'hôte)* you are likely to enjoy comfortable accommodation

Room in the Hôtel Le Square Michel-Latrille, Astaffort (p248)

in an attractive house, often in quiet or out-of-the-way places. Prices vary according to the degree of comfort and the facilities provided. Bear in mind that many guest houses are booked up a long time in advance. Another advantage of staying in a guest house is that breakfast is frequently included in the price and is often very filling. French guest-house associations include **Fleurs de Soleil**, whose members are expected to be friendly and helpful, and must offer a certain level of comfort in a limited number of rooms.

THALASSOTHERAPY & HYDROTHERAPY

Most of Aquitaine's health and fitness centres are in the Landes and Pays Basque. There are high-class establish-

ments near Biarritz, such as the new thalassotherapy centre at the Grand Hôtel in Saint-Jean-de-Luz *(see p253)*. There are also several spa resorts in the Pyrénées-Atlantiques, including Cambo-les-Bains, Les Eaux-Bonnes, Les Eaux-Chaudes and Salies-de-Béarn. With its 17 spa centres, Dax *(see p250)* is the Landes' health-treatment capital. Les Prés d'Eugénie spa in Eugénie-les-Bains *(see p251)* also has a high-class restaurant. There are also several thassalotherapy centres in the Gironde. Les Sources de Caudalie *(p245)*, near La Brède, offers vinotherapy treatments using vine and grape extracts. Some spa chains, such as **Accor Thalassa** and **Thermale de France**, operate a central-booking service. Another organization is **Chaîne Thermale du Soleil**, with a long list of members.

RELAIS SAINT-PIERRE

All establishments classed as Relais Saint-Pierre are of special interest to anglers *(see p280–81)*. The classi-fication is awarded by **Maison de la France** to hotels and campsites located near fishing lakes and in beautiful surroundings. These establishments issue fishing licences, and provide anglers with packed lunches.

Indoor swimming pool at the spa town of Salies-de-Béarn (see p216)

COUNTRY GÎTES

A country gîte *(gîte rural)* is a house or furnished detatched building, with one or more bedrooms, a dining-sitting room, a kitchen or kitchenette, and a bathroom. Gîtes can be rented for a few days or for a weekend, but are most often rented for a minimum of one week. **Gîtes de France** is an association that guarantees certain well-defined levels of comfort (indicated by 1–5 blades of wheat symbols) and whose members abide by a national charter. All the gîtes in this association are regularly checked and graded by Gîtes de France, which has five agencies in Aquitaine.

RENTED ACCOMMODATION

Another reliable organization is **Clévacances**, whose members offer high quality accommodation with an individual touch. This applies both to rented accommodation and to individual rooms in guest houses. There are five grades of comfort.

The website of **Aquitaine Location Vacances** is also useful for people who want to rent a house of character. Another good, internet-based rental agency is **Aquitaine on Line**, which has a directory of guest houses, gîtes, apartments and villas, some of which are available out of season. Some local tourist offices also issue lists giving full details of all rentable accommodation in their area.

Château d'Urtubie, a listed historic monument, at Urrugne *(see p253)*

YOUTH HOSTELS

Youth hostels offer inexpensive accommodation to anyone, regardless of their age. However, to stay in a youth hostel, you must have a membership card, the Carte de la Fédération Unie des Auberges de Jeunesse **(FUAJ)**, which can be obtained from any youth hostel. Although Bordeaux and Arcachon each have a youth hostel, most are concentrated in the region between the coast of the Pays Basque and its hinterland. The youth hostels at Anglet and Biarritz also organize surfing and hiking.

Through **CROUS**, students can arrange accommodation in Bordeaux University's halls of residence during the summer.

CAMPSITES

Aquitaine has a large number of campsites, which are often sited in beautiful, unspoilt countryside. Many belong to **Camping Qualité Aquitaine**. Members of this association must display, and adhere to, a clear pricing structure, and maintain high standards of hygiene and cleanliness. Their sites must also be well-organized, in quiet, secluded locations and have no negative impact on the environment.

DISABLED TRAVELLERS

Information about accommodation with facilities for disabled travellers is available from **Tourisme et Handicap** and **Association des Paralysés de France**. The latter has also

The 18th-century Auberge du Moulin de Labique in Saint-Eutrope-de-Born, near Villeréal *(see p250)*

teamed up with Gîtes de France to recommend country gîtes, guest houses and other places to stay that are suitable for people with physical disabilites. These places are listed on a national register that is available free of charge from its website or from the head office of Gîtes de France, and also appear in listings for each *département*. The Association des Paralysés de France also has branches in each *département*. APF Évasion organizes specially designed holidays.

Swimming pool at the Eskualduna campsite, near Hendaye *(see p197)*

DIRECTORY

GENERAL INFORMATION

Maison de la France
20 avenue de l'Opéra,
75041 Paris Cedex 01
Tel (01) 42 96 70 00

CHAIN HOTELS

Mercure
2 rue de la Mare Neuve,
91021 Evry Cedex
Tel 0825 88 33 33
www.mercure.com

Sofitel
www.sofitel.com

TRADITIONAL FAMILY-RUN HOTELS

Pierre et Vacances
Tel 0825 07 06 05
www.
pierrevacances.com

Fédération Nationale des Tables et Auberges de France
2 rue Lanternières, BP 47,
31012 Toulouse Cedex 06
www.
tables-auberges.com

Logis de France
*Tel (01) 45 84 83 84
(central booking)*
www.logis-de-france.fr

Relais du Silence
17 rue d'Ouessant,
75015 Paris
*Tel (01) 44 49 90 00
(central booking)*
www.silencehotel.com

LUXURY HOTELS

Châteaux et Hôtels de France
Tel 0892 23 00 75 (central booking)
www.
chateauxhotels.com

Relais et Châteaux
Tel 0825 32 32 32 (central booking)
www.
relaischateaux.com

GUEST HOUSES

Fleurs de Soleil
www.
fleurs-soleil.tm.fr

THALASSOTHERAPY & HYDROTHERAPY

Centrales de Réservation Accor Thalassa
Tel 0825 007 777.
www.
accorthalassa.com

Chaîne Thermale du Soleil
www.sante-eau.com

Thalatel
*Tel 0826 887 099
(central booking)*
www.thalatel.com

Thermale de France
2 cours de Verdun,
40101 Dax Cedex
Tel 0800 40 00 40

COUNTRY GÎTES

Gîtes de France
59 rue Saint-Lazare, 75439
Paris Cedex 09
*Tel (01) 49 70 75 75 et
0891 16 22 22 (central booking)*
www.
gites-de-france.fr

RENTED ACCOMMODATION

Fédération Nationale des Locations Clévacances
54 boulevard de
l'Embouchure, 31000
Toulouse
Tel (05) 61 13 55 66
www.clevacances.com

Aquitaine Location Vacances
www.aquitaine-location-vacances.com

Aquitaine on Line
www.aquitaine-on-line.com

YOUTH HOSTELS

Fédération Unie des Auberges de Jeunesse (FUAJ)
9 rue Pajd, 75018 Paris

Tel (01) 44 89 87 27
www.fuaj.org

CROUS (Bordeaux)
166–192 cours
de l'Argonne,
33000 Bordeaux
Tel (05) 57 59 85 50
www.cercle-universitaire.com &
www.crous-bordeaux.fr

CAMPSITES

Camping Qualité Aquitaine
Camping Les Bo-Bains,
24150 Badefols-sur-Dordogne
Tel 05 53 73 52 52
www.campings-aquitaine.com

DISABLED TRAVELLERS

Association des Paralysés de France
17 boulevard Auguste-Blanqui, 75013 Paris
Tel (01) 40 78 69 00
*Tel (05) 56 08 67 30
(Gironde: Le Bouscat)*
*Tel (05) 58 74 67 92
(Landes: Dax)*
www.apf.asso.fr

Association Tourisme et Handicap
280 boulevard Saint-Germain, 75007 Paris
Tel (01) 44 11 10 41

Choosing a Hotel

Hotels have been selected across a wide price range for
their facilities, good value and location. The list covers all
the areas and price categories with additional information
to help you choose a hotel that best meets your needs.
Hotels within the same category are listed alphabetically.
For map references, *see back endpaper.*

PRICE CATEGORIES
Unless specified, price categories are for
a standard double room per night
during the high season, including
breakfast and taxes:
€ Under 70 euros
€€ 70–110 euros
€€€ 110–150 euros
€€€€ 150–200 euros
€€€€€ Over 200 euros

GIRONDE

ARCACHON Hôtel Le Dauphin   €€€
7 avenue Gounod, 33120 **Tel** *(05) 56 83 02 89* **Fax** *(05) 56 54 84 90* **Rooms** *50*   *Map B2*

This well-run hotel dating from the late 19th century is instantly recognizable from its red-and-white brickwork. It is
located a few blocks back from the sea in a quiet residential district. The pristine rooms have simple pine furnishings
and white walls. **www.dauphin-arcachon.com**

ARCACHON BASIN Le Grain de Sable   €€
37 avenue de la Libération, Arès, 33740 **Tel** *(05) 56 60 04 50* **Fax** *(05) 57 17 14 98* **Rooms** *14*   *Map B2*

Located on the north side of the Arcachon Basin is this simple, traditional hotel. Each room is decorated in a different
theme with pretty, fresh fabrics. Ask for a quieter room at the back overlooking the garden. There is a salon bar and
a breakfast room. **www.hotelgraindesable.com**

ARCACHON BASIN La Guérinière   €€€
18 cours de Verdun, Gujan Mestras, 33470 **Tel** *(05) 56 66 08 78* **Fax** *(05) 56 66 13 39* **Rooms** *25*   *Map B2*

This modern building stands in the centre of the local oyster farming capital. Inside the atmosphere is calm and
relaxed. The recently renovated rooms are well-equipped, spacious and bright, with contemporary décor. There is a
Michelin-starred restaurant that opens out onto a plant-filled terrace and overlooks the pool. **www.lagueriniere.com**

BLAYE Villa Prémayac   €€
13 rue de Prémayac, 33390 **Tel** *(05) 57 42 27 39* **Fax** *(05) 57 42 69 09* **Rooms** *5*   *Map C1*

This restored 18th-century villa in the heart of the city has individually styled bedrooms, with the rooms in the oldest
part named after mythological goddesses. The owner, a former artist, has created a chic, Bohemian ambiance inside.
There are two gardens outside, one Italianesque, the other contemporary Zen in style. **www.villa-premayac.com**

BLAYE Hôtel la Citadelle   €€€€
Place d'Armes, 33390 **Tel** *(05) 57 42 17 10* **Rooms** *21*   *Map C1*

Located in the centre of Blaye, this Logis de France hotel is situated on a site classed as an historic monument by
UNESCO. The 17th-century citadelle sits at the edge of the Gironde river with breathtaking views over the estuary
and is a great spot for nature lovers and sports enthusiasts. **www.hotel-la-citadelle.com**

BORDEAUX Acanthe   €
12–14 rue St-Remi, Quartier St Pierre, 33000 **Tel** *(05) 56 81 85 01* **Fax** *(05) 56 44 74 41* **Rooms** *20*   *Map C2*

The bright rooms in this recently-renovated hotel are of a decent size and all non-smoking, as well as being sound-
proofed against the city-centre traffic. Some rooms have balconies with a view of the Garonne, while others look
out over the rooftops. The staff are friendly and helpful. Public parking nearby. **www.acanthe-hotel-bordeaux.com**

BORDEAUX La Maison du Lierre   €€€
57 rue Huguerie, 33000 **Tel** *(05) 56 51 92 71* **Fax** *(05) 56 79 15 16* **Rooms** *12*   *Map C2*

Close to Bordeaux's chic Golden Triangle, this small hotel has a homely atmosphere more like a *chambre d'hôte*. It
has been renovated with flair – the quiet rooms are stylish and decorated in warm colours. Generous home-made
breakfasts may be taken in the interior courtyard. Advance booking is recommended. **www.maisondulierre.com**

BORDEAUX La Maison Bord'eaux   €€€€
113 rue de Docteur Albert Barraud, 33000 **Tel** *(05) 56 44 00 45* **Fax** *(05) 56 44 17 31* **Rooms** *6*   *Map C2*

Located near the Jardin Public is this 18th-century hotel with ultra modern décor. A beautiful stone staircase leads to
spacious rooms. Owned by the wine-producing Lurton family, tastings of the *grands crus* are offered in the bar and
gourmet dinners can be reserved. Closed Jan. **www.lamaisonbordeaux.com**

BORDEAUX Tulip Inn Bordeaux Bayonne Etche-Ona   €€€€
4 rue Martignac, 33000 **Tel** *(05) 56 48 00 88* **Fax** *(05) 56 48 41 60* **Rooms** *63*   *Map C2*

This is two hotels in one: the contemporary Bayonne and, just round the corner, the more atmospheric Etche-Ona
with its Basque-inspired décor. Both occupy elegant 18th-century mansions in the heart of the Golden Triangle and
offer comfortable rooms and top-notch service. **www.bordeaux-hotel.com**

Key to Symbols *see back cover flap*

BORDEAUX Burdigala ⚅🎁🔆🗐🅿 €€€€€

115 rue Georges-Bonnac, 33000 **Tel** *(05) 56 90 16 16* **Fax** *(05) 56 93 15 06* **Rooms** *83*   **Map** *C2*

At this sophisticated hotel in an elegant 18th-century building near the shopping street, rue Ste Catherine, the rooms are stylish and decorated using rich fabrics, wood and marble. They are also equipped with the latest technology. The restaurant Le Jardin de Burdigala, in the rotunda dining room, serves classic gourmet cuisine. **www.burdigala.com**

BORDEAUX Hauterives & Restaurant St James ⚅🎁🔆🗐🅿🌢 €€€€€

Place Charles-Hostein, Bouliac, 33270 **Tel** *(05) 57 97 06 00* **Fax** *(05) 56 20 92 58* **Rooms** *18*   **Map** *C2*

Four pavilions around a 17th-century vinegrower's house make up this luxury hotel with a view of the city below. Jean Nouvel based his design on the ancient tobacco-drying sheds of the region. The rooms combine minimalist furnishings with high-tech comforts. There is a gourmet restaurant and an upmarket bistro. **www.saintjames-bouliac.com**

BOURG Hôtel Les Trois Lis 🔆 €

11 place de la Libération, 33710 **Tel** *(05) 57 68 22 86* **Fax** *(05) 57 68 31 10* **Rooms** *11*   **Map** *C2*

Centrally-located, this well-run hotel has bright, fresh rooms and is ideal for exploring the historic centre on foot. The rooms are well-maintained, with free Wi-Fi access and hairdryers. The rooms at the front look out over the ancient covered marketplace, where the Sunday morning market is still held. Public parking nearby. **www.les-trois-lis.com**

BOURG Château de la Grave 🎁🅿🌢 €€

2km (1 mile) from Bourg centre, 33710 **Tel** *(05) 57 68 41 49* **Rooms** *3*   **Map** *C2*

Perched on a hill, this winemaking domain has a stunning view over vineyards. Renovated in Louis XIII style and crowned with two Neo-Gothic towers, the building has a rustic interior and the rooms are charming. The owners (fourth generation) will explain the winemaking process on the estate. Closed Feb. **www.chateaudelagrave.com**

CAP-FERRET La Maison du Bassin 🎁🌢 €€€

5 rue des Pionniers, 33950 **Tel** *(05) 56 60 60 63* **Fax** *(05) 56 03 71 47* **Rooms** *7 (plus 4 annex rooms)*   **Map** *B2*

Ultra-chic and highly sought-after address at the end of the Cap-Ferret peninsula. A colonial ambience is achieved with highly polished wood, cane chairs and stylish accessories. Try one of the tasty tropical rums as an aperitif, before dining on the tropical veranda. Reservations by telephone only. **www.lamaisondubassin.com**

CREON Château Camiac ⚅🎁🎴🔆🗐🅿🌢 €€€€

Route de Branne, D121, 33670 **Tel** *(05) 56 23 20 85* **Fax** *(05) 56 23 38 84* **Rooms** *14*   **Map** *C2*

This charming 19th-century château situated in the Entre-Deux-Mer vineyards, about 6km northeast of the ancient *bastide* village Créon, has vast bedrooms furnished with antiques. Classic dishes are served in a beautiful dining room with works of art hung on the walls. Tennis courts and vast garden. Closed Oct–Apr. **www.chateaucamiac.com**

LACANAU-OCEAN L'Oyat ⚅🎁🗐🅿🌢 €€

Front de Mer, 33680 **Tel** *(05) 56 03 11 11* **Fax** *(05) 56 03 12 29* **Rooms** *30*   **Map** *B2*

L'Oyat is a family-friendly hotel located at the edge of the beach in this surfers' paradise. The rooms are unexceptional but comfortable and bright. All have a view of the ocean. The restaurant L'Imprévu serves both classic and oriental dishes, while the brasserie offers salads and snacks. Handy laundry room. Closed Nov–Mar. **www.hotel-oyat.com**

LIBOURNE Château de la Rivière 🎴🔆🅿🌢 €€€

8km (5 miles) northwest of Libourne, La Rivière, 33126 **Tel** *(05) 57 55 56 51* **Rooms** *5*   **Map** *C2*

This 19th-century château, restored by Viollet le Duc, is on a wine domain that produces Fronsac AOC wines. Well-equipped with elegant furnishings, the freshly decorated bedrooms are located in the Renaissance wing. Tastings and visits of the underground cellars are available. Closed mid-Dec–mid-Jan. **www.chateau-de-la-riviere.com**

MARTILLAC Les Sources de Caudalie ⚅🎁🎴🔆🗐🅿🌢 €€€€€

Chemin Smith Haut Lafitte, 33650 **Tel** *(05) 57 83 83 83* **Fax** *(05) 57 83 83 84* **Rooms** *50*   **Map** *C2*

Situated in the Smith Haut Lafitte vineyards, this hotel is a leading health, fitness and vinotherapy centre. The luxury rooms are individually decorated. La Grande Vigne, the gourmet restaurant, is decorated in the style of an 18th-century orangery. There's also an oak-beamed inn. Golf and wine tasting courses are available. **www.sources-caudalie.com**

PAUILLAC Château Cordeillan-Bages ⚅🎁🎴🔆🗐🅿🌢 €€€€€

Route des châteaux, 33250 **Tel** *(05) 56 59 24 24* **Fax** *(05) 56 59 01 89* **Rooms** *25*   **Map** *B1*

Set among vineyards, this 17th-century former Carthusian monastery is midway between a luxury hotel and a country guesthouse. The sophisticated and contemporary rooms, softened by sunny Italian influences, open out onto the courtyard. The renowned restaurant serves ultra-modern cuisine. Closed Dec–mid-Feb. **www.cordeillanbages.com**

SAINTE CROIX DE MONT Château Lamarque 🗐🎴🅿🌢 €

6km (4 miles) east of Cadillac, 33410 **Tel** *(05) 56 62 01 21* **Fax** *(05) 56 76 72 10* **Rooms** *2*   **Map** *C2*

A family wine domain nestled in the shade of a large cedar tree offers two suites, each sleeping up to four. They are simply furnished and one suite has 1930s décor. The owner Mme Darroman is proud of her well-kept rooms and home-made jams served at breakfast. Relax at the poolside with views of the nearby vineyards. **www.ch-lamarque.com**

ST-EMILION Au Logis des Remparts 🅿🎴🗐🌢 €€

18 rue Guadet, 33330 **Tel** *(05) 57 24 70 43* **Fax** *(05) 57 74 47 44* **Rooms** *17*   **Map** *C2*

Outside peak season, when prices drop, this modest hotel provides a comfortable overnight stop. Its main draws are the sizeable terraced garden and swimming pool. The rooms lack character, but those at the back benefit from views over the vineyards. **www.saint-emilion.org**

ST-EMILION Hostellerie de Plaisance   🖼 P 🍴 📺 🅰   €€€€€

Place du Clocher, 33330 **Tel** *(05) 57 55 07 55* **Fax** *(05) 57 74 41 11* **Rooms** *17 (plus 4 suites)*   **Map** *C2*

Upscale hotel in an exceptional location overlooking St-Emilion and its famous vineyards. Luxurious rooms boast the full range of amenities, including magnificent bathrooms. Some have private terraces. The service is top-notch and the restaurant is one of the region's best. **www.hostellerie-plaisance.com**

ST-MACAIRE Hôtel Les Feuilles d'Acanthe   🍴 🏃 P 🅰   €€

5 rue de l'Eglise, St-Macaire, 33490 **Tel** *(05) 56 62 33 75* **Fax** *(05) 56 73 24 65* **Rooms** *11*   **Map** *C2*

Located in the historic medieval centre of St-Macaire, 2km (1 mile) north of Langon, is this former merchant's house dating from the 16th century. The rooms have simple, elegant oak furniture and are tastefully decorated. The service is impeccable, yet unstuffy. There is a good restaurant. Closed Christmas–mid-Jan. **www.feuilles-dacanthe.com**

SAUTERNES Peyraguey Maison Rouge   🖼 🏊 🏃 P 🅰   €€

2km (1 mile) from Sauternes, Bommes-Sauternes, 33210 **Tel** *(05) 57 31 07 55* **Rooms** *3*   **Map** *C2*

An ancient winemaker's house with elegant bedrooms decorated in a minimalist style. "St-Emilion" faces the sun setting over the vines, "Sauternes" opens out onto the pool, while "Médoc" has a stunning view of the Garonne valley. Guests receive a complimentary bottle of Sauternes on arrival. **www.peyraguey-sauternes.com**

PÉRIGORD AND QUERCY

BERGERAC La Flambée   🍴 🏊 🏃 P 🅰   €€

153 avenue Pasteur, Route de Périgueux, 24100 **Tel** *(05) 53 57 52 33* **Fax** *(05) 53 71 07 57* **Rooms** *21*   **Map** *D2*

This hotel in an old Périgordian house and in its own park is a peaceful retreat just 3km (2 miles) from the centre of Bergerac. The rooms are spacious and individually decorated. Those in the outbuildings have their own terrace. The elegant restaurant serves classic and regional dishes and there's a lounge bar for apéritifs. **www.laflambee.com**

BERGERAC Château des Merles   🍴 🏊 🏃 P 🅰   €€€

12km (7 miles) east of Bergerac, Tulières, Mouleydier, 24520 **Tel** *(05) 53 63 13 42* **Rooms** *15*   **Map** *D2*

Built at the end of the 17th century and later modified by one of Napoleon's generals, the architecture of this château is typically Neo-Classical. The bedrooms were completely renovated in 2004 and are stylish with modern décor. Facilities include a 9-hole golf course and putting green, restaurant, bistro and creche. **www.lesmerles.com**

BEYNAC Hôtel du Château   🍴 🏊   €

La Balme, 24220 **Tel** *(05) 53 29 19 20* **Fax** *(05) 53 28 55 56* **Rooms** *15*   **Map** *E2*

Attractive rooms, a good restaurant and friendly service make this small hotel the best accommodation option in this picturesque village on the Dordogne. Front rooms overlook the river, though traffic might disturb light sleepers (despite insulated windows). Free internet connection. **www.hotelduchateau-dordogne.com**

BRANTOME Hôtel Chabrol   🍴   €€

57 rue Gambetta, 24310 **Tel** *(05) 53 05 70 15* **Fax** *(05) 53 05 71 85* **Rooms** *18*   **Map** *D1*

A nicely old-fashioned hotel ideally situated in the centre of Brantôme yet still benefitting from a riverside location. The prettily decorated rooms, all light, calm and airy, represent good value for money. Those on the front look across the river to the medieval abbey. **www.lesfrereescharbonnel.com**

BRANTOME Château de la Côte   🍴 🏊 🏃 P 🅰   €€€

5km (3 miles) south of Brantôme, Biras-Bordeilles, 24310 **Tel** *(05) 53 03 70 11* **Rooms** *16*   **Map** *D1*

Set in an enchanting Renaissance château standing in its own park, this chic yet unpretentious hotel has period furniture and paintings that once belonged to the archbishop of Arles. The bedrooms are vast and some are located in the towers. Meals can be taken in the elegant restaurant or outside on the terrace. Closed Nov–Mar. **www.chateaudelacote.com**

BRANTOME Le Moulin de l'Abbaye   P 🍴 🏃 📺 🅰   €€€€€

1 route de Bourdeilles, 24310 **Tel** *(05) 53 05 80 22* **Fax** *(05) 53 05 75 27* **Rooms** *19*   **Map** *D1*

Treat yourself to a night of luxury in this romantic, creeper-covered mill on the River Dronne. Rooms are in the mill and in two handsome old houses nearby, but all share the same fresh yet sophisticated décor. Terraced waterside gardens provide the perfect breakfast spot. **www.moulinabbaye.com**

CAHORS Le Grand Hôtel Terminus   🖼 🍴 📺   €€€

5 avenue Charles de Freycinet, 46000 **Tel** *(05) 65 53 32 00* **Fax** *(05) 65 53 32 26* **Rooms** *22*   **Map** *E3*

Cahors' top hotel occupies a grand mansion two minutes from the train station. Inside, you'll find 1920s-style décor, including stained-glass windows and a reassuring air of efficiency. Rooms have less character, though most have generous bathrooms. The restaurant has a vast wine cellar. **www.balandre.com**

CHANCELADE Château des Reynats   🖼 P 🍴 🏊 🅰   €€€€

Avenue des Reynats, 24650 **Tel** *(05) 53 03 53 59* **Fax** *(05) 53 03 44 84* **Rooms** *37*   **Map** *D1*

Just west of Périgueux, this charming 19th-century château makes for an agreeable night's stay. Standard rooms in the "Orangerie" annexe are bright and breezy, but for real atmosphere upgrade to the château rooms. There's also a top-notch restaurant and spacious grounds. **www.chateau-hotel-perigord.com**

Key to Price Guide *see p244* **Key to Symbols** *see back cover flap*

DOMME L'Esplanade
P 🍽 🖹   €€

Rue du Pont Carrel, 24250 **Tel** *(05) 53 28 31 41* **Fax** *(05) 53 28 49 92* **Rooms** *25*   **Map** *E2*

Perched on the edge of a cliff, the best rooms in this elegant hotel offer panoramic views of the Dordogne valley. Some have canopied four-poster beds to match the refined, opulent décor. Less dramatic but very comfortable rooms are among the streets of the medieval *bastide*. Closed mid-Nov–end Feb.

FIGEAC Hôtel des Bains
P 🖹 🖐   €€

1 rue du Griffoul, 46100 **Tel** *(05) 65 34 10 89* **Fax** *(05) 65 14 00 45* **Rooms** *19*   **Map** *E2*

A simple, welcoming and well-tended hotel immediately across the River Célé from Figeac's glorious medieval centre. The renovated rooms, some with balconies, offer excellent value. Breakfast and drinks are served on the terrace in fine weather. There are plenty of restaurants in the vicinity. **www.hoteldesbains.fr**

LA ROQUE GAGEAC Auberge de la Plume d'Oie
🍽 🖐   €€

Le Bourg, 24250 **Tel** *(05) 53 29 57 05* **Fax** *(05) 53 31 04 81* **Rooms** *4*   **Map** *E2*

This charming, restored stonebuilt inn stands between the cliffs and the Dordogne river in a pretty medieval village. Bright, stylish rooms are decorated in neutral tones with elegant wood furniture. Enjoy gourmet food in the restaurant while admiring the boats gliding by on the river. Closed mid-Nov–late Dec & mid-Jan–Apr.

LES EYZIES-DE-TAYAC Le Moulin de la Beune
P 🍽 🖐   €

2 rue du Moulin-Bas, 24620 **Tel** *(05) 53 06 94 33* **Fax** *(05) 53 06 98 06* **Rooms** *20*   **Map** *E2*

Shady gardens beside the River Beune provide a haven of peace tucked off Les-Eyzies' busy main road. The rooms, in a converted mill building, are simple and fresh, with crisp white cottons and large windows ensuring plenty of light. There's also an excellent restaurant.

LES EYZIES-DE-TAYAC Hôtel du Centenaire
🍽 ⛱ 🖈 🖹 P 🖐   €€€€

2 avenue de Cingle, 24620 **Tel** *(05) 53 06 68 68* **Fax** *(05) 53 06 92 41* **Rooms** *19*   **Map** *E2*

Tucked away in a pleasant garden, this family-run hotel is widely recognized as one of the finest hotel-restaurants in France. Despite this accolade, the atmosphere remains friendly and informal. The luxury rooms are ornately furnished and have canopied beds. The restaurant serves inventive regional cuisine. Closed Nov–Apr. **www.hotelducentenaire.fr**

MARTEL Relais Ste-Anne
P ⛱ 🖹 🖐   €€

Rue du Pourtanel, 46600 **Tel** *(05) 65 37 40 56* **Fax** *(05) 65 37 42 82* **Rooms** *16*   **Map** *E2*

Behind the discreet entrance hides a lovely old building, once a girls' boarding school complete with a chapel, in spacious grounds. Everything is designed for a relaxing stay, from the beautifully appointed rooms – some with private terrace – to the heated pool. Hearty breakfasts. **www.relais-sainte-anne.com**

MERCUES Château de Mercuès
🖂 P 🍽 ⛱ 🖈 📺 🖐   €€€€€

46090 **Tel** *(05) 65 20 00 01* **Fax** *(05) 65 20 05 72* **Rooms** *30*   **Map** *E3*

Dominating the Lot valley is this turreted 13th-century château where the bishops of nearby Cahors once lived. It is now a luxury hotel offering rooms on a suitably grand scale, gourmet dining among chandeliers or in the courtyard, tennis courts and extensive parkland. **www.chateaudemercues.com**

MOISSAC Le Moulin de Moissac
🖂 P 🍽 🖹   €€

Esplanade du Moulin, 82200 **Tel** *(05) 63 32 88 88* **Fax** *(05) 63 32 02 08* **Rooms** *30*   **Map** *E3*

Though not the most attractive building, this hotel in a former mill more than compensates with its quiet, riverside location, efficient service and well-equipped rooms. All come with DVD/CD player, Wi-Fi Internet and coffee machine. Central Moissac is a stroll away. **www.lemoulindemoissac.com**

MONTPAZIER Edward 1er
🍽 ⛱ 🖈 P 🖐   €€€

5 rue Saint Pierre, 24540 **Tel** *(05) 53 22 44 00* **Fax** *(05) 53 22 57 99* **Rooms** *12*   **Map** *D1*

A small 19th-century château named after the founder of this well-preserved *bastide* town now offers elegant bedrooms with antique furniture, canopied beds and rich fabrics. Some rooms have views of the historic centre while others overlook the garden. The restaurant features regional produce. Closed mid-Nov–Mar. **www.hoteledward1er.com**

NONTRON Le Grand Hôtel Pélisson
🖂 P 🍽 ⛱ 🖐   €

3 place Alfred Agard, 24300 **Tel** *(05) 53 56 11 22* **Fax** *(05) 53 56 59 94* **Rooms** *23*   **Map** *D1*

This well-run provincial hotel has been in the same family for 50 years. It is a friendly and unassuming place with guest rooms overlooking the market square or the pretty garden at the back. The restaurant serves good fare, either in the oak-beamed dining room or outside.

PERIGUEUX Hôtel Régina
🖂 P 🖹   €

14 rue Denis Papin, 24000 **Tel** *(05) 53 08 40 44* **Fax** *(05) 53 54 72 44* **Rooms** *41*   **Map** *D1*

This hotel opposite the train station is one of the better accommodation options in Périgueux, the "capital" of the Dordogne. The rooms are bright and airy, if lacking in character. Those at the front have insulated windows. It's a 10-minute walk to the centre with its choice of restaurants. **www.choicehotelseurope.com**

PUY-L'EVEQUE Hôtel Bellevue
🖂 P 🍽 🖹   €

Place de la Truffière, 46700 **Tel** *(05) 65 36 06 60* **Fax** *(05) 65 36 06 61* **Rooms** *11*   **Map** *E3*

The Bellevue is a modern hotel perched above the honey-coloured houses of Puy-l'Evêque, to the west of Cahors. The décor is contemporary and all rooms have panoramic views of the Lot valley and its neatly tended vineyards. The restaurant has a reputation for adventurous, cosmopolitan cuisine.

RIBERAC Hôtel de France

3 rue Marc-Dufraisse, 24600. **Tel** *(05) 53 90 00 61* **Fax** *(05) 53 91 06 05* **Rooms** *12*   **Map** *D1*

Book ahead for a room in this charming hotel tucked down a side street off Ribérac's market square. Imaginative décor and use of colour make even the smallest rooms bright and cheerful. The same artistic touches are apparent in the restaurant and in the small flower-filled garden. **www.hoteldefranceriberac.com**

ROCAMADOUR Domaine de la Rhue

46500 **Tel** *(05) 65 33 71 50* **Fax** *(05) 65 33 72 48* **Rooms** *14*   **Map** *E2*

A short drive from Rocamadour is this peaceful hotel in beautifully converted 19th-century stables. Exposed beams and stonework give the spacious rooms an upscale rustic charm. Some come with a terrace, others with a kitchenette. The nearest restaurants are in Rocamadour. **www.domainedelarhue.com**

SARLAT Hôtel des Récollets

4 rue Jean-Jacques Rousseau, 24200 **Tel** *(05) 53 31 36 00* **Fax** *(05) 53 30 32 62* **Rooms** *18*   **Map** *E2*

Though nothing fancy, this small hotel in the heart of medieval Sarlat is a reliable option for a quiet stay. Guest rooms are modern, but traces of the building's 17th-century origins can be found in the bare stone walls and the interior courtyard – once a cloister – where breakfast is served. **www.hotel-recollets-sarlat.com**

SARLAT Clos la Boëtie

97 avenue de Selves, 24200 **Tel** *(05) 53 29 44 18* **Fax** *(05) 53 28 61 40* **Rooms** *11*   **Map** *E2*

Located in the heart of Sarlat, this renovated mansion sits in private grounds. Contemporary and antique styles have been successfully combined and the décor of the rooms is romantic and refined. Some have terraces opening onto the garden. Sauna and fitness room available. Closed mid-Nov–mid-Mar. **www.closlaboetie-sarlat.com**

ST-CIRQ-LAPOPIE Hôtel de la Pélissaria

Le Bourg, 46330 **Tel** *(05) 65 31 25 14* **Fax** *(05) 65 30 25 52* **Rooms** *10*   **Map** *E3*

Situated in a medieval clifftop village above the Lot river, this intimate hotel in a 16th-century house features tiled or polished wood floors, exposed stone walls and oak beams. The most appealing rooms occupy separate buildings in the gardens. Most rooms have lovely views.

TAMNIES Hôtel Laborderie

Le Bourg, 24620 **Tel** *(05) 53 29 68 59* **Fax** *(05) 53 29 65 31* **Rooms** *39*   **Map** *E2*

Between Sarlat and Les Eyzies-de-Tayac lies this modern, family-run hotel. It has expanded over the years from the original *auberge* to offer a wide choice of rooms in three new annexes overlooking the pool. Children will also appreciate the large, grassy park. The restaurant is good, too. **www.hotel-laborderie.com**

TREMOLAT Le Vieux Logis

Route des Champs, Le Bourg, 24510 **Tel** *(05) 53 22 80 06* **Fax** *(05) 53 22 84 89* **Rooms** *25*   **Map** *D2*

This hotel near Cadouin has been home to the same family for four generations. The rooms are located in the main house, the tenanted farm and the outbuildings. Although freshly decorated, it still retains its authenticity, with some of the furniture dating from the 16th century. The restaurant serves classic regional cuisine. **www.vieux-logis.com**

LOT-ET-GARONNE

AGEN Le Colombier du Touron

6km (4 miles) west of Agen, 187 avenue des Landes, Brax, 47310 **Tel** *(05) 53 87 87 91* **Rooms** *9*   **Map** *D3*

This 18th-century stone building, with authentic dovecote, sits in its own park close to Agen. It is a friendly-family hotel with a good restaurant and a pleasant shady terrace for summer dining. The pretty bedrooms are individually decorated using bright fabrics. Some have balconies overlooking the garden. **www.colombierdutouron.com**

AGEN Hôtel Château des Jacobins

1 place des Jacobins, 47000 **Tel** *(05) 53 47 03 31* **Fax** *(05) 53 47 02 80* **Rooms** *15*   **Map** *D3*

Built in the early 19th century, this small, ivy-clad château with a walled garden is an oasis of calm in the city centre. The rooms are elegantly decorated with period furniture and chandeliers. There's secure parking and you'll find plenty of fine restaurants within easy walking distance. **www.chateau-des-jacobins.com**

ASTAFFORT Le Square Hôtel

5–7 place de la Craste, Astaffort, 47220 **Tel** *(05) 53 47 20 40* **Rooms** *14*   **Map** *D3*

This attractive hotel in the centre of quiet Astaffort, 13km (8 miles) southwest of Laplume, has stylish, modern bedrooms. There is also a fine gourmet restaurant that serves classic cuisine with a twist. The dining room opens out onto a patio with a panoramic view. Closed Jan. **www.latrille.com**

AUBRAC Le Comptoir d'Aubrac

Hermitage Himalaya, Le Bourg, 12470 **Tel** *(05) 65 48 78 84* **Fax** *(05) 65 48 78 92* **Rooms** *5*   **Map** *D3*

Catherine Painvin, the creator of "Tartine and Chocolat" in Paris, has created a chic, bohemian *chambre d'hôte* in this small village. The décor in the personally styled rooms is enhanced with objects gathered locally, as well as from Asia and Africa. The large rooms exude comfort and simplicity. *Table d'hôte* on request. **www.catherinepainvin.com**

Key to Price Guide *see p244* **Key to Symbols** *see back cover flap*

CASTILLONNES Hôtel Restaurant Les Remparts

26 rue de la Paix, 47330 **Tel** *(05) 53 49 55 85* **Fax** *(05) 53 49 55 89* **Rooms** *9* **Map** *D2*

The attractive hotel is set back from the road in the middle of Castillonnès, a medieval *bastide*. Through an arched entrance, the 15th-century building has been tastefully renovated to provide spacious, soothing rooms. There is a popular regional cuisine restaurant with a romantic setting.

CASTILLONNES La Maison Prideaux

10km (6 miles) east of Castillonnès, Le Bourg, Parranquet, 47210 **Tel** *(05) 53 49 01 19* **Rooms** *3* **Map** *D2*

This *chambre d'hôte* is housed in a cluster of stone buildings. Original features, such as the ancient bread oven, have been carefully renovated and each room has simple modern décor that retains its rustic charm. Breakfast is copious and *table d'hôte* is available, as well as gastronomic weekends and golf lessons. **www.gites-dordogne.com**

DURAS La Maison de la Halle

7km (4 miles) south of Duras, Lévignac-de-Guyenne, 47120 **Tel** *(05) 53 94 37 61* **Rooms** *4* **Map** *D2*

Located in the *bastide* village of Lévignac, this 18th-century house overlooks the square where a market is held each Wednesday. The upmarket *chambre d'hôte* has been personally decorated by the owners with neutral tones and antiques. The upper terrace at the rear has a wonderful view of the Dropt countryside. **www.maisondelahalle.com**

LAPLUME Château de Lassalle

12km (7 miles) southwest of Laplume, Brimont, 47310 **Tel** *(05) 53 95 10 58* **Rooms** *17* **Map** *D3*

A palm-tree lined alley leads to this charming 18th-century residence which is situated in the heart of the Agen countryside. Comfortable and with a relaxed ambience, the rooms are decorated in a country house style. The restaurant, L'Orangerie, serves regional gourmet cuisine. Closed Christmas and New Year. **www.chateaudelassalle.com**

LAUZUN Château de Péchalbet

6km (4 miles) west of Lauzun, Agnac, 47800 **Tel** *(05) 53 83 04 70* **Fax** *(05) 53 83 04 70* **Rooms** *5* **Map** *D2*

This Périgordian country guesthouse, which belonged to the counts of Ségur, is set in open countryside, ensuring a peaceful stay. The rooms are comfortable, some with four-poster beds. Relax in the lounge in front of the magnificent fireplace or stroll in woods and parkland. *Table d'hôte* on request. Closed early Nov–Mar.

LE TEMPLE-SUR-LOT Les Rives du Plantié

Route de Castelmoron, 47110 **Tel** *(05) 53 79 86 86* **Fax** *(05) 53 79 86 85* **Rooms** *10* **Map** *D3*

The pretty gardens of this delightful hotel slope down to the banks of the River Lot and there is a landing stage for guests arriving by boat. The bedrooms in the renovated 19th-century house have been decorated with Provence colours and patterned fabrics. In the restaurant, imaginative dishes stray from the regional classics. **www.rivesduplantie.com**

MARMANDE Château de Malvirade

8km (5 miles) south of Marmande, Grézet-Cavagnan, 47250 **Tel** *(05) 53 20 61 31* **Rooms** *5* **Map** *D3*

This Renaissance château set in its own estate was restored in the 15th and 17th centuries. The spacious rooms are beautifully decorated, in particular the Henri de Navarre room. The owners act as guides to this historic monument, which is open to the public from May–Sep. *Table d'hôte* on request. Closed Nov–mid-Apr. **www.malvirade.com**

MONCLAR D'AGENAIS Château de Seiglal

2km (1 mile) from Monclar, 47380 **Tel** *(05) 53 41 81 30* **Rooms** *5* **Map** *D3*

Set among ancient cedars and oak trees, this hotel in a 19th-century château has large rooms with views of the park. Simply furnished with rustic period pieces, it has a homely atmosphere and families are well received. The bathrooms are basic but functional. *Table d'hôte* on request. **www.chateau-de-la-seiglal.fr**

MONFLANQUIN Les Bourdeaux

2km (1 mile) from Monflanquin, 47150 **Tel** *(05) 53 49 16 57* **Fax** *(05) 53 49 16 57* **Rooms** *3* **Map** *D3*

Located near the *bastide* town of Monflanquin, this guesthouse has magnificent views that have inspired painters such as Peter Engels. The rooms are named after wines – "Sancerre" has a private terrace, "Fleurie" has a mezzanine and "Champagne" has some original features. Closed end Oct–Easter. **www.lesbourdeaux.com**

PUJOLS Hôtel des Chênes

4km (2 miles) southwest of Pujols, Lieu dit Bel-Air, 47300 **Tel** *(05) 53 49 04 55* **Rooms** *21* **Map** *D3*

A traditional well-run hotel with a peaceful, relaxing atmosphere set in a stunning location with panoramic views of the perched village of Pujols. The rooms have basic but bright furnishings and the best ones have terraces with views. Family rooms are available. The restaurant serves classic dishes. Closed Sun, Nov–Mar. **www.hoteldeschenes.com**

PUYMIROL Les Loges de l'Aubergade

52 rue Royale, 47270 **Tel** *(05) 53 95 31 46* **Fax** *(05) 53 95 33 80* **Rooms** *10* **Map** *D3*

This country house with adjoining cloister once belonged to the counts of Toulouse. The rooms, decorated in a contemporary style by Jacques Garcia, are large and comfortable. Vaulted ceilings, stone walls and courtyards contribute to the elegant atmosphere. There is also an acclaimed restaurant. Closed 3 weeks Nov. **www.aubergade.com**

ST-SYLVESTRE-SUR-LOT Château Lalande

Avenue Georges Robert, 47140 **Tel** *(05) 53 36 15 15* **Fax** *(05) 53 36 15 16* **Rooms** *25* **Map** *D1*

A romantic atmosphere reigns in this magnificent château dating from the 13th and 18th centuries, set in a vast park. The luxurious bedrooms have period furniture, tapestries and high ceilings. The intimate restaurant serves gourmet classic cuisine. *Hammam* (Turkish bath) and tennis court available. **www.chateau-lalande-perigord.com**

TONNEINS Côté Garonne ⬛🍴⬛🅿❶   €€

36–38 cours de l'Yser, 47400 **Tel** *(05) 53 84 34 34* **Fax** *(05) 53 84 31 31* **Rooms** *6*   **Map** *D3*

The rooms at this small, well-kept hotel situated on the banks of the Garonne are colourfully decorated and of a decent size. All have a view of the river. The restaurant is bright and contemporary with a relaxed, casual atmosphere and a beautiful panorama. Traditional dishes are on offer, as well as salads and tapas. **www.cotegaronne.com**

TOURNON D'AGENAIS Hôtel du Château de l'Hoste ⬛🏛🅿❶   €€

10km (6 miles) southwest of Tournon d'Agenais, St-Beauzeil, 82150 **Tel** *(05) 63 95 25 61* **Rooms** *29*   **Map** *E3*

The charming 18th-century manor house, with a lovely white-stone façade, is set in an immense park with ancient trees and exudes a warm atmosphere. There are several categories of rooms to choose from and the largest have a lounge and dressing room. Classic French cuisine is served in the restaurant. **www.chateaudelhoste.com**

VILLEREAL Auberge du Moulin de Labique ⬛🏛🧍🅿❶   €€€

8km (5 miles) south of Villeréal, Saint-Eutrope de Born, 47210 **Tel** *(05) 53 01 63 90* **Rooms** *5*   **Map** *D2*

A peaceful stay is guaranteed in this 18th-century domain set in its own 24-ha (60-acre) estate with lakes and meadows. The rooms are in the converted stables or in the main house where they have balconies. The décor is tasteful with quarry-tiled floors and Jouy fabrics. Delicious home-made cooking. **www.moulin-de-labique.fr**

LANDES

AIRE-SUR-L'ADOUR La Maison du Bos 🏛🏛🧍🅿❶   €€

9km (6 miles) southwest of Aire-sur-l'Adour, Miramont-Sensacq, 40320 **Tel** *(05) 58 79 93 18* **Rooms** *4*   **Map** *C4*

Set in the Tursan countryside is this ancient farmhouse that has recently been renovated with care and attention to detail. There is a pretty courtyard and fountain and two blue-shuttered buildings, one houses a gîte, the other the bedrooms. The rooms are tastefully decorated and each has its own private entrance and terrace.

AIRE-SUR-L'ADOUR Château de Bachen 🧍⬛🅿❶   €€€

Duhort-Bachen, 40800 **Tel** *(05) 58 71 76 76* **Fax** *(05) 58 51 10 10* **Rooms** *4*   **Map** *C4*

This hotel, in an 18th-century château set in Tursan vineyards, commands wide views of the Gers countryside. Owned and restored by chef Michel Guérard and his wife, the hotel has very comfortable bedrooms which are decorated and furnished in an elegant and sophisticated style. Wine tastings available. Closed Nov–Mar.

BISCAROSSE La Caravelle ⬛🧍🅿❶   €€€

3km (2 miles) north of Biscarosse, Route des Lacs, Ispe, 40600 **Tel** *(05) 58 09 82 67* **Rooms** *15*   **Map** *B3*

Near a golf course and beside Lac de Biscarosse, this small, old-fashioned and well-run hotel is a haven of tranquility. The rooms have good views of the lake either from the ground floor annexe rooms or the balconies in the main building. Half board is obligatory. Closed Nov–mid-Feb. **www.lacaravelle.fr**

CAPBRETON Cap Club Hôtel 📺⬛🏛🧍⬛🅿❶   €€€

85 avenue de Maréchal de Lattre de Tassigny, 40130 **Tel** *(05) 58 41 80 00* **Rooms** *75*   **Map** *A4*

Both sport and relaxation are on offer in this modern hotel that sits on the edge of the beach facing the ocean. A vast range of sport and fitness activities are available, or you can enjoy a relaxing massage. The rooms are well-equipped and contemporary, and the restaurant caters for all tastes with healthy and gastronomic menus. **www.capclubhotel.com**

CASTETS La Bergerie St Michel 🏛🅿❶   €€

4km (2 miles) west of Castets, route de Castets, St Michel-Escalus, 40550 **Tel** *(05) 58 48 74 04* **Rooms** *3*   **Map** *B4*

Surrounded by forest and close to the Etang de Léon, this pleasant *chambre d'hôte* is set in an ancient Landaise farmhouse. The comfortable bedrooms have low-key modern furnishings and contemporary paintings, and the breakfast is copious. It is an ideal spot for nature lovers to explore the Courant d'Huchet nearby. Closed Oct–May.

CREON D'ARMAGNAC Le Poutic 🅿❶   €

Route de Cazauban, 40240 **Tel** *(05) 58 44 66 97* **Rooms** *3*   **Map** *B3*

A warm welcome awaits you at this beautifully renovated Landaise farmhouse. The rooms are spacious and contemporary furniture and colours combine perfectly with the rustic charm of the original building. Breakfast is a feast of homemade jams and pastries. *Table d'hôte* on request, offering regional dishes. Jacuzzi available. **www.lepoutic.com**

DAX Au Fin Gourmet 📺⬛🧍   €€

3 rue des Pénitents, 40100 **Tel** *(05) 58 74 04 26* **Rooms** *20*   **Map** *B4*

Conveniently located in the centre of Dax, this simple town hotel has been pleasantly renovated with a mix of modern and traditional styles and offers rooms and studios with kitchen facilities. It houses two restaurants, one with slightly kitsch décor serving traditional French dishes and the other a bistro. **www.hotel-aufingourmet.com**

DAX Mercure Splendid 📺⬛🏛🧍⬛🅿❶   €€€

Cours Verdun, 40100 **Tel** *(05) 58 56 70 70* **Fax** *(05) 58 74 76 33* **Rooms** *106*   **Map** *B4*

This hotel was particularly popular in the 1930s and was favoured by French writer Guy de Maupassant. The Art Deco style has been preserved in the bar, rooms and reception. The dining room is majestic and reportedly inspired by a cruise liner. The modern part of the building has a casino, spa and thalassotherapy centre. Closed Jan–Feb. **www.mercure.com**

Key to Price Guide *see p244* **Key to Symbols** *see back cover flap*

EUGENIE-LES-BAINS La Maison Rose   P ⑪ ▣ ◐   €€€

334 rue René Vielle, 40320 **Tel** *(05) 58 05 06 07* **Fax** *(05) 58 51 10 10* **Rooms** *40*   **Map** *C4*

The illustrious chef Michel Guérard draws worshippers to Eugénie who flock to his highly acclaimed mini hotel chain and restaurants. This, the most modest of his three hotels, feels like a country house, from the rose-filled garden to the pretty guest rooms – not lavish but absolutely immaculate. **www.michelguerard.com**

EUGENIE-LES-BAINS Les Prés d'Eugénie   P ⑪ ▣ ▤   €€€€€

334 rue René Vielle, 40320 **Tel** *(05) 58 05 06 07* **Fax** *(05) 58 51 10 10* **Rooms** *22*   **Map** *C4*

The most luxurious of Michel Guérard's three hotels has six gorgeous suites in addition to its simple but luxurious bedrooms. The 19th-century manor is famed for its *"cuisine minceur"* restaurants, which offer residents the option of losing weight while revelling in some of France's finest cooking. **www.michelguerard.com**

GRENADE-SUR-L'ADOUR Pain, Adour & Fantaisie   ⑪ ♦ ▣ P ◐   €€€€

14–16 place des Tilleuls, 40270 **Tel** *(05) 58 45 18 80* **Fax** *(05) 58 45 16 57* **Rooms** *11*   **Map** *B4*

This fine 17th-century house is located in the heart of the *bastide* town. The comfortable rooms have well-equipped bathrooms complete with jacuzzis, and a view of either the main square or the river. The gourmet restaurant has an innovative menu and serves the best of Landais produce. A superb terrace overhangs the river. Closed mid-Nov–mid-Dec.

HAGETMAU Hôtel des Lacs de l'Halco   ⑪ ▣ ♦ ▣ P ◐   €€

Route de Cazalis, 40700 **Tel** *(05) 58 79 30 79* **Fax** *(05) 58 79 36 15* **Rooms** *24*   **Map** *B4*

An unusual modern structure, designed using glass, steel, wood and stone and standing on the edge of the forest and lake, is a hotel with comfortable rooms decorated in a modern style to achieve a Zen ambience. The glass-walled restaurant appears to float on the lake and serves excellent regional dishes. **www.hotel-des-lacs-dhalco.com**

HOSSEGOR Les Hortensias du Lac   ▣ ♦ P ◐   €€€€

1578 avenue du Tour du Lac, 40150 **Tel** *(05) 58 43 99 00* **Fax** *(05) 58 43 42 81* **Rooms** *16*   **Map** *A4*

Built in the 1930s, this small Landes-Basque hotel exudes Belle Epoque charm. The villa is surrounded by pine forest and has direct access to the beach. The rooms, which either have a terrace or balcony, have been redecorated in a modern style while the suites have a colonial feel. Closed Nov–Mar. **www.hortensias-du-lac.com**

LABASTIDE ARMAGNAC Domaine de Paguy   ▣ ⑪ ▣ P ◐   €€

2km (1 mile) east of La Bastide, Betbezer-d'Armagnac, 40240 **Tel** *(05) 58 44 81 57* **Rooms** *6*   **Map** *C4*

This attractive vine-clad 16th-century manor house, overlooking the vineyards on an extensive wine estate, has large comfortable rooms that are tastefully decorated. There are also gîtes available for longer stays. Peace and tranquillity are guaranteed in this farm-auberge, which makes its own armagnacs. **www.tourisme-landes.com**

MONT-DE-MARSAN Domaine d'Agès   ▣ ▣ ♦ P ◐   €€

12km (7 miles) northwest of Mont-de-Marsan, Ousse Suzan, 40110 **Tel** *(05) 58 51 82 28* **Rooms** *3*   **Map** *C4*

Tucked away in a vast pine forest is this ivy clad house with its exceptional colonial-style balcony. There are two bedrooms and a suite, furnished with period pieces from the Louis XIII and XVI era. Breakfast can be taken outside on the terrace. Good *table d'hôte* is available on request. **www.hoteslandes.com**

MONTFORT-EN-CHALOSSE Aux Tauzins   ⑪ ▣ ♦ ▣ P ◐   €€

Route de Hagetmau, 40380 **Tel** *(05) 58 98 60 22* **Fax** *(05) 58 98 45 79* **Rooms** *16*   **Map** *B4*

This classic family-run hotel is situated in the small village of Montfort, 18km (11 miles) east of Dax, in the heart of the Chalosse countryside. The rooms are standard and well-kept. Most have balconies with magnificent views of the valley. The dining room is old-fashioned but the cuisine is delicious. Closed two weeks in Oct. **www.auxtauzins.com**

PEYREHORADE Maison Basta   ▣ ▣ ♦ P ◐   €

335 chemin de Basta, Ortheville, 40300 **Tel** *(05) 58 73 15 01* **Rooms** *4*   **Map** *B4*

One of the oldest houses in the Orthe, Maison Basta has been carefully restored from near ruins by its present owners. The rooms are located in the renovated barn and each is decorated according to a theme. Good *table d'hôte* is available to guests who book in advance. Picnics on request. Closed Christmas & New Year. **www.gite-basta.com**

SABRES Auberge des Pins   P ⑪ ♦ ◐   €€€

Route de la Piscine, 40630 **Tel** *(05) 58 08 30 00* **Fax** *(05) 58 07 56 74* **Rooms** *25*   **Map** *B3*

From the moment you enter this attractive farmhouse, deep in the forests of the Landes Regional Park, you know you're in for a treat. This is country living at its best – old-style hospitality, homely rooms, open fires in winter and quiet corners to curl up with a book. Fine restaurant. **www.aubergedespins.fr**

SEIGNOSSE La Villa de l'Etang Blanc   ⑪ ♦ P ◐   €€€

2265 route de l'Etang Blanc, 40510 **Tel** *(05) 58 72 80 15* **Fax** *(05) 58 72 83 67* **Rooms** *10*   **Map** *B4*

This charming small hotel is set in a park with direct access to the Etang Blanc. Its elegant rooms are individually decorated in a romantic style. The good restaurant serves traditional dishes and the service is professional and discreet. Boats are available to use on the waterway joining l'Etang Noir. Closed mid-Nov–Apr. **www.letangblanc.com**

SOUSTONS Hôtel du Lac   P ⑪   €

63 avenue Galleben, 40140 **Tel** *(05) 58 41 18 80* **Fax** *(05) 58 41 29 84* **Rooms** *7*   **Map** *B4*

A refurbished and unpretentious restaurant-with-rooms facing Soustons lake and a short drive from the ocean. It's worth paying a little extra for a balcony room on the front to benefit from the expansive views. The restaurant is well-loved locally for its seafood and typical Landaise dishes. **www.hoteldulac-batby.com**

SOUSTONS Relais de la Poste

🔳 🏊 🎿 🗐 🅿 🄿 €€€€

10 km (6 miles) south of Soustons, 24 ave de Marenne, Magesq, 40140 **Tel** *(05) 58 47 70 25* **Rooms** 13 **Map** *B4*

This former staging post dating from the 19th century is listed by Relais & Châteaux. The recently decorated rooms have been individually styled and there is a superb, well-equipped fitness centre. The restaurant is renowned and serves classic gastronomic dishes. Closed mid-Nov–mid-Dec. **www.relaisposte.com**

VILLENEUVE DE MARSAN Hervé Garrapit

🔳 🏊 🗐 🅿 🄿 €€€

Place Boiterie, 40190 **Tel** *(05) 58 45 20 08* **Fax** *(05) 58 45 34 14* **Rooms** 8 **Map** *C4*

This former coaching inn has individually-styled, spacious rooms, some with balconies. Higher category rooms are equipped with the latest audio and visual technology. Enjoy a drink while taking in the view of the church on the wood-decked terrace outside. Classic gastronomic dishes are served in the Louis XVI dining room. **www.herve-garrapit.com**

PAYS BASQUE

AINHOA Ithurria

🅿 🔳 🏊 🗐 €€€€

Place du Fronton, 64250 **Tel** *(05) 59 29 92 11* **Fax** *(05) 59 29 81 28* **Rooms** 27 **Map** *A4*

This pretty 17th-century Basque inn was a stop on the pilgrimage route to Santiago de Compostela. Opposite is the village's *pelota* court. Rooms are comfortable and prettily decorated, and the cosy dining room has an open fireplace, oak beams and a menu with local specialities. **www.ithurria.com**

ANGLET Château de Brindos

🅿 🔳 🏊 🗐 🄿 €€€€€

1 allée du Château, 64600 **Tel** *(05) 59 23 89 80* **Fax** *(05) 59 23 89 81* **Rooms** 29 **Map** *A4*

Set in extensive, wooded grounds, this luxurious country house hotel offers gracious living beside a peaceful lake. Modern facilities include a weight room, sauna and *hammam* (Turkish bath), with the beach and a golf course a short drive away. Enjoy breakfast on the jetty over the lake. **www.chateaudebrindos.com**

BAYONNE Adour Hôtel

🔳 🎿 🗐 €€

13 place Sainte Ursule, 64100 **Tel** *(05) 59 55 11 31* **Fax** *(05) 59 55 86 40* **Rooms** 12 **Map** *A4*

A friendly, family-orientated, city-centre hotel that is just a few steps away from the train station. Completely renovated in 2005, the rooms are spotless and have good soundproofing. Each room is decorated in a different style and reflects Basque culture. Regional dishes are served at the *table d'hôte*. Bikes are available to hire. **www.adourhotel.net**

BAYONNE Grand Hôtel

🔣 🎿 🅿 €€€

21 rue Thiers, 64100 **Tel** *(05) 59 59 62 00* **Fax** *(05) 59 59 62 01* **Rooms** 54 **Map** *A4*

This 19th-century hotel, built on the site of a former Carmelite convent, occupies a prime spot in the heart of the medieval town, between Château-Vieux and the theatre. The well-equipped rooms are comfortable and decorated in an old-fashioned classic style. Breakfast can be taken in your room or in the dining room. **www.bw-legrandhotel.com**

BIARRITZ Maïtagara

🄿 €

34 avenue Carnot, 64200 **Tel** *(05) 59 24 26 65* **Fax** *(05) 59 24 26 30* **Rooms** 15 **Map** *A4*

Guests receive a warm welcome at this 19th-century hotel located opposite the public gardens. The rooms, some of which are furnished in Art Deco style, are well-maintained and functional. There is a pretty, flower-filled garden. Closed 1st two weeks Dec. **www.hotel-maitagara.com**

BIARRITZ Inter Hotel Windsor

🅿 🔳 €€€

Grande Plage, 64200 **Tel** *(05) 59 24 98 90* **Fax** *(05) 59 24 98 90* **Rooms** 48 **Map** *A4*

Standing above the Grande Plage of lively Biarritz, this comfortable town house property has spacious rooms, with fine views from those facing the sea. The hotel affords easy access to the beach and seafront public swimming pool. The restaurant serves good seafood and local dishes. **www.inter-hotel.com**

BIARRITZ Hotel du Palais

🅿 🔳 🏊 🎿 🗐 🄿 €€€€€

1 avenue de l'Impératrice, 64200 **Tel** *(05) 59 41 64 00* **Fax** *(05) 59 41 67 99* **Rooms** 132 **Map** *A4*

The grande dame of Biarritz's hotel scene has an ambience that harks back to the resort's Belle Epoque heyday. A magnificent heated seawater pool, direct beach access, a putting green, a playground and children's pool complement the lovely rooms and outstanding restaurants. **www.hotel-du-palais.com**

BIDARRAY Hôtel Barberaenea

🔳 🎿 🅿 🄿 €

Place de l'Eglise, 64780 **Tel** *(05) 59 37 74 86* **Fax** *(05) 59 37 77 55* **Rooms** 9 **Map** *B4*

This ancient authentic Basque *auberge* is located in the same square as the pretty 12th-century church. The hotel is family-run and has rustic furniture. Some of the charming bedrooms have a view of the church while others overlook the surrounding hills and valleys. The rustic restaurant serves local dishes. Closed Nov–Jan. **www.hotel-berberaenea.fr**

LARRAU Etchemaïté

🅿 🔳 🎿 🄿 €

Larrau 64560 **Tel** *(05) 59 28 61 45* **Fax** *(05) 59 28 72 71* **Rooms** 16 **Map** *B5*

A warm welcome awaits you at this lovely *auberge* situated at the foot of the Pic d'Orhy, at the edge of the Iraty forest. The rooms are well-kept and cosy in this simple family-run hotel. The restaurant has a lovely view of the valley and serves excellent regional cuisine that combines tradition and creativity. Closed Jan. **www.hotel-etchemaite.fr**

Key to Price Guide *see p244* **Key to Symbols** *see back cover flap*

ST-ETIENNE-DE-BAIGORRY Hôtel Arce

Route Col d'Ispeguy, 64430 **Tel** *(05) 59 37 40 14* **Fax** *(05) 59 37 40 27* **Rooms** *20*   **Map** *B5*

This welcoming Basque inn set in the Aldudes valley, in the foothills of the Pyrenees, is ideal for exploring the Basque country. The guest rooms have been renovated and there is a pleasant restaurant terrace. The pool is on the opposite bank of the river, along with a tennis court. Closed mid-Nov–mid-Mar. **www.hotel-arce.com**

ST-JEAN-DE-LUZ Château Urtubie

Rue Bernard de Coral, Urrugne, 64122 **Tel** *(05) 59 54 31 15* **Fax** *(05) 59 54 31 15* **Rooms** *10*   **Map** *A4*

Situated 4km (2 miles) southwest of Saint-Jean-de-Luz, this 14th-century castle boasts Louis X and Louis XVI among its past guests, followed later by Wellington who billetted here. The well-equipped, elegant bedrooms have furniture dating from the 18th and 19th centuries and wonderful views. Closed mid-Nov–mid-Mar. **www.chateaudurtubie.fr**

ST-JEAN-DE-LUZ Grand Hôtel

43 boulevard Thiers, 64500 **Tel** *(05) 59 26 35 36* **Fax** *(05) 59 51 99 84* **Rooms** *52*   **Map** *A4*

An early 20th-century seaside resort hotel with a pink Belle Epoque façade facing Saint-Jean-de-Luz bay. The recently renovated bedrooms are well-equipped and comfortable, and around half of them have a seaview. The spa-thalasso centre has been open since 2007. There is an excellent restaurant. Closed Jan. **www.luzgrandhotel.fr**

ST-JEAN-PIED-DE-PORT Hotel les Pyrénées

19 place du Général-de-Gaulle, 64220 **Tel** *(05) 59 37 01 01* **Fax** *(05) 59 37 18 97* **Rooms** *18*   **Map** *B5*

This 18th-century coaching inn stands at the French end of the Roncevaux pass, where the pilgrim's route to Santiago de Compostela crosses the Pyrenees. It offers immaculate rooms, a health club with heated outdoor pool and a restaurant with both gastronomic and budget menus. **www.hotel-les-pyrenees.com**

BÉARN

ESQUIULE Chez Chilo

7km (4 miles) west of Esquiule on D24, route de Barcus, 64130 **Tel** *(05) 59 28 90 79* **Rooms** *11*   **Map** *B5*

Hidden in the Béarn countryside, around 15km (9 miles) west of Oloron-Sainte-Marie, is this delightful, whitewashed traditional inn. The interior is rustic with authentic Basque furniture. The pleasant rooms have been refreshed and some of the bathrooms have a jacuzzi. M. Chilo prepares colourful Basque-Béarn dishes. Closed Jan. **www.hotel-chilo.com**

MONEIN Maison Canterou

Quartier Laquidée, 64360 **Tel** *(05) 59 21 41 38/(06) 32 38 80 98* **Rooms** *5*   **Map** *C4*

This traditional farmhouse with an inner courtyard is located on the rolling Béarn hills, in a wine estate that produces Jurançon wines. The rooms are tastefully decorated. One has a balcony opening out to face the Pyrenees while "Cupidon" is for romantics. *Table d'hôte* is available on request.

OLORON-STE-MARIE Hotel Alysson

Boulevard Pyrénées, 64400 **Tel** *(05) 59 39 70 70* **Fax** *(05) 59 39 24 47* **Rooms** *32*   **Map** *B4/5*

In a pleasant small town poised between the lowlands and the Pyrenees, this hotel has small, well-designed modern rooms, excellent cooking and an attractive open-air terrace-bar. The enormous restaurant opens onto the attractive gardens. **www.alysson-hotel.fr**

ORTHEZ Reine Jeanne

44 rue Bourg Vieux, 64300 **Tel** *(05) 59 67 00 76* **Fax** *(05) 59 69 09 63* **Rooms** *30*   **Map** *B4*

Occupying an 18th-century building in this historic Bearnaise town straddling the Gave de Pau river, this pleasant hotel has small guest rooms around a sheltered courtyard, as well as a modern wing with larger rooms. It has a country-style restaurant with traditional cooking. **www.reine-jeanne.fr**

PAU Hôtel Continental

2 rue Maréchal Foch, 64000 **Tel** *(05) 59 27 69 31* **Fax** *(05) 59 27 99 84* **Rooms** *75*   **Map** *C4*

This comfortable hotel in the centre of historic Pau has huge old-fashioned bedrooms and is situated just a couple of minutes' walk from the castle and a choice of restaurants. Opened in 1912, the Continental has old-world charm but with up-to-date facilities. Parking is available nearby. **www.continental-pau.com**

PAU Hotel du Parc Beaumont

1 avenue Edouard VII, 64000 **Tel** *(05) 59 11 84 00* **Fax** *(05) 59 11 85 00* **Rooms** *72*   **Map** *C4*

This luxurious modern hotel, part of the Concorde group, stands in beautiful grounds next to Pau's casino and palm-lined boulevard with great views of the Pyrenees. Rooms are lavishly furnished and there is a heated pool, whirlpool, sauna and *hammam* (Turkish bath). **www.hotel-parc-beaumont.com**

SAUVETERRE-DE-BEARN La Maison de Navarre

Quartier St-Marc, 64390 **Tel** *(05) 59 38 55 28* **Fax** *(05) 59 38 55 71* **Rooms** *7*   **Map** *B4*

This pink mansion house in a beautiful medieval village has bright, airy guest rooms. It is comfortable, good value for money and child-friendly. The family donkey, Zebulon, lives in the garden and the beaches of the Atlantic coast are not too far away. Excellent restaurant. **www.lamaisondenavarre.com**

WHERE TO EAT

The art of cooking is deeply rooted in the culture of Aquitaine, and the wealth of fine produce, specific to the region, is reflected in the wide range of superb local dishes. Some specialities, including beef from Bazas, black cherries from Itxassou and, of course, truffles from the Périgord, are celebrated at the many food festivals that punctuate the year here. Wherever you go, from the Médoc to the Pays Basque, and from the Arcachon Basin to the high Pyrenees, you are sure to enjoy excellent food, not only in restaurants and bistros, but also at more modest places, serving *table d'hôte* meals.

Les Loges de l'Aubergade, a restaurant in Puymirol *(see p265)*

TYPES OF RESTAURANT

In Aquitaine, there is a wide variety of places where you can enjoy good food. These range from top-class restaurants with famous reputations to brasseries, small taverns and tapas bars, and *salons de thé* (tea rooms). A good gauge of the quality of an establishment is often the display of a badge or logo, indicating membership of an association, such as the Fédération Nationale des Tables et Auberges de France *(see p243)* or **Restaurateurs de France**, which lists places that meet certain standards of gastronomy and service. One group, **Toques du Périgord**, accepts as members those restaurants in the Dordogne where professional chefs produce authentic dishes by traditional methods. Another reliable indicator of quality is a listing in Logis de France, Châteaux et Hôtels de France or Relais et Châteaux *(see pp240–43)*. Some websites, notably the **Association des Cuisiniers Landais** and **Balades en Aquitaine** also list recommended restaurants.

LOCAL PRODUCE

Besides its world-famous wines, Aquitaine is an abundant source of top-quality produce, such as lamb from Pauillac, ducks and geese from the Landes, beef from Bazas and capons from Grignols. All along the rivers Garonne and Dordogne, shad and lamprey, two species of migratory fish, are highly prized for their fine flavour. The region is also noted for its magnificent crayfish, bred from an imported New World variety, as the indigenous species is now protected. Oysters are gathered in the Arcachon Basin and on the Arguin sandbank, as are shellfish, including piddock, which is eaten either raw or cooked. Hake is fished in the Gulf of Gascony and sardines in the waters off Saint-Jean-de-Luz.
   Among the region's finest fruit and vegetables are prunes and melons from the Agenais, tomatoes from Marmande and asparagus from Blayais. Walnuts from the Périgord are a wonderful addition to *salade landaise*, made with gizzard confit. In the Pays Basque, strings of bright red, Espelette peppers, which add a touch of spice to many local dishes, are often hung up to dry across the fronts of houses. Several hundred different species of edible mushroom also grow in Aquitaine, including cèpes and the highly prized truffle – the "black diamond" of the Perigord.

SPECIALITIES

With every season, certain specialities come into their own. Autumn is the time to enjoy truffles cooked in goose fat with scallops, and wood pigeon is eaten either roasted or as salmi (a rich stew). If you like freshwater fish, you can feast on elvers, popularly known as "the white gold of the Adour". Foie gras *(see p256)*, lightly cooked or fried as escalopes and served with fruit, is probably the most famous delicacy of the region, and a popular, but more homely, dish is *garbure (see p257)*, a Béarnese vegetable soup made with confit of

Tables on the terrace of the Restaurant de la Poste near Terrasson-Lavilledieu *(see p263)*

Empress Eugénie's former summer palace in Biarritz, now the Hôtel du Palais *(see p268)*

goose. The cuisine of Aquitaine also features a host of pork products, such as Bayonne ham *(see p256)*, *ventrèche* (dried streaky bacon), grilled *tricandilles* (tripe) and *grenier médocain* (rolled pork belly).

In Basque auberges, you will be served tasty dishes in which colourful, sweet red Espelette peppers frequently feature. These range from *chipirons* (small stuffed squid) and *marmitako* (tuna casserole) to *txanguro* (stuffed crab) and *piperade* (a type of ratatouille). Some restaurants organize courses that aim to introduce visitors to the art of cooking, with the emphasis on the traditional preparation of local produce.

CHEESES AND DESSERTS

The most popular cheese in Aquitaine is *tomme de brebis*, a ewe's milk cheese from the Ossau valley, that is served with black cherry jam *(see p257)* or quince jelly. This is closely followed in popularity by *cabécou*, a creamy goat's cheese.

Traditional desserts include *cannelés de Bordeaux* (small fluted cakes with a soft, moist centre and caramelized shell), *tourtière aux pruneaux* (a crisp cake made with prunes), served flambéed in Armagnac, *gâteau basque (see p257)*, and *touron,* a specialist Basque confectionery *(see p273)*.

EATING OUT

The enjoyment of food in convivial surroundings is of central importance right across France. In restaurants, bread and a carafe of water will automatically be brought to your table. These are included in the price of the meal, as is service, even though it is still customary to leave a tip. In the high summer season, it is always advisable to book a table in advance. In the low season, particularly in country areas, many restaurants close for periods of a few weeks or several months. To check, call in advance.

Most establishments accept major credit cards, such as Visa, Mastercard, American Express and Diners' Club.

Interior of the Casino at Salies-de-Béarn *(see p216)*

WHEELCHAIR ACCESS

Any establishment that displays a "Tourisme et Handicap" sticker will have wheelchair access and facilities for people with disabilities. Brochures issued by tourist offices also give details of establishments participating in the Tourisme et Handicap scheme. Several other organizations also provide information on a range of restaurants, hotels and other establishments with facilities for people with disabilities *(see pp242–3)*.

CHILDREN

Almost all restaurants in Aquitaine welcome children, and most have special, cheaper children's menus. Some establishments also provide high chairs for very young children.

DIRECTORY

Balades en Aquitaine
www.balades-en-aquitaine.com

Les Toques du Périgord
www.toques-perigord.com

Association des Cuisiniers Landais
www.qualitelandes.com

Restaurateurs de France
www.restaurateursdefrance.com

The Flavours of Aquitaine

Southwestern France fulfils the requirements of the most demanding gourmet. The Atlantic coast supplies fine seafood, while inland forests are a rich hunting ground for game, truffles and wild mushrooms. Geese and ducks provide the fat that is key to local cuisine, as well as meat and *foie gras*. The Pyrenees offer beef and lamb grazed on mountain pastures, and the Basque country adds the spicy notes of red peppers and fine chocolate. Charcuterie and cheeses abound. Garlic, saffron and walnut oil contribute yet more flavour and colour. Bordeaux's world-class wines *(see pp258–9)* are the perfect accompaniment.

Black truffles

Fishermen opening oysters at a maritime festival in Arcachon

MEAT, GAME & SEAFOOD

Ducks and geese, fattened to produce *foie gras* and *confit* meat (preserved in fat), are highly prized, as are flavourful rosy *agneau de Quercy* lamb, raised on the grasslands of the Causses de Quercy, and milk-fed veal *(veau sous la mère)*. Regional charcuterie (preserved meat, usually pork

but also game) is superb, notably the sweet salted and dried ham of Bayonne. Pork also features in the *boudin blanc* and *boudin noir* of Quercy and is used with duck or goose liver in pâtés. The woodlands of the Dordogne and Lot are rich in game: *sanglier* (wild boar), *chevreuil* (roe deer), *faisan* (pheasant), *lièvre* (hare) and *perdrix* (partridge).

The pure, clear waters of the Arcachon Basin enhance the flavour of its oysters. They need no accompaniment other than lemon or shallot vinegar, but the citizens of Bordeaux like to eat them with little sausages. Mussels are also raised on the coast, and the sea yields a variety of fish. Eels, lamprey and sturgeon are caught in the Gironde estuary.

Chorizo — Garlic saucisson — Truffle saucisson — Wild boar saucisson — Wild boar ham — Bayonne ham — Bilberry saucisson

Selection of traditional southwestern charcuterie

REGIONAL DISHES AND SPECIALITIES

Pink garlic

As a starter, duck or goose *foie gras* may be served with a jelly of sweet Monbazillac wine. On the coast, a seafood soup such as *chaudrée* (with white wine and garlic) might be offered. In the Pays Basque there could be a dish of *chipirons* (little peppers stuffed with spicy salt cod). *Salades quercynoise, périgordienne* and *landaise* are all variants on salad with *foie gras*, smoked *magret* (duck breast fillet), *confit de gésiers* (preserved gizzards) and perhaps stuffed goose neck *(cou farci)*. Meat may be served with a *sauce Périgueux* (shallots, truffle shavings and Monbazillac) or *à l'Agennaise* (with prunes and Armagnac). Rocamadour goat's cheese is often served with a salad, dressed with walnut oil, while *fromage de brébis* (ewe's milk cheese) comes with cherry or quince jam *(pâte de coings)*. Desserts tend to be based on local fruits.

Salade landaise, *featuring* foie gras, *duck confit and* gizzards, *makes a good main meal in a bistro.*

Fattened Périgord geese, the source of *foie gras*

FRUIT, NUTS & VEGETABLES

The fruit that best characterizes the region is the plum or, rather, two plums: the round, green *reine-claude* (greengage) and the larger, purple plums that become *pruneaux d'Agen*, succulent black prunes used in tarts and patisserie or enveloped in chocolate. Other fruits include *fraises du Périgord* strawberries and the black cherries of Itxassou. Walnut trees are abundant in the Dordogne and Lot, where plantations hug the river valleys. Walnuts are served raw with cheese, as well as going into many traditional recipes, from sauces to bread, cakes and tarts. Walnut oil is never used in cooked dishes, but is delicious simply drizzled over lettuce.

Basque cuisine gets its spicy identity from the red Espelette pepper *(see p199)* which is dried and powdered for use in dishes such as *piperade*. Vegetables such as asparagus and early carrots thrive in the sandy soil of the Landes.

Harvest of walnuts from the Quercy region

TRUFFLES

The oak forests that cover much of the Périgord region conceal one of its most prized treasures, the black truffle or *truffe du Périgord*, also dubbed the "black diamond", which goes to flavour many luxury dishes. Truffles grow on the roots of oak trees and are located with the help of trained pigs or dogs. During the season, from November to March, truffles sell for astronomical prices at markets in villages such as Lalbenque and Limogne-en-Quercy.

ON THE MENU

Chipirones à l'encre Baby squid cooked in their own ink

Civet de lièvre Jugged hare

Entrecôte à la bordelaise Steak in a sauce of red wine, shallots and bone marrow

Garbure béarnaise Vegetable soup with *confit* of duck or goose and red wine

Matelotte d'anguilles Eel stewed in wine sauce

Pommes sarladaises Potatoes sautéed in goose fat with chopped garlic and parsley

Poule au pot béarnaise Chicken stuffed with giblets, garlic, onion, breadcrumbs and egg, stewed with vegetables

Ttoro Rich fish and shellfish stew with tomatoes, onions and Espelette pepper

Omelette aux truffes *is a simple dish transformed by its luxurious garnish of shaved black truffle.*

Piperade *is a Basque dish of stewed peppers, onions and tomatoes with eggs. Bayonne ham may be laid on the top.*

Croustade, *thin pastry layered with butter and sliced apples, is perfumed with Armagnac and vanilla.*

What to Drink in Aquitaine

For centuries, the vineyards of Aquitaine have been producing excellent wines and other alcoholic drinks, most notably the world-renowned wines of Bordeaux and the great Armagnacs. The fine wines produced in areas such as Bergerac, Cahors, Côtes-de-Duras and Jurançon are also recognized internationally for their high quality. Modern wine-making techniques, allied with age-old methods, are now widely used, resulting in an almost unequalled level of expertise. Eaux-de-vie is made by a dwindling number of travelling home-distillers, and the region is also noted for its spring and mineral waters and for its locally produced fruit juices.

Bottle of Izarra

Poster advertising Lillet, an aperitif

RED WINES

Bergerac   Côtes-de-Duras   Saint-Émilion

Wines produced in the Bordeaux region have several *appellations*: Haut-Médoc, Margaux, Saint-Estèphe, Graves, Fronsac, Saint-Émilion and Pomerol. Aquitaine has some famous wine châteaux and several *grands crus*, such as Mouton Rothschild. The CIVB (Conseil Interprofessionnel des Vins de Bordeaux; (05) 56 00 22 66), and the *maisons du vin* that have been set up in many vine-growing areas, work to promote the region's wines, and growers often open their cellars to visitors. Not far from the Bordeaux area are other, equally renowned wine-producing regions, including Buzet, Madiran, Bergerac and Côtes-de-Duras, one of the oldest AOCs in France. Thanks to a few enthusiasts, some lesser-known areas are returning to prominence. These include Estaing, in the Lot, and Domme in the Périgord. Cahors wines, which are already well known, are going from strength to strength.

WHITE WINES

The region's best-known dessert wine is undoubtedly Sauternes, whose producers include the legendary Château d'Yquem. Other excellent dessert wines include Sainte-Croix-du-Mont, Loupiac and, of course, Monbazillac. The two smooth, white wines of the Dordogne, Saussignac and Rosette, are both excellent accompaniments to fish and white meat, but they can also be enjoyed as dessert wines. The dry white wines of Entre-Deux-Mers, Tursan and Chalosse, go particularly well with cheese. Tariquet, between the Landes and the Gers, is a large estate well known for its Côtes de Gascogne *vins de pays* and for its brandies. The vineyards of the Jurançon area, at the foot of the Pyrenees, produce distinctive dry, sweet and dessert wines.

Bottle of Pacherenc

WINE-TASTING

Certain inter-professional organizations, including INAO (Institut National des Appellations d'Origine), have designed a set of glasses that allow the drinker to fully appreciate the colour, nose and other characteristics of each type of wine. For example, a brandy glass is wider than a red wine glass, and has a shorter stem. A white wine glass is taller and narrower.

INAO red wine glass   INAO white wine glass   Brandy glass

LIQUEURS AND BRANDIES

Aquitaine produces many different types of apéritif, including plum or walnut liqueurs and red or white Kina Lillet, a mixture of Peruvian quinine and local wine, made in the Bordeaux region since 1887. Armagnac is the oldest French eau-de-vie, and 6 million bottles of it are sold each year. Floc de Gascogne is an apéritif version of Armagnac. Izarra, a liqueur made from a blend of Pyrenean and Oriental plants, has been made in the Pays Basque since 1835. Pacharan, from Basse-Navarre, is an aniseed-flavoured liqueur in which wild sloes are macerated. Like Izarra, Pacharan is served either before or after a meal.

Lillet, an apéritif from Bordeaux

Bottle of Armagnac

Floc de Gascogne

Prune-based apéritif

NON-ALCOHOLIC DRINKS

Abatilles mineral water

With its well-preserved natural environment, southwestern France has several sources of pure spring and mineral water. Although the Lot's spa has closed, its spring is the source of Miers-Alvignac water. Being rich in beneficial minerals and having diuretic properties, this is available from chemists. Abatilles mineral water, from the Arcachon Basin, is ideal for everyday drinking. Drinks made from pure fruit juices, such as prune and apple, are produced by several makers, including Vallée Verte in Le Bugue, in the Périgord.

Café terrace in Mézin

READING A WINE LABEL

Estate

Vintage (the year when the grapes were harvested). Some labels also show the wine's alcohol content.

"Mis en bouteille au château" ("estate-bottled") is a guarantee of the wine's authenticity.

Château de Côme

Saint-Estèphe

APPELLATION SAINT-ESTÈPHE CONTRÔLÉE

CRU BOURGEOIS

2000

MAURICE VELGE S.A. PROPRIÉTAIRE
33180 SAINT ESTÈPHE

Mis en Bouteille au Château

750 ml

The château is sometimes shown on the label.

Appellation d'Origine Contrôlée indicates the area of production.

Classification

Bottle's capacity

Wines are mainly classified according to their country and region of origin, their category (AOC or *vin de pays*), their alcohol content and their vintage. Choosing a wine will depend on the type of dish it is to accompany, on price in relation to quality, and on age. You can invest in young wines for laying down or buy those that are ready to drink. The choice in Aquitaine ranges from little-known *vins de pays* to some of the world's greatest vintages.

Choosing a Restaurant

The restaurants, cafés and other food establishments listed here have been selected largely for the quality of their menus and their commitment to using local produce. The entries are listed by area and alphabetically within each price category. For map references, *see back endpaper.*

PRICE CATEGORIES
The following price categories are for a three-course meal for one, including half a bottle of house wine, service and tax.

€ Under 30 euros
€€ 30–45 euros
€€€ 45–65 euros
€€€€ 65–80 euros
€€€€€ Over 80 euros

GIRONDE

ARCACHON Chez Yvette
€€   *Map B2*
59 boulevard du Général Leclerc, 33120 **Tel** *(05) 56 83 05 11* **Fax** *(05) 56 22 51 62*

Seafood doesn't come much fresher than at this venerable Arcachon restaurant run by former oyster farmers. Success stories include lamprey *à la bordelaise* (cooked in wine) and roast turbot, but it is hard to resist the spectacular seafood platters. It's wise to make reservations in advance.

ARCACHON BASIN Chez Eliette-Xavier Jalade
€€   *Map B2*
19 avenue Commandant-Allègre, Andernos-les-Bains, 33510 **Tel** *(05) 56 82 16 77*

Former oyster farmer Xavier has transformed his fish shop into this delightful, good-value restaurant sitting on the jetty. A selection of the freshest seafood is beautifully presented and prepared. It is one of the best places to try oysters; the crab soup and tartare of tuna are also delicious. Xavier's wife, Sylvie, conjures up irresistible desserts.

ARCACHON BASIN Sail Fish
€€   *Map B2*
Rue des Bernaches, Lege-Cap-Ferret, 33970 **Tel** *(05) 56 60 44 84*

This trendy restaurant standing on the north side of the basin is popular with both the local smart set and visitors. The menu ranges from simple steak grilled on an open fire to more elaborate dishes using regional produce, such as duck and foie gras. There's good freshly-caught seafood too. As night falls the dancing begins.

ARCINS Le Lion d'Or
€€   *Map C2*
Place de la République, 33460 **Tel** *(05) 56 58 96 79*

Situated 6km (4 miles) from Margaux, on the Médoc wine route, is this animated bistro, which has a dining room decorated with wooden wine cases from the neighbouring estates. The delicious regional cuisine is served in large portions. The restaurant is small and popular with locals so book ahead. Closed Mon, Sun, Jul & public hols.

BAZAS Les Remparts
€€   *Map C3*
49 place de la Cathédrale, 33430 **Tel** *(05) 56 25 95 24*

A pleasant restaurant where the locals come *en famille*, Les Remparts has a lovely view of the cathedral's rose garden from the terrace. The good-value midday menus offer traditional cuisine prepared with an innovative touch. Veal cutlet with girolle mushrooms and tartare of scallops and salmon are among the choices. Closed Mon & Sun pm.

BORDEAUX Bistrot d'Edouard
€   *Map C2*
16 place du Parlement, 33000 **Tel** *(05) 56 81 48 87* **Fax** *(05) 56 48 51 74*

On one of Bordeaux's prettiest squares, this fuss-free bistro offers a broad range of inexpensive fixed-price menus. Don't expect gourmet dining, but the food is reliable, covering everything from salads, omelettes, vegetarian dishes and fish to regional specialities. Outside dining in summer.

BORDEAUX Estaquade
€   *Map C2*
Quai des Queyries, 33000 **Tel** *(05) 57 54 02 50*

A fashionable venue on the north bank of the Garonne, this restaurant is entirely made of wood, zinc and steel, and is raised on stilts. It has a waterside terrace with an unspoilt view of the Place de la Bourse. Breast of duck, rib beef and Atlantic fish are treated with imagination. Excellent value midday menu. Closed Christmas and New Year.

BORDEAUX Café Maritime
€€   *Map C2*
1 quai Armand-Lalande, Hangar G2, Bassin à Flot (berth) no. 1, 33000 **Tel** *(05) 57 10 20 40*

This smart, trendy café is located in a converted dockside boatshed. The bold decoration features tropical white-leaded wood, giant lamps and ephemera from faraway shores. Dishes are cooked in the state-of-the-art kitchen in view of the diners. The menu ranges from classic dishes to the more exotic, such as Thai mussels and sushi. Closed Sun.

BORDEAUX Le Café Gourmand
€€   *Map C2*
3 rue Buffon, 33000 **Tel** *(05) 56 79 23 85*

Patronized by local clientèle, this smart yet laid back bistro in Bordeaux's Golden Triangle serves local dishes prepared with a modern touch, such as stir-fried Landes chicken or lamprey *à la bordelaise*. Compose your own mini or maxi menu from a choice of five starters and five mains. For those with a sweet tooth, there is also a menu *"maxi sucrée"*.

Key to Symbols *see back cover flap*

BORDEAUX Le Chapon Fin

5 rue Montesquieu, 33000 **Tel** *(05) 56 79 10 10* **Map** *C2*

This establishment in the heart of the old city has long been a meeting place for politicians and artists, frequented for its superb gourmet cuisine as well as for its ornate Belle Epoque décor. The gastronomic cuisine has been brought into the 21st century, with great success, by chef Nicolas Frion. Closed Mon, Sun & Aug. **www.chapon-fin.com**

FRONSAC Le Bord d'Eau

Route de Libourne, 33126 **Tel** *(05) 57 51 99 91* **Map** *C2*

The menu at this riverside restaurant with a spectacular view features freshwater fish and aromatic meat stews. Lamprey *à la bordelaise*, Arcachon sole and herring caviar are some of the tasty dishes on offer. The cellar is stocked with Fronsac wines (some old vintages) and also the lesser known Lalande de Fronsac. Closed Mon, Wed pm & Sun pm.

LANGON Claude Darozze

95 cours du Général-Leclerc, 33210 **Tel** *(05) 56 63 00 48* **Fax** *(05) 56 63 41 15* **Map** *C2*

Inside this unassuming hotel-restaurant you'll find wonderfully over-the-top décor and some of the region's best food and wine. Depending on the season, you might be regaled with a *carpaccio de thon rouge* (red tuna) with cheese, followed by oysters and a stunning Grand Marnier soufflé, light as air.

LA REOLE Aux Fontaines

8 rue de Verdun, 33190 **Tel** *(05) 56 61 15 25* **Map** *C2*

Formerly a school where young ladies learned how to run a household, Aux Fontaines is now a good-value restaurant where the chef likes to experiment with textures and flavours. Grapefruit and melon soup, sardines stuffed with risotto, and *parmentier* of duck are some of the delicious propositions. Closed Mon, Wed pm & Sun.

MONSEGUR La Ferme Gauvry

10km (6 miles) west of Monségur, D16, Rimons, 33540 **Tel** *(05) 56 71 83 96* **Map** *C2*

This real working farm with chickens, cows and pigs, and vineyards now offers authentic home-made dishes to suit a variety of budgets and appetites, including panfried veal liver, grilled duck breast and more elaborate dishes such as *garbure (see p257)* of woodpigeon. Reservations recommended. Closed Mon, Tue & 1st two weeks Jan.

MONTAGNE ST-EMILION Le Vieux Presbytère

Place de l'Eglise, 33570 **Tel** *(05) 57 74 65 33* **Map** *C2*

An ancient presbytery standing at the foot of a Roman chapel now houses an elegant restaurant. Since the current owners' arrival in 2005, the cuisine has gained an excellent reputation. Inspired by regional products, the combination of tradition with modernism results in succulent dishes such as roast lamb with garlic confit. Closed Tue & Wed.

PAUILLAC Château Cordeillan-Bages

61 rue Vignerons, 33250 **Tel** *(05) 56 59 24 24* **Fax** *(05) 56 59 01 89* **Map** *B1*

Very much an up-and-coming restaurant in the heart of Bordeaux's vineyards – its third Michelin star is close. The Pauillac lamb is a signature dish, which might be preceded by an inventive *petit-pois* milkshake and followed by mint-chocolate finger served with a green-tea jelly and bitter chocolate pastry. Well worth splashing out for.

PORT DE MACAU La Guinguette du Bout d'Ile

7km (4 miles) from Margaux on D2, 33460 **Tel** *(05) 57 88 04 81* **Map** *C2*

Hidden away at the end of a road that weaves its way through the Gironde countryside (take the Chemin du Bord de l'Eau at Macau), is this traditional *guinguette* (open-air café or dance hall) sitting at the water's edge. Friendly and relaxed, locals come here to enjoy simply prepared regional dishes, such as meat and fish grilled over a wood fire.

PYLA-SUR-MER Gérard Tissier

35 boulevard de l'Océan, 33115 **Tel** *(05) 56 54 07 94* **Map** *B2*

Near the dunes and facing the ocean, this restaurant with a discreet nautical theme serves well-prepared, freshly caught seafood dishes with a modern twist. To awaken the palate try the smoked salmon with wasabi sorbet and for a main course, fillet of bass with Asiatic flavours. For dessert there is a more classic choice. Good Bordeaux wines.

ST-EMILION L'Envers du Décor

11 rue du Clocher, 33330 **Tel** *(05) 57 74 48 31* **Fax** *(05) 57 24 68 90* **Map** *C2*

Local wine producers rub shoulders with tourists in this delightful little bistro/wine bar. The menu runs the gamut, from omelettes and salads to more elaborate regional dishes, or you can choose from daily specials on the chalkboard. Winner of the award for the best wine list in France in its class.

SOULAC-SUR-MER Le Pavillon de la Mer

19 rue de la Plage, 33780 **Tel** *(05) 56 09 80 82* **Map** *B1*

One of the best restaurants in this popular Second Empire seaside resort. This traditional restaurant without pretention offers good quality, reliable cuisine. Freshly caught fish such as sea bass, seafood platters and succulent roast lamb are among the classics on offer. The service is attentive, even in high season. Closed Oct–Mar.

VERTHEUIL La Table d'Olivier

53 route de Lesparre, Gaillan-en-Médoc, 33340 **Tel** *(05) 56 41 13 32* **Map** *B1*

Situated 14km (9 miles) northwest of Vertheuil is this restaurant beside a lake. The dining room has a simple homely feel with large rustic wooden tables. Refined, quality cuisine includes dishes such as Blaye asparagus with spring herb flavoured butter. Classic desserts. Resonably priced wines. Closed Mon, Sat lunch, Sun pm, two weeks Feb & mid-Jul–Aug.

PÉRIGORD AND QUERCY

BERGERAC La Cocotte des Halles

Place du Marché-Couverte, 24100 **Tel** *(05) 53 24 10 00* **Fax** *(05) 53 24 10 00*   **Map** *D2*

Red-and-white checked tablecloths set the tone in this popular little restaurant in the market hall. Choose from daily specials featured on the chalkboard. Typical dishes include duck *confit* with *pommes sarladaises* (potatoes fried with parsley and garlic). A lovely spot for a light lunch.

BRANTOME Le Moulin du Roc

7km (4 miles) northeast of Brantôme, Le Pont, Champagnac de Belair, 24530 **Tel** *(05) 53 02 86 00*   **Map** *D1*

Set in a 17th-century walnut oil mill on the Dronne, this restaurant's cuisine has a high reputation. Installed on the waterside terrace or in the luxurious dining room, diners enjoy such delicacies as crispy artichoke and *foie gras* tart. Delicious desserts. Good selection of Bergerac and Bordeaux wines. Closed Tue, Wed lunch & mid-Oct–mid-May.

BRANTOME Les Frères Charbonnel

57 rue Gambetta, 24310 **Tel** *(05) 53 05 70 15* **Fax** *(05) 53 05 71 85*   **Map** *D1*

The restaurant of the Hôtel Chabrol has a well deserved reputation for its upscale regional cuisine and excellent service. Black périgord truffles add style to omelettes and to the house special, pike-perch *vol-au-vent*. These can be enjoyed in the dining room, or on the riverside terrrace.

BRANTOME Le Moulin de l'Abbaye

1 route de Bourdeilles, 24310 **Tel** *(05) 53 05 80 22* **Fax** *(05) 53 05 75 27*   **Map** *D1*

Dine in luxury on innovative dishes such as duck *foie gras* poached in walnut liqueur, or grilled pigeon flavoured with almond oil and Jamaican pepper. Luscious desserts might include a gratin of strawberries with white chocolate. A magical setting and impeccable service. Closed Nov–Apr.

CAHORS Le Lamparo

76 rue Georges-Clémenceau, 46000 **Tel** *(05) 65 35 25 93* **Fax** *(05) 65 23 83 45*   **Map** *E3*

Bustling first-floor restaurant opposite the market hall, with a large terrace for fine-weather dining. The menu ranges from pasta and wood-fired pizza to copious salads, grills and local fare, with a few fish dishes for good measure. It's nothing fancy, but reliable with generous portions.

CAHORS Le Balandre

5 avenue Charles-de-Freycinet, 46000 **Tel** *(05) 65 53 32 00* **Fax** *(05) 65 53 32 26*   **Map** *E3*

For fine dining in Cahors, head for the restaurant in the Hôtel Terminus, where 1930s décor complements refined Quercy cuisine. Rustic dishes, such as roast Quercy lamb laced with juniper juice, are given a modern twist. Or try egg poached with *foie gras* and truffle sauce. Cahors wines feature strongly.

CHANCELADE L'Oisan

15 avenue des Reynats, 24650 **Tel** *(05) 53 03 53 59*   **Map** *D1*

There's a hushed, starchy atmosphere in this grand dining room with chandeliers and rich furnishings, but the cuisine is full of pleasant surprises. Dishes such as *foie gras* with lemon *confit* and pistachios reflect the imagination and skill of the chef. The good wine list features up-and-coming producers. Closed Mon, Sat lunch & Sun pm.

DOMME L'Esplanade

Le Bourg, 24250 **Tel** *(05) 53 28 31 41* **Fax** *(05) 53 28 49 92*   **Map** *E2*

Welcoming and efficient service, well-presented dishes and an unbeatable panorama of the Dordogne valley keep customers coming back to this hotel-restaurant. Ask for a window or terrace table. Signature dishes include lamb with *foie gras* and truffles, and the delectable chocolate trilogy.

FIGEAC La Cuisine du Marché

15 rue Clermont, 46100 **Tel** *(05) 65 50 18 55* **Fax** *(05) 65 50 18 55*   **Map** *E2*

In a former wine cellar in the heart of Figeac's medieval core, this attractive restaurant takes pride in using only the freshest ingredients. Star billing goes to its wide range of fish dishes, though you'll also find plenty of local classics, all prepared in the open kitchen. The set menus represent good value.

LES EYZIES-DE-TAYAC Le Vieux Moulin

2 rue du Moulin-Bas, 24620 **Tel** *(05) 53 06 94 33* **Fax** *(05) 53 06 98 06*   **Map** *E2*

Dine on well-priced regional cuisine in a 17th-century mill with its rustic interior, or beside the river in peaceful, flower-filled gardens. Among the simple but beautifully prepared dishes choose from *escalope* of *foie gras* with truffle sauce or truffle risotto, with pigeon casserole to follow. Closed Nov–Apr.

MONBAZILLAC La Tour des Vents

Moulin de Malfourat, 24240 **Tel** *(05) 53 58 30 10* **Fax** *(05) 53 58 89 55*   **Map** *D2*

Book a window or terrace table to enjoy the wonderful views over the Dordogne valley to Bergerac. Good-value menus offer local specialities, including *foie gras* and duck, but also fish and seafood. There is even a vegetarian option. Treat yourself to a glass of sweet Monbazillac with *foie gras*.

Key to Price Guide *see p260* **Key to Symbols** *see back cover flap*

MONPAZIER La Bastide

52 rue St-Jacques, 24540 **Tel** (05) 53 22 60 59 **Fax** (05) 53 22 09 20 **Map** D2

Real, old-school French cookery at its best. Gleaming tableware and starched cloths announce that you're in for a treat. Crusty walnut bread, *foie gras*, sweetbreads and truffles, rounded off with a refreshing sorbet – it's all ultra-fresh and skilfully prepared. Prices are very reasonable.

MONTIGNAC-LASCAUX La Roseraie

11 place d'Armes, 24290 **Tel** (05) 53 50 53 92 **Map** E2

In the heart of Périgord Noir, this hotel-restaurant combines the charm of the past with modern tastes. Classic ingredients are prepared in a contemporary manner, such as trilogy of *foie gras* and tartare of goose breast with walnuts and raspberry vinegar. Gourmet chidren's menu. Closed lunch Mon–Fri (except 15 Jul–15 Aug), Nov–Mar.

PERIGUEUX Le Clos Saint-Front

5 rue de la Vertu, 24000 **Tel** (05) 53 46 78 58 **Fax** (05) 53 46 78 20 **Map** D1

Reservations are recommended at this restaurant near Périgueux's prehistory museum, with its inventive, inexpensive cuisine and peaceful courtyard garden. According to the season, you could opt for lamb flavoured with spices and rosemary, or sole served with an onion, thyme and lemon *compôte*.

PERIGUEUX L'Essentiel

8 rue de la Clarté, 24000 **Tel** (05) 53 35 15 15 **Fax** (05) 53 35 15 15 **Map** D1

Another city-centre restaurant where it's wise to reserve. The dining room's sunny southern colours complement southwestern dishes perfectly, such as grilled duck breast served with a delicious *gâteau* of foie gras, asparagus and potatoes. There's also a pretty, pocket-sized garden.

RIBERAC Le Chevillard

Gayet, route de Bordeaux, 24600 **Tel** (05) 53 91 20 88 **Map** D1

For that quintessential French experience, try this friendly *auberge* in a lovely old farmhouse west of Ribérac. Famous for its groaning buffets (*hors-d'oeuvre*, seafood and dessert), it also offers a good range of meat and fish dishes. Prices are reasonable; the lunch menu represents exceptional value.

ROCAMADOUR Jehan de Valon

Cité Médiévale, 46500 **Tel** (05) 65 33 63 08 **Fax** (05) 65 33 65 23 **Map** E2

An elegant restaurant perched on the edge of a gorge in the middle of medieval Rocamadour. Consistently well-prepared and presented dishes showcase local delicacies: smoked duck, succulent Quercy lamb and Rocamadour's very own goats' cheese served with a crunchy walnut salad.

SARLAT Le Régent

6 place de la Liberté, 24200 **Tel** (05) 53 31 06 36 **Fax** (05) 53 59 03 91 **Map** E2

Watch the world go by from the pavement terrace of this popular brasserie on Sarlat's main square. The food is nothing fancy, but reliable and not expensive, considering the location. The menu covers everything from salads to regional cuisine. Nov–Easter: open for lunch only.

SARLAT Le Couleuvrine

1 place de la Bouquerie, 24200 **Tel** (05) 53 59 27 80 **Map** E2

This restaurant is in a tower that once formed part of Sarlat's medieval ramparts. Classic dishes, such as duck breast with figs, are served in the dining room with period furniture, oak beams and a large open fireplace. The jazzy bistro in the vaulted cellar proposes simpler dishes, and a good selection of wines by the glass. Closed Mon, Tue lunch & Jan.

SORGES Auberge de la Truffe

Le Bourg, 24420 **Tel** (05) 53 05 02 05 **Fax** (05) 53 05 39 27 **Map** D1

Sorges is the self-proclaimed truffle "capital" of France, and this auberge is the perfect place to sample Périgord's "black diamond." The top-price menu features truffles with every course. Less expensive fare is on offer too, and the set menus start at a reasonable price. Truffle-hunting weekends are offered.

ST-LEON-SUR-VEZERE Le Dejeuner sur l'Herbe

Le Bourg, 24290 **Tel** (05) 53 50 69 17 **Map** E2

This unusual establishment is open all day. It is ideal for picnics as meals are available to take away and tables and chairs are provided. The menu includes bread-based snacks, traditional Périgordian dishes and goats' cheese salad. There is a lovely terrace and garden overlooking the Vézère river. No toilets. Closed Wed (except in summer).

TERRASSON-LAVILLEDIEU Restaurant de la Poste

7 avenue Georges Haupinot, Le Lardin St Lazare, 24200 **Tel** (05) 53 50 32 27 **Map** E2

This small, friendly hotel-restaurant, in a former coaching inn west of Terrasson-Lavilledieu, is a practical place to stop after visitng the nearby Jardins de l'Imaginaire. The menu centres on traditional cuisine and features a dish of the day, which might be Périgordian omelette, fresh *foie gras* or *mique*, a local meat casserole. Closed Fri pm, Sat & Sun.

TREMOLAT Le Vieux Logis

Halfway between Les Eyzies-de-Tayac and Bergerac, Le Bourg, Trémolat, 24510 **Tel** (05) 53 22 80 06 **Map** E2

Charming hotel-restaurant with a shaded terrace, surrounded by pretty gardens. The restaurant, housed in a former tobacco *séchoir*, serves classic cuisine prepared by talented chefs. Dishes feature high-quality produce, such as white truffles, pigeon breast and *marrons glacés*. The classic wine list includes the best from Bordeaux and Bergerac.

LOT-ET-GARONNE

AGEN Le Cauquil
 €

9 avenue du Générale-de-Gaulle, 47000 **Tel** *(05) 53 48 02 34*   **Map** D3

The daily-changing menu is chalked up on the blackboard in this unpretentious bistro. Fresh produce is used to prepare local dishes that can be enjoyed in a friendly, relaxed atmosphere. Simple but tasty: duck breast with Griotte cherries or *daurade* with garlic. The prices are reasonable and the portions generous. Closed Sun & 1st two weeks Aug.

AGEN L'Atelier
€€

14 rue Jeu de Paume, 47000 **Tel** *(05) 53 87 89 22*   **Map** D3

Tables and chairs have replaced the work benches in this former carpenter's workshop. The restaurant is decorated in an eclectic style and at midday it offers a good value *"formule rapide"*. In the evening, count on a bigger budget. Well-prepared dishes are on offer such as pigs' trotters coated in sesame seeds. Closed Sat & Sun.

AGEN Mariottat
 €€€

25 rue Louis-Vivent, 47000 **Tel** *(05) 53 77 99 97* **Fax** *(05) 53 77 99 79*   **Map** D3

It comes as a surprise to find this elegant restaurant tucked down a very ordinary backstreet, but inside the 19th-century mansion, with its chandeliers and high ceilings, you're in for a treat. Duck reigns supreme – *assiette tout canard* is the signature dish, alongside succulent Agen prunes and summer fruits.

AIGUILLON Le Jardin des Cygnes
€

Route de Villeneuve, 47190 **Tel** *(05) 53 79 60 02*   **Map** D3

Housed in a former wine warehouse at the confluence of the rivers Lot and Garonne, this hotel-restaurant serves typical regional dishes, many accompanied by the locally produced plums and prunes. Options might include *foie gras*, duck *confit*, pork with prune chutney and wild boar in season. Closed Fri pm & Sat.

ASTAFFORT Une Auberge en Gascogne
€€€

9 faubourg Corné, 47200 **Tel** *(05) 53 67 10 27*   **Map** D3

The passionate chef here is a veritable artist, creating inventive dishes in which the different flavours can each be savoured separately. *Copeaux* (shavings) *de foie gras*, *turbot meunière* and farmed Pyrenean lamb are among the ingeniously presented specialities. There's a good selection of local wines. Variable opening times so call ahead.

ASTAFFORT Le Square
€€€€

5–7 place de la Craste, 47220 **Tel** *(05) 53 47 20 40*   **Map** D3

This elegant hotel-restaurant has two dining rooms, one that opens onto a patio, and the other on the first floor with a panoramic view. Michel Latrille's cuisine wavers between classicism and modernism. Savour dishes such as *langoustines raviolis* and asparagus with truffle juice. Good selection of regional wines. Closed Mon, Tue lunch & Sun pm.

BUZET-SUR-BAISE Le Vigneron
€

Boulevard de la République, 47160 **Tel** *(05) 53 84 73 46* **Fax** *(05) 53 84 75 04*   **Map** D3

A village restaurant with old-fashioned cooking. Most people opt for the excellent-value four-course *menu du jour* (not served on Sundays), which includes an *hors-d'oeuvre* buffet and an impossibly wicked selection of desserts – the *gâteau* of layered *crêpes* and cream, covered in meringue, is not to be missed.

CASTELJALOUX La Vieille Auberge
€€

11 rue Posterne, 47700 **Tel** *(05) 53 93 01 36*   **Map** C3

This charming stone-built *auberge*, with a gaily decorated dining room, stands in one of the tiny streets in the *bastide* town. The menu features classic regional dishes such as Périgord duck breast and Quercy lamb, but also diversifies with such dishes as scallops and king prawns with *confit* of fennel. Carefully selected wine list. Closed Wed.

CLAIRAC Auberge de Clairac
€€€

12 route de Tonneins, 47320 **Tel** *(05) 53 79 22 52*   **Map** D3

The chef here uses the best local produce, as well as herbs from his own "aromatorium". His passion for seeking out new aromas, combined with a talent for modern culinary techniques, results in innovative dishes such as Quercy veal with a tobacco infusion and Aquitaine caviar served on a fillet of fish with celery cappucino. Closed Mon, Wed & Sun pm.

DURAS Le Don Camillo
€

Place Marguerite-Duras, 47120 **Tel** *(05) 53 83 76 00*   **Map** D2

A simple family-orientated restaurant in the centre of town that is well-known for its unbeatable midday menus. Delicious home-made dishes and pizzas are served in copious portions. There is a pleasant shady terrace for outdoor eating in summer. The staff are efficient and friendly. Reservations recommended, especially for lunch. Closed Tue.

FRANCESCAS Le Relais de la Hire
€€€

11 rue Porte-Neuve, 47600 **Tel** *(05) 53 65 41 59* **Fax** *(05) 53 65 86 42*   **Map** D3

The chef of this upmarket village restaurant near Nérac makes full use of his herb garden and edible flowers to create dishes that are a feast for all the senses. Try the tempting artichoke soufflé with *foie gras* or zander (freshwater perch) stuffed with crayfish, followed by desserts that look almost too good to eat.

Key to Price Guide *see p260* **Key to Symbols** *see back cover flap*

LAPLUME Château de Lassalle

3km (2 miles) from Laplume, Brimont, 47310 **Tel** *(05) 53 95 10 58*   **Map** *D3*

The orangery of an 18th-century château houses a restaurant serving high-quality cuisine. Themed seasonal menus include specialities such as panfried *foie gras* with quince or lamb with a herb crust and an Armagnac-based sauce. Good selection of regional wines, and also a wide range of Armagnacs. Oct–Mar: closed Fri pm, Sat lunch & Sun.

MARMANDE Le Moulin d'Ané

Virazeil, 47200 **Tel** *(05) 53 20 18 25* **Fax** *(05) 53 89 67 99*   **Map** *D3*

Consistently excellent seasonal cuisine is served in this restored 18th-century watermill near Marmande. Typical southwestern dishes include succulent *blonde d'Aquitaine* beef, tender fillets of duck breast and apple tart laced with armagnac. Be sure to try the exceptionally plump and juicy Marmande tomatoes.

MARMANDE Le Prianon

Avenue Hubert Ruffe, 47200 **Tel** *(05) 53 20 80 94*   **Map** *D3*

This charming rustic establishment with an authentic warm welcome offers a good choice of excellently prepared dishes made with local produce. The lamb cutlets flavoured with thyme are particularly recommended. Closed Sat lunch, Sun & Dec.

NERAC La Chaumière d'Albret

6km (4 miles) north of Nérac, Lavardac, 47230 **Tel** *(05) 53 65 51 75*   **Map** *D3*

Situated in Lavardac, once a port for unloading Armagnac barrels, this countryside restaurant serves local specialities at modest prices. The menus offer a good choice, including home-made fish soup, oysters, *salade Gasconne* (with duck breast and foie gras) , quail and *blanquette de canette* (duckling) with prunes. Closed Mon, Sun pm & Oct.

NERAC Aux Délices du Roy

7 rue du Château, 47600 **Tel** *(05) 53 65 81 12*   **Map** *D3*

Not far from the château, situated in the old town, this rustic restaurant serves traditional fish dishes. The talented chef prepares carefully selected langoustine, sea bream, sea bass, sole, tuna and turbot with skill. The menu changes regularly. There's a good selection of white wine to accompany the fish dishes. Closed Mon & 1st Nov–1st Apr.

PENNE D'AGENAIS La Maison sur la Place

10 place Gambetta, 47140 **Tel** *(05) 53 01 29 18*   **Map** *D3*

The former grocery store on the main square now houses this delightful restaurant. The dining room is elegant and modern, and the cuisine is traditional with a hint of the exotic, with such dishes as fish marinated in coconut milk, stuffed pork Polynesian style or simply grilled *entrecôte*. Cookery courses available. Closed Mon & Sun pm.

PUJOLS Auberge Lou Calel

Le Bourg, 47300 **Tel** *(05) 53 70 46 14* **Fax** *(05) 53 70 49 79*   **Map** *D3*

The sister-restaurant to Pujol's famous La Toque Blanche offers less exalted but nevertheless fine dining at an affordable price. To kick off the meal, try the apple and *foie gras tatin* drizzled with a honey vinaigrette. On fine days tables spill onto the terrace with views over the Lot valley.

PUYMIROL Les Loges de l'Aubergade

52 rue Royale, 47270 **Tel** *(05) 53 95 31 46* **Fax** *(05) 53 95 33 80*   **Map** *D3*

One of the southwest's great restaurants is set in a beautiful medieval lodge on a hilltop. Here Michel Trama creates sublime works of art, such as potato and *foie gras* parcels and wafer-thin slices of green apple. The setting is equally theatrical, with Baroque drapes, exposed stone and a gorgeous Italianate courtyard.

ST-ETIENNE-DE-FOUGERES Auberge de Feuillade

Feuillade, 2 km (1 mile) outside St Livrade-sur-Lot, 47380 **Tel** *(05) 53 01 09 84*   **Map** *D3*

A typical farmhouse in the Lot valley 25km (16 miles) west of Villeneuve-sur-Lot, serving traditional farmhouse fare. Dishes are prepared with home-grown farm produce and might include *foie gras*, salads and *confit* of duck, served with vegetable gratin or flan, as well as home-made desserts. Reservations obligatory. Closed Wed & Sun pm.

TOURNON D'AGENAIS Le Beffroi

Place de la Mairie, 47370 **Tel** *(05) 53 01 20 59*   **Map** *E3*

An old stone building in the centre of this *bastide* town now houses this contemporary restaurant. The young, talented chef prepares tasty, imaginative dishes. The *menu du marché* is good value, and the childrens' menu is a scaled down version of this. The *menu gastronomique* has dishes such as pumpkin soup with diced *foie gras*. Closed Mon & Sun pm.

VILLENEUVE-SUR-LOT Les Rives du Plantié

Route de Castelmoron, Le Temple-sur-Lot, 47110 **Tel** *(05) 53 79 86 86*   **Map** *D3*

This 19th-century house set in wooded parkland, with views of the Lot river, houses a pleasant hotel-restaurant. The updated menu now includes both traditional dishes and more modern choices, such as *millefeuille* of mozzarella served with a tomato *compôte* and strawberry *gazpacho* with melon *gelée*. Nov–Apr: closed Sat lunch & Sun pm.

VILLENEUVE-SUR-LOT La Toque Blanche

4km (2 miles) south of Villeneuve, Pujols, 47300 **Tel** *(05) 53 49 00 30*   **Map** *D3*

This hillside restaurant offers panoramic views of the 13th-century *bastide* town and the Mail valley. Classic southwest dishes with a touch of modernism are prepared using regional produce. The menu includes warm lobster salad garnished with truffle and *foie gras* shavings. Extensive wine list. Closed Mon, Tue lunch & Sun pm.

LANDES

BELIN-BELIET Plaisirs des Landes

2km (1 mile) on the right after leaving centre of Saugnacq-et-Muret **Tel** *(05) 58 08 21 52*   **Map** *B3*

One of the few authentic farmhouse inn in Les Landes serves home-made regional dishes. There is only one menu which starts with an *apéritif*, moves on to *foie gras*, Landaise salad, then duck breast, followed by cheese and dessert; wine included. The Landaise platter is a lighter option. Telephone at least the day before to reserve.

CAPBRETON Le Bistro

Place des Basques **Tel** *(05) 58 72 21 98*   **Map** *A4*

Just as stone's throw from the fishing port is this bustling yet relaxed bistro. The menu, which is written up on a blackboard, changes regularly. Simple dishes, such as steak with shallots, are offered at midday. In the evening, more elaborate dishes include honeyed fillet of pork with Mirabelle plums. Closed Mon, Sat lunch & Sun (except Jul & Aug).

CASTETS Ferme-Auberge Lesca

428 chemin des Tucs, 40260 **Tel** *(05) 58 89 41 45*   **Map** *B4*

In the former barn of the first farm-auberge to open in Les Landes, there are three menus. All include dishes prepared using the farm's produce: *foie gras*, breast and *confit* of duck, asparagus and for dessert, a delicious *tourtière*. Farm visits can be booked in Jul & Aug. Closed Nov–Mar; call for opening hours at other times. Reservations only.

DAX La Chaumière

3km (2 miles) north of Dax, Saint-Paul-lès-Dax, 40990 **Tel** *(05) 58 91 79 81*   **Map** *B4*

This traditional, rustic restaurant is dedicated to the Basque-Landaise bullfighting culture. During the bullfighting season, it is filled with Spanish bullfighters, who come to enjoy the specialities of the southwest. The extensive menu features such dishes as *foie gras* flan, seafood soup and *garbure (see p257)*. Open lunch only unless booked ahead.

DAX La Table de Pascal

4 rue Fontaine-Chaude, 40100 **Tel** *(05) 58 74 89 00*   **Map** *B4*

Excellent Parisian-style, city-centre bistro with a retro décor and convivial atmosphere. The menu features fresh regional produce. Expect to see old favourites such as poached egg with *foie gras*, frogs' legs with *persillade* (parsley vinaigrette) and duck breast. Delicious desserts. Reservation advisable. Closed Mon, Sun, Mar & Sep.

DAX Une Cuisine en Ville

11 avenue Clémenceau, 40100 **Tel** *(05) 58 90 26 89*   **Map** *B4*

Creativity abounds here, in both the contemporary decoration and the innovative cuisine. This revolves mainly around a *tapas*-style menu, which presents an assortment of mini-portions of quality seasonal produce, meticulously prepared by the skillful chef. Service is friendly and attentive. Good wine selection. Closed Mon, Tue & Sun pm.

DAX Le Moulin de Poustagnacq

3km (2 miles) north of Dax, route de l'Oustalot, Saint Paul lès Dax, 40990 **Tel** *(05) 58 91 31 03*   **Map** *B4*

Overlooking a lake, and situated at the edge of a forest, this charming old flour mill provides a peaceful setting for regional cusine with a modern touch. The innovative menu offers dishes such as crispy asparagus risotto with clams, and breast of pigeon with a Pomerol-flavoured sauce. Good selection of wines. Closed Mon, Tue lunch & Sun pm.

EUGENIE-LES-BAINS La Ferme aux Grives

111 rue Thermes, 40320 **Tel** *(05) 58 05 05 06* **Fax** *(05) 58 51 10 10*   **Map** *C4*

The more "rustic" of Michel Guérard's much acclaimed restaurants *(see below)* still serves sublime food. Normally heavy southwestern dishes are reinvented for a modern palate, from the terrine of wild mushrooms and *foie gras* to the feather-light apricot and almond *feuilletée*.

EUGENIE-LES-BAINS Les Prés d'Eugénie

Le Bourg, 40320 **Tel** *(05) 58 05 06 07*   **Map** *C4*

Chef Michel Guérard, considered by many to be a gastronomic genius, doesn't follow trends but sets them himself. This is a temple to refined dishes cooked with passion such as the succulent lobster in Armagnac, or crab *à la japonaise*, in saki. Closed Mon & lunch Tue–Fri.

GRENADE-SUR-L'ADOUR Pain, Adour et Fantaisie

14–16 place des Tilleuls, 40270 **Tel** *(05) 58 45 18 80*   **Map** *C4*

Regional produce is used in the meticulously prepared dishes that hint at tradition and modernism at the same time. Tuna *brochette* with sesame accompanied by passion fruit sauce is just one option. Imaginative desserts. Excellent choice of Bordeaux wines; Madiran and Jurançon are also well represented. Closed Mon, Wed lunch & Sun pm.

HOSSEGOR Le Pavillon Bleu

1053 avenue du Touring Club de France, 40150 **Tel** *(05) 58 41 99 50*   **Map** *A4*

This modern, elegant restaurant sits at the edge of a lake and has a wooden-decked terrace. The chef uses fresh seasonal produce for his innovative dishes. Panfried *foie gras* with Pyrenean honey or bass stuffed with spicy fennel served with roast pineapple are some of the choices. Oct–Easter: closed Mon & Tue lunch; also New Year to end Jan.

Key to Price Guide *see p260* **Key to Symbols** *see back cover flap*

MAGESQ Relais de la Poste
 €€€€€

24 avenue de Marenne, 40140 **Tel** *(05) 58 47 70 25* **Map** *B4*

In the heart of the Landes forest, in a magnificent former staging post, this restaurant is the standard bearer for classic gastronomic French cuisine. Seasonal dishes include Adour salmon, white Magesq asparagus and warm duck *foie gras* with grapes. Panoramic terrace. Good selection of wines, especially older vintages. Call for opening times.

MIMIZAN Hôtel Atlantique
 €€

38 avenue de la Côte d'Argent, 40200 **Tel** *(05) 58 09 09 42* **Fax** *(05) 58 82 42 63* **Map** *B3*

Very popular, modestly priced restaurant in a hotel on the seafront at the north end of the beach. Seafood is a speciality, with good *soupe de poisson* as well as regional gastronomic favourites such as *magret de canard, confit de canard* and wild boar with prunes.

MONT-DE-MARSAN Didier Garbage
 €€

RN 134, Uchacq-et-Parentis, 40090 **Tel** *(05) 58 75 33 66* **Fax** *(05) 58 75 22 77* **Map** *C4*

One of France's up-and-coming chefs turns out authentic Landaise cuisine in his convivial, slightly rustic restaurant outside Mont-de-Marsan. Look forward to lamprey, elvers (freshwater eels) and expertly crafted fish dishes, in addition to meats and luscious desserts. There's also a bistro for casual dining.

MONT-DE-MARSAN Les Clefs d'Argent
 €€€

333 avenue des Martyrs de la Résistance, 40000 **Tel** *(05) 58 06 16 45* **Map** *C4*

This restaurant has two dining rooms – one cosy and intimate with a large fireplace, the other colourful. The chef is a native of the town who uses locally sourced produce, while taking inspiration from his wife's African origins, to create tasty refined dishes. Asparagus, *foie gras*, veal and strawberries feature regularly. Closed Mon, Sun pm & Aug.

PISSOS Café de Pissos
€€

42 rue du Pont-Battant, 40140 **Tel** *(05) 58 08 90 16* **Map** *B3*

At the centre of the Parc Régional des Landes, this village café has a pleasant terrace shaded by ancient plane trees and a vaulted dining room. The menu includes timeless dishes such as duck served with a cep mushroom sauce, and for dessert chocolate profiteroles. Wine list features wines from the southwest. Closed Tue pm, Wed, Sun pm & Nov.

ROQUEFORT Auberge du Jardin de Violette
 €€

8km (5 miles) northwest of Roquefort, Lencouacq, 40120 **Tel** *(05) 58 93 03 90* **Map** *C4*

The dining room of this delightful farmhouse inn is located inside the renovated stables. Almost-forgotten varieties of home-grown vegetables (Chinese artichoke, golden purslane) and flowers (violets, acacia, courgette) are prepared with know-how and talent, and served with delicious farm-raised chicken and duck. Reservations necessary.

SABRES Auberge des Pins
 €€

Route de la Piscine, 40630 **Tel** *(05) 58 08 30 00* **Fax** *(05) 58 07 56 74* **Map** *B3*

In this attractive Landaise farmhouse, run by a friendly family, the oak-lined dining room provides the perfect setting for typical Landaise cuisine. This ranges from flavourful asparagus and fresh fish to duck in all its guises. Best of all, though, is the boned pigeon stuffed with *foie gras*. Good selection of local wines and Armagnac.

SAINT-SEVER Le Relais du Pavillon Costedoat
 €€€

Route de Grenade, 40500 **Tel** *(05) 58 76 20 22* **Map** *C4*

One of the best restaurants in the Chalosse serves tasty, simply prepared dishes to be enjoyed in the dining room or on the shady terrace. Savour the local produce used to prepare such dishes as cep mushrooms served on a slice of cured ham with an egg, grilled duck breast and roast lamprey. Closed Mon, Sun pm.

SAUBUSSE Villa Stings
 €€€€

Rue du Port, 40180 **Tel** *(05) 58 57 70 18* **Map** *B3*

In a grand 19th-century house overlooking the Adour river, this discreet restaurant with an elegant dining room serves classic quality produce, prepared to today's tastes. Main courses include fillet of plaice served with stir-fried asparagus and spring vegetables with a light seaweed sauce. Closed Mon, Sat lunch, Sun pm & Feb.

SEIGNOSSE Les Roseaux
 €€

Route Louis de Bourmont, 40510 **Tel** *(05) 58 72 80 30* **Map** *B4*

A favourite with local families, this restaurant is hidden away beside the Etang Blanc with a lovely view over the lake. The menus are especially good value and copious: *piperade* (with tomato and pepper) omelette, eels with *persillade* (parsley vinaigrette) and *confit* of duck feature. Boats for hire. Reservations recommended. Closed Tue (except Jul & Aug).

SOUSTONS Marinero
€€

8km (5 miles) east of Soustons, 15 Grand Rue, Vieux Boucau, 40480 **Tel** *(05) 58 48 14 15* **Map** *B4*

This family-run restaurant is located on a pedestrianized street in the centre of town and has a pleasant terrace. The chef revisits the classics, mainly fish, but also includes Spanish specialities such as a selection of *tapas* and an Iberian platter. The set menus offer better value and more generous portions than *à la carte* dishes. Closed Mon, Tue & Oct–Apr.

VILLENEUVE-DE-MARSAN Hervé Garrapit
€€€

21 avenue Armagnac, 40190 **Tel** *(05) 58 45 20 08* **Map** *C3*

Situated in Bas Armagnac this former staging post has an elegant dining room decorated in Louis XVI style and a beautiful garden. The cuisine is classic, paying hommage to the best produce that the southwest can offer, and includes dishes such as terrine of *foie gras* and fillet of Aquitaine beef with *sauce bordelaise*. Extensive wine list.

PAYS BASQUE

ANGLET Château de Brindos €€€€
1 allée du Château, 64600 **Tel** *(05) 59 23 89 80*   **Map** *A4*

The vast dining room in this unusual 1920s château has views of the park and lake. Using the freshest produce, the chef creates compositions such as oyster capuccino with Aquitaine caviar served with seaweed bread. Desserts receive the same attention. Smaller tasting portions are an option. Bordeaux and Jurançon wines. Closed last two weeks Feb.

BAYONNE Le Bayonnais €
24 rue Marengo, 64100 **Tel** *(05) 59 25 61 19* **Fax** *(05) 59 59 00 64*   **Map** *A4*

With a handful of tables on the terrace and more inside, this small restaurant has a well-deserved reputation for imaginative dishes, such as sole with lentils, pig's head with apple and pastilla with figs. The well-chosen wine list emphasizes regional wines and major names from elsewhere in France.

BAYONNE Auberge du Cheval Blanc €€€
68 rue Bourgneuf, 64100 **Tel** *(05) 59 59 01 33* **Fax** *(05) 59 59 52 25*   **Map** *A4*

Stray from the set menu to eat *à la carte* at this well-regarded hotel in the riverside Petit Bayonne quarter. The menu changes with the seasons, with local dishes, such as *xamano* (ham and mashed potatoes), fine Atlantic seafood, interesting soups and casseroles, and delicious desserts. Respectable wine list.

BIARRITZ Le Clos Basque €
12 rue L. Barthou, 64200 **Tel** *(05) 59 24 24 96* **Fax** *(05) 59 22 34 46*   **Map** *A4*

Regional specialities are the order of the day at this small, cheerful tavern, with its Spanish-style whitewashed walls, coloured tiles and summer terrace. Reserve a table in advance because the place fills up quickly with local diners as well as visitors, especially in high season and at weekends.

BIARRITZ Chez Albert €€
Port des Pêcheurs, 64200 **Tel** *(05) 59 24 43 84* **Fax** *(05) 59 24 20 13*   **Map** *A4*

From the terrace of Chez Albert there are superb views of Biarritz's picturesque fishing harbour and the surrounding cliffs and beaches, making this fine seafood restaurant popular. Arrive early for the best tables. Piled platters of seafood, freshly caught lobster, sole, sea bream, tuna and sardines are among the treats here.

BIARRITZ Le Sissinou €€
5 avenue Maréchal Foch, 64200 **Tel** *(05) 59 22 51 50* **Fax** *(05) 59 22 50 58*   **Map** *A4*

Managed by chef Michel Cassou-Debat – a veteran of some of France's top establishments – Sissinou is one of Biarritz's most talked-about restaurants. Elegant in a minimalist way, it serves wonderful seafood, such as tuna carpaccio and red mullet in an emulsion of green peppers, and desserts that invite indulgence.

BIARRITZ Hôtel de Palais €€€€
1 avenue de l'Impératrice, 64200 **Tel** *(05) 59 41 64 00*   **Map** *A4*

The restaurant in what was Empress Eugénie's summer palace offers traditional cuisine, served in exceptionally pleasant surroundings with views of the Atlantic. Simply prepared dishes use the finest ingredients. The menu includes lobster with tomato *gazpacho*, roast langoustines and Pyrenean *agneau de lait*. The wine selection is also classic.

BIDARRAY Auberge Iparla €€
Chemin de l'Eglise, 64780 **Tel** *(05) 59 37 77 21*   **Map** *C4*

Alain Ducasse, one of the best chefs in France, may be the owner, but Iparla still retains the ambiance of a village inn. In the large dining room with its spectacular mountain view, try traditional dishes prepared *"à la Ducasse"*. Basquaise tripe, local Aragon ham and Banka trout. Booking advisable. Closed Wed, (except Jun–Oct) & Jan–Mar.

BIDART Les Frères Ibarboure Guéthary €€€€
Chemin de Ttaliénèa, Guéthary, 64210 **Tel** *(05) 59 54 81 64*   **Map** *C4*

The finest restaurant in the Pays Basque is a fraternal affair: Philippe produces the savoury dishes while Martin prepares the tempting desserts. The harmony of Basque culinary traditions and the chefs' creativity and passion makes for a memorable experience. Good choice of wines by the glass. Closed Wed, Sun pm, mid-Nov–Dec & Jan.

HENDAYE-PLAGE La Cabane de Pecheur €
Quai de la Floride, 64700 **Tel** *(05) 59 20 38 09*   **Map** *A4*

Diners at this relaxed, unpretentious restaurant enjoy fine views of the fishing port and the bay, with the coast of Spain in the background. The interesting menus offers mainly seafood and fish: fish soup, scallops, seafood platters and the catch of the day. Grilled meats too. A good place to have lunch before exploring the Pays Basque. Closed Mon.

LARRAU Etchémaïté €€
Larrau, 64560 **Tel** *(05) 59 28 61 45* **Fax** *(05) 59 28 72 71*   **Map** *B5*

This family-run mountain inn and restaurant is set in a spectacular location and has a cosy dining room with an open fireplace and great views. Favourites are lamb and duck dishes garnished with apples, *cep mushrooms* or *foie gras* and there is usually a good choice of Atlantic seafood too. Varied wine list.

Key to Price Guide *see p260* **Key to Symbols** *see back cover flap*

ST-JEAN-DE-LUZ Restaurant Petit Grill Basque

2 rue St-Jacques, 64500 **Tel** *(05) 59 26 80 76* **Fax** *(05) 59 26 80 76* **Map** *A4*

One of the most affordable eating places in normally pricy St-Jean-de-Luz, with the accent on simple, good Basque home-cooking using fresh local ingredients. The fish soup is excellent, as are the grilled squid, the peppers stuffed with cod and the many other Basque dishes. Well-priced and unassuming wine list.

ST-JEAN-DE-LUZ Le Kaïku

17 rue République, 64500 **Tel** *(05) 59 26 13 20* **Map** *A4*

Situated in a 16th-century house, the oldest in St-Jean-de-Luz, this restaurant is a local institution. The menu includes locally caught fish and seafood, and regional produce. Grilled fish, seafood and guinea fowl feature regularly. It is popular with visitors so it fills up quickly and at peak times the service, although efficient, lacks charm. Closed Tue & Wed.

ST-JEAN-DE-LUZ Chez Txalupa

Place Corsaires, 64500 **Tel** *(05) 59 51 23 34* **Map** *A4*

Chez Txalupa is a favourite with locals. Expect the best catches of the Atlantic coast, prepared in dishes such as king prawns in a hot vinegar dressing, sardines in tomato salsa, oysters and lots of other shellfish, tuna, cod and monkfish. Extensive wine list and imaginative desserts. Reservations recommended.

ST PEE SUR NIVELLE Le Fronton

Quartier Ibarron, 64310 **Tel** *(05) 59 54 10 12* **Map** *A4*

There's a friendly welcome at this village inn with a large well-kept dining room. The classic regional dishes attract a regular clientele. Quality products are carefully chosen and the menu includes a deliciously light and flaky anchovy *tartelette*, duck breast with crushed potatoes and *cèpes*, and chocolate tart *à l'ancienne*. Closed Mon & Sun pm.

URT La Galupe

Place du Port, route de Bayonne, 64240 **Tel** *(05) 59 56 21 84* **Map** *B4*

Located at the port is this former fishermen's inn with a charming rustic interior. The tasty regional menu, featuring locally caught fish and seasonal produce, is prepared with precision by the creative chef. Dishes include salmon fished from the Adour, langoustines *à la plancha* and home-made *boudin noir*. Ecclectic wine list. Call for opening times.

BÉARN

BOSDORROS Auberge Labarthe

Rue Pierre Bidau, 64290 **Tel** *(05) 59 21 50 13* **Map** *C5*

At this charming restaurant behind the church the menu includes simple, well-prepared dishes with a modern twist, such as pork fillet served with a spicy Thai sauce, smoked eel terrine and creamed cod fish soup. Presentation is precise, service is friendly and the prices are reasonable. Closed Mon, Tue, Sun pm & Jan.

JURANÇON Chez Ruffet

3 avenue Charles-Touzet, 64110 **Tel** *(05) 59 06 25 13* **Map** *C5*

At Chez Ruffet the chef uses fresh market produce to concoct regional dishes that show great personality, including carpaccio of goose breast with basil and broad beans, and Chalosse beef served with a *compôte* of Tresson onions. The décor is both modern and rustic. There are well-chosen wines from the best local producers. Closed Mon & Sun pm.

OLORON-STE-MARIE Le Chaudron

18 avenue Lattre-de-Tassigny, 64400 **Tel** *(05) 59 39 76 99* **Map** *B5*

Generous portions of traditional cuisine are served in this convivial restaurant with an attractive terrace. The good value set menus offer a wide choice of dishes. The *"tout au canard"* menu presents duck in all its guises; grilled, *confit*, foie gras. Other specialities include *garbure* and, if you have room, a giant peach melba.

ORTHEZ Au Temps de la Reine Jeanne

44 rue Bourg-Vieux, 64300 **Tel** *(05) 59 67 00 76* **Fax** *(05) 59 69 09 63* **Map** *B4*

This rustic eating-place is attached to a comfortable country inn. The menu is equally rustic, with plenty of local dishes, including offal and rich meaty dishes. Liver, black pudding, suckling pig, foie gras, *cassoulet* and monkfish all make an appearance. Good value.

PAU La Planche de Boeuf

30 rue Pasteur, 64000 **Tel** *(05) 59 27 62 60* **Fax** *(05) 59 27 62 60* **Map** *C5*

La Planche de Boeuf is popular with local diners, especially in winter, and you will need to arrive early to get a table next to the open fire. The menu is meaty, with tasty beef from the farms of the surrounding Béarn countryside and lamb from the Pyrenees, accompanied by a good wine list that emphasizes the southwest.

PAU Le Jeu de Paume – Hôtel Parc Beaumont

1 avenue Edouard VII, 64000 **Tel** *(05)59118400* **Map** *C5*

Luxury and refinement pervade this restaurant situated in the town centre, near Parc Beaumont. The young chef, who has learned his craft from some of the most talented chefs in France, stays faithful to the best traditional produce, but diversifies to add a touch of modernism to the preparation and presentation of the dishes. Excellent wines.

SHOPS AND MARKETS

Aquitaine is a mainly agricultural region, with an abundance of food specialities. These are often sold by the producers themselves at local markets. Here you will find foie gras from the Périgord or the Landes, oysters from Arcachon, strawberries and prunes

Specialities of Aquitaine

from the Lot-et-Garonne, goat's cheese from Quercy, wines from the Bordeaux area, and Armagnac. Many local artists and craftspeople offer their work for sale, and some open their studios to visitors. There are also numerous antiques shops and flea markets.

A lively market in Saint-Jean-de-Luz, selling local produce

MARKETS

Markets are friendly, lively places, where all sorts of tempting delicacies are on offer. Small producers set out their home-grown vegetables and fruit, which may include some vineyard peaches and old-fashioned varieties of apple. Other stalls are loaded with charcuterie, jars of foie gras and jams, such as those made by **Francis Miot**, and a range of local specialities, many of them made with organic produce. Markets vary according to season and to the area, and there are frequent speciality events, such as the cèpes market in Villefranche-du-Périgord, the truffle market in Lalbenque, various foie gras markets, and fish auctions in coastal towns. The Fête du Piment, devoted to sweet red peppers, takes place in Espelette in October, after the harvest. Powdered red pepper is available from **Ttipia** and **Xavier Jauregui**'s farm, both in Espelette. Farmers' markets usually start at around 7am and most are over by about 12.30pm.

WINE

Wine-producers whose estates are on official wine routes open their cellars to visitors, as do several Maisons des Vins and wine co-operatives. Here visitors may taste the wine and buy direct from the producer.

Local wine merchants stock such regional wines as Bordeaux, Bergerac (particularly **Julien de Savignac**, in Le Bugue), Cahors, Côtes-de-Duras and Jurançon, and spirits such as eau-de-vie and Armagnac. Information is available from **Bordeaux Tourist Office**, with details of **wine tours** at www.winetravelguides.com.

Jam produced by Francis Miot

SHOPS AND CRAFTS STUDIOS

Besides outlets for gastronomic specialities, the southwest has a host of shops selling handicrafts and traditional health and beauty preparations. Some local produce has surprising uses.

Both walnuts and salt from Salies-de-Béarn are used in cosmetics, and grape extracts feature in the treatments offered by **Les Sources the Caudalie** (see p245).

Crafts stalls are often found at produce markets in certain villages, particularly in summer. Hatters, metalworkers, stringed-instrument makers, enamellers, and glass-blowers at **Verrerie de Vianne**, welcome visitors to their studios. Individual events are also devoted to certain crafts. There are pottery fairs, weaving and basketry markets, and cutlery fairs. A craftworkers' festival takes place in July at La Bachellerie, in the Dordogne. Aquitaine also has a long pottery-making tradition. **Cazaux**, in Biarritz, is one of several outlets where original pieces can be found. **Madilar**, in Bayonne, is one of several Basque jewellers who use traditional designs. *Makhilas*, Basque shepherd's crooks with decorative finials, are custom-made by Ainciart Bergara. Boxwood-handled knives, made in Nontron, are another Périgordian classic. Traditional makers include **Coutellerie Nontronnaise**.

Interior of Confiserie Pierre Boisson, a confectioner's in Agen

REGIONAL PRODUCE

Aquitaine produces a wide variety of fine foods. This includes the beef from Chalosse, ham from Bayonne and caviar from **Estudor**, the Périgordian fish-farming business, as well as poultry, cheese, such as ewe's milk cheese from Ossau-Iraty, and fruit and vegetables, such as chasselas grapes from Prayssas, tomatoes from Marmande and black cherries from Itxassou. While some producers have roadside stalls, others have joint outlets in certain villages.

The region is also known for its sweet delicacies, such as prunes, produced by **Pierre Boisson** in Agen; *cannelés*, baked by **Baillardran** in Bordeaux; and the famous *Les Pyrénéens* chocolates, made by Lindt in Oloron-Sainte-Marie. Macaroons, the

Ducks at the Musée du Foie Gras in the Lot-et-Garonne

speciality in Saint-Jean-de-Luz, are made at **Maison Adam** and the confectioner **Pariès**.

LINEN

Colourfully striped Basque linen *(see p205)* is sold in interior decoration shops such as **Tissages Moutet**, who use leading designers. Rope-soled espadrilles, everyday footwear in the Pays Basque, are made in fashionable versions by **Fabrique Prodiso**.

At **Béatex**, in Oloron-Sainte-Marie, Basque bérets are still made from Pyrenean wool. This is especially warm, like the mohair that is woven at **Ferme du Chaudron Magique**, in Brugnac.

Largely because of the popularity of surfing, sportswear is now another speciality of the region. T-shirts by the Spanish Kukuxumusu label are in popular demand.

Window display at a Basque linen shop in Saint-Jean-de-Luz

FARM SHOPS

The popularity of countryside holidays has benefited many farms in Aquitaine. All over the region you will see "Bienvenue à la Ferme" signs by the roadside. Farms displaying this have campsites or rooms to let, and they also provide open-air activities, meals and tasty snacks for children.

Many farmers sell their produce by opening their premises to visitors and giving free tastings. At these farms you are likely to find everything from fruit juice, wine honey and walnut cake, to goat's cheese, free-range eggs and chickens, preserves and aromatic and medicinal herbs.

DIRECTORY

SPECIALITIES

GIRONDE

Baillardran
Galerie des Grands-Hommes, Bordeaux
Tel (05) 56 79 05 89

Bordeaux Tourist Office
12 cours 30 juillet, Bordeaux
Tel (05) 56 00 66 00

Wine tours
www.winetravel guides.com

PÉRIGORD-QUERCY

CIVRB
1 rue des Récollets, Bergerac
Tel (05) 53 63 57 57

Estudor
Les Moulineaux, Montpon-Ménestérol
Tel (05) 53 80 61 10

Julien de Savignac
Avenue de la Libération, Le Bugue
Tel (05) 53 07 10 31

LOT-ET-GARONNE

Confiserie Pierre Boisson
20 rue Grande-Horloge, Agen *Tel (05) 53 66 20 61*

PAYS BASQUE

Xavier Jauregui
Ferme Erreka, Espelette
Tel (05) 59 93 80 29

Maison Adam
6 rue de la République, Saint-Jean-de-Luz
Tel (05) 59 26 03 54

Pariès
14 rue du Port-Neuf, Bayonne
Tel (05) 59 59 06 29

Ttipia
Merkatu Plaza, Espelette
Tel (05) 59 93 97 82

BÉARN

Les Confiture (Francis) Miot
48 rue Joffre, Pau
Tel (05) 59 35 05 56

CLOTHES & HANDMADE ITEMS

GIRONDE

Les Sources de Caudalie
Chemin de Smith Haut-Lafitte, Bordeaux-Martillac
Tel (05) 57 83 83 83

PÉRIGORD-QUERCY

Coutellerie Nontronnaise
Place Paul-Bert, Nontron
Tel (05) 53 56 01 55

LOT-ET-GARONNE

Ferme du Chaudron Magique
Brugnac
Tel (05) 53 88 80 77

Verrerie de Vianne
Av. de la Verrerie, Vianne
Tel (05) 53 65 83 30

PAYS BASQUE

Cazaux
10 rue Broquedis, Biarritz
Tel (05) 59 23 15 01

Madilar
58 avenue Maréchal-Soult, Bayonne
Tel (05) 59 63 38 18

BÉARN

Béatex
Rue Rocgrand, Oloron-Sainte-Marie
Tel (05) 59 39 12 07

Fabrique Prodiso
3 rue du Jeu-de-Paume, Mauléon-Licharre
Tel (05) 59 28 28 48

Tissages Moutet
Route de Biron, Orthez
Tel (05) 59 69 14 33

What to Buy in Aquitaine

Aquitaine will tempt you with a great range of souvenirs, from Basque linen and Médoc confectionery to Périgord foie gras and studio ceramics. Small shops in villages all over the region offer a wide variety of local products and specialities. Also, the farmers' markets, craftsmen's workshops and farm shops are particularly good places to buy, as producers are always happy to pass on a little of their knowledge and to explain their methods.

Mohair gloves and scarf from Lot-et-Garonne

Espadrilles

BASQUE ITEMS

Besides espadrilles, berets and woollen items, linen is one of the finest of all Basque items. Woven from flax, it has seven coloured stripes for the seven Basque provinces. T-shirts made by Kukuxumusu are very fashionable in the Pays Basque, and the popularity of surfing has given sportswear by Quiksilver, 64 and other makers a fresh cachet.

T-shirts made in the Pays Basque

Basque berets

Basque linen

Painted plate

Basque crockery

Most Basque crockery consists of white porcelain decorated in green and red, the traditional colours of the Pays Basque. The principal manufacturers are located on the Adour river.

Ceramic vase

Key fob with Basque cross

Basque jewellery

The Basque cross is a motif that appears on rings, chokers, bracelets and many other items. An ancient sun symbol, it is known all over the world, and its four scrolled arms symbolize the movement of the stars. Basque crosses, known as Lauburu *(Four Heads), are supposed to be good-luck charms.*

Brooches and pendants featuring traditional motifs

Silver bracelets

NATURAL PRODUCTS

A vinotherapy spa centre, with hot springs and health treatments using grape extracts, was established in Bordeaux in the 1990s. It now produces a range of cosmetics based on these spring waters and grape extracts. Other spas in Aquitaine also produce many of their own health products, such as salt and clay extracts, for use at home.

Honey soaps from La Cité des Abeilles, Saint-Faust, Béarn

Fine salt from Salies-de-Béarn

Coarse salt from Salies-de-Béarn, for hydrotherapy

Caudalie health product

REGIONAL SPECIALITIES

Aquitaine has a great gastronomic tradition. Its many specialities include Périgordian truffles and foie gras, Arcachon oysters, Agen prunes, Bayonne ham, Béarnese ewe's milk cheese, Espelette red peppers, Basque cakes and Bordeaux wines. Besides such factory-made products as Lindt chocolate, a wide range of traditionally made products are available, straight from the maker.

Box of Basque macaroons

Stuffed Agen prunes

Walnuts in liqueur

Agen prune purée

Chocolate and Médoc hazelnut spread

Lindt chocolate, made in Oloron-Sainte-Marie

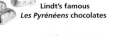

Lindt's famous *Les Pyrénéens* chocolates

Médoc hazelnut chocolates

Almond sweets made by Francis Miot

***Tourons*, traditional Basque confectionery**

ENTERTAINMENT

A festive spirit pervades many aspects of daily life in Aquitaine. Basque *bandas* play in the streets, and even enjoying a drink in a local *bodega* is likely to be enlivened by music. From jazz and film to bullfighting and Basque choral singing, the region offers a wide choice of entertainment all year round. The many dance and drama festivals, as well as concert halls and art galleries, also play an important part in this vibrant cultural scene.

Flamenco dancer

GENERAL INFORMATION

Regional daily newspapers, local radio stations and tourist organizations *(see pp285 and 286)* are good sources of up-to-date information about cultural events. **Clubs et Concerts**, a free fortnightly events bulletin published in Bordeaux, also has a website.

BUYING TICKETS

Tickets for most mainstream events are available from outlets such as **FNAC**, the large books and music store, and hypermarkets, including **Carrefour. France Billet**, an online ticket agency, allows you to purchase tickets either over the internet or from one of the region's agencies.

THEATRE AND DANCE

One of the region's leading cultural attractions is the **Opéra National de Bordeaux**, at the city's Grand Théâtre *(see pp 70–71)*, with a regular programme of opera, operetta, classical ballet and contemporary dance. Outside large towns, a large number of **festivals** take place throughout the summer. These include Jeux du Théâtre, in Sarlat *(see p33)*, and the major international contemporary mime festival, Mimos, in Périgueux, *(see p99)*. Dance companies come to Biarritz to take part in Le Temps d'Aimer, and to Mont-de-Marsan for the Festival d'Art Flamenco *(see p33)*. The Festival de Pau *(see p33)* features drama, music and dance.

A production of the ballet *Sleeping Beauty* at Opéra National de Bordeaux

MUSIC

The region's concert halls cater for every musical taste. The **Scène Nationale de Bayonne et du Sud Aquitain**, among others, hosts a wide range of events, but it is in the **Zénith de Pau**, the region's largest concert hall, that the biggest stars usually perform.

Classical recitals take place in the Médoc's vine-growing châteaux and Romanesque churches, and jazz is played at various festivals in the Gironde (at Pauillac, Fort-Médoc, Uzeste and Monségur, for example) and at **Comptoir du Jazz** in Bordeaux. The Festival de Musique Baroque du Périgord Noir takes place in some of the area's finest churches. Les Nuits Lyriques en Marmandais *(see p154)* is a concert series, given by top soloists.

CINEMA

The regional daily newspaper *Sud-Ouest (see p285)* provides information about films throughout the region. **Jean-Vigo**, in Bordeaux, shows art-house films and also puts on *cinéconcerts* (silent films

Traditional Basque fanfare at the Fêtes de Bayonne

with live music). Art-house films are also shown at **Utopia**, in a deconsecrated

Utopia, a cinema in Bordeaux

church. The **Jean-Eustache** cinema in Pessac hosts a festival of films on historical themes. **Ciné-Passion** is a mobile cinema that shows

films at venues around Brantôme, in the Périgord, with open-air showings in summer. The Festival des Jeunes Réalisateurs, held in Saint-Jean-de-Luz in October, is a showcase for films by young directors.

Casino de la Plage, in Château Deganne, in Arcachon

ART GALLERIES AND CRAFT STUDIOS

Bordeaux has about 30 art galleries, including **Arrêt sur l'Image**, which is devoted to photography. Art studios in Monflanquin (Lot-et-Garonne) are highly sought after, and some major European artists have set up studios in the **Domaine d'Abbadia** in Hendaye. Art galleries on the south coast are filled with paintings with a strong regional character.

The **Route des Métiers d'Art** was created to help promote the region's crafts studios. A guide to workshops along it is published by the regional tourist authority *(see p285)*.

CASINOS

Several towns, including **Arcachon, Biarritz, Saint-Jean-de-Luz, Pau** and Hossegor, have grand houses that have been converted into casinos, with slot machines and roulette.

DIRECTORY

GENERAL INFORMATION

www.
clubsetconcerts.com

TICKETS

Carrefour
www.
carrefourspectacles.com

FNAC
www.fnac.com

France Billet
www.
francebillet.com
Tel 0892 692 192

THEATRE, DANCE & MUSIC

Comptoir du Jazz
Le Port de la Lune,
58 quai de Paludate,
33800 Bordeaux
Tel (05) 56 49 15 55

Festivals d'Aquitaine
Aquitaine en Scène
http://
festivals.aquitaine.fr

Opéra National de Bordeaux
Grand Théâtre
Place de la Comédie,
33000 Bordeaux
Tel (05) 56 00 85 95
www.opera-bordeaux.com

Scène Nationale de Bayonne et du Sud Aquitain
Place de la Liberté,
64100 Bayonne
Tel (05) 59 59 07 27

Zénith de Pau
Boulevard du Cami-Salié,
64000 Pau.
Tel (05) 59 80 77 50
www.zenith-pau.fr

CINEMAS

Cinéma Jean-Eustache
Place de la Ve-République,
33600 Pessac
Tel 0892 687 021

Ciné-Passion en Périgord
La Fabrique.
Rue Amiral-Courbet,
24110 Saint-Astier
Tel (05) 53 02 41 96
www.cine-passion24. com

Jean-Vigo
6 rue Franklin,
33000 Bordeaux
Tel (05) 56 44 35 17

Utopia
5 place Camille-Jullian,
33000 Bordeaux
Tel (05) 56 52 00 15

ART GALLERIES & CRAFT STUDIOS

APRASAQ
Association pour la Promotion de Métiers d'Art d'Aquitaine
353 boulevard du Président-Wilson, 33200 Bordeaux
Tel (05) 57 22 57 36
www.route-metiers-d-art-aquitaine.com

Domaine d'Abbadia
64700 Hendaye
Tel (05) 59 20 37 20

Galerie Arrêt sur l'Image
Quai Armand-Lalande,
33300 Bordeaux
Tel (05) 56 69 16 48

Website for the arts and art galleries of the southwest
Lists galleries, art festivals and exhibitions.
www.articite.com/
aquitaine/galeries_dart/
galeries_aquitaine.htm

CASINOS

Arcachon
163 boulevard de La Plage
Tel (05) 56 83 41 44

Biarritz
1 avenue Édouard-VII
Tel (05) 59 22 77 77

Pau
Parc Beaumont
Tel (05) 59 27 06 92

Saint-Jean-de-Luz
Place Maurice-Ravel
Tel (05) 59 51 58 58

OUTDOOR ACTIVITIES

For visitors, both rugby, in which Aquitaine excels, and Basque pelota are likely to be spectator sports. However, the region offers a range of other sporting and outdoor activities. In summer, the Pyrenees are ideal for hiking, handgliding and mountaineering and, in winter, they offer superb skiing and snow-walking. The

Surfer on the beach at Anglet

coastline, the flat expanses of the Landes and the gentle hills of the region's vineyards are pleasant to explore by bicycle or on horseback, the leisurely pace enabling you to take in the spectacular scenery. Aquitaine is also a top destination for golfing enthusiasts, being home to several of the finest courses in Europe.

Hiking in the Massif de la Rhune, in the Pays Basque

WALKING

From the coast to the Pyrenees, through the vineyards of Bordeaux and across the Landes, more than 6,000km (3,730 miles) of waymarked footpaths criss-cross Aquitaine. For example, the GR653 and GR65 are two good, long-distance paths on the ancient pilgrim routes to Compostela. They are all managed by the Association de Coopération Interrégionale.

In the Pyrénées-Atlantiques, the legendary GR10, from Hendaye to the Cirque de Litor, and the GR8, from Urt to Sare, lead through pristine valleys and tracts of unspoilt countryside. Information can be obtained from the **Fédération Française de la Randonée Pédestre**. Official footpaths in Aquitaine also include those known as the Sentiers d'Émilie, and guides to these are available from bookshops. Some organizations offer hiking trips with a donkey to carry your luggage. Full information about this is available from departmental tourist authorities (see p286).

CYCLING

Aquitaine has a total of 2,000km (1,240 miles) of cycle tracks and mountain-biking routes, which are graded by level of difficulty. The disused railway lines along the coast and around the Arcachon Basin have been made into cycle tracks. These are particularly good, with the densest network between Pointe de Grave and Bayonne. With their gentle hills and picturesque *bastide* towns, the Périgord, the Lot-et-Garonne, the Pays Basque and Béarn are all perfect for leisurely cycling. In the more mountainous areas, cycling is of course more arduous, although steep climbs are rewarded by exhilarating descents. *À Vélo*, a brochure issued by the regional tourist authority (see p285), gives details of various short cycling circuits and longer tours. Another source of information is the **Fédération Française de Cyclotourisme**.

HORSE RIDING

One of the best ways of exploring the countryside is on horseback. There are several thousand kilometres of official bridleways in the region and a good number of riding centres. Escorted rides, on horses, ponys or *pottoks* (small Pyrenean horses), follow the many picturesque bridleways. In the Pyrenees, there are also escorted rides along the routes used by local shepherds and their flocks. Covering over 1 million ha (2471,000 acres) the forests of the Landes offer ideal terrain for horses. Information about opportunities for horse riding in the southwest is available from the **Comité Régional**.

Cycling on a quiet country road in the Dordogne

An escorted ride in
the Pays Basque

GOLF

The first golf course on the
Continent was built at Pau
in 1856. Since then, about
50 others, including several
putting greens, have been
created. The diversity of the
region's landscape has made
it possible to build golf courses
with widely different terrain.
Most are in set beautiful
surroundings, in the heart of
verdant countryside in Pau and
Arcangues, or in the midst of
vineyards in the Médoc. The
Chiberta golf course at Anglet,
just a few hundred yards from
the beaches, is one of the finest
golf courses on the Basque
coast. Chantaco, at Saint-Jean-
de-Luz, is another. The well-
known courses at Hossegor,
Seignosse and Moliets are
regarded as being among
the 50 best in Europe. The
Bordeaux-Gironde Golf-Pass

and Biarritz Golf-Pass allow
visiting golfers to play on
several courses in one zone
at preferential rates. The **Ligue
d'Aquitaine de Golf** provides
information on all aspects of
golfing in the region.

WINTER SPORTS

With several Pyrenean
mountain resorts, the
southwest has much to offer
winter sports enthusiasts.
There is downhill skiing at
La Pierre-Saint-Martin,
Artouste and Gourette, at an
altitude of 2,400m (7,877ft),
and cross-country skiing at
Issarbe, Le Col du Somport
and the Forêt d'Iraty. The
Comité Régional offers
detailed information.

HANGGLIDING

Hanggliding can offer
spectacular views of the
Pyrenean valleys. Centres at
Accous and Saint-Jean-Pied-
de-Port welcome beginners,
but they may prefer to go to
the Dune du Pyla. Here you
only need to run a few yards
to take off and float high
above the Arcachon Basin.
Several hanggliding schools are
members of the **Fédération
Française de Vol Libre**.

Golf course at the Château de
Montal, in the hills of Quercy

DISABLED VISITORS

Various organizations
promote sport for people
with disabilities. While
Handisport has a special
interest in people with restricted
mobility or impaired sight, the
**Ligue du Sport Adapté
d'Aquitaine** is concerned
with mentally handicapped
people. Tourisme et Handicap
is a useful source of
information on wheelchair
access. Through **APF Évasion**
(see p243) the **Association
des Paralysés de France**
organizes holidays for people
with disabilities.

DIRECTORY

WALKING

**Association
de Coopération
Interrégionale**
Les Chemins de
Saint-Jacques-
de-Compostelle
4 rue Clémence-Isaure,
31000 Toulouse
Tel (05) 62 27 00 05
www.chemins-
compostelle.com

**Fédération
Française de la
Randonée Pédestre**
14 rue Riquet,
75019 Paris
Tel (01) 44 89 93 93

CYCLING

**Fédération
Française
de Cyclotourisme**
12 rue Louis Bertrand,
94207 Ivry-sur-Seine
Tel (01) 56 20 88 87

HORSE RIDING

Comité Régional
Hippodrome du Bouscat,
BP 95, 33492 Le Bouscat
Cedex *Tel (05) 56 28 01 48*

GOLF

**Ligue d'Aquitaine
de Golf**
15 Avenue Pasteur,
33185 Le Haillan
Tel (05) 56 57 61 83
www.ffg-aquitaine.org

MOUNTAIN
SPORTS

**Comité Régional
du Club Alpin
Français**
5 rue René-Fournets,
64000 Pau
Tel (05) 59 27 71 81
www.clubalpinorthez.
com

**Comité Régional
de la Montagne
et de l'Escalade**
7 rue de Rossini,
64000 Pau
Tel (05) 59 80 22 70
www.ffme.fr

**Fédération
Française de Vol
Libre**
33700 Méignac
Tel (05) 56 46 07 58

DISABLED
VISITORS

**Association
des Paralysés
de France**
www.apf.asso.fr

**Association
Tourisme et
Handicap**
www.gihpnational.org/to
urisme/ath.htm

**Comité Régional
d'Aquitaine
Handisport**
119 bd Wilson, 33200
Bordeaux-Caudéran
Tel (05) 57 22 46 11
www.handisport.org

**Ligue du Sport
Adapté d'Aquitaine**
(as for Handisport)
Tel (05) 57 22 42 18

Watersports

The beaches of southwest France, which stretch for over 250km (155 miles), are renowned for having the best breakers in Europe. This makes them very popular for surfing, although the sea here is also ideal for other watersports. Sheltered by dunes and pine forests, the lakes of the Landes and Gironde are perfect for sailing. The white-water rivers of the Pyrenees, the Périgord and the Leyre, as well as their calmer stretches, offer excellent opportunities for canoeing. Sea fishing and angling in streams or lakes, are other options.

Windsurfer on the Étang de Léon, in the Landes

Canoeing in the lower Vézère valley

SEA-KAYAKING AND SURF-KAYAKING

The whole of the region's coastline is suitable for sea kayaking. In "frenzy", a more energetic form of surf-kayaking, a light unsinkable craft is used to skim along the crest of breakers at exhilarating speed. While the slow-moving waters of the Dordogne and lower Vézère rivers are perfect for novice canoeists, the Auvézère, upper Dronne and upper Isle present a suitable challenge for the more experienced. The **Fédération Française Canoë-Kayak de Gironde** co-ordinates information, and some organizations, such as **Vallée de la Vézère** and **Canoë Dordogne**, rent canoes and arrange themed routes.

SAILING, WINDSURFING AND SAND-YACHTING

La Teste-De-Buche, **Arcachon** and **Hendaye** are coastal resorts identified as *stations voile* (windsurfing, sailing and sand-yatching centres) by the Fédération Française.

The region's many natural and man-made lakes also offer superb watersports facilities and, unlike coastal resorts, they are not affected by the tide. Carcans-Hourtin, Lacanau, Cazaux, Sanguinet, Parentis, Soustons, Hossegor and Biscarrosse are resorts that offer ideal conditions for catamaran sailing, as well as for windsurfing and funboarding. Surrounded by maritime pines, these sheltered lakes are also ideal for bathing, and young children can play at the water's edge in complete safety. The Gironde estuary also offers opportunities for watersports enthusiasts. Each year, between March and late November, the **Club Nautique Bourquais** organizes regattas. Aquitaine's wide Atlantic beaches offer vast spaces for sand-yachting,

particularly in autumn, when the wind is most favourable. Information about these sports is posted on the **Ligue d'Aquitaine** website.

DEEP-SEA DIVING

Between the Pays Basque and the Arcachon Basin, there are several diving centres. Those on the Arcachon Basin, where the **Fédération Française d'Etudes Sports Sous-marin** is based, are very popular. Diving in the shallow waters off the coast is organized from the jetty at La Croix des Marins, while diving in deeper waters, further out at sea, is organized from the marina. Off the Plage des Gallouneys, the water is up to 15–18m (50–60 ft) deep, and here old World War II blockhouses, now covered with sea anemones, have become home to a variety of marine life. You can also go diving in the Étang de Sanguinet, which is 7–8m (23–26ft) deep. It harbours a wreck, half buried in sand, that is home to freshwater fishes. For several years now, the Association de Défense et d'Études Marines de la Côte has been working to install an artifical reef, 25m (80ft) down in the sea off Mimizan. Degraded by over-fishing and oil pollution, this area of the seabed is gradually recovering, and is being recolonized by marine plants and animals.

A twin-hulled sailing dinghy

Kite-surfers at Lacanau, one of the region's greatest surfing resorts

SURFING

More than simply a sport, surfing in this part of France is almost a way of life. The waves hitting the beaches here are at their highest and most powerful in the autumn. **Anglet, Biarritz**, Hossegor and **Lacanau** are major venues for international competitions, and each of them has a number of surfing clubs. One of the best centres for surfers, however, is **Capbreton**, which is also well known as a diving spot because of the Gouf, an underwater canyon, more than 3,000m (9,846ft) deep.

There are also a large number of surfing schools dotted along the coast, that offer instruction for both beginners and experienced

surfers. Many of these are members of the **Fédération Française de Surf**.

You can hire surfing equipment at almost any resort. Information on all aspects of surfing in the southwest is given in an annually updated booklet, *Surfer en Aquitaine*, issued by the **Ligue d'Aquitaine de Surf**. The waves here are also perfect for bodyboarding, in which you ride the waves lying on a surfboard, and for kite-surfing, in which you skim along the waves, towed, and sometimes lifted, by a kite. Kite-surfing is especially popular at Arcachon, Biscarrosse and Lacanau. **Surf Report**, accessible by telephone or via the internet,

gives daily reports on the best surfing spots and on weather conditions. Other websites provide information on conditions along the whole of the region's coastline.

Pupils from one of the region's many surfing schools

Surfer on breakers at a beach in the Pays Basque

DIRECTORY

WHERE TO SURF

Ligue d'Aquitaine
1 avenue de la Côte-d'argent,
40200 Mimizan
Tel (06) 74 82 74 17
www.surfingaquitaine.com
www.ecoledesurf.com

Fédération Française de Surf (FFS)
Plage Nord, BP 28, 40150 Hossegor
Tel (05) 58 43 55 88.
www.surfingfrance.com

Anglet Surf Club
Place du Docteur-Gentilhe,
64 600 Anglet
Tel (05) 59 03 01 66

Biarritz Surf Club
Plage de la Milady,
64200 Biarritz
Tel (05) 59 23 24 42

Capbreton Surf Club
Boulevard François-Mitterrand,
40130 Capbreton
Tel (05) 58 72 33 80

Lacanau Surf Club
Boulevard de la Plage, 33680
Lacanau-Océan
Tel (05) 56 26 38 84

Surf Report
Tel 0892 68 13 60
www.surf-report.com

White-water rafting on the Gave de Pau, near Bétharram

WHITE-WATER RAFTING AND CANYONING

Many clubs and other organizations have special programmes tailored for beginners, as well as for experienced enthusiasts. In Béarn, the rivers that rush down the Pyrenean valleys offer a thrilling challenge to skilled rafters and canyoners. Also, the Nive river, close to the Basque coast, is an excellent site, and offers opportunities for a host of other watersports as well.

Whether you choose a demanding or a more gentle descent, you must be able to swim and must obey your guide at all times.

Many organizations, including **Eaux Vives, Canoë-Kayak de Mer** and **Loisirs 64**, will provide all the essential information.

CANAL BOATING

The Canal de Garonne, the continuation of the Canal du Midi, as well as the Lot, Dordogne and Baïse rivers are either partly or wholly accessible by motor boat. Those who enjoy exploring a region off the beaten track will be interested in the choice of options available (*see pp298–9*). These range from a short trip on the river to a cruise in a hired boat. Sailing down the Leyre, which winds through the forests from the Landes in Gascony to the Arcachon Basin in the Gironde, offers a voyage of discovery at a leisurely pace. There are 12 boat-hire centres along this river, which has been aptly nicknamed "the little Amazon". You can enjoy trips of just a few hours or of several days, accompanied by a qualified leader.

FISHING

The region's lakes and rivers offer fishermen almost limitless opportunities to indulge their passion. They are divided into three grades. The best waters are home to trout and salmon. In the second- and third-grade waters, carp, tench, roach, pike and black bass can be found.

Fishing is controlled by law, so as to protect fish stocks across all species and preserve the environment. To fish in Aquitaine, you must purchase a licence, which is available from fishing-tackle shops and other outlets. Fishing licences are available for one day, for two weeks (*forfait vacances*) or for a year.

There are a huge number of lakes in this region of France. Among the best for fishing are the large ones along the coast of the Gironde and the Landes. The Garonne and the Dordogne are rich in such migratory species as salmon, shad and meagre. The still waters of the Lot-et-Garonne, the canal parallel with the Garonne and many lakes are also good fishing spots.

Whether using a rod and reel or fly-fishing, the more active anglers will usually head for the Pyrénées-Atlantiques, which has some of the best fishing waters in Europe. The Gave d'Oloron is one of the finest salmon-rivers in France.

On the coast, anglers can catch turbot, sole and bream. Boats taking visitors further out on tuna- and shark-fishing expeditions leave from Saint-Jean-de-Luz and Biarritz. A more unusual kind of fishing is surf-casting. This is done from beaches at night or at dawn, using 4.50-m (15-ft) rods to cast into the surf.

Every *département* in France has a **Fédération de Pêche** (fishing association), to which approved fishing clubs and organizations belong.

Barge on the Baïse, below the lock at Lavardac

Anglers on the jetty leading to the lighthouse at Capbreton

SAFETY AT SEA

Every year, accidents in the Atlantic happen as the result of holidaymakers disregarding basic safety rules. The main danger to swimmers is being swept out to sea by the strong currents that form in large bays as the tide turns. To be safe, swimmers should bathe only on beaches that are supervised (from June to September). Swimming is forbidden outside areas marked by blue pennants. Surfing and bodyboarding are only permitted outside bathing areas, and some beaches have specially marked surfing and bodyboarding zones, where swimmers are not allowed. If you want to go sailing, you should always check the **sea forecast** (*météo marine*) before setting out, as weather conditions at sea can change rapidly. Inexperienced sailors should always be supervised by professionals. **CROSS** (Centre Régional Opérationnel de Surveillance et de Sauvetage) will come to the rescue of sailors or swimmers in difficulty.

Green flag, the signal for safe bathing

WATERSPORTS FOR DISABLED PEOPLE

Some beaches in the Pays Basque have been made accessible to people with disabilities thanks to **Handiplage**, an association that also publishes *Handi Long*, a guide for visitors with disabilities. Among the outdoor activities that have been especially adapted through **Handisport** (*see p277*) are surfing (contact Handisurf), canoeing and deep-sea diving.

DIRECTORY

USEFUL NUMBERS

CROSS Atlantique
29770 Audierne
Tel (02) 97 55 35 35

Sea Forecast
http://plages-landes.info

Visitors with Disabilities Handiplage
39 rue des Faures,
64100 Bayonne
Tel (05) 59 59 24 21
www.handiplage.fr

CANOEING

Canoës Vallée de la Vézère
10 promenade de la Vézère, 24620 Les Eyzies-de-Tayac
Tel (05) 53 05 10 11
www.valleevezere.com

Canoë Dordogne
24250 la Roque-Gageac
Tel (05) 53 29 58 50

Fédération Française de Canoë-Kayak de Gironde
Bordeaux
Tel (05) 56 44 82 08
Aire sur l'Adour, Landes
Tel (05) 58 71 75 04

RAFTING

Canoë-Kayak de Mer
Maison de la Nature du Bassin d'Arcachon, 33470 Le Teich
Tel (05) 56 22 80 93

Eaux Vives
Le Pont,
64190 Navarrenx.
Tel (05) 59 66 04 05.

Loisirs 64
21 rue de Hirigogne,
64600 Anglet
Tel (05) 59 03 42 92

SAILING

Ligue d'Aquitaine
Boulevard du Parc-des-Expositions, 33520 Bordeaux-Lac.
Tel (05) 56 50 47 93

Cercle de Voile d'Arcachon
Marina (port de plaisance), 33120 Arcachon
Tel (05) 56 83 05 92

Club Nautique Bourquais
2 bis quai des Verreries, 33710 Bourg-sur-Gironde
Tel (05) 57 68 44 44

Centre Nautique d'Hendaye
Marina , 64700 Hendaye
Tel (05) 59 48 06 07

SAND YACHTING

Ligue d'Aquitaine
45 rue du Périgord, 33160 Saint-Médard-en-Jalles
Tel (06) 26 90 54 19

DEEP-SEA DIVING

Comité Interrégional Atlantique-Sud
119 bd Wilson 33200 Bordeaux-Cauderan
Tel (05) 56 17 01 03

Club d'Exploration Sous-marine d'Aquitaine
69 avenue d'Arès, 33000 Bordeaux
Tel (05) 56 99 46 26

Fédération Française d'Etudes Sports Sous-marin
209 rue 14 juillet, 33400 Talence
Tel (05) 56 96 67 52

FISHING

Fédérations Départementales de Pêche

Dordogne
16 rue des Prés,
24000 Périgueux
Tel (05) 53 06 84 20

Gironde
299 cours de la Somme,
33800 Bordeaux
Tel (05) 56 92 59 48

Landes
102 allée Marine,
40400 Tartas
Tel (05) 58 73 43 79

Lot-et-Garonne
BP 225, 47006 Agen
Tel (05) 53 66 16 68

Pyrénées-Atlantiques
12 bd Hauterive, 64000
Pau *Tel (05) 59 84 98 50*

SURVIVAL GUIDE

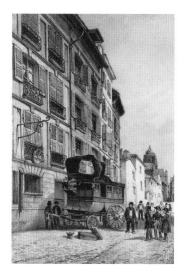

PRACTICAL INFORMATION

Because of its gentle climate, southwest France attracts tourists all year round. But it is during the summer, particularly in the coastal resorts, that it sees the largest number of visitors. Covering an area as large as the Netherlands, the region offers many different types

Traditional Basque dress

of scenery, including mountains, a beautiful coastline, forests and vineyards, as well as a wide choice of activities. It also has a rich cultural heritage, with several major prehistoric sites, many grand, imposing châteaux, and numerous picturesque, medieval towns and villages.

Beach and Fort de Socoa at Saint-Jean-de-Luz, in the Pays Basque

WHEN TO GO

During summer, southwest France welcomes a constant stream of visitors, and the areas along the coast become particularly crowded. The whole of Aquitaine is enlivened with festivals and fairs, and it is also the high season for watersports.

Autumn is the best time of year for golf, surfing, hunting and fishing, and is also when truffles and cèpes are gathered, and grapes harvested in the vineyards. By contrast to the coastal resorts, which are now fairly quiet, large towns and cities remain lively places. In Bordeaux, for example, theatre, concerts and exhibitions are in full swing, shops are busy and just taking a stroll in the streets is pleasant.

In the Pyrenees, between November and Easter, the snow-covered peaks draw winter-sports enthusiasts. The resorts are particularly busy during school holidays.

VISAS

Whether you need a visa to visit France depends on your nationality and length of stay. Citizens of European Union countries do not need one. Citizens of the USA,

Canada, Australia and New Zealand do not need a visa for stays of up to three months. All foreign visitors need an identity card or valid passport.

ANIMALS

There is no bar to bringing pets to France, so long as the animal is at least three months old, has microchip identification and has been vaccinated against rabies. A certificate of vaccination, issued by a qualified, registered vet must be shown.

Some beaches have a no-dogs policy. In coastal resorts, it is an offence to allow your dog to foul pavements and other public areas, and transgressions are likely to

be punished by a 70-euro fine. Particularly "aggressive" dogs, such as pit bull terriers, are outlawed in France.

TAX-FREE GOODS

Visitors resident outside the European Union can reclaim the sales tax TVA, or VAT, of 12 per cent on certain goods, if the total value of their purchases, on a single day in one shop, is 175 euros or more. TVA is much lower in the Basque part of Spain – just 7 per cent, as opposed to 19.6 per cent or even 33.3 in France. Many people from Béarn and the Pays Basque, therefore, cross the border to buy alcohol and cigarettes, or for short breaks.

CUSTOMS DUTIES

If you are travelling within the European Union, there is no limit to the amount of goods you can buy so long as they are for your personal use. (This does not apply to new vehicles.) However, you should not take home more than 3,200 cigarettes, more than 10 litres of spirits or more than 90 litres of wine. Plants, ivory, counterfeit

One of the region's many important museums and galleries

◁ **The fishing harbour at Saint-Jean-de-Luz**

A tourist office in a historic building

items and works of art are subject to particular restrictions. If you have doubts about anything, it is advisable to check with the **Service des Douanes**.

ADMISSION CHARGES

Admission charges for most museums, monuments and archaeological and other sites range from 2 to 7 euros. There are reductions for children up to 12 years old, and usually no charge for children under six. Students under the age of 26 and people over 65 are also entitled to reductions. Consult **Centres d'Information pour la Jeunesse** for further details of the range of concessions available to young people.

TOURIST INFORMATION

Information on everything, from the region's coast and countryside to its villages, towns and cities, as well as the passes of the Pyrenees and local wine routes, is available from the **Comité Régional du Tourisme**. This

organization can also give advice on where to go, what to do and where to stay.

Each *département* has a **Comité Départemental du Tourisme**, which coordinates information from all local business involved in tourism, and which can also help you book accommodation. To contact a **tourist office**, no matter where you are in France, dial 3265 and you will be put through to the relevant branch. The **Maison Aquitaine** in Paris is another good source of information for planning your stay.

OPENING TIMES

Most archeological sites, museums and other visitor attractions are closed on Mondays or Tuesdays. In summer, however, museums open every day, and shops are likely to stay open at lunchtime or later in the evenings. Out of the high season, shops open from 9am to 7:30pm, and close at lunchtime. Hypermarkets are open all day and many also open on Sunday mornings. Apart from those in major coastal resorts, large towns and on motorways, most petrol stations close on Sundays. In restaurants, it can sometimes be difficult to order a meal after 2pm at lunchtime and after 10pm in the evening.

Brochures with tourist information on the southwest

MEDIA

The principal French national daily newspapers, such as *Le Monde*, go on sale at newsagents from opening time every morning. The best way of getting the feel of local life in Aquitaine is to read *Sud Ouest*, a regional daily with more than 1 million readers that is published in 22 local editions.

Many kiosks, especially in larger towns, also sell a wide range of foreign newspapers, and most 3- and 4-star hotels provide newspapers for their foreign guests. Bars and bistros also put out a copy of the local newspaper for customers to read.

The best-known and most widely read regional magazine is the bimonthly *Pyrénées Magazine*, which carries features on mountain hiking and local culture. Others include *Pays Basque Magazine* and *Le Festin*, an art journal devoted to the cultural heritage of the region. Both are published quarterly.

Aquitaine also has a number of radio stations. Among them is France Bleu, which has local stations in the Gironde, the Périgord, Béarn and in the Pays Basque.

Logo of TV7 Bordeaux and France Bleu

Local television stations include FR3 Aquitaine and FR3 Pau-Béarn, and TV7, which covers the area in and around Bordeaux. Satellite channels, including a wide range of foreign channels, are also usually available in 3- and 4-star hotels.

The daily newspaper *Sud Ouest* and the magazine *Pyrénées*

A ride at the Parc d'Attractions Walibi

TRAVELLING WITH CHILDREN

Children are welcome almost everywhere in southwest France, including hotels, campsites and gîtes. The time when there is most on offer for children is, of course, during school holidays.

Besides its many activity and entertainment centres, the region has several theme parks. These include the **Parc Animalier** in Capbreton, the **Haras National de Gelos** (horse-breeding centre) near Pau, the **Parc d'Attractions Walibi** *(see p161),* near Agen,

and the **Parc Préhistorique de Fontirou**, with the largest exhibit devoted to prehistoric animals anywhere in Europe.

As in other countries, children in cars are legally required to travel in child car seats. Swimming pools in public places should also be fenced. On the beach, parents should protect children from strong sun and obey safety rules imposed by lifeguards. If you would prefer to avoid beaches with large waves, keep to the Arcachon Basin, the bay at Saint-Jean-de-Luz or any of the large coastal lakes *(see pp278–9).*

SMOKING

Smoking is forbidden in public places, such as cinemas, museums, galleries, historical monuments and buildings that are open to visitors, and on public transport. Restaurants, in theory, should have smoking and non-smoking areas, but this is not rigidly enforced.

DISABLED TRAVELLERS

Two websites, **handiweb** and **handitec**, offer detailed information about the legal provision in France for disabled travellers, and other practical details. They also provide useful information and relevant addresses that will help you to plan your trip and make the most of your stay. For details on sport for people with disabilities, see p277.

ELECTRICITY

As elsewhere in Europe, the current in France is 220v-AC. Two-pin plugs, with rounded prongs, are used.

DIRECTORY

TOURIST INFORMATION

Centre d'Information Jeunesse Aquitaine (CIJA)
125 cours Alsace-Lorraine,
33000 Bordeaux
Tel (05) 56 56 00 56
www.info-jeune.net

Maison Aquitaine
21 rue des Pyramides,
75008 Paris
Tel (01) 55 35 31 42

Service des Douanes
Tel 0820 024 444
www.douane.gouv.fr/

Comité Régional du Tourisme
Cité Mondiale,
23 parvis des Chartrons,
33074 Bordeaux Cedex
Tel (05) 56 01 70 00
www.tourisme-aquitaine.fr

DISABLED TRAVELLERS

www.handiweb.fr
www.handitec.com

COMITÉS DÉPARTEMENTAUX DU TOURISME

Dordogne
25 rue du Président-Wilson,
24009 Périgueux Cedex
Tel (05) 53 35 50 24
www.dordogne-perigord-tourisme.fr

Gironde
21 cours de l'Intendance,
33000 Bordeaux
Tel (05) 56 52 61 40
www.tourisme-gironde.cg33.fr

Landes
4 rue Aristide-Briand, BP 407, 40012
Mont-de-Marsan Cedex
Tel (05) 58 06 89 89
www.tourismelandes.com

Lot-et-Garonne
271 rue Péchabout, BP 30158,

47005 Agen Cedex
Tel (05) 53 66 14 14
www.lot-et-garonne.fr

Béarn-Pays Basque
4 allées des Platanes
BP 811, 64108 Bayonne Cedex
Tel (05) 59 46 52 52
www.tourisme64.com

CHILDREN

Haras National de Gelos
1 rue du Maréchal Leclerc,
64110 Gelos.
Tel (05) 59 35 06 52

Parc Animalier
Avenue de l'Océan, 40530 Labenne
(south of Capbreton)
Tel (05) 59 45 43 93

Parc d'Attractions Walibi
Château de Caudouin,
47310 Roquefort
Tel (05) 53 96 58 32

Parc Préhistorique de Fontirou
Fontirou, RN 21, 47340 Castella
Tel (05) 53 40 15 29

Personal Security and Health

Its well-run local authorities and public services make Aquitaine a generally safe place to visit. But you should always guard against petty crime by taking a few simple precautions, such as locking your car and not flaunting valuable personal possessions. Pharmacies are almost everywhere, and all large towns have modern, well-equipped hospitals, such as the CHU in Bordeaux.

PERSONAL SECURITY

If you are involved in an accident, call the **police**, and take statements from witnesses. This may be useful if you need to provide a report. If you are the victim of assault or robbery, contact the nearest police station. Your country's consulate or embassy may also be able to help you. If you lose your passport or other important documents, report this to the nearest police station. If your credit card is lost or stolen, you must notify the police of this too *(see pp288–9)* and, of course, contact the company that issued the card.

Pharmacy sign

EMERGENCIES

In an emergency, call **SAMU** (Service d'Aide Médicale d'Urgence) by dialling 15, or the **Sapeurs Pompiers** (fire brigade) by dialling 18. Unless they are in immediate danger, do not try to move someone who is injured before medical help arrives. If you are involved in an emergency in the mountains, call **PGHM** for the Pyrénées-Atlantiques. This is the police force in charge of high mountain areas. You can summon help by dialling 112, the central, European-wide number of the **emergency service**, which operates via mobile phones. For difficulties at sea, contact **CROSS**, which will notify the lifeguard and lifeboat organizations.

MEDICAL CARE

No vaccinations are needed to visit France. If you come from a European country, apply for a European Health Insurance Card (EHIC). You can do this online or at post offices in the UK, before you leave. It will enable you to claim for state health service treatment in European Union countries, should you need it. You can receive hospital treatment, consult a doctor at a surgery or even ask one to visit. Outside normal hours, there will always be a doctor on call and a duty pharmacy that is open. Details of these services are posted outside surgeries and published in local papers, and are also available from police stations. While some medicines can be obtained by prescription only, others are sold over the counter.

OUTDOORS

Every summer the ocean claims more lives. On beaches, always heed lifeguards' safety instructions and only swim in supervised areas. If the red pennant is flying, the sea is dangerous and you should not enter the water.

Never venture off into the mountains alone, and always check conditions first with the **local weather station**. A mobile phone, good map and sturdy boots are essentials.

Lifeguards on a beach, along the Atlantic coast

DIRECTORY

EMERGENCY NUMBERS

CROSS Étel
Tel (05) 56 73 31 31

PGHM for Pyrénées-Atlantiques
Quartier Saint-Pée,
64400 Oloron-Sainte-Marie
Tel (05) 59 10 02 50

SAMU
Tel 15

Police and Gendarmerie
Tel 17

Sapeurs Pompiers (Fire)
Tel 18

Emergency Service
Tel 112
(Europe-wide number)

Local Weather Station
Tel 0892 68 02 XX
(for XX dial the number of the relevant département)
Tel 0892 68 08 77
(shipping forecast)
Tel 0892 68 10 20
(snow & avalanche information)

MAIN HOSPITALS

Bordeaux
Place Amélie-Raba-Léon
Tel (05) 56 79 56 79

Périgueux
80 avenue Georges-Pompidou
Tel (05) 53 45 25 25

Mont-de-Marsan
Avenue Pierre-de-Coubertin
Tel (05) 58 05 10 10

Agen
21 route de Villeneuve
Tel (05) 53 69 70 71

Bayonne
13 avenue Interne Jacques-Loëb
Tel (05) 59 44 35 35

Pau
4 boulevard Hauterive
Tel (05) 59 92 48 48

CONSULATES

UK
353 blvd du Président Wilson,
Bordeaux
Tel (05) 57 22 21 10

USA
10 place de la Bourse,
Bordeaux
Tel (05) 56 48 63 80

Banking and Local Currency

Because of the large number of tourists it attracts, the southwest of France is well served by banks and bureaux de change, where visitors can change travellers' cheques or foreign currency. It is also possible to obtain euros at post offices and to withdraw cash from automatic cash machines, which can be found in all towns and many villages. Those who come from a country where the euro (€) is the national currency, can also withdraw cash from any bank.

CURRENCY

Visitors from countries outside the Euro-Zone can change currency in banks and post offices, and at bureaux de change in department stores in large towns, as well as in railway stations, airports and around tourist resorts. A commission is usually charged when changing currency, even if the rate is fixed, and this should be clearly displayed. It is always advisable to look around for the most favourable rates. You may like to consult an internet currency converter, which uses the most up-to-date exchange rates to make its calculations. Changing banknotes is as economical as changing travellers' cheques, but if you use a debit card to obtain cash, you may have to pay an additional charge of 1 per cent of the amount drawn.

TRAVELLERS' CHEQUES

Travellers' cheques from **Travelex** or **American Express** are a safe and convenient way of carrying large amounts of cash. Travellers' cheques can be cashed at any bank or bureau de change and, subject to certain conditions, their value is refundable in case of loss or theft. Remember to keep the record of your cheques' serial numbers in a safe place, separate from the cheques themselves, as you will be asked to provide these should you need to claim a refund. You must countersign each cheque when you exchange it for cash or use it to make a purchase.

BANK CHEQUES

Paying by bank cheque when you are abroad is not a viable option. Most bureaux de change do not accept bank cheques in exchange for currency.

CREDIT CARDS

Credit and debit cards are accepted in many shops, hotels and restaurants. However, some establishments will not accept cards for amounts below a certain figure, and this policy should be displayed. The most commonly used cards are **Visa** and **Eurocard-Mastercard**, although hotels and restaurants also accept **American Express** and **Diner's Club**.

There are ATMs (automatic teller machines) in every town in the region. Bear in mind, however, that ATMs may run out of cash over a long weekend, such as Easter, or when a public holiday falls on a Friday or a Monday.

A branch of the bank Crédit Agricole, in a historic building

BANKING HOURS

Most banks in France are open for business from 9am to 12:30pm and from 1:45pm to 4:45pm, Tuesday to Sunday. Remember that on the eve of public holidays, such as Bastille Day (14 July) and Assumption (15 August), banks close early. The major French banks have branches in most towns in Aquitaine.

DIRECTORY

BUREAUX DE CHANGE

American Express Bordeaux
11 cours de l'Intendance
Tel (05) 56 00 63 33

Change Plus, Biarritz
9 rue Mazagran
Tel (05) 59 24 82 47

Travelex, Bordeaux airport
Hall A 33700 Mérignac
Tel (05) 56 34 03 40

Thomas Cook Périgueux
10 allée d'Aquitaine
Tel (05) 53 35 95 00

Thomas Cook Pau
Place Clemenceau
Tel (05) 59 11 86 86

INTERNET CURRENCY CONVERTERS

www.xe.com/ucc
www.x-rates.com/
calculator.html

LOST CARDS AND TRAVELLERS' CHEQUES

Eurocard-Mastercard
Tel 0800 90 23 90
www.eurocardmastercard.tm.fr

Visa
Tel 0892 70 57 05
www.carte-bleue.com

Diner's Club
Tel 0810 314 159
www.dinersclub.fr

American Express
Tel (01) 47 77 72 00 (cards)
Tel 0800 90 86 00 (cheques)
www.americanexpress.fr

Travelex
Tel 0800 90 83 30.
www.travelex.com

THE EURO

Since the beginning of 2002, the euro, the European single currency, has been in use in 13 countries of the European Union. Austria, Belgium, Eire, Finland, France, Germany, Greece, Italy, Luxembourg, the Netherlands, Portugal, Spain and Slovenia have all gone over to the single currency. The United Kingdom, Denmark and Sweden have retained their respective currencies, with an option to review their decision in the future.

Euro notes are identical across all 13 countries. Euro coins, by contrast, have one side identical (the value side) and one side unique to each country. Notes and coins are valid and interchangeable in each of the 13 countries that are currently using the euro.

Banknotes

Euro banknotes have seven denominations. The 5€ note (which is grey) is the smallest, followed by the 10€ (red), 20€ (blue), 50€ (orange), 100€ (green), 200€ (yellow) and 500€ (purple). All notes shows the stars of the European Union.

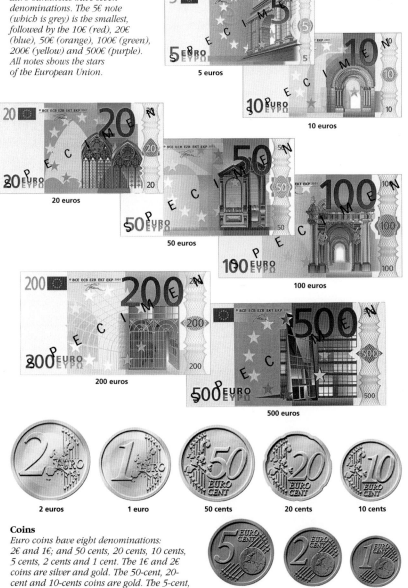

5 euros

10 euros

20 euros

50 euros

100 euros

200 euros

500 euros

2 euros

1 euro

50 cents

20 cents

10 cents

Coins

Euro coins have eight denominations: 2€ and 1€; and 50 cents, 20 cents, 10 cents, 5 cents, 2 cents and 1 cent. The 1€ and 2€ coins are silver and gold. The 50-cent, 20-cent and 10-cents coins are gold. The 5-cent, 2-cent and 1-cent coins are bronze.

5 cents

2 cents

1 cent

Communications

French telecommunication systems are reliable and efficient. Most public telephones are now operated using pre-pay cards, that are available from post offices and tobacconist-newsagents. The mobile phone network has also expanded. With the growth of the internet, cafés have opened all over the region, offering inexpensive access to the web and allowing users to enter chat rooms and check their email. La Poste, the French postal service, is reliable and relatively inexpensive, and there are post offices all over Aquitaine, even in remote rural areas.

Distinctive yellow French mail box, a 1960s design

TELEPHONING IN FRANCE

All French telephone numbers have 10 digits. The first two digits indicate the region: 01 indicates Paris and the Île de France; 02 the northwest; 03 the northeast; 04 the southeast (including Corsica); and 05 the southwest. When phoning from outside France, dial 00 33 and omit the initial zero from the 10-digit number (for example, 00 33 3 45 67 89 10).

To use a payphone (cabine téléphonique), you usually need a phone card (télécarte). These are available in 25, 50 or 120 telephone units. Very few public telephones are now coin-operated, and these are only likely to be found in the most out-of-the-way places.

With a **France Télécom** card, you can make calls from any private or public phone, the cost of the call being transferred to your own telephone bill. The card can be used both in France and in about one hundred other countries as well. All types of phonecards (from pre-pay cards to top-up cards for mobile phones) are available at post offices and at most newsagents and tobacconists.

To call another country from France, dial 00, followed by the country code, then the number. All call charges and country codes are printed in telephone directories and also appear on the website of France Télécom. In case of difficulty, you can be connected by an **operator.**

MOBILE PHONES

France is well covered by the three main French mobile phone operators: SFR, Bouygues and France Télécom. Information on obtaining a service from one of these is available from your own operator.

Mobile phones that use a pre-pay card service are also available for hire in France, from specialist shops.

INTERNET ACCESS

You will have no trouble finding internet cafés. Among them are **Cyberstation** in Bordeaux and **Madiba Café** in Dax, but there are many others. Tourist offices have details of them. The cost will be in proportion to the time you spend online. All large hotels offer guests internet access, which is charged at a flat rate.

USING A PHONECARD TELEPHONE

1 Lift the receiver and wait for the dialling tone.

2 Insert the *télécarte*, arrow side up.

3 The display will show how many units are stored on the card.

4 Key in the number and wait to be connected.

5 If you want to make another call, do not replace the receiver: simply press the follow-on button.

6 When you have finished the call, withdraw your card.

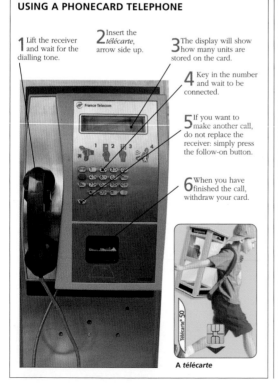

A *télécarte*

Some post offices have internet terminals known as **Cyberposte**. There are 800 of these in France, and you can use them to surf the web and check your email. Information about Cyperposte is given on La Poste's website.

USING LA POSTE

To send a letter, use one of La Poste's distinctive yellow mailboxes. These are found in the street and also outside every post office. Collection times are indicated on them.

Stamps are available from post offices, newsagents and tobacconists. They are sold individually or in books (carnets de timbres) of 10. Postage rates vary according to the weight of the letter or parcel and its destination. The postal service is fast and reliable. A letter to a destination within France will arrive in 24 to 48 hours; from France to another country allow one to five days, unless you have paid for express delivery.

Some post offices have facilities that obviate the need to queue. These include stamp machines, franking machines and cash dispensers.

POSTE RESTANTE

French post offices, right across the country, also provide a mail-holding service (poste restante), so that you can receive mail while travelling, without the need for a fixed address. Letters and parcels sent to you at a poste restante should be addressed with the name of the addressee, the words "poste restante", the name of the relevant post office, the town and the postcode. To collect mail, you will need some form of identification.

You can also arrange to have your mail forwarded to an address of your choice, when you are away from home. There is a charge for this service, and you should allow about four days for it to come into effect.

An internet café, one of a growing number in the southwest

La Poste also provides banking services. You can withdraw cash and change foreign currency, but as elsewhere you will need identity for both these transactions.

EXPRESS PARCELS

Two courier companies, Colissimo and Chronopost, work in conjunction with La Poste to deliver express parcels. These services are very efficient. They guarantee delivery within 12 to 48 hours and you can track your parcel on the internet by using a number that you will be given when you consign it. However, using them is much more expensive than sending parcels by ordinary post.

Stamp with Eleanor of Aquitaine

POSTCODES

Each district of Aquitaine has a five-digit postcode. In an address, this number should appear in front of the name of the town or village, and should be on the same line. The first two digits correspond to the number of the *département*, and the three others to the relevant sorting office. The postcode 24 corresponds to the Dordogne, 33 to the Gironde, 40 to the Landes, 46 to the Lot (part of Quercy), 47 to the Lot-et-Garonne, and 64 to the Pyrénées-Atlantiques.

DIRECTORY

USEFUL NUMBERS

Directory enquiries for France and French overseas departments
118 712

International directory enquiries (including French overseas territories)
3212

Country codes
UK: 44
USA: 1
Belgium: 32
Switzerland: 41

Sending a telegram by phone
Within France: 3655
international telegrams:
0800 33 44 11

Reverse-charge call
(Appel en PCV) 3006

Translation Services
Tel *(01) 48 78 43 32*
www.sft.fr

WEBSITES

www.laposte.fr
www.francetelecom.fr

INTERNET CAFES

Cyberstation
23 cours Pasteur,
33000 Bordeaux
Tel *(05) 56 01 15 15*

Madiba Café
Rue Gambetta,
40100 Dax
Tel *(05) 58 74 98 53*

TRAVEL INFORMATION

It is easy to travel to and around Aquitaine. There are major international airports at Bordeaux, Biarritz and Pau, and there are also three smaller, regional ones, sited at Bergerac, Agen and Périgeux. The TGV (high-speed, long-distance train) and the TER (the regional express

Bordeaux airport

train) services, together with the seaports at Bordeaux and Bayonne and an excellent network of major roads and motorways, also provide speedy access to most parts of region, as well as good links with the rest of Europe, particularly with Spain and Portugal.

Bordeaux airport, serving 3 million passengers a year

AIRPORTS

Several international, national and regional airlines operate flights to airports in Aquitaine. Average flight times are about one hour from a destination within France, and about two hours from any European city. Passengers from North America will change at Paris for frequent connections to the region's airports.

Bordeaux-Mérignac airport handles 3 million passengers a year and about 200 aircraft a week take off and land

there. From Bordeaux, there are 15 international connections to destinations such as Florence, Lisbon, London and Munich, and daily internal flights to about 10 French towns, as well as many charter flights. The national French airline, Air France, operates direct flights to Spain, Belgium and Portugal from Bordeaux.

A shuttle service operates between Bordeaux airport and the city centre. There are departures every 45 minutes, and the journey time is about 30–45 minutes.

Biarritz airport handles 1 million passengers a year, with direct flights from Paris, Clermont-Ferrand, Lyon, Geneva and other European cities. Buses run into central Biarritz and Bayonne, and to the coastal towns of Hendaye and Saint-Jean-de-Luz.

AIRPORT	INFORMATION	DISTANCE FROM CITY	TAXI TO CITY (APPROX.)
DORDOGNE			
Bergerac-Roumanière	(05) 53 22 25 25 www.bergerac.aeroport.fr	5km (3 miles) SW of Bergerac	12–15 € to the centre of Bergerac
Périgueux-Bassillac	(05) 53 02 79 70 www.aeroport-perigueux.com	12km (7 miles) E of Périgueux	15 € to the centre of Périgueux
GIRONDE			
Bordeaux-Mérignac	(05) 56 34 50 50 www.bordeaux.aeroport.fr	15km (9 miles) W of Bordeaux	25–30 € to the centre of Bordeaux
LOT-ET-GARONNE			
Agen-la-Garenne	(05) 53 77 00 88 www.aeroport-agen.com	3km (2 miles) SW of Agen	8–12 € to the centre of Agen
PYRÉNÉES-ATLANTIQUES			
Biarritz-Anglet-Bayonne	(05) 59 43 83 83 www.biarritz.aeroport.fr	2km (1 mile) SE of Biarritz	13–20 € to Biarritz, Anglet or Bayonne
Pau-Pyrénées	(05) 59 33 33 00 www.pau.aeroport.fr	7km (4 miles) N of Pau	30 € to Pau

Pau-Pyrénées airport by night

Pau airport, which handles 1 million passengers a year, is used by Air France and such international airlines as Transaria, to Amsterdam, and Ryanair, to destinations in the UK. There is also a good shuttle bus service into the city centre.

Although it is much smaller, **Bergerac airport**, in the Dordogne, handles flights to a number of destinations in Britain, including London, Southampton, Birmingham, Liverpool, Exeter and Bristol. **Périgueux airport** and **Agen airport** are used mostly by business people travelling in private planes.

CONNECTIONS

Many regular airlines, as well as the low-cost airlines Ryanair, Easyjet, Flybe and bmibaby, operate flights to southwest France. Most flights from Paris (Roissy-Charles de Gaulle and Orly Sud) are provided by the national carrier **Air France**, which also operates flights from the southwest to Geneva, London, Madrid, Barcelona and Amsterdam.

Most of the foreign airlines that serve the region provide flights to Bordeaux and Pau. The low-cost airlines serve a wide range of destinations. **Ryanair** operates flights from London-Stansted to Biarritz, Bergerac and Pau, and also from the cities of Nottingham, Liverpool and Exeter to Bergerac. **bmibaby.com** runs regular services from both Nottingham and Manchester to Bordeaux. **Flybe** operates flights from Southampton, Leeds, Birmingham, Exeter and Bristol to Bergerac; and **Air France** has flights to Brussels and Lisbon from Bordeaux.

AIR FARES

The low-cost airlines have dramatically reduced the price of travelling by plane. A number of websites, such as **cheapflights.com/co.uk**, allow travellers to compare fares offered by several different airlines. In general, the further in advance you buy your ticket, the cheaper it will be. However, low-cost airlines do not offer all the comforts and facilities that are usually provided by the regular airlines.

Regular airlines also offer reduced fares, mainly for families, and people under 25 and over 60. Children under two travel free, although they are not allocated a seat. Bear in mind that certain types of ticket are not exchangeable or refundable, and that others are valid only for return journeys or require your stay to include a Saturday night.

Cheap flights to internal and international destinations are available from Air France, which offers last-minute cut-price tickets from midnight on Wednesdays.

FORMALITIES

Check-in for passengers and their luggage usually closes 30 minutes before the flight's departure, but it is best to arrive at the airport at least an hour before boarding time.

Passengers in the hall at Pau-Pyrénées airport

Each passenger usually has a baggage allowance of 20kg (44lb) in economy class, and 30kg (66lb) in business class. Special rates apply to golfing and winter-sports equipment. Passengers are allowed one piece of hand luggage each. Anything that can be used as a weapon, such as a sharp or pointed object, cannot be carried in hand luggage.

Children between the ages of 4 and 12 can travel alone, provided they have their own passport and wear some form of identity. Airlines will take good care of them for their complete journey.

Animals usually travel in the hold, in special cages. Those weighing less than 5kg (11lb) may travel with their owner, in a carrier, although this will be at the airline's discretion.

Travelling by Train

Thanks to an excellent rail network, whose backbone is the high-speed TGV Atlantique service, the region forms a key link in Europe's north–south transport axis. By train, Bordeaux is now less than three hours from Paris, Lille five hours and Brussels under seven. Quick, convenient and comfortable, the high-speed train service, along with an efficient network of regional express trains (the TER), offers an ideal way of exploring Aquitaine, especially in high season, when roads can be congested.

The concourse at Bordeaux's TGV station

RAIL SERVICES

French trains are generally punctual and reliable. The timetables for TGV and TER services are available at all stations, including the main southwestern regional ones at **Agen, Bayonne, Bordeaux, Mont-de-Marsan, Périgueux** and at **Pau.**

The SNCF, French national railways, offers a **luggage-delivery service** *(service d'enlèvement des bagages à domicile),* which is particularly useful to older people. This allows travellers to arrange for their luggage, including cases, pushchairs, bicycles and other items, to be taken directly to wherever they are staying.

Most trains have a bar or a restaurant car. For passengers who want to take their car on the train, an **auto-train** service runs between Paris and Bordeaux (all year), and to Biarritz (in summer) and to Tarbes. SNCF also offers special **Train + Location voiture** rates for rail travellers who need to hire a car at their destination. Similar deals apply to bicycle hire. Information is available from station concourses.

HIGH-SPEED TRAINS

About 20 high-speed train services run between Paris and Bordeaux every day, with an average journey time of 3 hours. There are also 12 daily Paris–Agen services (4 hours), four Paris–Pau services (5 hours), and seven to the Basque coast (4 $\frac{1}{2}$ hours), including a sleeper service. Planned improvements to the Tours–Bordeaux stretch of the TGV Atlantique route should cut the journey time from Paris to Bordeaux down to two hours. Smoking is prohibited on all TGV trains and all seats must be pre-booked.

REGIONAL EXPRESS TRAINS

Aquitaine's network of regional express (TER) services covers 2,647km (1,645 miles). There are 163 stations and 26 lines, for a total of 360 towns and villages. Whether you are off to Pau for a major sporting event or simply want to get away for a relaxing break on the Arcachon Basin, regional express trains allow you to travel economically, with no worries about congested roads or parking problems.

Twenty return services run between Arcachon and Bordeaux every day, and the journey time is 45 minutes. From Bordeaux, the journey takes 1 hour 15 minutes to Périgueux, 1 hour 20 minutes to Dax, 1 hour 30 minutes to Agen, and 2 hours to Pau.

TICKETS

Tickets can be purchased at railway stations, at SNCF-approved travel agents, and from automatic machines. A telephone information line, that is open seven days a week, provides details of train times and allows you to buy a ticket, which will be sent to you free of charge, and is valid for two months.

You can also reserve a seat, buy an electronic ticket, book a hotel and arrange car hire by visiting SNCF's website.

FARES

A reduction of 25 to 50 per cent on rail fares is available for children under the age of 12, people

A TER regional express train

The SNCF railway station at Biarritz

between the ages of 12 and 25, and those over 60. This applies to TGV train journeys so long as seats are still available, and on Corail and TER trains out of peak times *(périodes bleues)*. When your tickets are checked, you may be asked to show proof of your age. For frequent rail travellers, there are special passes (such as Enfant + and Senior) that allow cheaper travel. If you buy your ticket two months to two weeks in advance, this will be a "Prem" ticket, with a reduction of 30 to 40 per cent.

Special tickets are also available to foreign visitors. These, which include Euro Domino and Inter Rail, provide reductions on Thalys and Eurostar trains. They can be purchased when booking your tickets in your home country. Aquitaine Temps Libre is a pass that gives a reduction of 25 per cent for return journeys on TER trains and buses during the summer.

ANIMALS

For an extra 5 , you can take a small dog or a cat with you on a train. However, dogs must be muzzled and cats must not weigh more than 6kg (13lb), and must be carried either in a bag or a basket.

For animals that weigh more, you will have to pay half the cost of a second-class ticket. This also applies to first-class travel. Be sure that fellow-travellers do not object to your pet, as they can refuse to share a carriage with any animal. Guide dogs travel for free.

BICYCLES

On main rail routes and on TER trains, bicycles are carried free. On TGVs, they must be dismantled, placed in a carrying bag and stored in luggage spaces.

On trains other than TGVs, bicycles can be carried in the guard's van or other designated places, and do not need to be dismantled. If your bicycle is stored in a guard's van, you will be responsible for lifting it in, securing it and lifting it out at your destination.

DISABLED TRAVELLERS

To help plan their journey, people with disabilities can call the freephone number for the **SNCF Accessibilité Service**. As well as giving practical help and information, this service can arrange to have tickets sent to your home address. To ensure that the help you need is available at the appropriate time and place, it is best to make any arrangements at least 24 hours in advance. **Les Compagnons du Voyage** is an association that can provide a suitable companion to travel with you on any train journey outside the Paris area.

Ticket-stamping machine

SCENIC JOURNEYS

The most scenic journey by tourist train is the ride up to Lac d'Artouste *(see p231)*, which offers spectacular views of the highest peaks in the Pyrénées-Atlantiques. The

rack railway up the Rhune *(see p198)* also offers breathtaking mountain views.

Travelling by Road

Road sign

The extensive network of roads and motorways that serve Aquitaine include all the main routes between Paris and Spain, and the Atlantic and Mediterranean coasts. Both major and minor roads in the southwest are well maintained, well sign-posted and generally pleasant to drive along. Some, especially in the Pyrénées-Atlantiques, pass through stunning countryside.

A trunk road through open countryside

DRIVING

Drivers should carry a registration certificate, insurance documents and a valid driving licence. At peak times on the roads, or at the start of major holiday periods, town centres and ringroads are likely to be congested. For information on traffic conditions go to the "Wily Bison" website (**Bison Futé**), tune into to *Autoroute FM* on 107.7, or contact **CRICR**.

DISTANCES BY ROAD

The most direct road route from Paris to Bordeaux is the A10 motorway. From there, the N10 and the A63 motorway lead south to Biarritz, Saint-Jean-de-Luz and Hendaye. The A62 motorway, or Autoroute des Deux-Mers, is another quick route to the region's Mediterranean side.

The journey from Paris to Bordeaux is 584km (363 miles); Bordeaux to Pau, 200km (124 miles); Bordeaux to Bayonne, 190km (118 miles); Bayonne to Périgueux, 317km (197 miles); Dax to Agen, 179km (111 miles); Arcachon to Villeneuve-sur-Lot, 200km (124 miles); and Paris to Bayonne, 736km (457 miles).

SPEED LIMITS

The speed limits are 50km/h (30mph) in towns; 90km/h (55mph) on open roads, but 80km/h (50mph) if it is wet or foggy; 110km/h on dual carriageways, but 90km/h (55mph) when wet or foggy; and 130km/h (80mph) on motorways, but 110km/h (70mph) if wet or foggy.

ROAD SAFETY

Seat belts must be worn by the driver and by passengers travelling both in the front and the back seats. Before you set off on a long journey, check your tyre pressure. Children must travel in child car-seats, and the use of mobile phones while driving is prohibited. Legal levels of alcohol in the blood are up to 0.5g, equivalent to two small glasses of wine. If you plan to drive in the

Speed-limit sign

Pyrenees in the ski season, you must carry snow chains. On motorways and major roads, beware of heavy trucks travelling at speed. As much of the region is inhabited by wild animals that may jump out onto the road, be especially vigilant wherever you see warning signs.

FUEL

Fuel stations on motorways clearly display their prices, There is little variation between them, and they are relatively high. Supermarkets such as Carrefour, Géant and Hyper U, located just outside towns, sell fuel cheaper. Bear in mind that in rural areas few fuel stations open late, and often close Sunday to Monday and on public holidays.

BREAKDOWN

Breakdown services, such as the **AA** and **RAC** in the UK and the **AAA** in the USA, sell policies that provide 24-hour cover in Europe. Some car manufacturers also offer a 24-hour breakdown service, whatever the make of your car. If you do not have a mobile phone, there are emergency phones along all motorways. You can use them to call for assistance.

TOLLS

At the entrance to a stretch of motorway where there is a toll (*péage*), you must collect a ticket, which you

Road signs in French and Basque

A minor road in the Ossau valley, in Béarn

A pay-and-display parking area in a town square

hand in at the motorway exit, when you pay the toll. This varies according to the type of vehicle and distance travelled. Automatic toll booths accept credit cards. Information on motorways is available on www.autoroutes.fr

HIRING A CAR

To hire a car you must be at least 21 years old and have a valid driving licence, which you must have held for at least a year. The main car-hire companies have offices in major railway stations, at airports and in town centres. Charges vary according to mileage and hire period and whether you return the car to another office. Car-hire companies in France, that have a comprehensive network of offices and pick-up sites, include **ADA**, **Avis**, **Hertz** and **Europcar**.

PARKING

Few town car parks are free. When you park, you must buy a ticket from a machine and place it in full view on the dashboard. Most towns have underground car parks.

CAMPER VANS

The overnight parking of camper vans is tightly regulated. In some districts there are special areas for camper vans, with water and other facilities. *Camping-Car Magazine* give details of 17,000 such areas in France.

ROAD MAPS

You will find a roadmap of the region on the inside covers of this guide. If you want to drive on minor roads or go touring off the beaten track, the more detailed Michelin or IGN maps are recommended. The **Michelin** and **Mappy** websites are also useful for planning routes.

BUSES

The region is served by a network of bus routes, operated by several different companies. **CITRAM**, for example, covers the Pyrénées-Atlantiques as well as 365 towns and rural areas in the Gironde. **RDTL** operates in the Landes, and **CFTA** in the Dordogne. Information on bus routes and timetables is available at all bus stations.
  Eurolines is a long-distance coach company that runs regular services between Britain and the Continent.

HITCHING AND CAR-SHARING

If you would like to give a hitch-hiker a lift, contact **Allostop Bordeaux**, which gives useful information. You are entitled to a contribution to cover fuel costs, and this is a maximum of 20 centimes per km (about 15p a mile) for each passenger you carry. **123envoiture.com** organizes car-sharing all over the region.

Travelling by Boat

The Arcachon Basin, the Gironde estuary and the lakes of the Landes and the Gironde are all excellent places for sailing. Also, cruising along the extensive network of navigable waterways formed by Aquitaine's rivers and canals is a perfect way to explore the unspoilt countryside of the region. You may hire a boat to enjoy these calm waters and their beautiful scenery, even without a sailing licence.

Salako, one of many ferries in the Arcachon Basin

Capbreton, a seaport and coastal resort in the Landes

MARINAS

The marina at **Arcachon** is the second-largest in western France, after the marina at La Rochelle. It has 2,600 moorings, including 250 for visitors, on 28 fully equipped pontoons.

Hendaye, where boats can put in whatever the weather conditions, has 720 pontoon moorings, including 120 for visitors. **Capbreton**, which is unuseable in rough seas, has 950 pontoon moorings, including 61 for visitors.

At Bayonne and Bordeaux, cruise liners can dock in the harbour, right in the heart of the city itself.

SAILING AND BOATING

You need a licence to sail a pleasure boat with an engine more powerful than 6HP. Three types of licence are available: *permis mer côtier* (coastal licence), *carte mer* (sea licence) and *permis mer hauturier* (ocean-going licence). Further information is available on the French government website: **www.mer.gouv.fr**.

Every evening, the port authority posts the weather forecast for the following day, and the outlook for the next few days. The website of the **Fédération Française de Voile** gives times of high water at each harbour as well as contact details for boat trips and boat hire.

For boating on canals and rivers, you do not need a licence, and hire companies will show you the basics of navigating a boat, as well as how to go through a lock. The regional tourist authority issues a brochure with details of navigable waterways, boat trips and boat-hire companies.

BOAT TRIPS AT SEA

The Arcachon Basin, with its oyster farms, huts on stilts, Cap-Ferret, the Île aux Oiseaux (Bird Island) and the Leyre delta, offers a great deal to explore by boat, either aboard a fishing smack or on one of the cruisers run by the Basin's boatmen. A meal is included in the price for some of these trips.

Boats from the jetty at Thiers and Eyrac, or from Le Pyla or Le Mouleau, take you to Banc d'Arguin, where you spend the day (bring a picnic). Another memorable trip is to the Phare de Cordouan *(see p60)*, in the open sea between Le Verdon-sur-Mer and Royan. Boats for this lighthouse, which include the cruiser **La Bohême**, leave from Pointe de Grave.

SEA LINKS

The local ferry company **Bateliers Arcachonnais** provides convenient sea links between Arcachon and Cap-Ferret, between Le Mouleau and Cap-Ferret, and between Arcachon and Andernos. The Arcachon–Cap-Ferret service runs all year, with services from 9am to 1am in the high season.

From Hendaye, ferries run between the Spanish port of **Fontarrabia** all year round, every half-hour out of season and every 15 minutes during the summer. The fares are very reasonable.

The ferry on the upper Gironde estuary, at Blaye

RIVER AND CANAL CRUISES

The Dordogne, Baïse, Isle and Adour rivers, the Gironde estuary and the Canal Latéral **À LA** Garonne can all be explored on short boat trips, or on cruises aboard hired boats. Two sources of information on river cruises are the **Direction Départementale de l'Équipement du Lot-et-Garonne** and the **Direction Interrégionale du Sud-Ouest**.

Sailing along the Canal du Midi (which, with the Canal Latéral **À LA** Garonne, forms the Canal des Deux-Mers) you can make frequent stops, to visit the many historic monuments and other places of interest, or to swap the peace of the river for the bustle of a picturesque town. You will also pass through several locks. Boat-hire

Gabare (sailing barge), on the Dordogne

companies include **Bateau Ville de Bordeaux**, **Croisières Les Caminades** in the Périgord, **Gabare Val-de-Garonne**, and **Croisadour** in Dax. You can hire a barge or cabin cruiser by the week (no licence is needed) from **Aquitaine Navigation** or **Crown Blue Line**. Prices are

900 €–3,500 € a week for a six-berth boat. You can also hire boats by the day. **En Péniche** is a company that runs upmarket barges, with all the facilities of a good hotel or guest house, including really comfortable berths.

For day trips through magnificent scenery, you can also book a ride on traditional river craft, such as the *gabares* (local sailing boats) that still cruise along the Dordogne. **Bateliers de Léon** take visitors on trips to the stunningly beautiful nature reserve at the Courant d'Huchet (*see p175*), aboard a *galupe*, a local type of flat-bottomed craft.

DIRECTORY

MARINAS

Arcachon
Tel (05) 56 22 36 75
www.port-arcachon.com

Capbreton
Tel (05) 58 72 21 23
www.port-capbreton.com

Hendaye
Tel (05) 59 48 06 07
www.hendaye.com

FERRY SERVICES

Les Bateliers Arcachonnais
Arcachon Basin
Tel (05) 57 72 28 28
www.bateliers-arcachon.asso.fr

Fontarrabia (Spain)
Bateau Marie-Louise, 7
64700 Hendaye
Tel (06) 07 02 55 09

BOAT TRIPS

Vedette La Bohême
Phare de Cordouan
Le-Verdon-sur-Mer, 33123
Tel (05) 56 09 62 93
www.vedettelaboheme.com

Bateliers de Léon
Courant d'Huchet
Rue des Berges-du-Lac,
40550 Léon
Tel (05) 58 48 75 39

GENERAL INFORMATION

Licences and rules at sea
www.mer.gouv.fr

Fédération Française de Voile
www.ffvoile.org

CANAL-BOAT HIRE

Aquitaine Navigation
47160 Buzet-sur-Baïse
Tel (05) 53 84 72 50
www.aquitaine-navigation.com

Crown Blue Line
47430 Le Mas-d'Agenais
Tel (05) 53 89 50 80
www.crownblueline.com

BARGES

En Péniche
Tel (04) 67 13 19 62
www.en-peniche.com

RIVER CRUISES

Direction Interrégionale du Sud-Ouest
2 port Saint-Étienne,
31000 Toulouse
Tel (05) 61 36 24 24

Direction Départementale de l'Équipement du Lot-et-Garonne
1722 avenue de Colmar,
47000 Agen
Tel (05) 53 69 33 33

Bateau Ville de Bordeaux
Quai Louis-XVIII, 33000 Bordeaux
Tel (05) 56 52 88 88

Croisières Les Caminades
24250 La Roque-Gageac
Tel (05) 53 29 43 08

Gabare Val-de-Garonne
47200 Fourques-sur-Garonne
Tel (05) 53 89 25 59

Croisadour
40100 Dax
Tel (05) 58 74 87 07

General Index

Acknowledgments

Main Contributors

Suzanne Boireau-Tartarat

Suzanne Boireau-Tartarat is the director of communications for Périgueux city council, and has contributed to many publications about the Dordogne. She is the author of the chapters on the Périgord and Quercy.

Pierre Chavot

Pierre Chavot, who lives near Bordeaux, is a freelance writer. He contributed to the chapter on the Landes for this guide, and has also written for several travel guides published by Hachette.

Renée Grimaud

Renée Grimaud, who lives in Bordeaux, is the author of several illustrated books and of travel guides to various regions of France. She is also a regulator contributor to Hachette's *Guides Voir*. She wrote the chapter on the Gironde.

Santiago Mendieta

Santiago Mendieta is a freelance journalist and writer. With the photographer, Étienne Follet, he has produced several illustrated books on the Pyrenees. He is the author of the chapters on the Pays Basque and Béarn.

Marie-Pascale Rauzier

A historian and journalist, Marie-Pascale Rauzier has written many books and travel guides, including the *DK Eyewitness Guide* to Morocco. She wrote the chapter on the Lot-et-Garonne.

Marguerite Figeac

Dr Marguerite Figeac has a PhD in history from the Sorbonne and teaches at the Institut de Formation des Maîtres d'Aquitaine in Bordeaux. She wrote the chapter on the history of Aquitaine.

Wilfried Lecarpentier

Wilfried Lecarpentier is the French correspondent of the *Los Angeles Times* and a member of the Association Professionnelle des Critiques et Informateurs Gastronomiques. He wrote the Travellers' Needs and Survival Guide chapters.

Gaëtan du Chatenet

Entomologist, ornithologist, member of the Muséum National d'Histoire Naturelle de Paris, draughtsman and painter, Gaëtan du Chatenet is the author of many works published by Delachaux & Niestlé and Gallimard.

Other Contributors

Xavier Becheler, Marie-Christine Degos, Isabelle De Jaham, Natacha Kotchetkova, Paulina Nourissier, Lyn Parry, Nicolas Pelé, Natasha Penot, François Pinassaud, Adam Stambul, Roger Williams.

For Dorling Kindersley

Douglas Amrine (Publisher), Jane Ewart, Fay Franklin (Publishing Managers), Uma Bhattacharya, Mohammad Hassan, Jasneet Kaur, Casper Morris (Cartography), Vinod Harish, Vincent Kurien, Jason Little, Azeem Siddiqui (DTP), Delphine Lawrance, Jude Ledger, Dora Whitaker (Editorial), Julie Bond (Design), Rachel Barber (Picture Research).

Editor

Cécile Landau.

Proofreader

Cate Casey.

Photography

Philippe Giraud.

Studio Photography and Additional Photography

Pierre Javelle, Éric Guillemot, Andrew Holligan, Roger Moss, Ian O'Leary.

Picture Research

Marie-Christine Petit.

Cartography

Cyrille Suss.

Illustrations

François Brosse

Architectural drawings pp 60, 86–7, 92–3, 110–11, 126–7, 134–5, 148–9, 196.

Jean-Sylvain Roveri

Architectural drawings pp24–5, 70–71, 104–05, 192–3, 222–3.

Éric Geoffroy

Illustrations on "Exploring" and "At a Glance" maps, on small town plans and tour maps.

Emmanuel Guillon

Façades and perspectives on pp20–21 and 22–3.

Rodolphe Corbel

Street-by-street maps: pp78–9, 98–9, 158–9, 188–9.

Index

Marion Crouzet.

Special Assistance

The publishers would like to thank the following people and institutions, whose assistance has made the preparation of this book possible: Mme Cappé and M. Caunesil, at the tourist office in Verdon-sur-Mer; M. Laurent Croizier and Mme Valentina Bressan at the Grand-Théâtre de Bordeaux; M. Alain Gouaillardou at the Château de Pau; Mmr Marie-Lou Talet at the town hall in Fumel; M. Yves-Marie Delpit at the Château de Bonaguil; Mme Patricia Fruchon at the Château de Castelnaud; Mme Yvette Dupré and Mme Sophie Maynard at the Jardins du Manoir d'Eyrignac and at the Château de Hautefort; M. Serge Roussel and M. Bertrand Defois at the Grotte du Pech-Merle; Mme Larralde of the parish of Saint-Jean-de-Luz; Mme Anne Mangin-Payen at SDAP 64; M. François Caussarieu and Mme Christiane Bonnat at CDT Béarn Pays Basque; the municipal authories of the Tursan; Mme Cécile Van Espen at the town hall in Lescar; the tourist office at Lescar; M. Gérard Duhamel at CAUE Dordogne; M. Roger Labiano at Kukuxumusu; M. Jean-Sébastien Canaux at the tourist office in Monflanquin; M. Christophe Pichambert at CLS Remy Cointreau; M. Daniel Margnes and M. Jean-François Gracieux at Maison Aquitaine; M. Éric Badets at the tourist office in Parentis-en-Born; Mme Anne Pregat at the Musée des Beaux-Arts de Pau; Mme Françoise Henry-Morlier at the Château de Cadillac; the Centre des Archives Historiques du Lot-et-Garonne; Mme Maïté Etchechoury at the Archives Départementales de Dordogne; M. Louis Bergès and Mme Detot at the Archives Départementales de Gironde, Mme Caroline Féaud at France 3 Rhône-Alpes-Auvergne; Mme Anne Le Meur of *Guide Hachette des Vins*.

For their hospitality and helpfulness, the publishers would like especially to thank Mme la Vicomtesse and M. le Vicomte Sébastien de Baritault du Carpia, owners of the Château de Roquetaillade, and Mme and M. Élséar de Sabran-Pontevès, owners of the Château de Cazeneuve. The publishers also extend their thanks to all those who sent in regional produce; they are too numerous to acknowledge individually.

Photography Permissions

The publisher would like to thank the following owners, curators, guides and other site staff, transport networks, shops, organisations and institutions who have given permission to photograph on their premises:
Phare de Cordouan and boat *La Bohême II*; the animal park *La Coccinelle* at La Hune; Parc Ornithologique du Teich; Grand-Théâtre de Bordeaux; Hrottes de Pair-Non-Pair; Château de Vayres; the tourist office at Saint-Émilion; Abbaye de la Sauve-Majeure; the Gallo-Roman villa at Loupiac; Château de La Brède; Mme Valérie Lailheugue at Château d'Yquem; M. Max de Pontac at Château Myra; M. Dominique Befve at Château Lascombes; Château Margaux; M. Philippe Dourthe at Château Maucaillou; M. Éric Derluyn at Château de Mascaraas; the tourist office at Lescar; the Musée de l'Abeille at Monein; the Maison du Jambon de Bayonne at Arzacq; Château de Morlanne; the Musée du Béret in Nay; the Musée des Beaux-Arts de Pau; the Artouste train; the Musée Basque in Bayonne; the Réserve du Pottock at Bidarray; the Comité des Fêtes d'Espelette; Château d'Abbadia; the Grottes de Kakouetta; Prodiso, the espadrille factory in Mauléon; Ona Tiss, the weaving workshop in Saint-Palais; the Rhune train; Château de Ravignan; the Musée de l'Hydraviation in Biscarosse; the Comité des Fêtes de Gabarret et de Roquefort; the Musée de l'Aviation Légère de l'Armée de l'Air in Dax; the Musée de Borda in Dax; the boatmen on the Courant d'Huchet; the Musée de la Chalosse in Monfort-en-Chalosse; the Écomusée de la Grande Lande; the Atelier Jacques et Louis Vidal in Luxey; the Musée de l'Estupe-huc in Luxey; the Musée de la Dame de Brassempouy; the Musée de la Faïence in Samadet; Château de Duras; Château Molhière; M. Bertrand de Boisseson at Château de Montluc; the Musée du Pruneau in Granges-sur-Lot; Mme Valérie Duguet-Parickmiler at Château de Nérac; M. Jean de Nadaillac at Château de Poudenas; M. Michel Trama de l'Aubergade in Puymirol; Mme Geneviève and M. Yves Boissière at the Musée du Foie Gras in Souleilles; M. Joël Gallot, glass-maker in Vianne; the national stud at Villeneuve-sur-Lot; Mme Hélène Lages at the Musée de Gajac in Villeneuve-sur-Lot; M. Bruno Rouable de Caudecoste and St-Nicolas-de-la-Balerme; the Musée du Tabac in Bergerac; M. Jean-Max Touron at Grotte du Roc de Cazelle and La Roque-Saint-Christophe; M. Patrick Sermadiras at the Château de Hautefort; M. Armando Molteni at Grotte du Grand-Roc; Mme and M. Jean-Luc Delautre at Château de Fénelon; Grotte de Proumeyssac; Mme Angélique de Saint-Exupéry at Château des Milandes; Château de Montal; M. François Gondran at the Gallo-Roman villa in Montcarret; Grotte du Pech-Merle; Château de Puyguilhem; Mme Nicole de Montbron at Château de Puymartin; Mme Nadia Lincetto at the Musée d'Art Sacré Francis-Poulenc in Rocamadour; Château de Montaigne; Les Jardins de l'Imaginaire in Terrasson-Lavilledieu; the Préhisto Parc in Tursac; Mme Marie and M. Dominique Palué at Château de l'Herm.

Picture Credits

The publisher would also like to thank the following individuals and institutions who have given their permission for their photographs to be used in this guide:

h = top; c = centre; b = bottom; l = left; r = right. Every effort has been made to trace the copyright holders and we apologize in advance for any unintentional omissions. We would be pleased to insert the appropriate acknowledgments in any subsequent edition of this publication.

4CORNERS IMAGES: SIME/Giovanni Simeone 10cla.

BORDEAUX AIRPORT: 292tc: Burdin L'Image; 292clt: Nihat Akgoz.
PAU AIRPORT: 293tl and 293bc: Studio Vu.
AFP: 50cl and 50crb.
AKG-IMAGES: 39crb and 41tl: British Library; 40bl: Jean-François Amelo; 42br: Jean-Pierre Verney; 49br.
ALAMY IMAGES: Cephas Picture Library/Hervé Champollion 10br; JLImages 10tc; nagelestock.com 11br.
APRASAQ: 285bll.
ARCHIVES DÉPARTEMENTALES DE LOT-ET-GARONNE: 24tl and 158tl: Bib. d'Agen Ms 42; 239c: 10 PH4.
ARCHIVES DE VILLENEUVE-SUR-LOT: 051bc and 108bl: R. Delvert.

BIARRITZ CULTURE: 34br: Ballet de Lorraine-Laurent Philippe.
BNF PARIS: 40tl, 40—41, 41ct, 42tl, 42bc, 105bc, 135bl, 181bc.
BRIDGEMAN ART LIBRARY: 26tr: Archives Charmet; 36, 37ct, 038bg, 43br, 47tc abd 48br: Giraudon/Lauros; 43bc and 70tr: Giraudon; 204cb: Sally Greene; 30tl and 49tr: Bridgeman Art Library.

CASINO D'ARCACHON: 275ctl: Marcel Partouche.
CAUDALIE: 273tr.
CAVE DES PRODUCTEURS DE JURANÇON: 31bc.
CCIP BORDEAUX: 047crb: Selva/Leemage.
CDT GIRONDE: 285 clb: B. P. Lamarque.
CÉRAMIQUES CAZAUX & FILS: 272c and 272crb.
CHÂTEAU DE CÔME: 259bl.
CHÂTEAU DE FARGUES: 46clb and 46crb: Archives Familiales de Lur Saluces.
CHÂTEAU MARTINENS: 31tc.
CINÉMA UTOPIA: 275tc.
CONSEIL GÉNÉRAL DU LOT: 123tr: Nelly Blaya.
CRT AQUITAINE: 285blr.

G. DAGLI ORTI: 37clb, 45br, 46bl, 195tc, 206cl, 206br.
F. DESMESURE: 274crt.
DOMAINE DES CASSAGNOLES: 259tcr.

DORLING KINDERSLEY: 115crb, 120tl, 120bl, 121bc, 281chtr, 287ct, page 289, 290tr, 290bl, 295cl, 296cr, 297ct, 297cc, 297cb.

EAU DES ABATILLES: 259cl.
ÉDITIONS CLOUET: 15tl and 258tr.
FESTIVAL ART FLAMENCO DE MONT-DE-MARSAN: 32b and 274tc: Sébastien Zambon/CG40.
E. FOLLET: 28tl, 28bc, 28br, 28–9, 29cl, 29cr, 29bf, 29br, 33cdt, 35c, 35bc, 55bl, 209tl, 228bl, 230ct, 232tl, 232br, 233bl, 233tr, 234tl, 234tr, 234clb, 234bc, 235tr, 235cr, 235bl, 237tc, 237crt, 237cl, 237c, 237crb, 237bl, 237bc.
FRANCE BLEU GIRONDE: 286cl.
FRANCE TELECOM: 290bc: 1998 PhotoDisc, Inc. All rights reserved. Images provided by: 1998 Nick Rowe - France Telecom.

GAÏA IMAGES: 208br: A. Senosiain; 171cr: Marlène Meissonnier.
GAMMA: 051hr: Politique Image/Gamma.
GOUFFRE DE PADIRAC: 119tl: Cliché POUX, SES Padirac.
GROTTES DE BÉTHARRAM: 229bl.
GROTTES PRÉHISTORIQUES DE COUGNAC: 131tr: Francis Jach.
E. GUILLEMOT: 009tr, 256tl, 256cg, 256ctr, 256cbr, 256bl, 256bc, 256br, 257hg, 257tr, 257ctr, 257cbl, 257cbc, 257cbtr, 257clb, 257btl, 257blb, 257bldh, 257blrb.

HEMISPHERE IMAGES: Pierre Jacques 11tr; Patrice Thomas 11cl.
HOA-QUI: 18tr: André Le Gall/Jacana; 18tl: CJ. Pache/Age/Hoa-Qui; 176cr: J. Cancalosi/Age/Hoa-Qui; 18br: JA Jimenez/Age/Hoa-Qui; 19br: J. Cancalosi/Nature Pl/Jacana; 172cl: José B. Ruiz/Nature Pl/Jacana; 18crb: Mike Wilkes/Nature Pl/Jacana; 19clb: Morales/Age/Hoa-Qui; 19bcl: Philippe Prigent/Jacana; 16clb: Pierre Petit/Jacana; 173tr: Rodriguez/Age/Hoa-Qui; 19crb: S. Raman/Age/Hoa-Qui; 18bl: U. Walz Gdt/Age/Hoa-Qui; 171br: W. Bollmann/Age/Hoa-Qui.

JARDINS D'EYRIGNAC: 111br: D. Reperant; 110l and 111tl: J.-B. Leroux.
P. JAVELLE: 30cr, 31cr, 138bl, 180tl, 219cr, 225tl, 256tl, 258tl, 258cll, 258clc, 258clr, 258bl, 258brl, 258brc, 258brr, 259tl, 259tcl, 259tr, 270tc, 270crb, 272tl, 272crt, 272clt, 272tr, 272clb, 272bl, 273tl, 273tcl, 273tcr, 273chg, 273cbl, 273ctr, 273cbr, 273cbcl, 273bcl, 274bcdt, 273cbcr, 273bl.

KEYSTONE-FRANCE: 45cb.
KHARBINE-TAPABOR: 44b, 63br, 155bc, 172tr.

LEEMAGE/SELVA: 13c, 170tl, 195crt, 195cr.
LIBRAIRIE MEGADENDA: 29tr: Éditions Erein.

MAIRIE DE DAX: 33bl: Philippe Salvat.
MAIRIE DE SOULAC: 61cl.
MAISON PARIÈS: 257ctl, 257br abd 273br.
MOUTON ROTHSCHILD: 31tl.
MUSÉE BASQUE ET DE L'HISTOIRE DE BAYONNE: 185b.
MUSÉE CHAMPOLLION DE FIGEAC: 124cr: Nelly Blaya.
MUSÉE D'AQUITAINE: 38br and 44cl: DEC,
Bordeaux-B. Fontanel; 38br: DEC,
Bordeaux-B. Fontanel & L. Gauthier; 038ct: DEC,
Bordeaux-Hugo Maertens, Bruxelles;
39tc and 039bc: DEC, Bordeaux-J.-M. Arnaud;
40clb and 41bl: DEC, Bordeaux-J. Gilson; 67crt:
CAPC-Frédéric Delpech.
MUSÉE D'ART SACRÉ DE ROCAMADOUR: 206bl:
J.-L. Nespoulous.
MUSÉE DE CAHORS HENRI MARTIN: 129cr:
J.-C. Meauxsoone.
MUSÉE DE GAJAC DE VILLENEUVE SUR LOT: 150cr.
MUSÉE DES ARTS DÉCORATIFS DE BORDEAUX: 72ctr:
DMB-L. Gauthier.
MUSÉE DES BEAUX-ARTS D'AGEN: 154cl, 159br and
160cl: Hugo Maertens, Bruges; 160tr.
MUSÉE DES BEAUX-ARTS DE BORDEAUX: 45tr and
48tl: M.B.A. Bordeaux-Lysiane Gauthier.
MUSÉE DESPIAU-WLÉRICK: 182crt: Studio Ernest,
Mont-de-Marsan.
MUSÉE DU PÉRIGORD DE PÉRIGUEUX: 101tr: B. Dupuy.
MUSÉE DU PRUNEAU DE LAFITTE: 153rb.
MUSÉE GEORGETTE-DUPOUY: 178cl: S. Dom Pedro Gilo.

J.-B. NADEAU: 8 c, 80bc and 81bc :
J.B. Nadeau/Appa.

OFFICE DE TOURISME D'ESPELETTE: 34c.
OFFICE DE TOURISME DE SAINT-JEAN-DE-LUZ: 32tc.
OFFICE DE TOURISME DE SOULE: 210l.

PARC NATUREL RÉGIONAL DES LANDES DE GASCOGNE,
BELIN-BELIET: 49cb, 50bcr and 173b.
PARC WALIBI AQUITAINE: 286tl.

PHOTOTHÈQUE HACHETTE: 7c, 43br, 46t, 46br, 053c,
86b, 113tl, 200cb and 283c: Hachette Livre; 47br:
Hachette Livre-Lacoste.
PHOTOTHÈQUE VILLE DE CAHORS: 128br: Nelly
Blaya; 128tl.
C. DE PRADA: 211tl and 210br.
PRESSE-SPORTS: 13b, 16tl.
PYRÉNÉES MAGAZINE: 285brr : Étienne Follet-Milan.

RMN: 44tl, 89tr, 147cr and 180tr; 072tl:
A. Danvers; 221br: Bellot/Coursaget; 218br:
Bulloz; 41ctb: D. Arnaudet and J. Schormans;
157cb: Franck Raux; 42cr, 48cb, 93br, 129tl and
146bl: Gérard Blot; 222tl: H. Lewandowski; 43ct: J.
G. Berizzi; 189ct, 191tl, 191tr, 191bl, 222tr, 222clt,
223cdh and 223crb: R. G. Ojéda; 220tl and 222clb:
V. Dubourg. ROGER-VIOLLET: 195br; 50tl: Lapi;
195br: Lipnitzki; 195clt: Branger.

SIBA: 22tr and 65br: Brigitte Ruiz.
SNCF: 294br: CAV-Patrick Leveque; 294clt:
CAV-Philippe Fraysseix.
SNTP: 291cl.
STUDIO VIDAL: 27c and 27bl: Cyrille Vidal.
SUD-OUEST: 285brl.
SYNDICAT VITICOLE DE SAINT-ÉMILION: 34clt:
Agence APPA; 81t: Office de Tourisme de la
Juridiction de Saint-Émilion-Xochitl.

S. TARTARAT: 134bl.
TAVERNE DU WEB: 291tl.
TV7: 285cr.

JACKET:
Front – ALAMY IMAGES: Eric Nathan main image;
DK IMAGES: Philippe Giraud clb.
Back – DK IMAGES: Philippe Giraud bl, cla, clb,
tl.
Spine – ALAMY IMAGES: Eric Nathan t; ETIENNE
FOLLET: b.

SPECIAL EDITIONS OF DK TRAVEL GUIDES

DK Travel Guides can be purchased in
bulk quantities at discounted prices for
use in promotions or as premiums.
We are also able to offer special editions
and personalized jackets, corporate
imprints, and excerpts from all of our
books, tailored specifically to meet
your own needs.

To find out more, please contact:
(in the United States) **SpecialSales@dk.com**
(in the UK) **Sarah.Burgess@dk.com**
(in Canada) DK Special Sales at
general@tourmaline.ca
(in Australia)
business.development@pearson.com.au

Picture Credits

The publisher would also like to thank the following individuals and institutions who have given their permission for their photographs to be used in this guide:
h = top; c = centre; b = bottom; l = left; r = right.
Every effort has been made to trace the copyright holders and we apologize in advance for any unintentional omissions. We would be pleased to insert the appropriate acknowledgments in any subsequent edition of this publication.

4CORNERS IMAGES: SIME/Giovanni Simeone 10cla.

BORDEAUX AIRPORT: 292tc: Burdin L'Image; 292clt: Nihat Akgoz.
PAU AIRPORT: 293tl and 293bc: Studio Vu.
AFP: 50cl and 50crb.
AKG-IMAGES: 39crb and 41tl: British Library; 40bl: Jean-François Amelo; 42br: Jean-Pierre Verney; 49br.
ALAMY IMAGES: Cephas Picture Library/Hervé Champollion 10br; JLImages 10tc; nagelestock.com 11br.
APRASAQ: 285bll.
ARCHIVES DÉPARTEMENTALES DE LOT-ET-GARONNE: 24tl and 158tl: Bib. d'Agen Ms 42; 239c: 10 PH4.
ARCHIVES DE VILLENEUVE-SUR-LOT: 051bc and 108bl: R. Delvert.

BIARRITZ CULTURE: 34br: Ballet de Lorraine-Laurent Philippe.
BNF PARIS: 40tl, 40—41, 41ct, 42tl, 42bc, 105bc, 135bl, 181bc.
BRIDGEMAN ART LIBRARY: 26tr: Archives Charmet; 36, 37ct, 038bg, 43br, 47tc abd 48br: Giraudon/Lauros; 43bc and 70tr: Giraudon; 204cb: Sally Greene; 30tl and 49tr: Bridgeman Art Library.

CASINO D'ARCACHON: 275ctl: Marcel Partouche.
CAUDALIE: 273tr.
CAVE DES PRODUCTEURS DE JURANÇON: 31bc.
CCIP BORDEAUX: 047crb: Selva/Leemage.
CDT GIRONDE: 285 clb: B. P. Lamarque.
CÉRAMIQUES CAZAUX & FILS: 272c and 272crb.
CHÂTEAU DE CÔME: 259bl.
CHÂTEAU DE FARGUES: 46clb and 46crb: Archives Familiales de Lur Saluces.
CHÂTEAU MARTINENS: 31tc.
CINÉMA UTOPIA: 275tc.
CONSEIL GÉNÉRAL DU LOT: 123tr: Nelly Blaya.
CRT AQUITAINE: 285blr.

G. DAGLI ORTI: 37clb, 45br, 46bl, 195tc, 206cl, 206br.
F. DESMESURE: 274crt.
DOMAINE DES CASSAGNOLES: 259tcr.

DORLING KINDERSLEY: 115crb, 120tl, 120bl, 121bc, 281chtr, 287ct, page 289, 290tr, 290bl, 295cl, 296cr, 297ct, 297cc, 297cb.

EAU DES ABATILLES: 259cl.
ÉDITIONS CLOUET: 15tl and 258tr.
FESTIVAL ART FLAMENCO DE MONT-DE-MARSAN: 32b and 274tc: Sébastien Zambon/CG40.
E. FOLLET: 28tl, 28bc, 28br, 28–9, 29cl, 29cr, 29bf, 29br, 33cdt, 35c, 35bc, 55bl, 209tl, 228bl, 230ct, 232tl, 232br, 233bl, 233tr, 234tl, 234tr, 234clb, 234bc, 235tr, 235cr, 235bl, 237tc, 237crt, 237cl, 237c, 237crb, 237bl, 237bc.
FRANCE BLEU GIRONDE: 286cl.
FRANCE TELECOM: 290bc: 1998 PhotoDisc, Inc. All rights reserved. Images provided by: 1998 Nick Rowe - France Telecom.

GAÏA IMAGES: 208br: A. Senosiain; 171cr: Marlène Meissonnier.
GAMMA: 051hr: Politique Image/Gamma.
GOUFFRE DE PADIRAC: 119tl: Cliché POUX, SES Padirac.
GROTTES DE BÉTHARRAM: 229bl.
GROTTES PRÉHISTORIQUES DE COUGNAC: 131tr: Francis Jach.
E. GUILLEMOT: 009tr, 256tl, 256cg, 256ctr, 256cbr, 256bl, 256bc, 256br, 257hg, 257tr, 257ctr, 257cbl, 257cbc, 257cbtr, 257cblb, 257btl, 257blb, 257bldh, 257blrb.

HEMISPHERE IMAGES: Pierre Jacques 11tr; Patrice Thomas 11cl.
HOA-QUI: 18tr: André Le Gall/Jacana; 18tl: CJ. Pache/Age/Hoa-Qui; 176cr: J. Cancalosi/Age/Hoa-Qui; 18br: JA Jimenez/Age/Hoa-Qui; 19br: J. Cancalosi/Nature Pl/Jacana; 172cl: José B. Ruiz/Nature Pl/Jacana; 18crb: Mike Wilkes/Nature Pl/Jacana; 19clb: Morales/Age/Hoa-Qui; 19bcl: Philippe Prigent/Jacana; 16clb: Pierre Petit/Jacana; 173tr: Rodriguez/Age/Hoa-Qui; 19crb: S. Raman/Age/Hoa-Qui; 18bl: U. Walz Gdt/Age/Hoa-Qui; 171br: W. Bollmann/Age/Hoa-Qui.

JARDINS D'EYRIGNAC: 111br: D. Reperant; 110l and 111tl: J.-B. Leroux.
P. JAVELLE: 30cr, 31cr, 138bl, 180tl, 219cr, 225tl, 256tl, 258tl, 258cll, 258clc, 258clr, 258bl, 258brl, 258brc, 258brr, 259tl, 259tcl, 259tr, 270tc, 270crb, 272tl, 272crt, 272clt, 272tr, 272clb, 272bl, 273tl, 273tcl, 273tcr, 273chg, 273cbl, 273ctr, 273cbr, 273cbcl, 273bcl, 274bcdt, 273cbcr, 273bl.

KEYSTONE-FRANCE: 45cb.
KHARBINE-TAPABOR: 44b, 63br, 155bc, 172tr.

Leemage/Selva: 13c, 170tl, 195crt, 195cr.
Librairie Megadenda: 29tr: Éditions Erein.

Mairie de Dax: 33bl: Philippe Salvat.
Mairie de Soulac: 61cl.
Maison Pariès: 257ctl, 257br abd 273br.
Mouton Rothschild: 31tl.
Musée basque et de l'histoire de Bayonne: 185b.
Musée Champollion de Figeac: 124cr: Nelly Blaya.
Musée d'Aquitaine: 38br and 44cl: DEC,
Bordeaux-B. Fontanel; 38br: DEC,
Bordeaux-B. Fontanel & L. Gauthier; 038ct: DEC,
Bordeaux-Hugo Maertens, Bruxelles;
39tc and 039bc: DEC, Bordeaux-J.-M. Arnaud;
40clb and 41bl: DEC, Bordeaux-J. Gilson; 67crt:
CAPC-Frédéric Delpech.
Musée d'Art Sacré de Rocamadour: 206bl:
J.-L. Nespoulous.
Musée de Cahors Henri Martin: 129cr:
J.-C. Meauxsoone.
Musée de Gajac de Villeneuve sur Lot: 150cr.
Musée des Arts Décoratifs de Bordeaux: 72ctr:
DMB-L. Gauthier.
Musée des Beaux-Arts d'Agen: 154cl, 159br and
160cl: Hugo Maertens, Bruges; 160tr.
Musée des Beaux-Arts de Bordeaux: 45tr and
48tl: M.B.A. Bordeaux-Lysiane Gauthier.
Musée Despiau-Wlérick: 182crt: Studio Ernest,
Mont-de-Marsan.
Musée du Périgord de Périgueux: 101tr: B. Dupuy.
Musée du Pruneau de Lafitte: 153rb.
Musée Georgette-Dupouy: 178cl: S. Dom Pedro Gilo.

J.-B. Nadeau: 8 c, 80bc and 81bc :
J.B. Nadeau/Appa.

Office de Tourisme d'Espelette: 34c.
Office de Tourisme de Saint-Jean-de-Luz: 32tc.
Office de Tourisme de Soule: 210l.

Parc Naturel Régional des Landes de Gascogne,
Belin-Beliet: 49cb, 50bcr and 173b.
Parc Walibi Aquitaine: 286tl.

Photothèque Hachette: 7c, 43br, 46t, 46br, 053c,
86b, 113tl, 200cb and 283c: Hachette Livre; 47br:
Hachette Livre-Lacoste.
Photothèque Ville de Cahors: 128br: Nelly
Blaya; 128tl.
C. de Prada: 211tl and 210br.
Presse-Sports: 13b, 16tl.
Pyrénées Magazine: 285brr : Étienne Follet-Milan.

RMN: 44tl, 89tr, 147cr and 180tr; 072tl:
A. Danvers; 221br: Bellot/Coursaget; 218br:
Bulloz; 41ctb: D. Arnaudet et J. Schormans;
157cb: Franck Raux; 42cr, 48cb, 93br, 129tl and
146bl: Gérard Blot; 222tl: H. Lewandowski; 43ct: J.
G. Berizzi; 189ct, 191tl, 191tr, 191bl, 222tr, 222clt,
223cdh and 223crb: R. G. Ojéda; 220tl and 222clb:
V. Dubourg. Roger-Viollet: 195br; 50tl: Lapi;
195br: Lipnitzki; 195clt: Branger.

SIBA: 22tr and 65br: Brigitte Ruiz.
SNCF: 294br: CAV-Patrick Leveque; 294clt:
CAV-Philippe Fraysseix.
SNTP: 291cl.
Studio Vidal: 27c and 27bl: Cyrille Vidal.
Sud-Ouest: 285brl.
Syndicat Viticole de Saint-Émilion: 34clt:
Agence APPA; 81t: Office de Tourisme de la
Juridiction de Saint-Émilion-Xochitl.

S. Tartarat: 134bl.
Taverne du Web: 291tl.
TV7: 285cr.

JACKET:
Front – Alamy Images: Eric Nathan main image;
DK Images: Philippe Giraud clb.
Back – DK Images: Philippe Giraud bl, cla, clb,
tl.
Spine – Alamy Images: Eric Nathan t; Etienne
Follet: b.

SPECIAL EDITIONS OF DK TRAVEL GUIDES

DK Travel Guides can be purchased in
bulk quantities at discounted prices for
use in promotions or as premiums.
We are also able to offer special editions
and personalized jackets, corporate
imprints, and excerpts from all of our
books, tailored specifically to meet
your own needs.

To find out more, please contact:
(in the United States) SpecialSales@dk.com
(in the UK) Sarah.Burgess@dk.com
(in Canada) DK Special Sales at
general@tourmaline.ca
(in Australia)
business.development@pearson.com.au

Phrase Book

In an Emergency

Help!	Au secours!	oh se**koor**
Stop!	Arrêtez!	aret-**ay**
Call a doctor!	Appelez un médecin!	apuh-**lay** uñ med**sañ**
Call an ambulance!	Appelez une ambulance!	apuh-**lay** oon oñboo-**loñs**
Call the police!	Appelez la police!	apuh-**lay** lah poh-**lees**
Call the fire department!	Appelez les pompiers!	apuh-**lay** leh poñ-**peeyay**
Where is the nearest telephone?	Où est le téléphone le plus proche?	oo ay luh tehleh**fon** luh ploo prosh
Where is the nearest hospital?	Où est l'hôpital le plus proche?	oo ay l'opee**tal** luh ploo prosh

Communication Essentials

Yes	Oui	wee
No	Non	noñ
Please	S'il vous plaît	seel voo **play**
Thank you	Merci	mer-**see**
Excuse me	Excusez-moi	exkoo-**zay** mwah
Hello	Bonjour	boñ**zhoor**
Goodbye	Au revoir	oh ruh-**vwar**
Good night	Bonsoir	boñ-**swar**
Morning	Le matin	ma**tañ**
Afternoon	L'après-midi	l'apreh-**meedee**
Evening	Le soir	swar
Yesterday	Hier	eeyehr
Today	Aujourd'hui	oh-zhoor-**dwee**
Tomorrow	Demain	duh**mañ**
Here	Ici	ee-**see**
There	Là	lah
What?	Quel, quelle?	kel, kel
When?	Quand?	koñ
Why?	Pourquoi?	poor-**kwah**
Where?	Où?	oo

Useful Phrases

How are you?	Comment allez-vous?	kom-moñ tal**ay voo**
Very well, thank you.	Très bien, merci.	treh byañ, mer-**see**
Pleased to meet you.	Enchanté de faire votre kon-ay-sans.	oñshoñ-**tay** duh fehr votr kon-ay-**sans**
See you soon.	A bientôt.	byañ-**toh**
That's fine	Voilà qui est parfait	vwalah kee ay par**fay**
Where is/are...?	Où est/sont...?	oo ay/soñ
How far is it to...?	Combien de kilomètres d'ici à...?	kom-**byañ** duh keelo-metr d'ee-see ah
Which way to...?	Quelle est la direction pour...?	kel ay lah **deer**-ek-syoñ poor
Do you speak English?	Parlez-vous anglais?	par-**lay** voo oñg-**lay**
I don't understand.	Je ne comprends pas.	zhuh nuh kom-**proñ** pah
Could you speak slowly please?	Pouvez-vous parler moins vite s'il vous plaît?	poo-**vay** voo par-**lay** mwañ veet seel voo play
I'm sorry.	Excusez-moi.	exkoo-**zay** mwah

Useful Words

big	grand	groñ
small	petit	puh-**tee**
hot	chaud	show
cold	froid	frwah
good	bon	boñ
bad	mauvais	moh-**veh**
enough	assez	ass**ay**
well	bien	byañ
open	ouvert	oo-**ver**
closed	fermé	fer-**meh**
left	gauche	gohsh
right	droit	drwah
straight ahead	tout droit	too drwah
near	près	preh
far	loin	lwañ
up	en haut	oñ oh
down	en bas	oñ bah
early	de bonne heure	duh bon urr
late	en retard	oñ ruh-**tar**
entrance	l'entrée	l'on-**tray**
exit	la sortie	sor-**tee**
toilet	les toilettes, les WC	twah-**let**, vay-**see**
free, unoccupied	libre	leebr
free, no charge	gratuit	grah-**twee**

Making a Telephone Call

I'd like to place a long-distance call.	Je voudrais faire un interurbain.	zhuh voo-dreh fehr uñ añter-oorbañ
I'd like to make a collect call.	Je voudrais faire une communication PCV.	zhuh voo**dreh** fehr oon komoonikah-**syoñ** peh-seh-veh
I'll try again later.	Je rappelerai plus tard.	zhuh rapel-**eray** ploo tar
Can I leave a message?	Est-ce que je peux laisser un message?	es-**keh** zhuh puh leh-**say** uñ mehsazh
Hold on.	Ne quittez pas, s'il vous plaît.	nuh kee-**tay** pah seel voo play
Could you speak up a little please?	Pouvez-vous parler un peu plus fort?	poo-**vay** voo par-**lay** uñ puh ploo for
local call	la communication locale	komoonikah-**syoñ** low-**kal**

Shopping

How much does this cost?	C'est combien s'il vous plaît?	say kom-**byañ** seel voo play
I would like ...	je voudrais...	zhuh voo-**dray**
Do you have?	Est-ce que vous avez?	es-kuh voo zavay
I'm just looking.	Je regarde seulement.	zhuh ruh**gar** suhl**moñ**
Do you take credit cards?	Est-ce que vous acceptez les cartes de crédit?	es-kuh voo zaksept-**ay** leh kart duh kreh-**dee**
Do you take traveler's checks?	Est-ce que vous acceptez les chèques de voyage?	es-kuh voo zaksept-**ay** leh shek duh vwa**yazh**
What time do you open?	A quelle heure vous êtes ouvert?	ah kel urr voo zet oo-**ver**
What time do you close?	A quelle heure vous êtes fermé?	ah kel urr voo zet fer-**may**
This one.	Celui-ci.	suhl-wee-**see**
That one.	Celui-là.	suhl-wee-**lah**
expensive	cher	shehr
cheap	pas cher, bon marché	pah shehr, boñ mar-**shay**
size, clothes	la taille	tye
size, shoes	la pointure	pwañ-**tur**
white	blanc	bloñ
black	noir	nwahr
red	rouge	roozh
yellow	jaune	zhohwn
green	vert	vehr
blue	bleu	bluh

Types of Shops

antiques shop	le magasin d'antiquités	maga-**zañ** d'oñteekee-**tay**
bakery	la boulangerie	booloñ-**zhuree**
bank	la banque	boñk
book store	la librairie	lee-**brehree**
butcher	la boucherie	boo-**shehree**
cake shop	la pâtisserie	patee-**sree**
cheese shop	la fromagerie	fromazh-**ree**
dairy	la crémerie	krem-**ree**
department store	le grand magasin	groñ maga-**zañ**
delicatessen	la charcuterie	sharkoot-**ree**
drugstore	la pharmacie	farmah-**see**
fish seller	la poissonnerie	pwasson-**ree**
gift shop	le magasin de cadeaux	maga-**zañ** duh ka**doh**
greengrocer	le marchand de légumes	mar-**shoñ** duh lay-**goom**
grocery	l'alimentation	alee-moñta-**syoñ**
hairdresser	le coiffeur	kwa**fuhr**
market	le marché	marsh-**ay**
newsstand	le magasin de journaux	maga-**zañ** duh zhoor-**no**
post office	la poste, le bureau de poste, le PTT	pohst, booroh duh pohst, peh-teh-teh
shoe store	le magasin de chaussures	maga-**zañ** duh show-**soor**
supermarket	le supermarché	soo pehr-**marshay**
tobacconist	le tabac	tabah
travel agent	l'agence de voyages	l'azhoñs duh vwayazh

Sightseeing

abbey	l'abbaye	l'abay-**ee**
art gallery	la galerie d'art	galer-**ree** dart
bus station	la gare routière	gahr roo-tee-**yehr**

cathedral	la cathédrale	katay-**dral**
church	l'église	l'ay**gleez**
garden	le jardin	zhar-**dañ**
library	la bibliothèque	beeblee**o**-tek
museum	le musée	moo-**zay**
tourist information office	les renseignements touristiques, le syndicat d'initiative	roñsayn-**moñ** too-rees-**teek**, sandee-ka d'eenee-sya**teev**
town hall	l'hôtel de ville	l'ohtel duh veel
train station	la gare (SNCF)	gahr (es-en-say-ef)
private mansion	l'hôtel particulier	l'ohtel partikoo-**lyay**
closed for	fermeture	fehrmeh-**tur**
public holiday	jour férié	zhoor fehree-**ay**

Staying in a Hotel

Do you have a vacant room?	Est-ce que vous avez une chambre?	es-kuh voo-**zavay** oon shambr
double room, with double bed	la chambre à deux personnes, avec un grand lit	shambr ah duh pehr-**son** avek un groñn lee
twin room	la chambre à deux lits	shambr ah duh lee
single room	la chambre à une personne	shambr ah oon pehr-**son**
room with a bath, shower	la chambre avec salle de bains, une douche	shambr avek sal duh bañ, oon doosh
porter	le garçon	gar-**soñ**
key	la clef	klay
I have a reservation.	J'ai fait une réservation.	zhay fay oon rayzehrva-**syoñ**

Eating Out

Have you got a table?	Avez-vous une table libre?	avay-**voo** oon tahbl leebr
I want to reserve a table.	Je voudrais réserver une table.	zhuh voo-**dray** rayzehr-**vay** oon tahbl
The check please.	L'addition s'il vous plaît.	l'adee-**syoñ** seel voo **play**
I am a vegetarian.	Je suis végétarien.	zhuh swee vezhay-**tehryañ**
Waitress/ waiter	Madame, Mademoiselle/ Monsieur	mah-**dam**, mah-demwah**zel**/ muh-**syuh**
menu	le menu, la carte	men-**oo**, kart
fixed-price menu	le menu à prix fixe	men-**oo** ah pree feeks
cover charge	le couvert	koo-**vehr**
wine list	la carte des vins	kart-deh vañ
glass	le verre	vehr
bottle	la bouteille	boo-**tay**
knife	le couteau	koo-**toh**
fork	la fourchette	for-**shet**
spoon	la cuillère	kwee-**yehr**
breakfast	le petit déjeuner	puh-**tee** deh-**zhuh-nay**
lunch	le déjeuner	deh-**zhuh-nay**
dinner	le dîner	dee-**nay**
main course	le plat principal	plah prañsee-**pal**
appetizer, first course	l'entrée, le hors d'oeuvre	l'oñ-**tray**, or-duhvr
dish of the day	le plat du jour	plah doo zhoor
wine bar	le bar à vin	bar ah vañ
café	le café	ka-**fay**
rare	saignant	say-**noñ**
medium	à point	ah **pwañ**
well-done	bien cuit	byañ **kwee**

Menu Decoder

l'agneau	l'an**yoh**	lamb
l'ail	l'eye	garlic
la banane	ban**an**	banana
le beurre	burr	butter
la bière, bière	bee-**yehr**, bee-**yehr**	beer, draft
à la pression	ah lah pres-**syoñ**	beer
le bifteck, le steack	beef-**tek**, stek	steak
le boeuf	buhf	beef
bouilli	boo-**yee**	boiled
le café	kah-**fay**	coffee
le canard	kan**ar**	duck
le chocolat	shoko-lah	chocolate
le citron	see-**troñ**	lemon
le citron pressé	see-**troñ** press-**eh**	fresh lemon juice
les crevettes	kruh-**vet**	prawns
les crustacés	**kroos**-ta-say	shellfish
cuit au four	kweet oh foor	baked
le dessert	deh-**ser**	dessert

l'eau minérale	l'oh **meeney**-ral	mineral water
les escargots	leh zes-kar-**goh**	snails
les frites	freet	chips
le fromage	from-**azh**	cheese
le fruit frais	frwee freh	fresh fruit
les fruits de mer	frwee duh mer	seafood
le gâteau	gah-**toh**	cake
la glace	glas	ice, ice cream
grillé	gree-**yay**	grilled
le homard	om**ahr**	lobster
l'huile	l'weel	oil
le jambon	zhoñ-**boñ**	ham
le lait	leh	milk
les légumes	lay-**goom**	vegetables
la moutarde	moo-**tard**	mustard
l'oeuf	l'uf	egg
les oignons	leh zon**yoñ**	onions
les olives	leh zol**eev**	olives
l'orange	l'oroñzh	orange
l'orange pressée	l'oroñzh press-**eh**	fresh orange juice
le pain	pan	bread
le petit pain	puh-**tee** pañ	roll
poché	posh-**ay**	poached
le poisson	pwah-**ssoñ**	fish
le poivre	pwavr	pepper
la pomme	pom	apple
les pommes de terre	pom-duh **tehr**	potatoes
le porc	por	pork
le potage	poh-**tazh**	soup
le poulet	poo-**lay**	chicken
le riz	ree	rice
rôti	row-**tee**	roast
la sauce	sohs	sauce
la saucisse	soh**sees**	sausage, fresh
sec	sek	dry
le sel	sel	salt
la soupe	soop	soup
le sucre	sookr	sugar
le thé	tay	tea
le toast	toast	toast
la viande	vee-**yand**	meat
le vin blanc	vañ bloñ	white wine
le vin rouge	vañ roozh	red wine
le vinaigre	vee**naygr**	vinegar

Numbers

0	zéro	zeh-**roh**
1	un, une	uñ, oon
2	deux	duh
3	trois	trwah
4	quatre	katr
5	cinq	sañk
6	six	sees
7	sept	set
8	huit	weet
9	neuf	nerf
10	dix	dees
11	onze	oñz
12	douze	dooz
13	treize	trehz
14	quatorze	ka**torz**
15	quinze	kañz
16	seize	sehz
17	dix-sept	dees-**set**
18	dix-huit	dees-**weet**
19	dix-neuf	dees-**nerf**
20	vingt	vañ
30	trente	tront
40	quarante	ka**roñt**
50	cinquante	sañk**oñt**
60	soixante	swas**oñt**
70	soixante-dix	swasoñt-**dees**
80	quatre-vingts	katr-**vañ**
90	quatre-vingt-dix	katr-vañ-**dees**
100	cent	soñ
1,000	mille	meel

Time

one minute	une minute	oon mee-**noot**
one hour	une heure	oon urr
half an hour	une demi-heure	oon duh-mee urr
Monday	lundi	luñ-**dee**
Tuesday	mardi	mar-**dee**
Wednesday	mercredi	mehrkruh-**dee**
Thursday	jeudi	zhuh-**dee**
Friday	vendredi	voñdruh-**dee**
Saturday	samedi	sam-**dee**
Sunday	dimanche	dee-**moñsh**

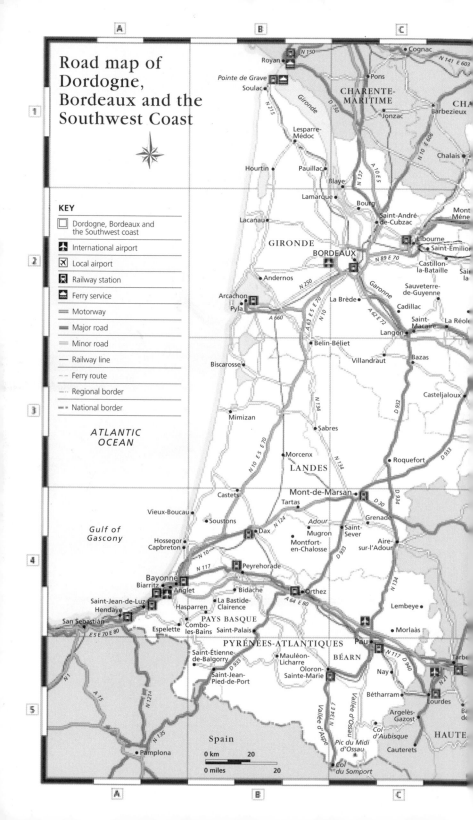